Birthright Citizens

Birthright Citizens tells how African American activists transformed the terms of citizenship for all Americans. Before the Civil War, colonization schemes and raced-based laws threatened to deport former slaves born in United States. *Birthright Citizens* recovers the story of how African American activists remade national belonging through battles in legislatures, conventions, and courthouses. They faced formidable opposition, most notoriously from the US Supreme Court decision in *Dred Scott*. Still, Martha Jones explains, no single case defined their status. Former slaves studied law, secured allies, and conducted themselves like citizens, establishing their status through local, everyday claims. All along they argued that birth guaranteed their rights. With fresh archival sources and an ambitious reframing of constitutional lawmaking before the Civil War, Jones shows how, when the Fourteenth Amendment constitutionalized the birthright principle, black Americans' aspirations were realized.

Martha S. Jones is the Society of Black Alumni Presidential Professor and Professor of History at Johns Hopkins University. She was formerly a Presidential Bicentennial Professor at the University of Michigan, and was a founding director of the Michigan Law School Program in Race, Law & History. She is the author of *All Bound Up Together: The Woman Question in African American Public Culture, 1830–1900* (2007) and coeditor of *Toward an Intellectual History of Black Women* (2015).

STUDIES IN LEGAL HISTORY

See the Studies in Legal History series website at
http://studiesinlegalhistory.org/

Studies in Legal History

EDITORS

Sarah Barringer Gordon, University of Pennsylvania
Holly Brewer, University of Maryland, College Park
Michael Lobban, London School of Economics and Political Science
Reuel Schiller, University of California, Hastings College of the Law

Other books in the series:

Cynthia Nicoletti, *Secession on Trial: The Treason Prosecution of Jefferson Davis*

Edward James Kolla, *Sovereignty, International Law, and the French Revolution*

Assaf Likhovski, *Tax Law and Social Norms in Mandatory Palestine and Israel*

Robert W. Gordon, *Taming the Past: Essays on Law and History and History in Law*

Paul Garfinkel, *Criminal Law in Liberal and Fascist Italy*

Michelle A. McKinley, *Fractional Freedoms: Slavery, Intimacy, and Legal Mobilization in Colonial Lima, 1600–1700*

Mitra Sharafi, *Law and Identity in Colonial South Asia: Parsi Legal Culture, 1772–1947*

Karen M. Tani, *States of Dependency: Welfare, Rights, and American Governance, 1935–1972*

Stefan Jurasinski, *The Old English Penitentials and Anglo-Saxon Law*

Felice Batlan, *Women and Justice for the Poor: A History of Legal Aid, 1863–1945*

Sophia Z. Lee, *The Workplace Constitution from the New Deal to the New Right*

Michael A. Livingston, *The Fascists and the Jews of Italy: Mussolini's Race Laws, 1938–1943*

Birthright Citizens

A History of Race and Rights in Antebellum America

MARTHA S. JONES
Johns Hopkins University

CAMBRIDGE
UNIVERSITY PRESS

CAMBRIDGE
UNIVERSITY PRESS

University Printing House, Cambridge CB2 8BS, United Kingdom

One Liberty Plaza, 20th Floor, New York, NY 10006, USA

477 Williamstown Road, Port Melbourne, VIC 3207, Australia

314–321, 3rd Floor, Plot 3, Splendor Forum, Jasola District Centre,
New Delhi – 110025, India

79 Anson Road, #06-04/06, Singapore 079906

Cambridge University Press is part of the University of Cambridge.

It furthers the University's mission by disseminating knowledge in the pursuit of
education, learning, and research at the highest international levels of excellence.

www.cambridge.org
Information on this title: www.cambridge.org/9781316604724
DOI: 10.1017/9781316577165

© Martha S. Jones 2018

First published 2018
Reprinted 2018

Printed in the United States of America by Sheridan Books, Inc.

A catalogue record for this publication is available from the British Library.

Library of Congress Cataloging-in-Publication Data
Names: Jones, Martha S., author.
Title: Birthright citizens : a history of race and rights in antebellum America / Martha S. Jones.
Description: Cambridge, United Kingdom; New York, NY: Cambridge University Press, [2018] |
Series: Studies in legal history | Includes bibliographical references and index.
Identifiers: LCCN 2018002423| ISBN 9781107150348 (hardback) |
ISBN 9781316604724 (paperback)
Subjects: LCSH: African Americans – Legal status, laws, etc. | African Americans –
Civil rights – History – 19th century. | Citizenship – United States – History – 19th century. |
Race discrimination – Law and legislation – United States – History.
Classification: LCC KF4757.J67 2018 | DDC 342.7308/3–dc23
LC record available at https://lccn.loc.gov/2018002423

ISBN 978-1-107-15034-8 Hardback
ISBN 978-1-316-60472-4 Paperback

To Jean Hébrard, and to Baltimore

Contents

Illustrations

Preface

First the Streets, Then the Archives

My thinking about this book began during my years as a public interest lawyer. Even then, my questions were about race and rights, although my research was conducted not in the reading rooms of ivied law libraries but in the soot-covered structures of lower Manhattan's halls of justice. It was the 1980s, and a radical legal culture focused on civil rights and the War on Poverty was being displaced. New social categories drove the dynamics of New York's trial courts: the homeless, the deinstitutionalized mentally ill, and people living with AIDS. Those men and women were also my neighbors, colleagues, and clients. Our lives and the litigation they generated tested the outer limits of law's capacity to dispense justice. My job was to press those limits, insisting that even those relegated to the margins had fundamental rights.

Scores of New York's public interest lawyers worked in just this way, many of us coming out of community-based legal services and legal aid programs. Our expertise was in the gritty fisticuffs of legal culture's trenches. We inhabited the lowest courts, venues with ghettoized jurisdictions, such as housing and family courts. Ours was a practice wrought from a potent mix of constitutional claims, rules of civil procedure, and gamesmanship. We didn't always give a lot of thought to the past, particularly if it didn't involve a relevant precedent. History was invoked instrumentally, as a highly selective measure of advocacy.[1] Most days, our sights were on the present and the future – winning a case, reforming the law, and changing the world, or at least a small piece of it.[2] Hours spent in the courthouse meant hours spent observing New York's disproportionately black and brown poor people navigate legal culture, often without the assistance of counsel. From security screenings to the clerk's counter, and from lengthy calendar calls to fraught hallway negotiations, they told their stories. Theirs were everyday problems that rarely rose to the level of high jurisprudential consequence.[3] Still, this was where many people encountered law – battling for heat and hot water, custody and care of their children, or public benefits.

FIGURE P.I Home of New York County's Housing Court. Manhattan's Housing Court is located in the borough's Civil Court Building, depicted here, at 111 Centre Street. When originally installed, the chain-link perimeter fence displaced an encampment of homeless people who had taken up residence against the building's façade. In 2012, renovation of the adjacent Collect Pond Park exposed foundation remnants from the nineteenth-century Tombs. Image courtesy of Martha S. Jones.

In the local courthouse, race met rights in the lives of people that class-action litigation and appellate courts rarely reached. Still, they were complex proceedings in which interests converged. Individual litigants asserted claims for personal and familial well-being.[4] For judges, opinions penned led to intellectual distinction, engagements with appellate courts, and expanding reputations. Lawyers worked toward numerous aims: law and public policy reform, a larger client base, or an appointment to the bench.[5] The social world was also present. Rent strikers, parents' associations, and welfare rights activists viewed court proceedings as an extension of their work in communities, in legislatures, and in the streets.[6]

At some moments the courthouse and the social world appeared to collide. For many months in the late 1980s, I encountered each morning an encampment of homeless people tucked up against the Housing Court's south façade – cardboard boxes, plastic bags, and the detritus of urban life assembled into shelter.[7] I knew about my city's economy and politics – gentrification and deinstitutionalization were thrusting thousands of New Yorkers onto the streets.[8] Still, I asked, why here, in a place seemingly far from family, neighborhood, and community services? How had *homeless* people come to take shelter in the shadow of the city's *housing* court? There was an intimacy on display: an edifice built to ensure tenants' rights and safe shelter locked in an awkward embrace with people who lived beyond the reach of legal rights and reason.[9]

I scrutinized constitutions, pored over state and federal statutes, and studied policy and regulation. Finally, it was history that rendered this scene fully legible. The Housing Court building, at first glance, appeared to be no more than one part of an endless grid of modern courthouses and administrative buildings. It was a monument to transparency and order. Still, as I hurried to nearby coffee shops for lunch, another landscape came into view. There, I walked narrow, curved, nineteenth-century streets with names like Mulberry, Mott, Bayard, and Pell. These were signs of an older neighborhood on top of which the modern courthouse had been built.

Pre–Civil War America's most notorious neighborhood was New York's Five Points. Irish immigrants lived alongside newly emancipated slaves; anti-abolitionist riots sometimes targeted black businesses; a burgeoning vice trade catered to white men of all classes; and complicit, affluent landlords knew that vice always paid the rent. Charles Dickens in his *American Notes* derided the neighborhood's "squalid streets," "wretched beds," "fevered brains," and "heaps of negro women," who forced the "rats to move away in search of better lodgings." Dance halls greeted patrons with a gaiety that promised drink, bawdiness, and intimacy across lines of color and class.[10]

Nineteenth-century reformers deemed Five Points a place in need of disciplining. Reform came about by way of razing the neighborhood, a process that began in 1838. By the time it was done, a new jail and courthouse building replaced saloons and brothels: The Tombs.[11] By the century's end all that remained were a few crooked streets, as law's edifices dominated the landscape. Most residents were displaced to the Lower East Side. But some returned. Poverty and vice were their tickets home, and their new hosts were sheriffs and judges rather than madams and barkeeps. They returned not to dank basement rooms but overcrowded jail cells. This crossroads of lower Manhattan – the Five Points turned courthouse cluster – still pulsed to the beat of violence and vice. But in The Tombs, cages, locked doors, and the movement of bodies by jailers and bailiffs regulated such interactions.

By the 1960s, the courthouse neighborhood I would come to know was in place. Major court reform beckoned another generation of the New York's marginalized to Five Points.[12] New venues, such as the housing and family courts, promised due process and justice to the city's poor and working people. The old Tombs complex was razed to make way for modern structures with windows, waiting rooms, and pro se clerks to guide the uninitiated through legal culture's maze. Dockets swelled and, with a jurisdiction that stretched from one end of Manhattan to the other, the Housing Court became one of the most complex crossroads in New York. Lawyers and court personnel worked side by side with the city's black and brown working poor and jobless. In hallways and anterooms, stories were told and retold.[13] The social world pressed in, and the courthouse pressed back. I still recall the week that metal detectors were installed.[14]

But what of the people in the encampment just outside? How had the homeless come to make their home at the Housing Court? In a historical sense, they had always been there. Call them Five Points hustlers, inmates of The Tombs, or litigants making claims to housing rights, New York's most marginalized residents had always occupied this place. All the efforts to erase them were betrayed by the presence of packing boxes, trash bags, and Five Points' newest residents, the homeless.

Finally, court administrators installed a six-foot-high chain-link fence around the building, displacing the homeless encampment. In that act, the past and the present became entwined in what Joseph Roach has termed surrogation.[15] In such encounters law's social processes of memory and forgetting produce culture. Collective, highly selective shared memories are constructed, in part, by public acts of forgetting or erasure – the renaming of a courthouse, the razing of a structure, the transfer of a deed, or the termination of a lease. Roach presses us to see in these acts a long history of law's rituals and practices – its theaters of courthouse squares and courtroom wells. Even as we enact these rituals of forgetting, we retain an imperfectly deferred sort of memory.

Our work as legal historians is to understand those sites where history's unspeakable, inexpressible past still lives. Roach gently chides us to go beyond the archives, to "spend more time in the streets." He might very well have had the image of homeless people at the Housing Court in mind.[16] We might cringe, furrow our brow, and avert our gaze from that homeless encampment. Or we might pause to ask how the sight of human beings huddled in cardboard boxes is a sign of the past. Then we can return to the archives, where we learn how the dynamics of race, power, and inequality have always lived there.

Acknowledgments

Out my window, just to the south, I can see the near corner of the Baltimore courthouse. It sits just a few short blocks away from my home. I could not know when I began this book that I would put on its finishing touches as a resident of Baltimore. I have long been a historian of this city, having walked its streets and alleys, scavenged in its cemeteries and historic sites, and gotten blissfully lost in its archives. But today the rhythms of my daily life play out in the very place that was a key site for early American struggles over race and rights. This book is an effort to bring that story to light, to take us beyond stark narratives about a city's progress and decline or about journeys from injustice to justice, to reveal the dynamics of quotidian struggles that in turn reveal battles that are epic if not eternal. Citizenship – the thorny problem of who belongs and by what terms – is one such problem.

It is only right that I should now recognize that this book is first and foremost dedicated to the city of Baltimore and its people, those living there today, along with those of 1868. It has always been the streets of today's city and the lives that make their way along them that have driven this history. How else might we understand the twenty-first century's entrenched indignity, inequality, and injustice if we do not explore that which is at its root. How might we find the spirit and the necessity of struggle if we do not know that it has always been this way. My history of Baltimore offers no easy or sure answers, but it does affirm that there has always been struggle here. Thank you to this city for giving me, the lapsed radical lawyer, a place in which to strive like a historian for the justice that comes from setting aside despair and cynicism and telling a truth, as best I can.

This book is also dedicated to my husband, historian Jean Hébrard, a constant and true companion on all my journeys, epic and otherwise. Jean has always supported how my work aims to extend justice to those who have been historically deprived of making their own record, often violently so. He has done those things that only a devoted historian-partner might do: he has made archive road trips, read draft chapters, and posed new challenges during the question-and-answer period. Jean has set aside his own demanding projects time and again to help me push through another barrier, be it the close reading of a document or the refinement of an insight or interpretation. And now he too has made Baltimore home, all the while reveling in its complexity and encouraging me to find my purpose in this place.

I have been accompanied by fellow travelers, writers who also have taken Baltimore as their subject matter, with the trouble of racism as a central concern. Their work has pushed me to recognize the power of the everyday to reveal much more than daily happenings. Readers will be most familiar with the writings of Frederick Douglass, who was awed by the city even before he laid eyes upon it. Douglass would go on to wring from Baltimore's structured injustice a way toward freedom of mind and of body. William Watkins, writing as "A Colored Baltimorean," devotedly chronicled events in the antebellum city, making its life and times a subject relevant to a wide audience. Baptist minister Noah Davis published a narrative that permitted me to peer inside the establishment of black religious communities, with all their meaningful wranglings.

Contemporary authors have kept my thinking focused on the resonances between Baltimore's nineteenth-century past and its present. Literary historian Lawrence Jackson and journalist Ta-Nehisi Coates both have related their coming-of-age narratives set in Baltimore, teaching us about the city as a setting for life stories that are epic and even transcendent. What better affirmation might there be for my enduring sense that in this city's quotidian happenings are events of great consequence? The *Baltimore Sun*'s Justin Fenton offered me insight into life on the ground in Baltimore, long before I called the city home. His coverage of legal culture writ large, from the courthouse to the streets, is a model for a historian wrestling with how to craft a relationship between the two.

The lessons of Sherrilyn Ifill's book *On the Courthouse Lawn* have never been far from my thinking. History matters, and Ifill explains how one legacy of lynching in Maryland has been the suppression of African American voting across generations. History matters because the effects of past injustices endure through memory, lore, and fragmentary retellings. Today, Ifill continues to guide my understanding of how racism perverts justice as she fills the shoes of another towering Baltimorean, Thurgood Marshall, in her role as president and director-counsel of the NAACP Legal Defense and Education Fund. Tiya Miles offered me a most moving formulation of how historical writing fits with the work of such lawyers. Beyond explaining the past, our studies are their own acts of justice, the correction of a historical record that otherwise left too much distorted, unsaid, and shrouded in myth.

This book began as an essay, one dedicated to my advisor, mentor, and friend, Eric Foner. Eric has always quietly believed in my capacity to tell law's stories with a grounding in the social and political history of black Americans. I presented work from this book in 2004 at a celebration of Eric's career. When it appeared in print three years later, a rereading persuaded me that Baltimore and its rich archives had more to offer those of us longing to understand better the history of race, rights, and citizenship. Eric has been a devoted teacher through all our years together, one of the best fortunes of my professional life.

This book has benefited immensely from exchanges at conferences, workshops, and seminars in the United State and Europe. Thank you to the hosts, commentators, and participants at the American Bar Foundation; American Historical Association; Association for the Study of African American Life and History; American Society for Legal History; Baltimore Bar Library; Brown University Center for the Study of Slavery and Justice; Le Centre International de Recherches sur les Esclavages et les Post-esclavages (CIRESC); City University of New York (CUNY) Graduate Center; Duke University School of Law; École des Hautes Études en Sciences Sociale; Emory University Department of History; Henry Ford Museum; Johns Hopkins University Department of History; Law and Society Association; National Humanities Center; New York University Department of History; Organization of American Historians; Penn State University Department of History; Princeton University Department of Religion and Center for African American Studies; Rice University Department of History; Rutgers-Newark Law School; Sorbonne Paris Cité Project on Writing History from the Margins; Statuts, "Race" et Couleurs dans l'Atlantique de l'Antiquité à nos jours (STARACO); Triangle Legal History Seminar; United States Attorney's Office for the Eastern District of Michigan; University of Detroit–Mercy Department of History; University of Maryland Center for Global Migration Studies; University of Miami Law School; University of Michigan Eisenberg Institute for Historical Studies, Law School, and Legal History Workshop; University of North Carolina Law School; University of Pennsylvania Law School, History Department, and McNeil Center for Early American Studies; University of Southern California Law School and Department of History; University of Virginia Law School; Washington University in Saint Louis School of Law; University of Wisconsin Law School; and Yale University.

I came to legal history late in my training, and despite having spent lots of time in local courthouses, I needed a new tool kit with which to tackle the archives. From the outset, the work of Ariela Gross captured the spirit of what I hoped to say, and still today I turn to her ideas for inspiration and guidance. She does not recall the first time we met, but I do. And from that day, Ariela has been a teacher, mentor, model, and friend. Her insistence on scholarly excellence along with a generousness of spirit have transformed my work, while her unflinching commitment to justice has set a high bar for the work of writing history. Kate Masur has been my most generous and most challenging reader, and a model of fierce collegiality and friendship.

Kate shared her own important work on the history of the antebellum culture of rights to lend a critical eye to this book, and this work is much better for it.

Many of the ideas here were developed in an exacting community of legal historians. At the University of Michigan Law School, Susanna Blumenthal, Tom Green, Bill Novak, and Rebecca Scott welcomed me, often seeing the best in my work before I did. In the circles of the American Society for Legal History I found opportunities to test my ideas and make them speak to broader audiences. ASLH also introduced me to the remarkable Sarah Barringer Gordon, a devoted mentor, sharp interlocutor, and an unparalleled series editor. To Sally I owe a debt for her commitment to this book that cannot be easily repaid. I promise to try. My legal history community has also included the generous collaborators associated with the Legal History Consortium, in particular Jane Dailey, Sally Gordon, Dan Hamilton, Bill Novak, Richard Ross, and Barbara Welke.

Friends who are also scholars have supported this work and made it better. Thank you to Mia Bay, Rabia Belt, Ira Berlin, Mary Frances Berry, Al Brophy, Kathleen Canning, Chris Capozzola, John Carson, Nathan Connolly, Myriam Cottias, Adrienne Davis, Alejandro de la Fuente, Erica Armstrong Dunbar, Laura Edwards, Sam Erman, Dan Ernst, Ada Ferrer, Tony Frazier, François Furstenberg, Kevin Gaines, Thavolia Glymph, Risa Goluboff, Dena Goodman, Annette Gordon-Reed, Sally Greene, Chuck Grench, Steven Hahn, Leslie Harris, Nancy Hewitt, Evelyn Brooks Higginbotham, Tera Hunter, Steve Kantrowitz, Kelly Kennington, Jeff Kerr-Ritchie, Tiya Miles, Jessica Millward, Julian Mortenson, Kunal Parker, Dylan Penningroth, Richard Primus, Patricia Reid, Hannah Rosen, Daryl Michael Scott, Mitra Sharafi, Manisha Sinha, Rogers Smith, Carroll Smith-Rosenberg, Miranda Spieler, Chris Tomlins, Penny Von Eschen, François Weil, Judith Weisenfeld, Barbara Welke, Jonathan Wells, and Diana Williams. I was very fortunate to write in the company of a remarkable writing group, the #GraftonLine, and I am immensely grateful for their support. Thank you also to my editor, Debbie Gershenowitz, and the anonymous readers at Cambridge University Press. All shortcomings in the book are mine alone.

The archives at the heart of this book are rich and generous, if also too often stretched financially. Thank you to the staffs and supporters of the Baltimore Bar Library, the Baltimore City Archives, the Library of Congress, the Maryland Historical Society, the Maryland State Archives, the National Archives and Records Administration, and the William L. Clements Library. I received financial support from the American Council of Learned Societies, the American Historical Association, Johns Hopkins University, the National Constitution Center, the National Humanities Center, and the University of Michigan. Students with the University of Michigan Undergraduate Research Opportunity Program and I thank Anna Clark, Alison Eitman, Avery Johnson, Alexandra Ladwig, Keegan McDonald, Anya Parfenoff, Skye Payne, and Brie Starks for their research assistance.

Family and friends have lived with my stories of Baltimore cheerfully, for a long time. Thank you to my community: Susanne Baer, Emily Clark, Kelly Cunningham, Laurent Dubois, Alvia Golden, Clayton Lewis, Angela Dillard, Lynda Kaplan, Amanda Krugliak, Deborah Labelle, Catherine Minds, Kary Moss, Michele Norris, Marianetta Porter, Richard Rabinowitz, Daria Roithmayr, Michelle Schreiber, and Meryl Schwartz. My families Jones and Hébrard are sources of inspiration and joy. Special thanks to my brother Paul Jones and his wife, Heidi, for their love, support, and our shared life. To my mother-in-law, Blanche "Mimi" Hébrard, merci de prendre si affectueusement soin de moi et de mon travail.

In 1845, Frederick Douglass described his feelings upon seeing Baltimore for the first time:

"I had the strongest desire to see Baltimore. Cousin Tom, though not fluent in speech, had inspired me with that desire by his eloquent description of the place. I could never point out any thing at the Great House, no matter how beautiful or powerful, but that he had seen something at Baltimore far exceeding, both in beauty and strength, the object which I pointed out to him."

I think I know that of which Douglass wrote. Thank you, Baltimore, for your beauty and strength.

Abbreviations

The following abbreviations are used for archives frequently referenced in the endnotes.

BCA   Baltimore City Archives, Baltimore, MD

MHS   Maryland Historical Society, Baltimore, MD

MSA   Maryland State Archives, Annapolis, MD

NARA   National Archives and Records Administration, Washington, DC

Introduction

Rights of Colored Men: Debating Citizenship in Antebellum America

The title of William Yates's 1838 treatise, *Rights of Colored Men*, aptly captures the subject of this book. The nineteenth-century Americans for whom Yates wrote were fascinated by a juridical puzzle: Not slaves nor aliens nor the equals of free white men, who were former slaves and their descendants before the law?

None were more interested in this question than black Americans themselves, and *Birthright Citizens* takes up their point of view to tell the history of race and rights in the antebellum United States. The pressures brought on by so-called black laws and colonization schemes, especially a radical strain, explain why free people of color feared their forced removal from the United States. In response, they claimed an unassailable belonging, one grounded in birthright citizenship. No legal text expressly provided for such, but their ideas anticipated the terms of the Fourteenth Amendment. Set in Baltimore, a place between North, South, and the Atlantic world, this book traces the scenes and the debates through which black Americans developed ideas about citizenship and claims to the rights that citizens enjoyed. Along the way they engaged with legislators, judges, and law's everyday administrators. From the local courthouse to the chambers of high courts, the rights of colored men came to define citizenship for the nation as a whole.

Yates authored the very first legal treatise on the rights of free black Americans.[1] It was 1838 when *Rights of Colored Men to Suffrage, Citizenship, and Trial by Jury* was published in Philadelphia.[2] He was not one of antebellum America's highly regarded legal minds. Some say he read law for a time, although there is no evidence he was admitted to the bar. Instead, Yates's career began with a short-lived stint as a newspaper publisher in his hometown of Troy, New York.[3] His bona fides on the subject of race and citizenship were best established during his years as an agent for the American Anti-Slavery Society.[4] While many abolitionists maintained a self-conscious distance from

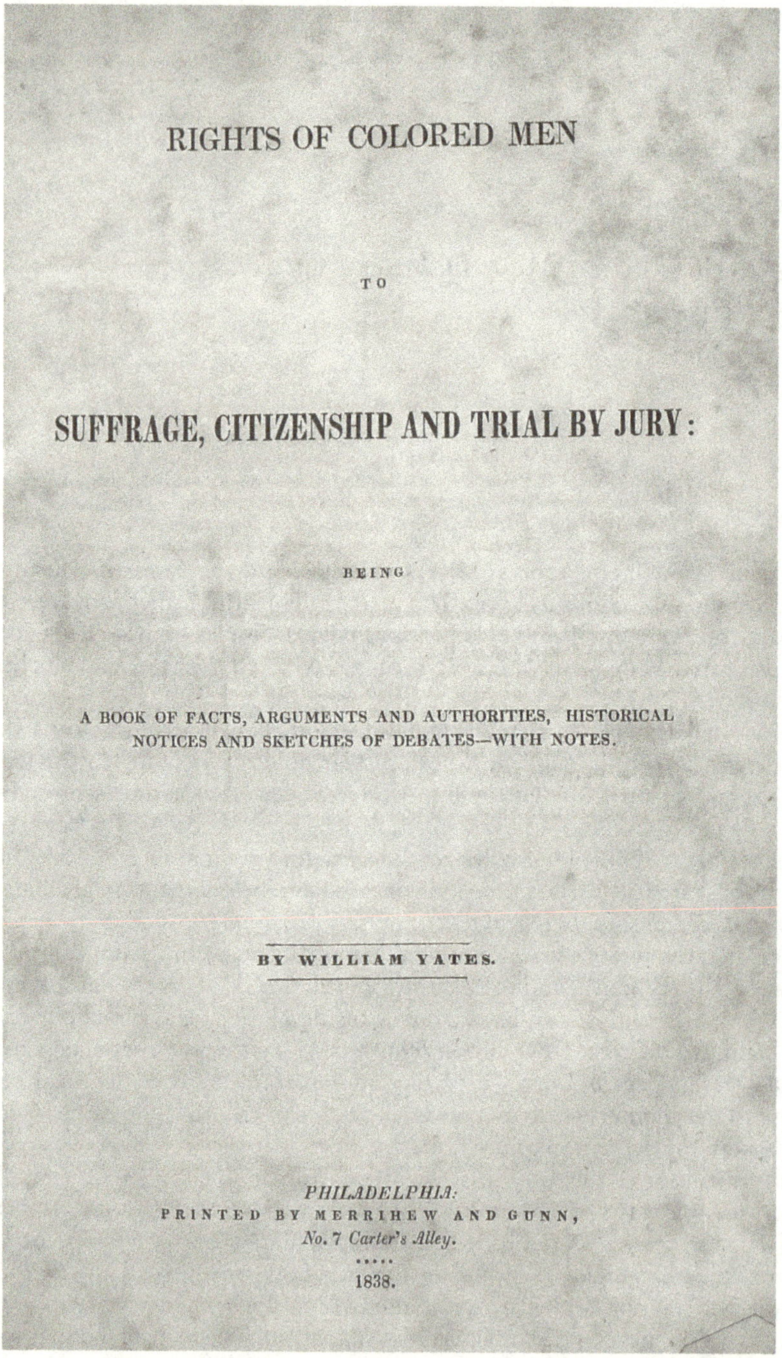

RIGHTS OF COLORED MEN

TO

SUFFRAGE, CITIZENSHIP AND TRIAL BY JURY:

BEING

A BOOK OF FACTS, ARGUMENTS AND AUTHORITIES, HISTORICAL
NOTICES AND SKETCHES OF DEBATES—WITH NOTES.

BY WILLIAM YATES.

PHILADELPHIA:
PRINTED BY MERRIHEW AND GUNN,
No. 7 Carter's Alley.

* * * * *

1838.

FIGURE I.I William Yates, *Rights of Colored Men*. American Anti-Slavery Society
agent William Yates made a case for the status of black Americans as citizens, consoli-
dating arguments made in conventions, legislatures, and courtrooms. The result, *Rights
of Colored Men*, was the first legal treatise on the subject. Image courtesy of the William
L. Clements Library.

free black communities, Yates centered his work there.[5] The oppression of free people of color was a companion to slavery, in Yates's view, with antislavery work necessarily extending into questions of free people's status.[6] Penning *Rights of Colored Men* was the pinnacle of this mission.

Yates placed a powerful instrument of authority in the hands of free African Americans and their allies. The antebellum legal treatise was a key tool in the standardization and dissemination of legal knowledge and was typically devoted to the comprehensive synthesis of a single branch of law.[7] By the late 1830s, Yates was following on the success of James Kent's *Commentaries* and Joseph Story's treatise series.[8] The genre had come to be associated with the concepts of law as scientific knowledge, legal education as systematic, and the profession as respectable.[9] Yates successfully adopted legal culture's own tool to such a degree that readers from the nineteenth century until today have regarded him as an authority on free black legal status. But Yates's text was also a work of advocacy.[10] *Rights of Colored Men* received prominent notices in the black and abolitionist press and could be purchased at local antislavery society offices.[11] As a result, the work served as a probing legal treatise that fueled activist arguments.[12]

Yates provides a window onto the position that some activists – black and white – took on race and citizenship at the end of the 1830s. Law was an instrument of change, and Yates forthrightly explained his objective: to undermine prejudice against color. Racism had led to "legal disability": exclusion from militia service, naturalization, suffrage, public schooling, ownership of real property, office holding, and courtroom testimony. Yates was especially unsettled by the disfranchisement of free black men in New Jersey, New York, Connecticut, and, more recently, Pennsylvania. Assembling evidence from legal culture, he believed, would help establish the rights and citizenship of free black people.[13]

Yates began with a story of the nation's origins. The establishment of the United States, he said, had been at the outset a revolutionary, republican, and enlightened undertaking that was untainted by racism or distinctions among and between races. This had been possible in the wake of the American Revolution because the founding generation knew firsthand the contributions black people had made to independence, through military service and labor. American law had originally been color-blind, as evidenced by the absence of racial distinctions in founding documents, such as the federal and state constitutions.[14]

Change came in the early nineteenth century, at the fault line between generations. A forgetting occurred, Yates posited. Lawmakers of the early republic did not know how black people had contributed to the nation's founding and hence were entitled to the privileges and immunities of citizens. In this sense, Yates's aim was partly to restore that past to the nation's political and legal memory. To achieve this, he compiled a history of lawmakers and their deliberations in which he found the development of antiblack prejudice in courts, constitutional conventions, and legislatures. He followed the profes-sional lives of men whose work included roles from low-level administrator to convention delegate and judge. Their ideas about free black people moved with them.

Most powerful was Yates's argument about how law, though suffering from amnesia, could be made right. The same instruments that had woven racism into the nation's legal fabric – courts, conventions, and legislatures – could now be used to recraft it. Legal culture was also capable of reform, of itself and of the status of black Americans. With the restoration of revolutionary-era mem-ories would come the reestablishment of racial equality. Lawmakers needed only to recall the past to restore racial justice, and Yates's treatise aimed to be an agent of that remembering.[15]

Looking back, it is easy to conclude that Yates's ideas were naïve. His faith in the power of historical knowledge, on the one hand, and the malleability of antiblack racism, on the other, seems like a misreading, given what we know of the rise of anti-free Negro thought and legislation in the 1840s and 1850s. But from Yates's point of view in 1838, he had prominent lawmakers who were sympathetic to his view. He built his arguments on the published opinions of judges, legislators, and constitutional framers who also advocated that free black Americans had rights. Yates amplified their ideas, giving them visibility and volume, all the while hoping he might help convert others to an affirmative position on black citizenship.[16]

Yates made a bold claim: Free black Americans could not be removed – banished, excluded, or colonized – from the borders of the individual states or the United States. With this he confronted head on the thorniest legal question of the antebellum period: Were free African Americans citizens with a claim to place? His answer was yes. Citizenship, he wrote, was distinct from political rights. It "strikes deeper" than, for example, the right to vote.[17] Denied the status of citizens, free black people were not secure in their "life, liberty, and property," or what he termed "personal rights."[18] At its core, citizenship was a claim to place, to enter and remain within the nation's borders. Citizenship, Yates believed, would protect free black people from expulsion.[19]

Yates adopted his most authoritative tone when discussing citizenship. The sections of his treatise on the vote and jury service leaned heavily on the published words of lawmakers. His discussion of citizenship was original, a structured synthesis that brought together a close reading of the Constitution with congressional debates and learned commentary. He began with four broad principles. First, no authority countered the view that free people of color were citizens, as contemplated by article 4, section 2, clause 1 of the Constitution. They were thus entitled to the "privileges and immunities of citizens." Nothing in the common law of England, the principles of the British constitution, or the Declaration of Independence recognized a distinction of color. Second, public-law jurisprudence recognized two classifications of persons: citizens and aliens. All those born within a jurisdiction were citizens with an allegiance to the state that demanded both obedience and protection. Third, to be deprived of the vote did not mark one as a noncitizen; nonpropertied men, women, and children were citizens even though in some jurisdictions ineligible to vote. Fourth and finally, Yates rejected any analogy between the status of free black people and that of Indians or slaves. The legal position of Indians was murky, though largely, he thought, governed by treaty and related law. Slaves were property and categorically not citizens.[20]

Yates provided case studies. Congress's 1820 debate over Missouri's admission to the union had turned in part on whether the new state could bar free black people from entering the state without violating the United States Constitution's guarantee of privileges and immunities. Then Major-General Andrew Jackson's proclamations to the "free colored inhabitants of Louisiana" during the War of 1812 which implied that soldiers of color were citizens like their "white fellow-citizens." In the example of Prudence Crandall, whose Connecticut school was said to have operated in violation of the state's black laws by admitting children of color from outside the state, the citizenship of free persons of color had been a "turning hinge." Crandall's attorneys argued that such a distinction denied free black children, as citizens, their guaranteed privileges and immunities.[21]

Rights of Colored Men remained an influential text throughout the antebellum years.[22] Other antislavery and African American activists would come to publish their own arguments about free black men and women as citizens. But few would adopt a form more cloaked in legal authority than that of the treatise. Yates's text fueled understandings of the role that law might play in claims for free black rights. It was also an example of how formal lawmaking by white men was connected to the vernacular legal culture of free black communities. Yates made a record that suggests how close to agreement highly placed lawmakers and free African American activists could be in their thinking.[23]

Yates and his treatise were forgotten after the Civil War, as was the threat of removal that so concerned him. The Civil Rights Act of 1866 and then the Fourteenth Amendment made clear that those who were US-born were citizens, whether they were formerly free or formerly enslaved. Persons born in the United States were citizens of the United States and of the individual state in which they resided.[24] The Civil Rights Act underscored that birthright was independent of "race, color, or previous condition of slavery or involuntary servitude."[25] It was a momentous turn of events by every measure. Birthright citizenship, a principle that African Americans had long argued was embedded in the Constitution, was affirmed. Yates's treatise survived but only in a literal sense, as a bound text tucked away on shelves that lined parlors and libraries.[26]

One century later, Yates and *Rights of Colored Men* were rediscovered. In the modern civil rights era, Yates's treatise took on renewed relevance as the United States again confronted the dilemma of African American citizenship. Nineteenth-century ideas served as evidence of an origins story about how the black freedom struggle had begun in the decades before the Civil War. Historians of race and rights dusted off the past of early African American and antislavery activism. They found William Yates.

Charles Wesley was the first historian to recover Yates. Wesley was a prolific scholar, a minister in the African Methodist Episcopal (AME) Church, and leader of the Association for the Study of Negro Life and History (ASNLH), known today the Association for the Study of African-American Life and History, or ASALH. Wesley was trained at Fisk and Yale, and received his PhD from Harvard in 1925. His scholarly energy was nearly boundless, and he published more than twenty books and many more articles, including survey-style works on black history. Wesley's subject matter was sweeping, from labor to the Civil War, citizenship, and Reconstruction. Within the ASNLH, Wesley served as director of research and publications, president, and executive director.[27]

Wesley set out to document how black thinkers had forged a long tradition of historical writing. The occasion was the 1963 ASNLH presidential address. The practice, Wesley explained, had been "associated with the building of nationalism and group pride." His starting point was comparative. Irish and Jewish people, like black Americans, had turned to historical writing to provide facts and combat oppression. Wesley's "Creating and Maintaining an Historical Tradition" was a call to arms that urged ASNLH members to pursue historical scholarship and teaching with political commitment and insight. Wesley placed historical writing during the civil rights era on a continuum that dated back to the earliest decades of the nineteenth century. To write history in the 1960s was, for Wesley, to continue that critical work.[28]

Wesley turned to some of the first works by black historians to make his case. Their earliest efforts had not been academic, at least not by twentieth-century standards. Black history had been told, in Wesley's view, before the publication of tracts and texts. African American orators were the first historians. Addresses delivered by men such as William Hamilton, Alexander Crummell, and Henry Highland Garnet "were evidence of the beginnings of the creation of an heroic tradition for Negro-Americans." A written tradition by "Negro Americans" then emerged, with writers including Robert B. Lewis, author of *Light and Truth* (1836); James W. C. Pennington, author of the *Text Book of the Origin and History of the Colored People* (1841); William Cooper Nell, author of *Services of Colored Americans, in the Wars of 1776 and 1812* (1851); and William Wells Brown, author of *The Black Man: His Antecedents, His Genius, and His Achievements* (1863) at the fore.[29] The first of these "Negro Historians" to be singled out by Wesley was William Yates, author of *Rights of Colored Men*. Yates had been a pioneering black historian.

Other historians also took notice of Yates, though they did not see him as Wesley had. John Myers included Yates in his study of American Anti-Slavery Society agents and their attention to the circumstances of free African Americans. Myers explained how the society had been generally ambivalent about working with free people in the North. However, by the mid-1830s a small cadre of agents was assigned that task, William Yates among them. Myers's larger aim was to demonstrate this change in terms of antislavery activism.[30]

Yates was, Myers explained, "first secretary of the Troy Anti-Slavery Society," representing that organization at national anniversaries in 1835 and 1836, and secretary and nominating committee member of the New York State Anti-Slavery Society. Myers documented how men such as Yates worked: They "gained the confidence of the colored people of Troy and were acceptable as agents to the Negro leaders of the country." Myers did not directly address the matter of Yates's racial identity, and assumed that he had been a white man who worked closely with black Americans.[31]

Had Yates been black or white? As other historians varyingly relied on Wesley and Myers, confusion resulted. In some cases, it appeared not to matter. Yates's identity was no more than an embellishment. For example, when historian Harold Hancock published Yates's "Letter of 1837," a report about free black people in Delaware, he explained:

William Yates of Troy, New York, was a Negro minister who was one of two persons employed by the American Anti-Slavery Society in the fall of 1836 to assist Negroes in the larger towns east of the Appalachian Mountains. His headquarters were near New York City. In the middle of June 1837, he attended two conventions in Philadelphia and took the opportunity to visit a slave state, Delaware, for the first time. Most of his 18-month appointment was spent in gathering data for the *Rights of Colored Men*.[32]

Hancock appears to have read both Wesley and Myers and then developed a composite biography that wedded Wesley's view of Yates as black with Myers's explanation of his work as an antislavery agent. Could both be correct?

There was only one author of *Rights of Colored Men*, though the confusion is understandable. The evidence gleaned from early American Anti-Slavery Society reports supports Myers's conclusion that Yates was a white abolitionist, a memorable one for his having worked with black people in the North.[33] Indeed, the mix-up about Yates's identity stems in part from his participation in black political and religious gatherings, and his faithful reportage on those meetings for the black press. Black commentators admired Yates and promoted his treatise.[34] For example, when in October 1838 Yates attended a meeting of the New York Association for the Political Elevation and Improvement of the People of Color, he spoke from his book on "the legal disabilities of the colored man." But Yates was not a delegate.[35] Never in the writings of Yates does the pronoun usage shift – for example, from "them" and "theirs" to "us" and "ours" – in a way that would include Yates among black Americans.[36] Wesley's misapprehension of this unusual antislavery agent is understandable, but Myers was correct.

I was destined to return to *Rights of Colored Men* in researching this book. It is a singular text: the only nineteenth-century treatise devoted exclusively to the status of free African Americans. As I began my research, I dug deeper into Yates's story and initially found little more than Myers had a half century earlier. Yates first appears in 1831, founding an upstate New York newspaper, the *Troy Press*.[37] He was an antislavery agent in 1833 and can be found among the delegates to many local and national conventions.[38] Yates conducted research for his treatise, visiting libraries and black communities between 1835 and 1837.[39] With the publication of *Rights of Colored Men*, he became a familiar figure in African American religious and political gatherings.[40] And then Yates receded from public life.[41]

Poring over newspapers, I came upon the unexpected. There was William Yates in the pages of the black-edited San Francisco *Elevator*. A review of William Wells Brown's 1863 book, *The Black Man*, bore his name.[42] This makes sense, I thought. Yates had migrated west and was still engaged with print culture and black politics. I read on, observing the review's wide-ranging familiarity with African American political culture. Yates critiqued Brown for examining too narrow a slice of black leadership. There, I thought, was a reflection of Yates's knowledge gained through years spent in free-black communities.

I continued my search with a working hypothesis in mind. Yates had migrated to California, as had many from the East after 1848. He had remained connected to black politics, and in that city he would have found many familiar figures – black activists who had settled in San Francisco and Sacramento from New York and Philadelphia.[43] Yates had maintained an active interest in the rights of free black people and, in his characteristic way, was so deeply involved that he even wrote for the black press. It was a good hypothesis. But it could not have been more wrong.

My error was rooted in a simple fact. There had been two men named William Yates. The Yates who penned the *Elevator* review and the one who authored *Rights of Colored Men* were not one and the same. Still, their stories had parallels. Both had been involved in antebellum black politics and devoted their public lives to securing the rights of free people of color. Still, they could have not been more different. William Yates, the treatise writer, had been a gentleman of some means, enough to sustain himself as a volunteer for the antislavery movement. His institutional home had been the American Anti-Slavery Society, in which black men were marginalized in the 1830s. And he had been white.

William Yates the reviewer for the *Elevator* was born a slave and had an equally important story to tell about the history of race and rights. From Virginia, Yates purchased his freedom, migrated to Washington, DC, and began working as a porter at the United States Supreme Court.[44] He had a legal education, the kind acquired through the negotiations that secured his liberty and through observing the goings-on in the nation's high court. Yates understood the law of slavery and of freedom. His labors earned him enough to secure the manumission of his wife, Emeliner, and their three children.[45]

In the early 1850s Yates had moved to San Francisco, where he became a public figure.[46]

A columnist for the African American-owned news weekly the *Elevator*, writing under the pen name "Amigo," Yates's ideas circulated widely.[47] Yates led California's black political conventions as a man "possessed of great natural strength and ability" whose reputation was so widespread that "during the last days of a legislative debate, a state assemblyman would rise to support the right of black testimony by mentioning the name of William Yates as a man whose testimony would be as valid as any man's."[48] The former slave made his mark on the very terrain that the treatise writer had once occupied: in newspapers and at black political conventions. He was also a man of action. Yates led a mid-1850s challenge against a state law that barred black testimony against the interests of white people. In 1865 he headed the black state convention's committee on voting rights. His focus remained steadily fixed on the contours of black citizenship.

The discovery of a second William Yates is more than coincidence. It is an affirmation of the very premise of this book. Black Americans can serve as our guides through a history of race and rights. Never just objects of judicial, legislative, or antislavery thought, they are what drove lawmakers to refine their thinking about citizenship. On the necessity of debating birthright citizenship, black Americans forced the issue. Men like San Francisco's William Yates wrote for newspapers, engaged in the vernacular study of law, debated in political conventions, and conducted themselves like rights-bearing individuals, all the while pressing for a radical redefinition of citizenship.

This study is indebted to happenstance and what I learned when the search for one William Yates led to the discovery of another. It was Yates the former slave who pointed me back to the free men and women of Baltimore, Maryland, where his ideas about race and rights went to the core of their struggles for belonging.

Legal historians have examined race and citizenship from three perspectives. Close reading of the antebellum era's major treatises suggests that generally citizenship was not a major subject of legal commentary. To the degree the concept was relevant, it guaranteed few rights or privileges, with neither voting rights nor property ownership, for example, dependent on citizenship.[49] When examining high court decisions, historians have relied on the 1857 case of *Scott v. Sandford* to explain the legal status of black Americans. This view defers to the opinion of Chief Justice Roger Taney, who held that no African American, enslaved or free, was a citizen of the United States.[50] Still others have looked for the origins of African American citizenship in the era of Reconstruction, with the ratification of the Fourteenth Amendment's birthright citizenship provision. This view credits federal officials and Congress members with having devised and set in place the principle of jus soli in American law.[51]

Birthright Citizens confronts high court opinions and legislative edicts with the ideas of former slaves and their descendants.[52] They too were students of law, though of a less orthodox sort, gleaning ideas from the world around them. Their ideas about the terms of national belonging were expressed in newspapers and political conventions.[53] Their actions – petitioning, litigating, and actions in the streets – are a record of how people with limited access to legal authority won rights by acting like rights-bearing people. They secured citizenship by comporting themselves like citizens.[54] They developed legal consciousness – an understanding of their lives through law – and sought badges of citizenship.[55] This is not, however, a story of unbridled agency in a triumphalist sense.[56] Inhabiting rights and comporting themselves like citizens only sometimes secured justice.[57] Just as often, just ends remained elusive.

From shardlike courthouse records – dockets, minute books, and case files – this study pieces together the everyday ways in which African Americans approached rights and citizenship. Traces in the court archive do not speak for themselves, and rarely do they include narrative. To get these documents to speak requires building individual stories with particularity. The result is a history, told through a series of disruptive vignettes, that suggests how people without rights still exercised them. Quotidian courthouse appearances resonate with debates in legislatures, high courts, and political conventions. New characters in the history of race and rights – black Americans whose stories had long been buried in unopened leather books and case files tied up with red string – are linked to those of better-remembered figures – lawyers, judges, and legislators.

This approach is interesting for what it leaves out as well as for what it includes. Its grounding in the perspective of antebellum America's black activists gives *Birthright Citizens* a selective and sometimes partial view of the era's citizenship debate. A few dimensions of that debate, surely relevant to some lawmakers in the nineteenth century and of note for historians today, did not figure importantly in how African Americans understood citizenship. An important example is the federal circuit court decision of 1823 by Justice Bushrod Washington in *Corfield v. Coryell*.[58] Washington's explanation of the Constitution's privileges and immunities clause is said to have influenced Reconstruction-era rethinking on citizenship. Today, legal scholars regard *Corfield* as an early and essential touchstone for arbitrating the rights of citizens. Still, there is no evidence that *Corfield* influenced the thinking about free African Americans in Baltimore or elsewhere. Later deemed influential, *Corfield* is outside the scope of this book.

This study also departs from those before it by looking for the history of law in debate and conflict, rather than in a positivistic interpretation of texts.[59] Those who read *Birthright Citizens* looking for a new answer to an old question – Were black Americans citizens? – will find the answer is yes and no. Sometimes citizenship was defined in constitutions and statutes, although most of the time it was not. Courts disagreed and even changed their minds over who was a citizen and what rights might attach to that status. Commentators and treatise writers were never in accord and amended their writings to reflect

changed thinking. The only consensus that emerges is one about the importance of fixing the status of free black people. Whether for or against desig-
nating them as citizens, there was widespread agreement about the need to
situate former slaves in the nation's legal regime. Beyond that, this is a story of
how lawmakers and jurists fumbled, punted, confused, and otherwise failed to
settle the question. Free black activists were generally of one mind. But even if
they agreed that they were citizens, they did not agree about whether the state
might affirm that fact. Faced with uncertainty, some fled for Northern cities,
Liberia, or Canada. Many more stayed put.

Other studies have examined African American rights during the antebellum
period, although few have expressly linked rights to citizenship as this book
does.[60] For the historian this is a thorny matter, foremost because not all antebellum Americans saw the relationship between rights and citizenship in the
same way. For some, being a citizen was the gateway to rights. Citizenship
was a prerequisite to the right to vote. For others, exercising rights was evidence of citizenship. If a person exercised the right to vote, it was evidence
that he was a citizen. Often no relationship between rights and citizenship was
articulated, leaving these as separate notions under law. Texts are of little help
with this puzzle. In the absence of positive law – such as the later Civil Rights
Act of 1866 – the equation linking rights and citizenship was never fixed. Black
Americans' efforts were aimed at securing rights that evidenced their citizenship. Still, when rights were denied them, free people of color inverted the argument: citizenship was said to be a gateway to rights.

"Rights" as used here refers to a process by which black Americans imagined,
claimed, and enacted their relationship to law. Political theorist Bonnie Honig
characterizes the assumption of rights and privileges by outsider subjects as a
quintessentially democratic practice. Fundamental to democracy are the ways
in which those said to be without rights make claims and "room for themselves." Although Honig's case is that of aliens, or noncitizens, her approach
serves well a search for meaning in the rights claims of free people of color.
Their rights making was messy, contested, and sometimes violent. How else,
Honig asks, would those on the outside challenge the imbalance of power that
framed such dynamics? Well before any judicial or legislative consensus granted
their rights, free black men and women seized them, often in everyday claims
that set them on a par with other rights-bearing persons.[61] Only later did those
rights become enshrined in text. In antebellum America, rights holders were
those who did what rights holders did.[62]

This process of making rights was linked, for black Americans, to a broad
claim to the "privileges and immunities of citizenship." Rights, like citizenship,
were not self-evident in antebellum America. What were the rights of citizens?
One answer comes out of a study of high court doctrine. The Supreme Court
before the Civil War, for example, was slowly developing a right to interstate
travel.[63] Another answer lies in the nascent terms of foundational texts. Can
we say, for example, that there was a right to the free exercise of religion

before *Reynolds v. United States* was decided in 1878?[64] Another touchstone is the Civil Rights Act of 1866, the nation's first articulation of civil rights: "To make and enforce contracts, to sue, be parties, and give evidence, to inherit, purchase, lease, sell, hold, and convey real and personal property, and to full and equal benefit of all laws and proceedings for the security of person and property." These textual expressions of rights existed alongside a view of rights as secured through their performance. Free African Americans became rights holders when they managed to exercise those privileges that rights holders exercised. And often they did so in ways that local authorities were bound to respect and enforce. They traveled between the states, they gathered in religious assemblies, they sued and were sued, testified, and secured their persons and property before the law. Their routes to doing so were sometimes circuitous, and they would need to reestablish such rights over and again. Still, the rights they inhabited became the rights they held. Sometimes they even appeared to be like citizens.

Citizenship had a piecemeal quality in antebellum America, defined only as needed. Who was a citizen? White aliens could become naturalized citizens. But what of those who declared their intention to naturalize before state courts? Were they aliens, citizens, or persons somewhere in between? The president was required to be a "natural born" citizen. Did this imply that others might be citizens by virtue of birth as well? White women and children were said to be citizens, though most agreed that their rights should be determined as much by age or sex as by their status. Paupers, the infirm, the feeble, and the insane represented a litany of conditions that functioned to compromise access to rights for those otherwise deemed citizens. From time to time, free people of color even held in hand affirmations of their citizenship. Black sailors, patent holders, and passport bearers carried such documents.

Place matters for any telling of race and citizenship. *Birthright Citizens* is set in Baltimore, where the specifics of region, political economy, and jurisdiction were critical to how law was constructed at the intersection of formal edicts and lived experience. This study's approach to the history of law reflects insights gained from the many social histories of free African Americans that center on city- or countywide communities.[65] Legal historians have adopted a similar frame, one that is guided by jurisdiction as a manifestation of the local.[66] The authority that a locally grounded study cedes in terms of breadth, it gains many times over in depth and complexity. To burrow into the dynamics of a local legal culture is to open a window onto how ordinary people interpreted law, the important role of legal administrators, and the perspectives of everyday litigants. Local legal culture is an essential dimension of this story.

Baltimore may vie with Philadelphia and New Orleans for supremacy when it comes to studying free people of color. But for a study of race and citizenship, no city better lends itself to understanding this fraught intersection. Baltimore was the nation's third largest city, situated on what historians have termed the middle ground, between North and South.[67] Maryland was a slaveholding state with southern and eastern regions that relied on bound labor for staple-crop production. Yet Baltimore was more strongly linked to regions to the north where grain production was in the hands of free labor. The city sat closer to Philadelphia than to Richmond. Critically for this study, Baltimore was home to the nation's largest free black community: some 25,000 residents, who built a robust public culture. By the 1830s Baltimore was in the throes of what historian Steven Hahn suggests was a century-long process of abolition and emancipation in the United States.[68] The city was a cosmopolitan port, influenced by the influx of mariners and the news they carried. At the same time, it was a locality grappling with the questions posed by the shift toward a postslavery society. The city's legal culture was sophisticated, autonomous, and claimed the era's most celebrated jurist, Roger Taney, as one of its own. In nearly all his years on the Supreme Court, Taney lived in Baltimore, hearing cases in the city's federal court and presiding over bar proceedings. Taney knew Baltimore's streets, alleys, and free African Americans. His decision in *Dred Scott* reflected the tensions that free African Americans generated in Baltimore.

Baltimore's local courthouse was a main stage, the crucible in which many thousands of black Baltimoreans came to know something about race and law. It was the space in which free African Americans confronted the state.[69] Through quotidian civil proceedings, they entered legal culture, learned its rules and rituals, and secured allies. There they confronted lawyers, judges, clerks, adversaries, and a curious public. Often their cases were said to be of little note. But on closer examination, as they filled the court's dockets, black claimants pressed the question of their own status. Underlying their brief appearances were questions about fundamental rights and privileges. Often these were muted in the interest of expedient and efficient administration. Nevertheless, the halls of the Baltimore courthouse echoed with questions about African American citizenship.

Chapters 1 through 4 examine the development of legal consciousness among black Baltimoreans. Without access to formal training, activists none-theless studied law. Their primers were African American and antislavery newspapers and their classrooms, lawyers' offices, ships at sea, and political conventions. Their questions were about rights and citizenship. Neither slaves nor the equals of free white men, free people of color pondered how to combat African colonization schemes and black laws. Most urgent was a radical strain of colonization that surfaced in Maryland, one that threatened their forced removal. They used rights claims and birthright citizenship to counter their opponents. But as Baltimore became increasingly distanced from New York and Philadelphia, activists turned to local avenues of redress and discovered the courthouse.

Chapters 5 through 7 explore what happened when black Baltimoreans turned to the local courthouse. There, they carried themselves like rights-bearing citizens. Disputes over church property and leadership brought hundreds of the city's black Baptists and Methodists into the local courthouse.

Their gatherings were one manifestation of a right to public assembly, and ownership of church property led them to sue and be sued. These same men and women inverted the intention of the black laws. Oppressive permit and license requirements were opportunities to make lawyers and judges party to an exercise of the rights to travel and to own firearms. As participants in the city's associational economy, free people of color were woven into networks of debt and credit, and when they failed financially, petitions for insolvency were a route to extinguishing their obligations. The same proceedings stretched the limits of their rights: black men testified against the interests of whites and served as court-appointed trustees, roles that custom suggested they should not occupy. Families and friends sought court intervention to protect the interest of young apprentices. Family autonomy was at stake, and the writ of habeas corpus proved to be a powerful tool for bringing white indenture holders before a judge. Often the results were not what petitioners aimed for, but they filed claims, served as witnesses, and subjected to the rule of law schemes that threatened to operate much like enslavement.

Chapter 8 examines the era of *Scott v. Sandford*. Rather than a starting place, that notorious case was but a late volley in the antebellum story of race and rights. In Baltimore, the case was in one sense much anticipated, with local legal greats like Roger Taney and Reverdy Johnson playing important roles. Even as newspapers promoted the decision's significance, underscoring the holding that no black person was a citizen of the United States, nothing changed in Baltimore. Black residents continued to exercise rights and conduct themselves like citizens in the state court venues that had long been the primary arbiters of such questions. State lawmakers continued to promote the forced removal of free African Americans – but their schemes failed. When Maryland's high court had the opportunity to adopt the reasoning of *Dred Scott*, it declined and instead affirmed that free people of color had the right to protect their persons and property before the law. In the state capitol, a legislative push proposed reenslavement or expulsion as a remedy for the "free negro problem." It too failed after black men and women from Baltimore lobbied for its defeat.

Birthright Citizens concludes with a look at the early years of Reconstruction. For readers familiar with this later period, much of what precedes it will seem similar. Indeed, between 1820 and 1860, black Baltimoreans confronted the very questions that would take center stage during Reconstruction. Were they citizens, and if so, what rights flowed therefrom? As the Civil Rights Act of 1866 put it, "All persons born in the United States and not subject to any foreign power, excluding Indians not taxed, are hereby declared to be citizens of the United States." The claim to birthright citizenship was affirmed with a guarantee of civil rights. Free men and women of color likely recognized the claims they had already long been pressing. And they did not wait for Congress before seizing the opportunities presented by the new, postwar climate. They moved about, reuniting their families, they organized armed militias, and they lobbied for desegregated public schools. In the courthouse, they returned to challenge apprenticeship contracts and won the declaration that they were unconstitutional.

No work of history is a blueprint for the present, and too much has changed between the nineteenth and the twenty-first centuries to permit us to prescribe remedies for today based on lessons from the past. Still, the case of free people of color and their struggle for belonging will read to some as a cautionary tale. And *Birthright Citizens* is guided by questions that are resonant in our present day. How, we might ask now, as Americans asked 200 years ago, should we regard those among us whose formal relationship to rights and citizenship remains unsettled and a recurring subject of political debate? What cost is there to be paid by a nation that permits people to work, create families, and build communities within its geopolitical borders, but then declines to extend them membership in the body politic? Even as we attempt to contain these questions by way of piecemeal legal texts, why are we surprised that individuals and their communities will reach for the brass ring of citizenship in a society that metes out rights and privileges by way of that construct? Free black Americans and their nineteenth-century trials make clear the pitfalls of the country's incapacity to sustain deliberations and arrive at resolutions. On the eve of the Civil War, nearly half a million people, the majority of them born in the United States, lived with their rights always subject to political whim and their belonging always subject to the threat of removal. We might say that they were not unlike today's unauthorized immigrants and their children, at least to the degree that free people of color then were also a community that lived through episodes of punitive legislation and efforts to force their exile. *Birthright Citizens* is their story.

I

Being a Native, and Free Born

Race and Rights in Baltimore

George Hackett's first lessons about race and rights were learned in his family's Baltimore home. The story of his father, Charles, suggests how much there was to know. Charles Hackett had come of age in the years after the American Revolution, just as Maryland law began to limit the political and economic lives of free men of color. Charles and others like him faced a narrow labor market.[1] He could work as a domestic or at sea, though neither was an easy choice for a man with a family. Charles was left to perform manual labor: cleaning privies, repairing roads, sinking pilings, leveling streets, and digging ditches.[2] Custom, laced with racism, generally excluded free black men from the skilled trades and professions that fueled the city's manufacturing economy. He faced recurring efforts to enact legislation that would have formally barred free men of color from more lucrative and less dangerous vocations.

It is unlikely, however, that Charles Hackett would have recounted his story as simply one of laboring in the city's lowest ranks. His work as an activist told another tale, one about how men and women of color taught themselves how to wrestle with questions of race and rights. His church leadership demanded a spiritual calling and scriptural expertise. It also required legal acumen, and Charles Hackett's earliest legal education came in the form of institution building. He was a lay leader in the African Methodist Episcopal Church, representing hundreds of black Methodists. His congregation was at the vanguard of a movement that rejected the marginalization of black worshipers in white-led Methodism. They had sought independence of thought, especially on slavery, and leadership roles, including ordination to the ministry. In the last years of the eighteenth century, Charles was among those establishing separate, black-led class meetings. His group purchased a lot and small building, naming it Bethel Church.[3] Bethel's leaders purchased the freedom of their minister and hired him to operate Baltimore's first black-led school.[4] In 1816, when black Methodists from Philadelphia, New York, and Baltimore launched

THE FREEDOM'S JOURNAL,

Is published every FRIDAY, at No. 152 Church-street, New-York.

The price is THREE DOLLARS A YEAR, payable half yearly in advance. If paid at the time o subscribing, $2 50 will be received..

☞ No subscription will be received for a les term than One Year.

Agents who procure and pay for five subscribers, are entitled to a sixth copy *gratis*, for on year.

No paper discontinued until all arrearages ar paid, except at the discretion of the Editors.

All communications, (except those of Agents must be *post paid*.

RATES OF ADVERTISING.

For over 12 lines, and not exceeding 22, 1st
insertion, - - - - - 75cts.
" each repetition of do. - - - 38
" 12 lines or under, 1st insertion, - - 50
" each repetition of do. - - - 25

Proportional prices for advertisements which exceed 22 lines.

N. B. 15 per cent deduction for those persons who advertise by the year; 12 for 6 mos.; and 6 for 3 mos.

AUTHORISED AGENTS.

C. Stockbridge, Esq. North Yarmouth, Maine.
Mr. Reuben Ruby, Portland, Me.
" David Walker, Boston.
Rev. Thomas Paul, do.
Mr. John Remond, Salem, Mass.
" George C. Willis, Providence, R. I.
" Isaac Rodgers, New London, Conn.
" Francis Webb, Philadelphia.
" Stephen Smith, Columbia, Penn.
Messrs. R. Cooley & Chs. Hackett, Baltimore
Mr. John W. Prout, Washington, D. C.
Rev. Nathaniel Paul, Albany.
Mr. Theodore S. Wright, Princeton, N. J.
" James Cowes, New-Brunswick, N J.
Rev. B. F. Hughes, Newark, N. J.
Mr. W. R. Gardiner, Port-au-Prince, Hay
Mr. Austin Steward, Rochester.
Mr Paul P. Williams, Flushing, L. I.
Mr. Leonard Scott, Trenton, N. J.

FIGURE 1.1 Agents for *Freedom's Journal*. Black activists developed legal acumen through networks including the African American press. The first such publication, *Freedom's Journal*, was based in New York and employed a Baltimore-based agent, Charles Hackett, who also oversaw publishing for the African American Methodist Episcopal Church. Image courtesy of Martha S. Jones.

an independent denomination – the African Methodist Episcopal Church – Charles Hackett witnessed the culmination of his twenty-five years of religious activism.

Hackett also learned how to think about his community in legal terms. The incorporation of a church, the purchase of land and a building, and arranging for the manumission of an enslaved minister were tasks that offered lessons in law. These transactions demanded negotiations with attorneys, justices of the peace, and clerks. In this sense, law governed the life of Bethel Church. The church also made its own law, titled *The Doctrines and Discipline*, that governed the whole of the denomination and allowed local congregations to hold tribunals that would resolve internal disputes.[5] Charles Hackett was key to this when, in 1820, he was elected the church's book steward. In that role, he visited Baltimore's black Methodists, explaining the importance of church law and raising funds for its publication.[6]

Informal exchanges about law – in church halls, on street corners, over meals, and during the work day – while difficult to recover with any specificity, must have been important. Charles Hackett was only semiliterate, if that. He signed legal documents with an X rather than his name, suggesting that he and others relied on those who could read to assist with interpretation of legal texts. Charles knew the power of literacy and made sure that his son George received the best education black Baltimore could provide. In helping to found the Bethel Church school, he would certainly have had his son and other children like him in mind. Even that work was informed by the parameters of law. Maryland never outlawed the education of free people of color. Still, enough slaveholding states did so that those setting up schools needed a keen sense of what might be permissible.[7] Did the Hackett family talk about law during their regular gatherings? Some lessons were unavoidable. Home life, too, turned on the workings of legal culture. Charles Hackett acquired a small bit of property: a lot on Friendship Street. But by 1832 he faced a foreclosure suit brought by his mortgage holders. His family's economic life was made orderly, though neither stable nor secure, by way of law.[8]

African American print culture extended the legal education of black Baltimoreans like Charles Hackett. In his role as an agent for the nation's first African American newspaper, *Freedom's Journal*, Charles was responsible for connecting his city to an emerging network of free black communities. Published in New York City, the weekly's editors included Samuel Cornish, a Presbyterian minister who had been a missionary in Maryland before settling in Philadelphia and then New York.[9] Perhaps he and Hackett met in Baltimore. It may have been that the two met in a political meeting. However they became acquainted, Hackett was among the first to represent Cornish's paper to the world, selling subscriptions and distributing newspapers in Baltimore.[10] *Freedom's Journal* framed its mission and the struggles of black Americans in expressly legal terms: "We shall ever regard the constitution of the United States as our polar star." Cornish and Hackett brought news to the street corners and parlors of black Baltimore, and with it came ideas about how law was one weapon in their arsenal.[11]

In this chapter, we encounter black Baltimoreans as they developed a legal acumen that undergirded their claims to citizenship. Their first primer was the African American press, where they encountered examples of how the United States Constitution might be used to challenge local laws and thus take on meaning in their daily lives. They also looked to legislators, but there found a muddled scene that failed to fix the status of people of color.[12] In New York, for example, black people were citizens but with inferior voting rights. In Missouri, according to Congress, they could be regulated though not barred from the state. When a free sailor named Gilbert Horton was arrested in Washington, DC, and threatened with sale as a slave, black Baltimoreans were right to be alarmed. Horton was detained in the nation's capital under a Maryland law, and his liberty turned on the benevolence of white men in faraway New York City. Many insisted that Horton was a free citizen of New York and immune from sale. But in the streets and jails of Washington, as in Baltimore, free black people were especially vulnerable with legal authorities so divided.

Competing views about race and rights clashed in Baltimore. From the North came news about how states such as New York and Pennsylvania had implemented gradual emancipation schemes. There, free black men could sometimes vote. From the South, the fact of slavery's expansion was apparent, and a new domestic slave trade threatened the security of free black Baltimoreans. Still other perspectives on the life of free people of color entered by way of the port. Men and women connected to the maritime trades knew of how race and rights intersected in the Caribbean and South America. Throughout the Americas, free black men and women confronted dynamic and uncertain futures. Sailors and draymen related tales of rebellion and liberty in far-flung locales where slaveholding was reluctantly giving way to free soil. Making comparisons between Baltimore and other cities became yet another way to understand life and law in Baltimore.

Maryland's complex character, reflecting North and South, was forged through commerce, finance, trade, and shipbuilding.[13] The city was also a global port with ties to the Caribbean and the South Atlantic. Aboard ships of far-flung origins came goods, news, and thousands of mariners. Free people of color knew these dynamics well. Their churches and political organizations tied them to the North. Slavery linked them to the South. And their labor – as seamen, dockworkers, boardinghouse keepers, and carters – ensured that they knew well the talk in the port. Baltimore was the third largest city in the United States, and more so than in any other, it was a city that was sustained by a many-faceted economy of exchange with the Americas.[14]

Ties of water, steel, and paper shaped the city. Canals connected it with Washington, DC, in one direction, and Pennsylvania's Susquehanna Valley in another. Turnpikes carried stages, wagons, and buggies through Baltimore via the National Road and seven additional turnpikes constructed between 1798 and 1816 that linked Baltimore to the West. By the 1820s, railroad projects – the Baltimore and Susquehanna, the Baltimore and Washington, and the Baltimore and Ohio – were revolutionizing the city, the exchange and export of goods, and the in- and out-migrations of people.[15] Law was a partner to the development of the city's character. The example of how joint stock companies emerged illustrates how the city was increasingly linked to other regions. Between 1787 and 1815, Baltimore became home to ten insurance companies (five for marine risks), seven turnpike companies, two bridge companies, and a water company, along with three manufacturing companies.[16] Print culture was also key. Hezekiah Niles's weekly news magazine, *Niles' Register*, published in Baltimore, was the country's paper of record. The Quaker abolitionist Benjamin Lundy chose Baltimore as his base when he began publishing the *Genius of Universal Emancipation*. There, a young journalist and antislavery convert, William Lloyd Garrison, would join him in 1829.[17]

By 1800, Baltimore's connections to the Caribbean and South America were nearly two centuries old. Some links were wrought from the trade in goods. Maryland merchants exported staple crops – food, household wares, and manufactured items – to the British, Spanish, and French empires, and Maryland tobacco was packed and loaded for Caribbean destinations. Baltimore was known as the "granary of the West Indies," as staples produced in northern Maryland and southern Pennsylvania were shipped to Caribbean markets. In addition, ships built in Baltimore, especially the much-admired Baltimore Clipper, took the city's name, along with its artisanship, manufacturing, and mariners, throughout the hemisphere.[18]

For free black households, links to the North were reinforced through a rich African American public culture of churches, fraternal orders, and newspapers. No connection was stronger than that established by the founding of African American churches. Black Christians in Baltimore were part of a rich and growing religious culture that was bound together by doctrine and worship styles as well as revivals and conventions. Black Baltimoreans also relied on the circulation of newspapers and tracts. Antislavery newspapers and, by 1827, the African American press knit free blacks in Baltimore together with communities in New York, Boston, Newport, and Philadelphia. *Freedom's Journal* included regular reports about happenings in Baltimore. News of colonization-society activities and the kidnappings of free black Marylanders thus reached black readers throughout the North.[19] *Freedom's Journal* was also an outlet for local news. For example, the head of Baltimore's Sharp Street Methodist school, William Lively, advertised for black students in its pages.[20]

Cities like Philadelphia and New York were touchstones for free black Baltimoreans. Like enclaves in the Maryland city, Northern black communities had grown up out of the revolutionary era's wave of abolition. But their trajectories had diverged as slavery was slowly done away with in the North. In Massachusetts, enslaved litigants succeeded in undoing slavery by judicial decree by the 1780s. New York set in place a gradual emancipation scheme in 1799 and then abolished the institution altogether in 1827.[21] No example was more proximate than that of Pennsylvania. That state's 1780 abolition act freed the children of enslaved people and helped fuel the emergence of an important and thriving African American public culture. With Philadelphia just over a hundred miles from Baltimore by coach, African Americans were able to move between the two cities for work and to strengthen ties of politics, church, and family. The questions black Baltimoreans asked about rights and citizenship did not differ greatly from those being posed in New York and Philadelphia.[22]

Connections to the South were more difficult to maintain. Baltimore was a city of migrants, and in this sense the presence of former slaves and fugitives linked Baltimore to the South, especially to its nearest neighbor, Virginia. During the summer season, free black men and women from Baltimore labored at the region's resorts and spas, where they encountered other Southerners, black and white. Still, black laws increasingly restricted travel, and local authorities curbed the development of independent black institutions such as churches. Farther south in Charleston, for example, the Reverend Morris Brown and his AME congregation were harassed and their church was closed down by the city when officials discovered alleged plans for a slave uprising. Brown would relocate to Philadelphia and become the denomination's second bishop, but the demise of his Charleston church reflected how regionally restricted such institutions were.[23]

Free black Baltimoreans looked to the South and saw slavery gaining ground as a political and economic institution.[24] The success of cotton fueled a new demand for enslaved labor. Upper South states like Maryland were drawn into a new slave trade, a domestic one in which prices for enslaved people sold out of Baltimore were driven by the demand of markets in Natchez and New Orleans. These forces were being felt as early as 1790, and by 1820 a robust internal slave trade was in operation. Some Maryland commentators condemned it.[25] Journalist Hezekiah Niles "supremely hated" the trade for its overall inhumanity, and underscored how "wretches" were kidnapping free African Americans and selling them as slaves.[26] Maryland lawmakers attempted to prohibit the domestic trade beginning in 1780, later stepping up their efforts by prohibiting the out-of-state sale or transport of slaves who had been promised their freedom after a term of years.[27] Still, the traffic in persons continued. A local grand jury published its observations of widespread kidnapping. It was an "evil," the jury members explained, that persisted despite legislation to the contrary. The demand from markets further south led to the out-of-state sale of term slaves – those bound for a number of years rather than for life – and the kidnapping of "free negroes decoyed by stratagem or dragged by force . . . and sent away."[28]

Black Baltimore's far-reaching vantage point is perhaps best understood by way of the people who moved into and out of the city. Human migrations large and small linked Baltimore to a geography that stretched to the Caribbean and South America. Some journeys were solitary. Such was the case for free black sailors who passed through the port. Although their numbers are difficult to document, we can say something about the numbers of men from Maryland who became mariners. In 1810, for example, 7.4 percent of black heads of households were said to be seamen.[29] Such men were "vectors of experience and information" in regional networks of communication. Black seamen shared news by word of mouth, the passing of newspapers, and their very demeanor, which could generate rumors and debate about happenings in distant locales.[30] Other black migrants came into the city as parts of households and under compulsion or duress. When Caribbean planters migrated to Maryland, as many did during the Haitian Revolution, they established plantations south and east of Baltimore, bringing with them enslaved workers. Many labored as domestics; some lived independently and were hired out for wages. Some escaped, disappearing into the city's growing free black enclaves.[31]

White Baltimoreans did not agree about how to regard the growing free black population. Between 1790 and 1820 the free black population in Baltimore had exploded from just 323 persons to more than 10,000. The overall percentage of black households in the city had doubled, from 11.7 percent to 23.5 percent.[32] Some expressed alarm, like Luther Martin, an antifederalist member of the United States Constitutional Convention and former Maryland attorney general. Martin wrote that the city risked becoming "the head quarters of free blacks and people of colour, not only from other states in the Union, but from the islands."[33] He was especially distressed about a recent court proceeding in which a woman, alleged to be a fugitive slave, had been released. There were differences over the merits of the case, but Martin's true concern was how the city's free black community was growing by way of local manumissions and the in-migration of black people from the lower South and the Caribbean. Not everyone agreed with Martin, and he received a quick public retort. The pseudonymous "Humanity" defended the court's action in freeing the alleged fugitive, and then generally decried the presumption that black people were slaves. "Such a proposition," the writer urged, was "opposed to every principle of law, of justice, and of humanity and it is in vain to urge in support of it, that the colour of a negro alone is sufficient evidence of his being a slave."[34] Over time this position would be defeated and color would raise the presumption of slave status. Still, Humanity's perspective was important. It admitted that Baltimore was becoming a haven for free black people and then urged that they should expect due process and fairness. With people like Martin and Humanity at odds, Baltimore was an awkward haven.

In distributing the pages of *Freedom's Journal* in Baltimore, Charles Hackett disseminated a retort that sought to clarify how free black Americans fit into the landscape of the city and of the nation. Civil rights, readers learned, were "the greatest value," and the paper's editors vowed that "it shall ever be our duty to vindicate our brethren, when oppressed, and to lay the case before the publick."[35] Those rights, the paper's prospectus asserted, were rooted in the nation's founding document, the Constitution.[36]

The black quest for rights had a long history, *Freedom's Journal* reported. A story reprinted from the *Liverpool Mercury* illustrated how quotidian claims intersected with constitutional principles through the life of one of the early nineteenth century's most commercially successful and politically influential black leaders, Paul Cuffe. In 1780 Cuffe, a Dartmouth, Massachusetts, mariner, and his brother John had been called on by a local collector to pay a personal tax. The two puzzled over their obligation, knowing that the laws and the constitution of the state linked taxation to citizenship. If the law demanded the payment of a tax, they reasoned, the same laws should "much necessarily and constitutionally" invest them with the right of representing and being represented in the state legislature. The two decided to insist on such a recognition of their rights. The Cuffes, explained the paper, won their claim. There was for readers of *Freedom's Journal* an instructive quality to the link between a ministerial act, such as paying taxes, and the securing of rights as citizens.[37] In his influential though short life – he died in 1817 – Paul Cuffe was remarkable for his business acumen, his political deftness, and even his intellectual contributions to an "African" identity among black Americans. He was also remarkable for his quest for citizenship.[38]

The Cuffe brothers' experience as seamen during the American Revolution hinted at how they developed expectations about citizenship through exchanges during their service aboard whalers and their detention in cells of the British Empire. *Freedom's Journal* brought such vantage points home, inviting readers to share in knowledge that made possible a comparative and transnational point of view. Sometimes this took the form of speculation. "What will be the case, when the slaves in the West Indies and the Spanish states, become all free citizens?" the paper asked.[39] Haitian history provided an example of what slavery's abolition might bring. Readers were reminded how, for example, in 1791 the French National Assembly had extended to free people of color "all the privileges of French citizens," including the right to hold office.[40] In "South America and Hayti," readers learned, "the Man of Colour is seen in all the dignity of man, freed from the prejudices, and endowed with the rights, and enjoying all the privileges of citizenship."[41] Comparative thinking about citizenship opened minds to the prospect of colonization and migration to Liberia. It was a "mere waste of words to talk of ever enjoying citizenship in this country," the journal's editors declared, and the Liberian example provided an important counterpoint.[42] As one correspondent put it, these examples and others ensured that free black men and women were "so far enlightened, as to know that they are unjustly, in this land of liberty, denied the rights and privileges of free citizens."[43]

Freedom's Journal also brought questions about free black citizenship close to home for Baltimoreans. In 1828 a correspondent reported, after a short visit to the city, that a free man of color "may be respected in his business; he may be encouraged; but when we come to talk of liberty – of the rights of citizen-ship – of his evidence in a court of justice against his fairer brethren, we cannot but perceive that there is little justice doled out to him by the republican laws of the state of Maryland."[44] Men from cities such as New York or Philadelphia recognized their relative status. "Baltimore was never designed to be the abode of your humble servant," a correspondent wrote. "A man of colour, educated at the north, can never feel himself at home in Baltimore," learned the paper's readers.[45] This view had merit. Black Baltimoreans made their way in a world framed by a particular if not unique legal culture, one that offered no certainty about their status.

If geography opened Baltimore up to the world, legal culture threatened to close it off. The city's free black men and women lived at the crossroads of geography, culture, and politics. But legal culture worked to close off these influences. Lawmakers found it nearly impossible to fix the status of free black Marylanders. Instead, they put in place a piecemeal scheme of requirements and restrictions aimed at curbing the very mobility and independence that life in the port city might invite. This tension, between ambition and possibility on the one hand and repression and control on the other, led free black families to study law. Their rights and status, confused and uncertain, relied on no single text, ruling, or statute.

Constitutions were one touchstone, and founding texts seemed to suggest that free people of color might expect to live as fully rights-bearing persons, equivalent to their white counterparts. The constitutions of the United States and Maryland were silent on the status of free black people. The 1776 Maryland state constitution did not use the word "citizen," although it recognized inhabitants and free men. It ascribed differences among Marylanders: there were non-Christians whose religious liberty was not guaranteed, clergy members who could own property only with permission of the legislature, and those under twenty-one or without property who were politically disenfranchised. Free people of color appeared to stand on a par with whites. The United States Constitution elided the question of who was a citizen. Its broad categories distinguished among free people, enslaved people, and Indians. It did not address the status of those who, though descended from slaves or the formerly enslaved, were now free. The Constitution's only references to citizens were fragmentary and implicit: only citizens could serve as members of Congress; only "natural born" citizens as president; only citizens could sue in federal courts. The Constitution thus guaranteed privileges and immunities of citizens but did not delineate how to distinguish citizens from noncitizens. The matter of race and citizenship, in both state and federal terms, remained unsettled. For Baltimoreans, neither constitution expressly barred legal distinctions grounded in race, leaving an opening for legislative action.[46]

There was little express collaboration between state and federal lawmakers in the early nineteenth century on the question of free black people, and the character of what emerged from Congress and from the state assembly differed. Maryland reached aggressively into the lives of free black people in the early republic, but Congress was more restrained. When setting the terms of the first national census enumeration in 1790, Congress provided that enumerators should distinguish between "the sexes and colors of free persons." Hence, the census schedule was divided into the categories of free whites, "all other free persons" including free African Americans, and slaves.[47] Congress did immerse itself in more local questions through its governance of the new District of Columbia. In 1802 Congress limited the vote and service in the militia in the district to "free white male inhabitants of full age."[48] No single piece of congressional legislation was felt more in Baltimore than the Naturalization Act of 1790, in which Congress expressly limited naturalization to free white persons; free people of color were not eligible to become naturalized citizens of the United States.[49] Thus in Baltimore, a destination for free black people from throughout the Americas, especially seamen, prohibitions against naturalization distinguished free black men and women from their white counterparts.

State lawmakers also began to draw boundaries around black Marylanders, attempting to fix them in place and in status through what came to be termed black laws. These did not constitute a comprehensive or coherent code such as that governing slavery and free people of color in the French and Spanish Americas.[50] Between 1780 and 1820, Maryland lawmakers set in place a piecemeal series of regulations. That about which the constitution had been silent now regularly animated the state assembly in Annapolis, as lawmakers asked where free African Americans stood in Maryland's legal culture.[51]

Central to this new legal regime were restrictions on mobility. By 1820, Maryland had closed its border to the in-migration of free black people, rendering its own residents increasingly isolated. State laws defined free black men and women in part by restricting their comings and goings. Maryland began by first restricting the slave trade into and through the state. By 1783, the legislature codified what was already true in practice: importing slaves from other states or countries was strongly discouraged, first by prohibitive taxes and then by criminal penalties. It would be another twenty-plus years before lawmakers regulated the movement of free black people. When they did so, in 1806, they imposed a hefty ten-dollar-per-day fine on those who migrated into the state. To make the state's position all the more clear, the new law added extra discouragement: failure to pay such fines could result in being sold out of Maryland, in essence enslaving free people.

For those remaining in Maryland, no authority spoke directly to their citizenship. Still, their rights narrowed between 1780 and 1820. Free black men had voted until the last years of the eighteenth century, but that door gradually closed. Initially lawmakers drew a distinction between "historically" and "newly" free people. Those free before 1783 retained a broad set of rights, while those born or manumitted after 1783 were distinguished by the rights they did not possess: they could neither vote nor hold public office. By 1783, "newly" freed people were barred from testifying against whites, although, notably, "historically" freed people were not. This distinction did not hold very long, however. By 1801, the constitution had been amended to limit the vote in Maryland to "free white male citizens, and no other." All free black people were thus disenfranchised.[52]

This fissure and others suggest how courts remained more porous institutions even as political rights were being revoked. When Maryland's high court attempted to interpret the state's tangled laws regulating black testimony, it failed. In the case of *State v. Fisher*, a trial court had allowed a free "mulatto" woman to testify against the interests of the defendant, a "free born white Christian man." The verdict was guilty. On appeal the high court asked whether a free mulatto woman could so testify. The justices scrutinized the statutes going back to the early eighteenth century and found they "could not agree in opinion upon the question." There was, as the decision put it, "a diversity of opinion." The testimony and the verdict were thus permitted to stand.[53] Legislators also suggested that courthouses remained open venues for free black Marylanders. The laws of 1783 generally sought to limit the rights of "newly" free black people. But there were important exceptions. They could by positive law "hold property" and "obtain redress in law or equity for an injury to . . . person or property."[54]

Maryland's early black laws, adopted in fits and starts, were never comprehensive. Nor did they bar African Americans from the courthouse. Instead, omissions left spaces through which free black people might insert their interests in courtrooms that remained open to black litigants. Maryland allowed the education of free African Americans, and in Baltimore, church-sponsored schools were in place by the first decade of the nineteenth century. The state's borders, which were crowded with legal barriers, expressly retained important openings. Black seamen, along with wagoners and messengers, could enter the state while performing their duties without risking punishment. There were no formal restrictions on the movement of free black Marylanders themselves. They could leave and reenter the state at will, another avenue by which networks remained intact.[55]

The 1820s marked a turning point, and two poles of a debate emerged. One view was that free African Americans were citizens of the individual states and of the United States, entitled to the privileges and immunities of citizenship guaranteed by the Constitution. The opposing view was that they were persons other than citizens, perhaps aliens or denizens. As such, free black men and women were subject to black laws as well as policies promoting colonization, banishment, and other modes of removal from the United States. Citizenship and the rights that might attend it took on new saliency. Some saw in it a strategy for resisting removal. Others saw in it an extension of rights to persons who must not become part of the body politic. The issue was joined in 1821, in a congressional debate over Missouri's state constitution and in a New York State constitutional convention. Lawmakers faced off, charting out the terms by which the question would be debated going forward. Black Marylanders watched as arguments over their status heated up.

When Congress took up Missouri's admission to the union in 1821, no one anticipated how free black citizenship would nearly derail the process. A slaveholding territory, Missouri proposed a state constitution that mandated laws "to prevent free negroes and mulattoes from coming to and settling in the State, under any pretext whatsoever." The proposal was harsh, and it gave Congress members pause. Would a prohibition against the in-migration of free persons of color violate the US Constitution's "privileges and immunities" guarantee? The answer, all agreed, turned on the citizenship status of free African Americans. If African Americans were citizens, Missouri's proposal drew impermissible distinctions such that its constitution would be refused. Were they not, Missouri would be free to bar black Americans, and the proposed constitution would become law.

The resulting debate stretched over many days and fills scores of pages in the *Annals of Congress*. In the Senate and the House, lawmakers reasoned aloud about what rights flowed from citizenship and to whom such rights belonged. Free African Americans were the hard case; everyone was aware of the state black laws already in place. Citizenship had never before been subject to such exacting scrutiny, with such forceful advocates on both sides. Some lawmakers took the position that free black people were citizens. As one argued: "If a person was not a slave or a foreigner – but born in the United States, and a free man, going into Missouri, he has the same rights as if born in Missouri." This was jus soli, or birthright citizenship. Others saw no conflict in permitting Missouri to bar black migrants, the implication being that free black Americans were not citizens. These were remarkably serious, well-reasoned, and in some cases lengthy examinations of the question. Those present were immersed in nothing short of a primer on the history and the practice of citizenship.

Northern state legislatures weighed in, speaking on behalf of those black men and women whom they deemed citizens. From New York came the insistence: "If the provisions contained in any proposed constitution of a new State deny to any citizens of the existing States the privileges and immunities of citizens of such new State, that such proposed constitution should not be accepted or confirmed."[56] Vermont also cried foul, interpreting the Constitution's privileges and immunities clause. Missouri proposed to prohibit the in-migration of "citizens of the United States" solely "on account of their origin, color or features," Vermont legislators said, while their state deemed free men of color "citizens of the United States."[57]

On the floor of the Senate the debate over Missouri was an elaborate exegesis on how the privileges and immunities clause might apply to black Americans. Southern lawmakers, like William Smith of South Carolina, endorsed Missouri's effort to bar free black migrants who sought entry into the state. Smith opined that Missouri's constitution was "republican" and without "objection."[58] Lawmakers split along sectional lines, with men of the North explaining the status of black men and women in their states and then invoking on their behalf full protection under the Constitution. Rhode Island's James Burrill mocked Missouri's proposed constitution, pointing to black military service: "We have colored soldiers and sailors, and good ones, too, but under no pretext whether of duty or any other motive, can they enter Missouri." Citizenship, he went on to explain, turned on birthright: "If a person was not a slave but a foreigner – but born in the United States, and a free man – going into Missouri, he has the same rights as if born in Missouri."[59]

In the House of Representatives, the debate was similarly divided. Pennsylvania's John Sergeant, chair of the judiciary committee, delivered one of the most elaborate presentations, lasting "upwards of two hours." Much in his remarks went to defeating the suggestion that Congress should leave questions about the propriety of Missouri's constitution to the judiciary. Sergeant was emphatic that Congress was charged with safeguarding the Constitution and its privileges and immunities clause by way of its power to review Missouri's admission as a state. When he finally turned to the merits, Sergeant explained that he disagreed with Congressman William Lowndes of South Carolina: The privileges and immunities clause "made no distinction of classes, but extended equally to both classes." Free people of color were, in his view, citizens of individual states, including "North Carolina, New York, and Massachusetts." They did not vote when not freeholders, "yet no one would deny them to be citizens of those States." What he and others sought was the affirmation of "the humble simple privilege of locomotion . . . a right indispensable to citizenship."[60]

Maryland lawmakers were silent. And their silence is remarkable if only because, amid a great deal of speechmaking, they did not weigh in even as their state was invoked repeatedly in the House. The example of "the Jews of Maryland" was used to complicate who was a citizen and what rights might flow from that.[61] It was reported that under Maryland's "old constitution" free people of color had voted, only to have the terms later changed to exclude them.[62] Maryland's black laws were said to show that the states had always regulated free black people "wholly independent of any federal control."[63] The state's representatives did vote on the various interim motions and did so as a block with other Southerners. But what precisely they thought was not recorded.

The sixteenth US Congress fumbled, letting ambiguity prevail. Missouri would be allowed to retain the clause in question. The state could bar free African Americans from entering. Still, Congress went on to admonish Missouri not to enact any law that would impair the rights of citizens from other states, including citizens of color. Were free African Americans citizens protected by the privileges and immunities clause, or were they not? Congress tried to have it both ways, it seems. The result left Missouri to act on its own conscience and kept free African Americans in limbo.

New York's state lawmakers confronted the same thorny question: Were free black Americans citizens, and if so, what rights derived from that status?

An 1821 statewide convention met in Albany to revise the state constitution. Spurred by a Republican Party faction, the expansion of the franchise in New York was front and center. The state's property qualification was slated for elimination. How might this affect the rights of the state's 20,000 free people of color?[64] While a small number of property-holding free black men had long enjoyed the franchise, lifting the property qualification would open the door to widespread black voting. Some among the convention's delegates sought to ensure that it would not. Their objective became clear by way of a proposal to broadly extend voting rights to men who paid taxes, served in the militia, or worked on the public roads, the vast majority of whom were white.

The convention split. Proponents of a race qualification argued that black New Yorkers were incapable of exercising political judgment. On the other side were men who argued that free black men stood equal to their white counterparts when it came to political rights. Congress's Missouri debates were invoked; if black people were citizens then they could not be deprived of privileges and immunities. The United States Constitution, it was argued, barred the use of race as a voting qualification. The arguments were lengthy and eloquent, but the result was another awkward compromise. The attempt to include the qualification "white" was defeated. Claims that endorsed the political capacities and citizenship status of black Americans seemed to carry the day – at least until later in the convention. Before they adjourned, delegates set in place a freehold property qualification of $250 only for black men. Thus, in New York, free black people were citizens, and yet their citizenship was circumscribed in ways that the citizenship of white men was not. Lawmakers fumbled, enabling differing conclusions. Free black New Yorkers were citizens of the state, but citizens of a distinct or second class. Free black New Yorkers were not citizens at all, making their qualified disfranchisement permissible. Or they were citizens in a state where voting rights were determined by race rather than citizenship status. Whatever the interpretation, the end point was further confusion.[65]

New York's debate reached well beyond that state, circulating widely through the writings of a delegate named James Kent. Kent's *Commentaries on American Law* became a standard reference for antebellum practitioners and jurists, and he devoted extensive thought to the puzzle of free black citizenship, pulling together many of the small bits of lawmaking that shed light on the topic. Of the deliberations at his home state's constitutional convention, he wrote: "It is certain that the constitution and statute law of New-York, speaks of men of colour as being citizens, and capable of being freeholders, and entitled to vote." Kent's own opinion was uncharacteristically muddled, however. He began: "Negroes or other slaves, born within and under the allegiance of the United States, are natural-born subjects, but not citizens." But then he took the other view: "If a slave born in the United States be manumitted, or otherwise lawfully discharged from bondage, or if a black man be born within the United States, and born free, he becomes thenceforward a citizen, but under such disabilities as the law of the state respectively may deem it expedient to prescribe to free persons of color."[66] Jurists who consulted the era's most widely read commentaries found the question of black citizenship among the issues raised. What they did not find was a clear answer.

Back in Baltimore, debates over rights in New York and Missouri were instructive, though remote. The principles that were being worked out may have appeared abstract, at least until *Freedom's Journal* brought the case of Gilbert Horton to the attention of Baltimore readers. A free black mariner, Horton had been threatened with sale as a slave in Washington, DC. That city's proximity to Baltimore might have been enough to generate real concerns. As unsettling, however, was how law's intricacies left black Marylanders especially vulnerable. Horton had been detained as an alleged fugitive under an "old law of Maryland," one that had been repealed in the state but not in the District of Columbia, which had adopted Maryland law at its founding.[67] The case required both lay people and lawmakers to closely examine where free people of color stood.

The debate surrounding Horton's circumstances made plain how abstract constitutional interpretations could play out in the lives of free black men and women. Horton, a free man from New York, had been "travelling in the pursuit of his lawful business to Washington" when he was "seized and imprisoned as a run-away slave."[68] Horton's story – that of a free black man whose trade drew him across state lines and who was not able to document his liberty or pay his jail fees – paralleled the circumstances of many black Baltimoreans. They had to ask themselves: Were *they* citizens, or could they be sold as slaves without due process of law?

Gilbert Horton was still a young man when he found himself in a Washington jail facing his sale as a slave for life. Enslavement was not wholly unfamiliar to Horton. He had been born enslaved in Westchester County, New York, at the end of the eighteenth century, just as that state passed a gradual emancipation law.[69] Its terms provided that Horton would be manumitted at age twenty-eight.[70] However, in a turn of good fortune, Horton's father, Peter, struck a deal with his son's owner.[71] Peter Horton labored one year in exchange for his son's freedom. As his father later reported, Gilbert was around eight years of age when manumitted. His freedom was followed by a period of indenture. Gilbert spent many of his early years in service.[72] The complexities of slavery and freedom were thus not new to the young man, though likely nothing had prepared him for the auction block and reenslavement.

Horton made his living as a mariner, a vocation that required him to leave New York and enter less familiar slaveholding ports. In 1826 he was serving aboard the navy's USS *Macedonian*. He left the frigate's service that June in the port of Norfolk, Virginia. By July Horton was in Washington, where he was a relative stranger. On a July day, as he headed along the streets of the capital city wearing what were described as a "tarpaulin hat, linen shirt, blue cloth jacket and trowsers [*sic*]," Horton was detained.[73] Unable to produce evidence of his free status, he was presumed to be a fugitive slave. Horton insisted that he was not.

Horton's fate took a turn when a local marshal placed an ad in Washington's *National Intelligencer*. The notice generally assumed Horton to be a slave, urging his "owner or owners . . . to come and prove him, and take him away, or he will be sold, for his jail fees and other expenses, as the law directs." But something about his story rang true enough that the notice added Horton's assertion that "he was born free, in the State of New-York, near Peekskill." This caught the attention of editors throughout the North, and news of Horton's legal predicament spread. A Connecticut newspaper reprinted the notice beneath an excerpt from the Declaration of Independence, putting it to readers that if "all men are created equal," how could it be that, "for the colour of the skin . . . a man born free is attainted, cast into prison, and sold as a slave?"[74] A New York paper remarked that Horton's detention violated "every principle of humanity and justice, and of constitutional law."[75] Another New York newspaper, the *Commercial Advertiser*, most closely chronicled the case. Horton's capture symbolized how untenable was a nation divided between slaveholding and non-slaveholding states, especially when free black men were in some jurisdictions regarded as citizens. The paper captured the view that would drive the ensuing debate: "The declaration – 'I am a Roman citizen,' was once a passport to the respect and protection of the world. So let it be with respect to the citizens of New-York."[76]

Deeds followed words. James Brown of Peekskill issued a short note to those holding Horton, confirming his free status: "[he is] a native of this town, and a free man, and has a father living, who is anxious to have him released, and is willing to offer any testimony concerning him in his power."[77] Westchester County leaders organized to steer Horton's fate. Farmer Oliver Green invited "citizens of West Chester County" to meet at his home, where they would confirm Horton's status, obtain his "immediate liberation," and express "their sense of this outrage on personal liberty in a territory under the immediate jurisdiction and control of the government of the United States."[78] The men of Westchester were not the only ones to act on Horton's case. Papers reported how others had visited Horton in his cell, confirming what the original notice suggested: Horton was a free man whose father lived in Yorktown. He provided the names of white men in New York City who would confirm his story: a Judge Oglesby, a grocer named Abraham Pearce, and dairy operator Job Griffin. Horton had spent some time in New York City, enough time to have develop white allies who could corroborate his story. There was "little reason to doubt" the young man's story, Horton's visitors reported, adding that they would "of course be happy to lend our aid to release him."[79] News of Horton's case reached Baltimore at the end of August, by way of a notice in the *Baltimore Patriot*.[80]

Testimonials continued to surface, fueling the construction of legal arguments back in Westchester. John Owen of Somers, New York, wrote in to the *Commercial Advertiser* to advise that Horton was "unquestionably a free man," having been manumitted and then apprenticed.[81] With this and other witness statements in hand, Oliver Green and Judge William Jay, son of Governor John Jay, hosted Westchester's public meeting on the evening of August 30. The gathering issued eight resolutions, including one that turned on state citizenship and a reading of the US Constitution: "Resolved, that the fourth Article of the Constitution of the U. States, the citizens of each State, are entitled to all the privileges and immunities of citizens of the several States; and that it is the duty of the State of New York, to protect its citizens in the enjoyment of this constitutional right, without regard to their complexion."

Events unfolded quickly in the days that followed, made all the more complicated by the delay in transmitting news between New York and Washington. Governor DeWitt Clinton of New York was asked to issue a demand for Horton's release, which he did in a letter to President John Quincy Adams. Clinton reiterated the conclusions of the Westchester meeting: Horton was a citizen of New York being subject to a Washington law that was "at least void and unconstitutional in its application to a citizen."[82] Horton was released unconditionally, likely even before Clinton's letter arrived.[83]

At least one newspaper's editor advised that Horton's "friends" should "take immediate measure to enable him to prosecute the persons who have subject him to imprisonment, for the double purpose of doing him justice, and trying the question of the constitutionality, or unconstitutionality of the act under which he suffered." The editorial continued: "An action may be commenced before the District Court, and carried to the Supreme Court of the United States, where the specific question must be tried and determined."[84] William Jay issued a memorial to Congress consistent with the Westchester resolutions: "The outrage offered to a citizen of this county, and a violation of the constitutional rights involved in that outrage, afford to the meeting new and strong evidence of the impropriety of the continuance of slavery."[85]

Congress once again became a main stage. Horton's dilemma was resolved, but the debate continued. Exchanges about the rights of a free man of color and citizenship in New York crystallized the tension between state citizenship and those protections guaranteed to all citizens by the Constitution. The debates of 1821 – over the constitutions of New York and Missouri – were revived. Aaron Ward, a representative from Westchester County, set forth a resolution that embroiled Congress in a disagreement over the status of Horton and men like him. Ward's objective was amending the laws of the District of Columbia to prevent circumstances such as that which Horton confronted. The congressional Committee on the District of Columbia would, by the terms of the resolution, inquire into and consider the repeal of "any law that authorize[d] the imprisonment of any free man of color, being a citizen of any of the United States, and his sale as an unclaimed slave, for gaol fees and other charges." Ward explained that he was acting in accordance with his sense of duty to his constituents and reminded the members of Horton's case, describing the latter as "a free man of color, and a citizen of that county, and of the State of New York."[86]

Ward anticipated objections, and his extended remarks urged that it was "the duty of every Representative on this floor, to guard and protect the rights of this Union," including for free men of color. He alluded to the law under which Horton had been detained and threatened with sale, and then gave a brief treatise on its unconstitutionality. Article 2, section 3, protected a "free citizen" from servitude for life without a trial and the allegation of a crime. The Fourth, Fifth, and Sixth Amendments established the "absolute rights of persons, and secure to every free person, whatever may be his complexion, the right of personal security, personal liberty, and private property." All citizens, he concluded, were "entitled to the privileges and immunities of citizens in the several states," pursuant to article 4. To leave no doubt as to his position, Ward reiterated that the district could not "strip the free man of color of his privileges as a citizen of the free and independent State of New York." He challenged the House: "Is a free citizen, then, because his color happens to be dark, to be less protected by the laws than the poor debtor, in the fangs of a merciless creditor?"[87]

House members like John Forsyth Sr. of Georgia attempted to table or otherwise defer consideration of Ward's resolution. As Kentucky representative Charles Wickliffe explained: "He had no wish to see the Missouri Question brought back into this house." For those with memories of 1821, the resolution's terms – in particular, its claim that free men of color were citizens entitled to constitutional protections – were "calculated to rouse feelings and produce excitement."[88] And Wickliffe was right, if not about Ward's intent then about his effect. Forsyth captured the broad strokes of the debate, explaining that there was a "radical difference of opinion." Some, he reported, "claim as a matter of right, that black persons, held to be citizens of the United States, in the State of New York, should enjoy in every other state the same privilege." Southern delegates "deny this claim," he went on: "We hold that we have the right to exclude free People of Color, to eject them and to limit their privileges, when we admit them to reside among us."[89] Forsyth proposed a compromise. If Ward would admit that the laws of the district were constitutional, he would endorse an inquiry into altering them.[90]

Ward ultimately accepted the compromise, gaining an inquiry into the laws of the district at the expense of making citizenship for free black people a part of the formal record. Still, the debate exposed deep fissures among lawmakers about black citizenship. Indeed, the exchanges on the floor of Congress were broadly instructive as they reached a wide readership when published in newspapers. It would be two weeks before the Committee on the District of Columbia would return its recommendations. It proposed much of the substance that Ward initially sought, including a prohibition against the sale into slavery of free persons of color for "prison fees and other charges of apprehension." Gone, however, was any mention of citizenship. In place of Ward's bold conclusions were terms such as "any person" and "free persons of color."⁹¹ When the committee's final proposals made their way to the floor of Congress later in January, the same conservative position held sway. Horton's case, while a triumph in the sense that his liberty was restored, was also a defeat. Lawmakers had advocated that free black men and women were citizens entitled to constitutional protections, but they had compromised on that position when confronted with an entrenched opposition.⁹² Nothing in the language of the final bills denied free black citizenship, but the silence reflected a missed opportunity.⁹³

Freedom's Journal made the significance of Horton's case clear for black Baltimoreans. Lawmakers were divided in the wake of the mariner's arrest, moving closer to a legal regime that left free people of color presumptive slaves. In Washington, one paper suggested, Horton as a citizen of New York was as vulnerable to arbitrary treatment as he would be in "Algiers or Tunis . . . Carolina or Georgia." In a tone that bordered on outrage, *Freedom's Journal* urged its readers to sharpen their minds: "In common with other citizens, we have rights which are dear to us; and we shall never sit patiently; and see them trampled upon, without raising our feeble voice, and entering our protest against the unconstitutionality of all laws which tend towards curtailing them in the least degree."⁹⁴ Long after the debate faded, the antislavery press ensured that Horton's case remained instructive. William Lloyd Garrison's *Liberator*, in 1833 and 1834, recounted it and emphasized that lawmakers, from local judges like William Jay to New York governor DeWitt Clinton and Congress member Aaron Ward had asserted that Horton and men like him were citizens of New York and of the United States.⁹⁵ The story evidenced how free black men and women had attracted highly placed allies to their cause. Their assertions of citizenship were no mere flight of fancy. Horton's trial and the congressional debates that followed served as a lesson on how claims to citizenship might be seriously debated and nearly won.⁹⁶

Being smart about law was, as Horton's case illustrates, not enough. Judges and legislators predictably disagreed about the bounds of citizenship, leaving free black men and women to arm themselves with knowledge and then to hope for a lucky break if threatened with detention or worse. It was an uneasy climate. Arguments for citizenship and against the terms of black laws had become sophisticated and sometimes held sway. Still, Baltimoreans did not enjoy even the modest assumptions that New Yorkers did when it came to citizenship, and the pressure they faced would only increase. Baltimore's port was a gateway to knowledge. It was also a locus for exit schemes, be they designed as voluntary emigration or coerced colonization. Black activists there would craft their own strategies for self-defense and begin to draw on ties to local legal minds to build their claim to place.

2

Threats of Removal

Colonization, Emigration, and the Borders of Belonging

Ideas about emigration, colonization, and antislavery mixed during an 1824 gathering in Baltimore's Bethel Church. The catalyst was the visit of the Haitian military officer and government representative "Citizen" Jonathan Granville. The white-led Baltimore Emigration Society sponsored the Baltimore leg of a tour that also included Philadelphia, New York, and Boston. Granville's aim was to entice free black people to abandon the United States, for most their place of birth, and migrate to Haiti and a chance at belonging. Baltimore's critics of slavery – black and white – gathered in the city's most important African American sanctuary to consider the future.

Black men came to the meeting as heads of households, church leaders, journalists, entrepreneurs, and laborers. To them, the prospect of emigration was not wholly new; Haiti had been on the table for some years, pushed there by increasingly oppressive conditions in the United States. Now the Caribbean republic offered a new pull: enticements that contrasted with the dim prospects of a future in Baltimore. Foremost were promises of "economic opportunity, equality, and citizenship," the latter guaranteed by a constitutional provision.[1] There were material incentives as well. Haiti's president, Jean-Pierre Boyer, had authorized his emissary to defray the costs associated with relocation. On arrival, emigrants would receive land and provisions for setting up their households. The crowd at Bethel Church probed Granville, giving voice to their doubts. Once satisfied, they pledged to seek a "speedy" and "effectual" emigration. Twenty-five men – including Charles Hackett, James Deaver, Robert Cowley, and Moses Freeman – were appointed to "confer with the free people of colour" and continue the work.[2]

The consensus evidenced during Granville's visit covered over the indecision and insecurity that gripped black Baltimoreans.[3] In the weeks and months following the Bethel Church meeting, those who had signed on to support emigration veered off track. Some did try to keep their promise. For example,

CONSTITUTION

OF THE

AMERICAN SOCIETY

OF

FREE PERSONS OF COLOUR,

FOR IMPROVING THEIR CONDITION IN THE UNITED STATES;
FOR PURCHASING LANDS; AND FOR THE ESTABLISH-
MENT OF A SETTLEMENT IN UPPER CANADA.

ALSO

THE PROCEEDINGS OF THE CONVENTION,

WITH THEIR

ADDRESS

TO

THE FREE PERSONS OF COLOUR

IN THE

UNITED STATES.

———————

PHILADELPHIA:
PRINTED BY J. W. ALLEN, NO 26, STRAWBERRY-ST.
1831.

FIGURE 2.1 The first "colored" convention. The black convention movement was a crucible for ideas about black citizenship. Baltimore activists, including Hezekiah Grice, aided the movement's founding and drove thinking about birthright citizenship both within and outside of convention proceedings. Image courtesy of the Colored Conventions Project.

AME minister Moses Freeman asked to be sent to Haiti as a missionary, only to be refused.[4] More typical were the men who stayed put. Charles Hackett never left Baltimore and instead became an agent for *Freedom's Journal*. Thomas Green and Robert Cowley joined the black-led convention movement.[5] James Deaver joined with activists Hezekiah Grice and William Watkins to form a Legal Rights Association that aimed to establish black rights in the United States.[6]

By one measure, Granville's visit was not a success in that few Baltimoreans migrated to Haiti. Still, it was the sort of occasion that built relationships between black and white activists through debates about colonization, emigration, and antislavery. With this came new exchanges about law. The Haitian Emigration Association's secretary, Daniel Raymond, was a lawyer, political economist, and expert on race and law.[7] In the 1810s, Raymond represented enslaved people in a series of complex freedom suits.[8] He was briefly a proponent of colonization and emigration, but by 1825 Raymond was an antislavery organizer running for the Maryland State Assembly on a gradual-emancipation platform.[9] Newspaper editor Benjamin Lundy closely chronicled Granville's visit and more broadly reported on developing debates about race and rights. Lundy soon counted among his close associates Raymond, Hezekiah Grice, and William Watkins.[10] These were networks by which black activists further developed their insights about law, generally, and rights under the Constitution in particular.[11]

This chapter explores how the borders of African American belonging were tested in the 1820s.[12] The expansion of the colonization movement brought debates from Congress and attorneys generals' opinions into African American public culture. Since the 1810s, colonization advocates had promoted the view that there was no future for an interracial democracy in the United States. The movement's leaders supported slavery's gradual abolition but feared a further increase in the number of free African Americans. To avoid that demographic shift, there was but one solution, it was said: The removal of former slaves and their descendants to colonies in Africa or elsewhere. The American Colonization Society (ACS) held its first meeting in 1817, and by 1821 it had established the West African colony of Liberia. Committed to black expatriation, colonization remained premised in the consent of free black people; the movement did not call for large-scale, forced banishment from the United States. Still, free African Americans viewed proposals for their removal as undercutting their status as citizens, and they organized against the ACS.[13]

Emigration was, however, a notion apart from colonization. It was premised in voluntary decisions by African Americans to leave the United States for locales such as Haiti, Canada, and beyond. Emigration advocates lamented that, despite having proven their belonging through their labor and the construction of a black public culture, black Americans could not expect recognition of their rights as citizens. Colonization, in its most common form, had a paternal caste. Its proponents believed that black people would be happiest in a black-led republic, beyond the contempt of and competition with white Americans. Emigration advocates never conceded this point. Instead, they underscored the pressure on African Americans to leave their homeland in the face of the threats that black laws and colonization imposed on daily life. Emigration to Haiti, for example, offered a balm. Wounds inflicted in the United States would be healed, as William Watkins explained on an occasion marking France's diplomatic recognition of Haiti, by being "admitted as citizens of a republic."[14]

The line between colonization and emigration was real, distinguishing self-determination from compulsion. Still, not all black men and women were of one mind in the 1820s, and in Baltimore they returned time and again to debates over colonization. Views about citizenship marked the divide. One pro-colonization memorial lamented: "Our difference of color, the servitude of many and most of our brethren, and the prejudices which those circumstances have naturally occasioned, will not allow us to hope, even if we could desire, to mingle with you one day, in the benefits of citizenship."[15] This was the voice of those who were resigned to being noncitizens. Others – including Baltimore minister, educator, and activist William Watkins – thought otherwise. He mocked those who suggested that black men could never "enjoy the unalienable rights of man" and the "privileges of freemen." Rather than benevolence, Watkins asserted, colonization reflected an effort to be rid of a "dangerous element in the general mass of the free blacks . . . a greater nuisance than even slaves themselves."[16] Through debates over colonization, African American ideas about law and citizenship were, out of necessity, worked out.[17]

Colonization cut close to home for black Marylanders by 1830. Congress never formally supported the scheme, but in Maryland lawmakers gave the movement political support and public dollars. The state's colonization advocates – including the presiding City Court judge Nicholas Brice – split from the ACS. The resulting Maryland State Colonization Society secured a modest appropriation of $1,000 per year.[18] By 1831, its first expedition aboard the schooner *Orion* was bound for Monrovia, Liberia. It had attracted thirty-one emigrants, just half the ship's capacity, at best a modest success. Most free black people did not sign on. Some flirted with the movement, a reflection of their despair about a future in Baltimore, and many felt the effects of the movement as migrants bound for Liberia passed through on their way to the port.[19] Public meetings encouraged free black Baltimoreans to reconsider their prospects in Liberia.[20] This climate never drew black Baltimoreans to colonization in significant numbers, but it did make the movement and its drive to remove them ever present.

By 1831, even superficial support for colonization disappeared. Instead, organizing against the movement led to new, constitutionally grounded arguments against the displacement of free black Baltimoreans. Benjamin Lundy's *Genius of Universal Emancipation* noted that an anti-colonization movement among black activists was gaining full force in New York,

Philadelphia, and Boston. But first up was a gathering in Baltimore, a self-described "respectable meeting of persons of color." Leaders included itinerant minister William Douglass and teacher William Watkins.[21] Watkins had signed on to the 1824 call for emigration to Haiti. At the time of the Baltimore meeting he was leading the opposition. The meeting's resolutions urged "caution" and "distrust" and charged the ACS with being driven by "selfish policy" rather than "benevolence." Schemes to remove free black Baltimoreans were countered with claims to place: "Resolved, That we consider the land in which we were born, and in which we have been bred, our only 'true and appropriate home.'"[22] It was one element of an emerging claim to birthright citizenship.

Hezekiah Grice later termed his experience in these years his "*Dred Scott* case."[23] His ideas about the legal status of free African Americans were being tested, and the long-time Baltimorean stood at a crossroads. Should he remain in Maryland or venture to a place where citizenship and rights would not be denied because of color? There might be, he believed, some promise in staying put, if only he could be certain about his status as a citizen. Grice had come of age in the wake of Maryland's 1802 elimination of black voting rights. Freeborn in rural Calvert County, as a teen Grice had thrown off the obligations of apprenticeship and migrated to Baltimore. By the 1820s, he was a young man and formally schooled. Grice associated himself with Benjamin Lundy and William Lloyd Garrison, critics of slavery who edited the *Genius of Universal Emancipation*.[24] Like Charles Hackett, he was an agent for *Freedom's Journal*.[25] Though allied with early abolitionist thought, Grice's views were independent and a work in progress. He did not immediately reject the prospect of leaving the United States.[26] He studied migration to Canada, publishing a map of likely destinations in 1830.[27] And he was also an ally to those, like New York–based journalist John Russwurm, who volunteered for migration to Liberia under the auspices of the American Colonization Society.[28] Grice considered migration to Africa closely enough that he spearheaded the development of a black-owned trading company that proposed transporting goods and people between the United States and Liberia.[29]

In Baltimore, Grice, along with William Watkins and James Deaver, founded the city's Legal Rights Association. Watkins, raised in the city's black Methodist community, published commentary in Lundy's *Genius of Universal Emancipation*, and later in Garrison's *Liberator*, under the pen name "A Colored Baltimorean."[30] Deaver, like Grice and Watkins, was an AME Church activist and a seasoned leader who served as president of Baltimore's African American–led Friendship Society, whose members supported the city's early antislavery movement.[31] They put questions about rights into the air in Baltimore. Deaver, for example, presided over a Friendship Society gathering at which the toasts included: "Give us our rights, and our motto shall be also, 'Our Country right or wrong'" and "Emancipation without emigration, but equal rights on the spot."[32] These men asked whether the United States Constitution provided for birthright citizenship and thus promised black Americans its privileges and immunities as provided for in article 4.[33] Together, Grice, Watkins, and Deaver sought to learn what they needed to know and to secure allies in efforts to ascertain "the legal status of the colored man in the United States."[34]

Watkins explained the Legal Rights Association's ideas for readers of Lundy's *Genius of Universal Emancipation*. His reflections were provoked by the annual celebration of July 4th. Of the Declaration of Independence, he said:

This imperishable document, whose attributes are truth, justice, and benevolence, has declared to the world that liberty, in the full sense of the word, is the birth-right of "all men"; (consequently, of every colored man in the Union;) that we are not only "born free," but have, by virtue of our existence, "certain rights," which are emphatically termed "inalienable."[35]

Watkins posed a question about the degree to which the Constitution affirmed the Declaration's ideals: "The Declaration of Independence is our advocate, and we hope it will yet be ascertained, whether or not the Constitution of the U. States secures to us those rights which the Declaration so freely accords." This close reading led to important questions:

Why, I emphatically ask, should we not enjoy those rights which all must confess have been wrested from us without the shadow of a crime? What evil could possibly accrue from the adoption, by the white people of this nation, of a liberal, just, and humane policy towards three hundred thousand of the home-born citizens of the United States?[36]

Black laws and colonization were an abrogation of birthright, Watkins suggested.

Grice worked within the earliest African American political conventions, and there developed ideas about colonization and citizenship. Accounts vary on who initiated the movement's first meeting in 1830. Some historians credit Grice himself, whose circular called for a national convention.[37] Others say Grice was among the first to respond when men from New York issued a call to convene.[38] Whatever the movement's origins, Grice's leadership is understood to have been foundational to organizing against colonization and black laws.

Only a handful of men served as delegates to the first convention in 1830, and Grice was among them. There, they took up the question that had animated earlier debates in Congress and state constitutional conventions: What was their standing before the law?[39] Situated, as the question was, in the context of repressive statutes and schemes of removal to Africa, it took on new import. Delegates produced resolutions premised in their status as noncitizens of the United States. They held out northern Canada as an alternative for emigration because there, it was said, black men and women would enjoy rights unfettered by racism. By 1831, however, the convention's premise had changed. No longer did Canada alone promise citizenship. That convention's second resolution directed that "the Declaration of Independence and Constitution of the United States, be read in our Conventions; believing, that the truths contained in the former are incontrovertible, and that the latter guarantees in letter and spirit to every freeman born in this country, all the rights and immunities of citizenship."[40] Objectives were moving toward a bold claim: From birthright flowed an entitlement to the privileges and immunities of citizens for all Americans, black and white. Grice was captivated by this possibility.

At the same time, Grice, Watkins, and Deaver worked their connections to white legal analysts, building their case. They turned to a local authority who was controversial at best: John H. B. Latrobe. A lawyer and philanthropist, Latrobe had been a colonization advocate since at least 1822.[41] Latrobe read law with Robert Goodloe Harper and shaped practice in the state through publication of his 1826 *The Justices' Practice under the Law of Maryland*, which was many times republished.[42] By 1831 Latrobe was poised to become the first president of the Maryland State Colonization Society. He was not a likely ally. Latrobe was no expert on citizenship, and his commitment to the removal of free black Marylanders ran against the Legal Rights Association view. He was, however, an available accomplice.

There was some common ground between Latrobe and the Legal Rights Association. The man who would become Maryland's most devoted advocate of colonization had built his reputation as a lawyer in part by representing free black men and women. As a young lawyer in the early 1820s, Latrobe made himself visible on court days, hoping to pick up a case or two, thus building a practice and a reputation. As Latrobe wrote in his diary, his earliest clients were free black Baltimoreans. When accused of petty crimes and facing summary trials, black men and women were assigned counsel and Latrobe was among them. His first courtroom victory came when he represented a "colored" man accused of larceny. His defense was vigorous and the state's attorney finally abandoned the prosecution. Latrobe's client was acquitted.[43]

Once he was an established lawyer, Latrobe was sought out by black Baltimoreans for his advice. The case of Hamlet Nicholas offers a glimpse of how attorney Latrobe worked with black clients, and how they viewed the experience. Nichols visited Latrobe's office, reporting he had trouble paying his rent. Latrobe called on Nichols's landlord and negotiated a settlement by which the apartment was surrendered but the man's furniture was saved.[44] Soon Nichols was back in Latrobe's office explaining that his landlord had not honored their settlement. Latrobe again got between the parties, this time advising Nichols to pay part of his rent arrears and the related court fees as a means of ending the matter. Latrobe took the occasion to reflect on how Nichols had understood the dispute and what it meant to come before the "law." "The law," Latrobe wrote, "in the eyes of the lower classes, is a most powerful engine, and when engaged in it they fancy that they possess the very thunder bolts of destruction."[45] Nichols and men like him saw in law a power mighty enough to destroy their opposition. Latrobe was not sure they were right.

It was summer of 1827 when William Watkins called on Latrobe, and the timing was no accident. Baltimore's mayor, Jacob Small, had issued a "proclamation ordering the colored people to be taken up after 11 o'clock pm."[46] Published in the city's newspapers, the notice directed city watch men to "arrest . . . all persons of colour found in any of the streets, lands, alleys, or any open grounds in their respective Wards, at or after the hour of 11 o'clock, P.M. unless such person shall have a written permit, from his or her master or mistress."[47] It was a curfew that discriminated between black and white residents. Watkins's question: Was such an order "constitutional?"[48] Latrobe obliged with an answer. And while his notes do not reflect its substance, he provided Watkins with an opinion on "the mayor's notice ordering the watchmen to apprehend all colored people after 11 o'clock pm."[49] Seven months later, the Legal Rights Association was still paying off Latrobe's fee. The transaction may have had its origins in politics, but it was also good business for Latrobe.[50]

Hiring Latrobe was just a beginning for the Legal Rights Association. When Grice and Watkins next required a legal opinion, they did not, it seems, return to the office of the city's chief colonizationist. Perhaps his opinion did not please, or his fee was too high. In any case, they need not have gone to Latrobe again. Baltimore was home to many of the country's best legal minds. Just a half dozen short blocks west of the city courthouse, on Baltimore Street, lived a leading expert: William Wirt, the former US attorney general.[51] Wirt had settled into family life and private practice in Baltimore after more than twenty years in Washington.[52] His reputation was formidable. Early nineteenth-century Americans knew him as an author of political essays and biographical sketches.[53] As a trial lawyer and appellate advocate, he was admired for his affecting arguments in such landmark cases as *McCullough v. Maryland* and *Gibbons v. Ogden*.[54] Wirt firmly established the office of the attorney general through development of its structure and record keeping during his long period of service, from 1817 to 1829.[55]

Most relevant for Grice and his associates, Wirt was among the nation's greatest authorities on citizenship. This did not mean he was an ally; his record was mixed. In 1821, as attorney general, he was asked if a free black man could command an American merchant vessel when federal law barred noncitizens from commanding such ships. He reasoned that if free black Virginians were not full citizens of their state, they could not be citizens of the United States for this purpose.[56] His opinion left the door open to another conclusion: If a black person was deemed a citizen of his individual state, he could also be a citizen of the United States: "I am of the opinion that the constitution, by the description of citizens of the United States, intended those only who enjoyed the full and equal privileges of white citizens in the State of their residence."[57] Three years later, in 1824, Wirt was asked to render an opinion on South Carolina's Negro Seamen's Act, which provided that black mariners entering the state were subject to detention while their ship was at anchor. Wirt deemed the statute to be unconstitutional, holding that only Congress had authority to regulate such terms of commerce.[58] The decision was not a direct affirmation of free black rights, but it put Wirt on the right side of the question.

Black activists saw useful equivocation in Wirt's position. They pointed out that he had, also as attorney general, granted patents to African Americans. Federal patent law generally denied patents to those who were not citizens. The prohibition against issuing patents to "foreigners" had not been part of the original 1790 legislation and was inserted three years later.[59] New Yorker Thomas Jennings, Grice's colleague in the early convention movement, displayed his 1821 patent certificate in a gilt frame, hung on the wall of his home.[60] The certificate evidenced Jennings's skill and ingenuity in having invented "a method of renovating garments."[61] As important, the certificate enjoyed pride of place because it implicitly affirmed the free black clothier's United States citizenship, signed by Wirt and President John Quincy Adams.

It was Wirt's legal work in defense of Cherokee sovereignty that best established his reputation on constitutional questions. Wirt was not a political ally to the Cherokee. Indeed, he had previously undercut native sovereignty by, for example, ruling against the Cherokee on a question of that nation's power of taxation.[62] But in the early 1830s, he acted as a skilled advocate when arguing *Cherokee Nation v. Georgia* (1831) and *Worcester v. Georgia* (1832) before the Supreme Court.[63] The retired attorney general was clear with the Cherokee leadership that he was not a cause lawyer, and he charged his customary fees.[64] Still, Wirt loaned his reputation and skill to the Cherokees and succeeded in having Georgia's regulations deemed unconstitutional. Only Congress, the Supreme Court ruled, could regulate the relationship between the state, its citizens, and the Cherokee nation. It was a short-lived victory for native sovereignty, however. President Andrew Jackson and state lawmakers would conspire to circumvent the court's ruling. The subsequent removal of native peoples from the southeastern United States, remembered as the Trail of Tears for its mortal brutality, would only reinforce free blacks' fears about colonization's grave potential.

The two matters – Indian sovereignty and free black citizenship – were not closely linked in a doctrinal sense. Advocates for the Cherokee people relied principally on an interpretation of the Constitution's provision for treaty-making power, as set forth in article 2. Free black activists, alternatively, looked to the Constitution's implicit granting of birthright citizenship and the protections extended by way of article 4's privileges and immunities clause. The arguments were rooted in different premises: the Cherokee were protected as noncitizens of the United States, and African Americans were safeguarded precisely because they were birthright citizens. Still, black Baltimoreans drew an analogy between Indian removal and black colonization.[65] Both circumstances turned on questions about the authority of the United States, or an individual state, to remove residents from the land. In Baltimore, an 1831 gathering of black activists explained:

The American Colonization Society, then, stands in the same attitude to our colored population, as Georgia does to the Cherokees. It willfully disregards their earnest, unequivocal and reiterated desires, pretending at the same time to be actuated by the most disinterested and benevolent motives; promising to remove them to Africa only with their own consent; yet determinist by every artifice to render their situation so intolerable here, as to compel them to emigrate.[66]

The Cherokee example was a cautionary tale for free African Americans who worried that if "a colony was formed for the blacks in the United States, they would in a short time be removed, as has been the case with the poor Indians."[67] Missives about the dangers of colonization were, at times, aimed directly at men like Wirt, who had committed themselves to the interests of the Cherokee:

Finally, we hope that *those who have so eloquently pleaded the cause of the Indian,* will at least endeavor to preserve consistency in their conduct. They put no faith in Georgia, although she declares that the Indians shall not be removed but "with their own consent." Can they blame us if we attach the same credit to the declaration that they mean to colonize us "only with our consent"? They cannot use force; that is out of the question. But they harp so much on "inferiority," "prejudice," "distinction" and what not, that there will no alternative be left us but to fall in with their plans.[68]

The antislavery press lauded Wirt's arguments on behalf of the Cherokee: "William Wirt has done that for the unprotected Indian – that for humanity – that for the sacred chastity of our national honor, which entitles him to the deep gratitude, the exalted admiration of every American bosom."[69] Black activists saw how the former attorney general used the Constitution to defend the sovereignty of native people and the right of the Cherokee people to remain in place, as citizens of their own nation. Wirt argued that Georgia was barred from enforcing the laws by which it hoped to strip the Cherokee of national political powers and make them second-class citizens "of color."[70]

This is certainly what Hezekiah Grice had on his mind when he "called on" Wirt. First, the two talked dollars and cents, with Wirt explaining that the fee for his opinion would be fifty dollars. Grice replied he was prepared to pay that much for an "opinion on the legal condition of a free colored man in these United States."[71] Wirt then imposed a second condition, insisting that Grice's questions be "written out in proper form." Grice assented, and left to have his questions drawn up by John Tyson, a local trial lawyer, state legislator, and nephew of the Quaker antislavery philanthropist Elisha Tyson.[72] Tyson worked with Grice, drawing up "a series of questions, based upon the Constitution of the United States, and relating to the rights and citizenship of the free black." But when Grice returned with the questions, Wirt dodged. He deemed Grice's request a "delicate matter" for "an officer under the government."[73] As such, Wirt explained, he was not in a position to "answer these questions as they should be answered." It was a thinly veiled brush-off. Wirt was a private citizen, not a public official, and regularly offered legal opinions for a fee.[74] His work on behalf of the Cherokee evidenced how far he was willing to go in a "delicate matter." Still, he declined to assist Grice. In the end, Wirt offered Grice only a sliver of encouragement. Regarding his questions, the former attorney general agreed "they should be answered, and by the best legal talent of the land." With that, Writ sent Grice to Philadelphia attorney Horace Binney.[75]

Wirt frustrated Grice. Still, there was some sense in what he recommended. Wirt held Binney in high esteem, so much so that he consulted Binney on strategy in the Cherokee cases.[76] Binney would have been a familiar figure as a lawyer of great reputation. He had served as a legislator in Pennsylvania and Washington, DC, and was more independent of political interests than was Wirt.[77] For men like Grice, Binney's reputation included his leadership in the antislavery conventions of the 1820s. For example, Binney had served alongside Baltimore's Daniel Raymond as a counselor to the American Convention for Promoting the Abolition of Slavery in 1828.[78] Binney was likely admired by Baltimore's black Methodists for having defended Philadelphia's Bethel Church against takeover attempts by white church leaders in 1816.[79] Despite his remarkable track record of work with black activists, Binney, like Wirt, sidestepped Grice's request. He was, the lawyer advised, unable to take on the matter owing to "age and poor eyesight."[80] Binney then referred Grice to another colleague, attorney John Sergeant.[81] Sergeant, too, had a well-known reputation as an antislavery activist. He had, as Binney explained to Grice, the "requisite character and weight" that Grice's issue demanded.[82]

Again Grice received a rebuff that was cloaked in some truth. Sergeant had served as Wirt's cocounsel in *Worcester v. Georgia* and was developing a strong reputation before the Supreme Court. He also had been a "counselor" to the Pennsylvania Abolition Society.[83] In 1816, as a member of Congress, Sergeant presented a petition on behalf of the Abolition Society calling for a national law that would discourage the kidnapping of free African Americans.[84] Like Raymond, Sergeant had attracted the criticism of proslavery Southerners when he traveled south seeking to advocate on behalf of a man held as a fugitive slave.[85] His record distinguished him as an ally to free black Americans. Sargeant was, as Grice later told it, most amenable to providing an opinion. But he imposed a condition: Binney, too, must "allow his name to be associated as an authority in the replies." When Binney again declined, the matter "fell through."[86]

These were formative moments for the development of ideas about black citizenship. The scale of deliberations vacillated between grand public debates and intimate law office encounters. Men like Watkins and Grice were learning lessons that no text could teach: The Constitution provided a basis for their claim to citizenship. But the text alone would not suffice. There were arguments to be honed and minds to be influenced. And the stakes were high.

Colonization and black laws did not, on their face, require the removal of black Marylanders. But their effect was to create a climate in which pressure to consent to exile was heavy and persistent.

The situation in Baltimore took a sharp turn in the fall of 1831 that the Legal Rights Association could not have anticipated. A Southampton County, Virginia, slave uprising led by Nat Turner reverberated throughout Maryland. In August, Turner and upward of sixty enslaved people carried out what is remembered as the most deadly slave rebellion in the United States. Over two days, an organized band worked to foment open revolt, freeing slaves and killing whites. Eventually they were overwhelmed by local militias and naval artilleries, and in the hysteria that followed, scores more black Virginians were killed. The county convicted and then executed fifty-six slaves said to have been among the rebels, but even this did not quash white fears. Reprisals took many forms, including the enactment of new, stringent black laws aimed at suppressing the rebellious influence that free black men and women were said to present.[87]

Reverberations reached the mayor's office in Baltimore. Residents reported new fears about free black city dwellers. Whether accurate reports or apocryphal tales, their letters show how events in rural Virginia might have led to changes in urban Maryland. One report explained that, for "several nights past," a "number of Blacks" had been "assembling in military uniform – toward the west of Saratoga Street . . . about midnight with their captain at their head giving orders and putting them through their military exercise." The anonymous informant warned: "Citizens of Baltimore be on your guard – for this is a fact."[88] A crudely penned note explained that at a place about fourteen miles from the city "the colored people intend [illegible] her on Saturday next to go to Baltimore." As a "preacher," the writer pledged, "I will strive to stop dem when we gets to the city."[89] The mayor's records also include a letter alleged to be an exchange between free black men conspiring to bring Turner and his rebellion to Baltimore: "Brother Jon told me that there was eight hundred people in town that was going to help murder the damd [sic] white people."[90]

William Watkins took up pen and paper to fire back against renewed calls for radical, forced colonization. "We would rather die in Maryland under the pressure of unrighteous and cruel laws than be driven, like cattle, to the pestilential clime of Liberia . . . Our limits will not permit us to expatriate." Watkins felt himself "emboldened" and used his voice to expose what was soon to come from the state legislature. He warned that Maryland would seek to "colonize her own free blacks," but without the "usual qualification." Gone from the equation would be "consent."[91] He was right in anticipating what lawmakers in Annapolis had in mind.

The legislature's response was led by Octavius Taney, a member of the state senate's committee on the "condition of the colored population" and brother of then United States attorney Roger B. Taney. Octavius Taney took direct aim at Maryland's free African Americans, seeing in them the seeds of slave unrest.

His aim was the wholesale removal of free black men and women. For men like Grice and others associated with the Legal Rights Association, such a proposal provided one answer to the questions they had privately posed to lawyers, and it was crushing.

This was radical colonization. Taney set out his scheme to "facilitate the removal of the free persons of color from our state, and from the United States" in early 1832.[92] He proposed that Congress fund the effort, going so far as to urge an amendment to the United States Constitution that would authorize such an appropriation were it deemed otherwise beyond Congress's authority. Even this state-level lawmaker recognized the constitutional problems that forced removal might present. Taney's scheme might have sounded like no more than an effort to fund existing colonization programs, but there was no such conditional language in his resolution, no hint that removal would be voluntary. The matter was referred to a joint committee of the Maryland Senate and House of Delegates, at which point Taney showed his hand, exposing the tenor of his measure. He was proposing a stopgap that would, on behalf of the citizens of Maryland, hold "persons of color to service for a term of years," indenturing or transforming them into term slaves. Taney's aim: "to prevent their absconding." Rather than waiting to be removed from the state and the nation, Taney anticipated that free black Marylanders would flee the jurisdiction.[93] His was, it seemed, no benevolent, long-term colonization proposal.[94] It was a new strain and it was radical.

Baltimore's black activists watched with concern. Taney's proposal came back from committee dubbed the Hughlett bill, and passed in the Senate. No subsequent action was reported in the House of Delegates. Still, by March of the same year a joint committee had come back with what amounted to a code that regulated free African Americans in Maryland in newly wrought detail. Newcomers were barred from immigration into the state or sojourning therein for more than ten days. Those already in the state who ventured away for more than thirty days were to be deemed "aliens." Gun ownership required a license for free black people in Maryland. Religious meetings outside the presence of a white preacher were banned, except in the cities of Baltimore and Annapolis, where written authorization would suffice. Marylanders were prohibited from purchasing from free black people foodstuffs and staple crops, unless in possession of "written authority." Merchants faced fines if they sold "ardent spirits, gunpowder, shot, or lead" to any "free negro." Nor could free black men sell "spirits."[95] Although these black laws did not expressly amount to removal, free black men and women saw them as an effort to force them to flee the state's oppressive laws and the penalties for which they provided.

Taney did not wholly fail. Maryland stepped into the breach left by Congress's failure to fund colonization. State lawmakers created the Maryland State Colonization Society, which was rooted in consensual removal. People of color "willing to remove out of the state and to the colony of Liberia . . . or such other place" might be aided by the state's colonization organization and the public dollars appropriated for that purpose. Framed by new legislation that promised to constrain daily life, colonization might seem more attractive. Some black Baltimoreans continued to consider Liberia, for now they were more vulnerable than ever.

What only a few Marylanders likely knew was that at the same moment his brother was contemplating the forced removal of free black people from the state, Roger Taney was also considering what limits the Constitution might set when it came to free people of color. Secretary of State Edward Livingston requested that the attorney general provide an opinion on the constitutionality of South Carolina's Negro Seaman's Act. It was far from a settled matter, Taney explained: "My two immediate predecessors in the office of attorney general of the U. States have as you know differed in opinion on this question. It cannot therefore be regarded as a settled point. Nor free from difficulty." Taney would not venture how the nation's high court might rule: "It is impossible to foresee how it may ultimately be decided in the Supreme Court." Still, his conclusion was unequivocal:

In my opinion South Carolina or any other slaveholding state has a right to guard itself from the danger to be apprehended from the introduction of free people of colour among their slaves – and have not by the constitution of the U.S. surrendered the right to pass the laws necessary for that purpose. I think this right is reserved to the states & cannot be abrogated by the U. States either by legislation or by treaty.

Octavius and Roger Taney contemplated two sides of the same coin in 1832: the former considered how the Constitution viewed the removal of free African Americans, and the latter, how it viewed their exclusion.[96] The view of Octavius was a matter of public record. Roger Taney's opinion remained unpublished and known only to those with official dealings in Washington, at least for the moment.

Hezekiah Grice watched this with what certainly must have been a mix of disappointment and fear. He weighed options: Baltimore and the threat of schemes to reenslave or remove him, or Haiti and the prospect of full citizenship. He chose the latter. The man who had helped found the colored convention movement and created Baltimore's Legal Rights Association left the United States. Before doing so, he made one last public appearance at the 1832 black national convention. It was an awkward scene. Grice, who had played a key role in bringing such gatherings into being, was politely excused: "We tender to Mr. Hezekiah Grice, our sincere thanks for the valuable information contained therein, but that we respectfully decline any interference, as a body."[97] It is unclear what precisely preceded Grice's dismissal. What was his "interference"? Some scholars have suggested that he put the issue of Haitian emigration on the table. But the wording of the minutes suggests that it was the result of his consultations with Wirt, Binney, and Sergeant that did not fit with the convention's agenda: "It was moved that the documents or interrogatories of Mr. Grice, a representative of the

Legal Right Society of Baltimore be reconsidered . . . we sincerely hope that the Society will persevere in its laudable undertaking, and that as individuals we will give it our best support."[98] Disappointment surely characterized Grice's feelings. He had been rebuffed by some of the nation's legal greats and refused a full hearing by his own compatriots. He gave up his home in Baltimore and moved to Haiti's capital, Port-au-Prince. There, he arrived a free man and skilled worker with expectations of being a full and equal citizen.[99]

Their alliances with even sympathetic lawyers generated more frustration than progress. Colonization was unjust, they were sure. Still, black Baltimoreans did not forget that promise of the port. It might be a better gateway to citizenship elsewhere. Hezekiah Grice and other emigrants were a minority, but all black Baltimoreans understood why Grice took the step he did. The promise of rights in Canada, Liberia, and Haiti was a standard by which black men and women measured their own status. The contrast might lead them to organize at home, or it might lead them to board a ship and head to sea.

3

Aboard the *Constitution*

Black Sailors and Citizenship at Sea

William Watkins took the occasion of the "Anniversary of American Independence" to condemn the day's contradictions. While many white "freemen" celebrated "the 'self-evident' truths that all men were created equal, and endowed by their Creator with inalienable rights," Watkins found himself downcast and contemplative on the Fourth of July, "feeling the injustice done me by the law of my country." Maryland's growing support for colonization especially provoked him. The prospect of removal from the United States was "anti-christian and anti-republican," he wrote in the *Genius of Universal Emancipation*. Nothing in the past nor in the present dictated that black men and women would "never enjoy . . . the rights of freemen." Nevertheless, it was a day of solemn reflection for black Americans, and Watkins related that he would "retire from the exulting multitude . . . to contemplate the past and the present as connected with . . . history in the land of our nativity." [1]

In his commentary Watkins set out some of the ideas generated by his work with the Legal Rights Association. He was confident about the meaning of the Declaration of Independence. Its "light and power" extended "to the oppressed of every clime" and would "never permit . . . the perpetuation of our degradation." [2] But there was work to be done: "We hope it will be ascertained, whether or not the Constitution of the U. States secures to us those rights which the Declaration so freely accords. We shall then, perhaps, have a little more light upon the absurd doctrine of our everlasting degradation in America." Watkins explained that black Americans, by their own "unremunerated labor," evidenced their belonging, in building the nation, purchasing their freedom, and acquiring "something like a competency." The improvement of the minds of African Americans – "intellectual elevation . . . proficiency in the arts and sciences" – refuted the colonizationist view that black men and women were destined for "everlasting degradation in America." Citizenship was doctrine. It was an ideal. And in Watkins's view it could be claimed through the quotidian

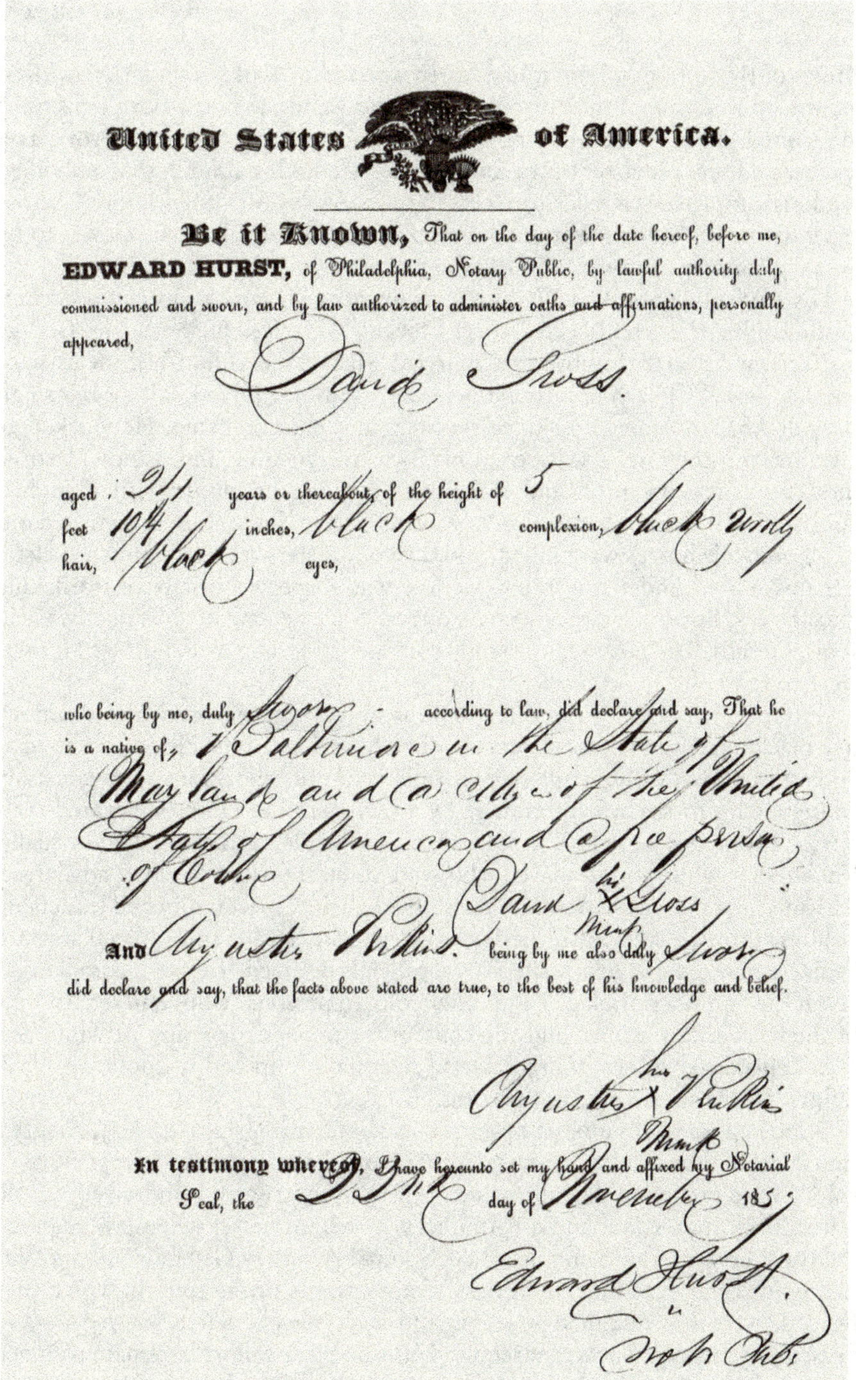

United States of America.

Be it Known, That on the day of the date hereof, before me, EDWARD HURST, of Philadelphia, Notary Public, by lawful authority duly commissioned and sworn, and by law authorized to administer oaths and affirmations, personally appeared,

David Gross

aged 24 years or thereabout, of the height of 5 feet 10 1/4 inches, black complexion, black woolly hair, black eyes,

who being by me, duly Sworn according to law, did declare and say, That he is a native of, Baltimore in the State of Maryland and a citizen of the United States of America and a free person of Colour

David his X mark Gross

And Augustus Perkins being by me also duly Sworn did declare and say, that the facts above stated are true, to the best of his knowledge and belief.

Augustus his X mark Perkins

In testimony whereof, I have hereunto set my hand and affixed my Notarial Seal, the 22nd day of November 185

Edward Hurst Not. Pub.

FIGURE 3.1 Seamen Protection Certificate. Protection certificates were intended to shield all American sailors from foreign impressment while at sea. For black seamen, such certificates also affirmed their status as birthright citizens of the United States in an era when most authorities otherwise openly debated black belonging. Image courtesy of the National Archives and Records Administration.

efforts of those from whom it had "been wrested."³ Watkins spoke as a citizen or, as he put it, one of the "three hundred thousand . . . home-born citizens of the United States."⁴ He also spoke as an educator, and it was his work as a teacher and schoolmaster of the Sharp Street Methodist Church that embodied Watkins's approach to securing rights in the everyday life of Baltimore.⁵ Across generations, in William Watkins's words, education enabled "the citizen to fly over the country as it were on the wings of the wind."⁶

His students embodied Watkins's vision of what education could accomplish. Among them had been George Hackett, Charles Hackett's son. George had grown up in Baltimore and married Mary Jane Gilliard, a member of another Bethel Church family, in the fall of 1828.⁷ He joined Baltimore's small class of African American skilled workers and entrepreneurs. He worked as a waiter and then in 1831 opened his own livery stable. In business, George showcased his education and training by signing his name with a studied flourish. Luck did not favor him, however. In 1837, his stable was washed out by a flood. His horses were killed, and the floodwaters revealed human skeletal remains buried under the stable. George was suspected briefly of trafficking in cadavers, but the charges were dropped. Still, he saw his business washed away, literally. The next year, his only son and namesake died. George Hackett went to sea.⁸

Seafaring was one of the three or four most common occupations among free black men in port cities from Maine to Maryland. Typically, they served as domestics aboard ship, while crew members in other positions were generally white. Going to sea was a strategy by which aspiring families elevated their status. The wages were fair; at least black and white sailors were paid equally. Unlike their white counterparts, who were often transients seeking adventure, African American seamen sought to establish their respectability and leadership at home through service on the sea.⁹ George Hackett became a naval steward in an era marked by racial strife. Naval officials received "frequent complaints" about the "number of blacks and other colored persons [who] entered at some of the recruiting stations, and the consequent under-proportion of white persons transferred to sea-going vessels." The navy imposed a quota on black sailors, setting the ceiling at 5 percent.¹⁰

Seamen posed a unique set of questions about citizenship. In 1803, congressional deliberations over seamen's protections had assumed "free persons of color" were protected like all seamen. Then, in the 1820s, some asked: Could a free black man command an American merchant vessel when law required that only citizens could command such ships? Attorney General William Wirt had opined that free black mariners, if not citizens of the state in which they resided, were not qualified to command such vessels. Some southern states passed Negro seamen acts that required visiting black sailors to remain confined aboard ship or in the local jail when in a city other than their home port. Courts approved. This was an awkward circumstance, because other authorities deemed free black sailors to be citizens. Many sailors carried Seamen's

Protection Certificates, federal government–issued documents that proved their citizenship when in foreign ports. We do not know if Hackett carried such a certificate, but surely some of the men around him did.[11]

Black Baltimoreans understood the world beyond the port through sailors' anecdotes and through the African American and antislavery press. Editors chronicled the unfolding story of slavery versus freedom in the Americas. Mexico was singled out for having abolished slavery, while opposition was expressed over the prospect of annexing Texas as a slaveholding territory.[12] Cuba detained black travelers accused of exciting "discontent among the slaves."[13] In Brazil, "enfranchised" former slaves were said to be property owners, professionals, and members of military regiments: "The benefits arising from them have disposed the whites to think of making free the whole negro population."[14] Men like George Hackett held a sophisticated, if incomplete, picture of the dynamics of race and rights beyond Baltimore.[15]

In spring 1839, US Navy commodore Alexander Claxton prepared to lead the Pacific Squadron aboard the flagship USS *Constitution*.[16] His orders included shuttling diplomats, suppressing the slave trade, and safeguarding the work of US vessels at work out beyond South America's west coast. As steward to the commodore, George Hackett joined dozens of men preparing the ship. He ensured that the commodore's accommodations were well stocked, carrying wine chosen especially for the voyage to Norfolk, where the *Constitution* was being readied.[17] The steward was a body servant, tending to the commodore's clothes and grooming. He was also a waiter, serving meals, pouring wine, delivering tea when called on, and a butler, attending to the laying out, washing, and pressing of uniforms, and the shining of shoes and boots.[18] Hackett's job as the commodore's steward meant he was present, however quietly, during the dictation of letters, the visits of dignitaries, and the conversations between the commodore and his officers. Space on board was highly regulated by status and rank. Most sailors never saw the inside of the wardroom where officers took their meals and socialized when off duty. Regular seamen lived their lives below deck.

The black abolitionist James McCune Smith penned a lighthearted description of the ship's steward for *Frederick Douglass' Paper*. While the captain "sailed the ship, the Steward hosted her," he wrote. His duties required "no little talent and expertise" and "much headwork" to ensure that the ship was property provisioned. He was expected to step in when others were unable to perform, becoming parson, lifesaver, or escort for an unaccompanied woman or child.[19] The *Constitution*'s administration reflected Hackett's exceptional position. When Captain Daniel Turner accounted for the ship's personnel to naval officials, as he did each month, he was careful to note that the commodore's staff was distinct from his regular crew. It included five people: the commodore himself, and his secretary, steward, coxswain, and cook.[20] Hackett's post was more isolated than most, but his station in the commodore's quarters ensured that he received another sort of education.

Following Hackett's journey reveals how he gained new perspectives on race and law. He observed as justice was carried out aboard the *Constitution*. From summary trials and floggings to elaborate court-martial proceedings, the commodore's steward learned about the administration of law. Among the lessons were ones about how, unlike in Baltimore, black seamen elsewhere were competent to testify against white interests. He heard stories of race and rights in foreign port cities, each a counterpoint to his home of Baltimore.[21] The slow and not always deliberate process of manumission and abolition was under way in the Americas, with free people of color generating consternation and contests over their status. When Hackett finally disembarked in Nantucket, Massachusetts, he arrived in the heart of radical abolitionist culture. Free people of color there were calling for slavery's demise, while they decried colonization and urged men like Hackett to stand firm in Baltimore and insist upon their belonging.

The *Constitution* became a courthouse for the adjudication of disciplinary infractions among crew members during their time at sea. The culprits were invariably white sailors. Black sailors, by contrast, figured in the proceedings as witnesses for the prosecution. Trouble often erupted in connection with episodes of leave that were liberally granted to seamen during the months the *Constitution* patroled South America's western seaboard. Naval law defined rights and obligations aboard ship and permeated day-to-day relations; from rank and hierarchy to protocol and diplomatic exchanges, law suffused the rituals and routines of the *Constitution*. Thus, rather than being immersed in a lawless space, their time at sea provided mariners with a legal apprenticeship – fragmentary and intermixed with custom – that emphasized the interplay between law and the assertion of rights.[22]

Legal proceedings were an exception to the casual racism that characterized life on the *Constitution*. White sailors derided black crew members, especially cooks and barbers, referring to them with sarcasm as "fashionable" and "colored gemman," a reaction to what were said to be the black men's respectable pretensions.[23] In contrast, disciplinary proceedings leveled the terms on which black and white seamen confronted each other. The frigate's mainmast was termed the "tribunal of justice." On one occasion, a first lieutenant gathered the crew there to inquire about the pilfering of food. The chief complainant was the owner of the dish in question, who accused two fellow sailors of stealing his much coveted meal of "dunderfunk." There was assembled a "whole posse of witnesses," black men being among them. "Swampseed," an African American cook, shared that the accused were regular food thieves, although he had not seen them lift the dish in question.[24] In addition to testifying, black sailors were also called on to witness punishments. Such was the case when four white "liberty men" failed to return from a day's break in the port of Callao, Peru. Ten days later, all hands were summoned to the deck to witness the punishment of the four for desertion and drunkenness. Each received twelve lashes, a sentence typically reserved for black men in US port cities like Baltimore.[25]

Hackett also observed the workings of complex legal proceedings and the discretion exercised by decision makers. Serious infractions led the commodore to convene courts-martial in cases of internal disciplinary infractions, and courts of inquiry to hear disputes between the ship's crew and civilians. These rested on the application of naval law.[26] Preliminary investigations were conducted, witnesses interviewed, and charges presented. Commodore Claxton determined whether a proceeding would go forward. When it did, he formally appointed the officers who would preside as president and advocate general. An 1839 case against James Morris alleged "mutinous conduct" in his aiding another marine, William Bambury, in an assault on an officer. The charges – violation of the "13th 14th and 15th articles for the better government of the Navy" – were signed by Lieutenant J. C. Rich and then transmitted to Claxton. In his letter of transmittal, Captain Daniel Turner appealed to Claxton. Morris had been acting pursuant to orders that required him to protect the prisoner, Bambury. Claxton exercised judge-like discretion, deciding against convening a court-martial.[27]

Claxton wasted little time organizing a court of inquiry, however, when he received a letter of complaint from Brazil's minister of foreign affairs to the Rio-based chargé d'affaires of the United States. Four officers were appointed to the inquiry: three presidents and an advocate general. The defendant, Commander French Forrest of the USS *St. Louis*, stood accused of negligence during a stopover in Rio, during which the Brazilian brig *Amisada* had suffered "immense damage." Claxton directed that Forrest answer the charges, and the tribunal was ordered to obtain testimony, record the facts, and prepare a written report. Over the course of three days in December 1839, Forrest's performance was evaluated. The final report's recommendations: "The damage done to the Guard vessel was very trifling and [the court] acquits Commander Forrest of negligence."[28] Power was expressed through law and through equity in the *Constitution*'s halls of justice.

Hackett also learned lessons about law in quotidian ways, absorbing them as he performed his duties within the inner workings of the flotilla's administration. On many days he was a silent witness to private conversations, pointed deliberations, and the formal execution of naval proceedings. On other days, he looked out from a distance at life in various port cities, each of which governed the lives of free black men and women by way its own history and its circumstances.

The first leg of the *Constitution*'s voyage was a diplomatic mission, shuttling Powhatan Ellis, the new United States minister plenipotentiary, to Mexico. The ship's time in port at Veracruz was just long enough to introduce Hackett to protocol and pomp. Ellis and his retinue received a seventeen-gun salute with the crew in uniform, positioned like sentries.[29] The *Constitution* departed early the next morning, cutting across the Gulf of Mexico bound for Cuba.[30] Arriving on July 3, the captain signaled for a pilot ship and then navigated the narrow harbor entrance. From above, the Morro and Punta forts watched over a harbor some described as the "safest, best defended, and most capacious in the world." At one end were the wharves of Havana that serviced merchant ships. Just opposite sat "the village of Casa Blanca, the notorious resort of the slavers" that frequented the Cuban port. Between the two there was space for several hundred ships to rest at anchor.[31] The *Constitution* took its place among them.

Hackett, along with the other black members of the *Constitution*'s crew, was confined aboard ship while they were in port. As a black correspondent to the *Colored American* had reported: "No colored seamen are allowed to come to this Island from the United States; if they do they are locked up in prison and tried for their lives; if convicted they are executed or else sold into perpetual slavery; if not convicted they are kept in prison until the ship is ready for sea, and then sent on board."[32] Hackett likely interacted with other black men, among them slaves, who carried goods to the frigate.[33] Otherwise, he was left to make sense of the place from the deck. One sight spoke volumes, however. Across the harbor was the HMS *Romney*, a hulk, no longer seaworthy, that served as a temporary hold for Africans seized by British antislavery patrols. Its free black British sailors, like Hackett, were barred from entering the port of Havana. The *Romney* provoked extended diplomatic wrangling, and its presence in the harbor aimed to draw attention to the dilemma that free black sailors confronted.[34]

Leaving Havana, the *Constitution* set her sights on the Pacific. It was a long journey that would take the frigate around Cape Horn to Valparaiso, Chile, but not before a respite in Rio de Janeiro.[35] Two weeks in Rio de Janeiro meant shore leave for many crewmembers who had not left the *Constitution*'s deck since New York. Sailors were allowed to disembark overnight, with their comings and goings carefully accounted for.[36] Hackett, however, remained confined to the ship, not by force of legal restrictions but because of his duties. Claxton's quarters were busier than usual, with diplomats and local dignitaries being ferried out to the frigate to make formal calls on the commander. Representatives of Sardinia, Russia, Britain, and the United States all paid formal visits to Claxton.[37] What might Hackett have learned from those who took liberty in Rio? The city was not unlike Baltimore, with a large free black population – the largest of any city in the Americas.[38] Free people of color in Rio were citizens by law. Still, laws constrained their rights.[39] Brazil's freed people had their own stories about families, work, property, businesses, and associational life, and their concerns paralleled those that black men and women wrestled with in Baltimore. Black laws aimed to fix their status. But in contrast, Rio's free people of color were also citizens who never faced the threat of removal from Brazil.

Hackett's time aboard the *Constitution* was cut short in March 1841. Commodore Claxton perished during an extreme bout of dysentery.[40] Hackett prepared to return to the United States; the commodore's death terminated any need for his services. Special arrangements were made for him to board a whaler out of Valparaiso, carrying with him 100 pounds of bread, 1 pound of port, and 5 gallons of vinegar.[41] Before he left, the steward had one last occasion to take part in naval maritime culture when he joined the commodore's funeral retinue. When Claxton was laid to rest in Valparaiso, it was a diplomatic affair. A procession ushered the body from the port to its final resting place, led by the ship's band, in uniform, with "the somber draper of death pendent from each instrument." Following were the marine guard, the chaplain, and eight naval officers who served as pallbearers. And then came Hackett and the rest of the commodore's staff, "body servants . . . their downcast countenances proclaiming how severely they felt this sudden and unexpected bereavement." Only after these men did foreign consuls and naval captains join the line.[42] The following day, Hackett boarded the whaler *Ann*, bound for Nantucket.[43]

There was no easing back into questions of race and rights for Hackett. After three and a half months at sea, the *Ann* arrived in Nantucket.[44] As he disembarked, Hackett stepped into a fray, the port's narrow streets teemed with the rhythms of African American public culture and antislavery activism. There, just months before, a young Frederick Douglass had delivered his first address to a predominately white antislavery audience. Agents and correspondents for the black and antislavery press, including Edward Pompey and George Bradburn, made their homes there. Above a general store was Nantucket's Anti-Slavery Library, which offered the public, "free of expense," publications intended to further the cause.[45] Perhaps Hackett heard the talk of Douglass's speech that still lingered on the island, or borrowed copies of the *Colored American* or the *Liberator* to catch up on events closer to home.

He need not have looked far because Maryland was in the news. The state's ongoing colonization movement drew the attention of black New Englanders, who followed such events closely. In New Bedford, Massachusetts, black men and women had just recently convened a meeting to decry the work of the Maryland State Colonization Society. They spoke sympathetically about the special plight of black Marylanders, "over whose heads the storm of persecution [was] now gathering" as they faced the threat of "expatriation from their native land." Black New Englanders counseled Marylanders "not to be intimidated by threats."[46] Still, Hackett would have learned that the threat of removal remained alive in his hometown.

On the table in Maryland was not a proposal for voluntary colonization but something more threatening. Maryland's colonization advocates were again pressing for the forced removal of black men and women from the state. Radical colonizationists had put forward a strongly worded resolution that was devoid of benevolence, editors of the *Colored American* reported. Lawmakers put forth a cynical lament: "It is most earnestly hoped that the free colored people of Maryland may see that their best and most permanent interests will be consulted by their emigration from this State." And then they backpedaled from an approach to colonization that was voluntary: "While this Convention would deprecate any departure from the principle which makes colonization

dependent upon the voluntary action of the free colored people themselves –
yet, if regardless of what has been done to provide them with an asylum, they
continue to persist in remaining in Maryland." Black Marylanders were mistaken if they expected to win "an equality of social and political rights." Forced
removal was on the near horizon, lawmakers warned: "THEY OUGHT TO BE
solemnly WARNED, that, in the opinion of this Convention, a day must arrive,
when circumstances that cannot be controlled, and which are now maturing,
WILL DEPRIVE THEM OF THE FREEDOM OF CHOICE, and leave them no alternative but removal."[47]

Hackett faced a hard choice, and black New Englanders pled with him and
men like him:

Let not a soul leave; stay by, and meet the hour like men, calmly, peaceably, firmly; it
will work your own, and the salvation of millions. They will never attempt, only three
to one, as they are, a removal by force; they cannot do it, and nobody will become
accessory to so foul a deed, as to come in and give them aid. Besides, humanity and God
are against them.[48]

He might have remained in Massachusetts, but instead Hackett headed home,
heeding the urgings of black activists across the North: "Stick to the ship, and
die where you were born." That was precisely what he did.[49] With a sea-borne
tour of the hemisphere's ports, new understandings about race and law, and a
close look at the radical abolitionist culture of the North behind him, Hackett
returned to the streets and alleys of Baltimore.

4

The City Courthouse

Everyday Scenes of Race and Law

Back in Baltimore, George Hackett took time to reestablish his connections after two years at sea. Some things had not changed very much. His parents, Charles and Charlotte, were in their home on Gay Street.[1] He likely also found there his wife, Mary Jane, and the couple's young daughters, Eliza Ann and Catherine Henrietta, though surely his girls were taller and had progressed in their studies. His city also had changed. Walking the ten short blocks from his home to Bethel Church, he could see how a scheme that mixed the push of colonization with pull of emigration had transformed his local congregation. In Hackett's absence, a group of just over 250 black Methodists had left for Trinidad. They were the latest wave of free people of color to emigrate, doubting that claims to citizenship would amount to anything in the United States. New England's black activists had been right to worry that black Marylanders would abandon their homeland when faced with threats of forced removal.[2] The departures of black Baltimoreans reflected how that city's residents remained vulnerable to emigration enticements even as New Yorkers resolutely resisted schemes to draw them away from the United States.

Planters in Trinidad and British Guiana (Guyana today) aimed to draw black laborers from the United States to their fields. Britain's abolition of slavery, and the anticipated end of the apprenticeship scheme that followed it, produced a new demand for workers. Colonial officials promised free passage and employment assistance, and sent agents to cities from Boston to Baltimore to promote migration.[3] They explained the labor conditions and climate. Of the political and legal status of black migrants, emigration agents described a world in which race did not constrain status: "No exclusive privilege now elevates a white man above his colored brethren. A Council of Government consisting of twelve gentlemen in which white and colored are mingled, are appointed by the queen . . . Judges are also appointed . . . [One] of these judges at the present time is a colored man."[4] Black journalists echoed this assessment: "The islands

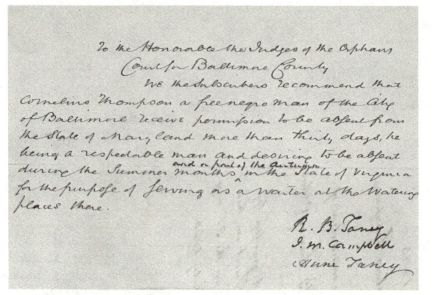

FIGURE 4.1 Travel permit application for Cornelius Thompson. Black men and women became more like rights-bearing citizens when they secured the travel permits as required by state black laws. Cornelius Thompson's application, pictured here, appropriated the authority of Chief Justice Roger Taney, his wife, Anne, and his son-in-law J. Mason Campbell, along with the power of the court, to ensure that Thompson could freely travel for work between Maryland and Virginia. Image courtesy of the Maryland State Archives.

of Hayti, and Trinidad are open to us; there [are] no distinctive persecuting laws [that] present insurmountable barriers to our advancement."[5]

Baltimoreans were not wrong to give emigration serious thought. Maryland's pro-colonization legislators encouraged this, and free people of color felt the push. Lawmakers eased the way to Trinidad and Guiana with a bill that gave free people of color the right to travel to foreign locales and, "if not pleased, to return" to the state.[6] They needed only "satisfy the orphans court . . . that they are visiting said places with a view of ascertaining whether they are suitable for emigration or settlement."[7] Annapolis legislators subsidized the earliest explorations by black Marylanders, allocating monies set aside for colonization to support "two black men of Annapolis, to enable them to visit Trinidad, with a view to ascertain its character, as a place for colored emigrants."[8] Emigration to the Caribbean did little to further the state colonization society's Liberia project. Still, its end result – the voluntary exit of free black people from the state – was consistent enough that it warranted public support.

Public meetings on emigration were called in African American houses of worship, the only large-scale political meetings convened by black Baltimoreans in this period. A November gathering at Bethel Church selected two lay leaders – Nathaniel Peck and Thomas Price – to undertake an exploratory excursion and then report back to the community at large.[9] They were supported by Baltimore's mayor, S. C. Leakin, and three judges: Nicholas Brice, W. D. G. Worthington, and U. S. Heath. By early spring, ads soliciting emigrants appeared in local papers.[10] A "government agent" for Trinidad was reported to be in Baltimore, "making arrangements for dispatching a vessel with emigrants." Local papers published a flattering portrait of life in the British colony that was said to draw on the voices of early emigrants themselves.[11] Crowds of those eager for a chance at life in Trinidad convened. An April 6 meeting was called at the Sharp Street Church, where George Hackett's father-in-law, Nicholas Gilliard, presided. A Trinidadian representative underscored that "slavery is totally and forever abolished in Trinidad." Anticipating questions about race and rights, he reassured black Baltimoreans: "In the Island of Trinidad you will enjoy every privilege, and your color will make no distinction . . . There are seventy-six schools where your children can be educated, free of charge."[12] One week later at Bethel Church, Peck and Price, who had returned, related their findings to "a densely crowded house [in which a] large number could not get near the door." The two promised to publish their observations in pamphlet form.[13] Among their findings were observations about race and rights. In Guiana, for example, Peck and Price reported observing criminal court proceedings during which they noted the role played by three assessors "who must be tax payers; [they] are called to take their place in rotation, without regard to color." They went on: "Many of the clerks in the public offices are coloured; also, tellers in the bank."[14] Emigration might lead to economic independence and even prosperity. It also promised equal rights.

By mid-April migrants from Baltimore were boarding ships by the dozens. There was the brig *Porpoise*, with 70 "colored emigrants." On another, 120 had booked passage.[15] The brig *Northerner* left with 93 people on board.[16] The *Belvidera* sailed with 135 "colored emigrants."[17] On May 22, "upward of one hundred emigrants left . . . for Trinidad."[18] Among the African American passengers' final acts was one that suggested how the prospective emigrants folded a bit of legal savvy into their preparations. Each appeared, often in a family group, before the clerk of the city court in Baltimore to secure a travel permit. No such permission of the court was required to simply leave Maryland. But someone had advised the travelers that if, however, they had even a distant hope of returning to Baltimore, they would need a permit to do so. By the score, those bound for Trinidad hedged their bets with small slips of paper that affirmed their enduring claim to place, even as they would venture far from Maryland.[19]

Emigrants' letters home showed that conditions in Trinidad were less than ideal. Still, missives to loved ones in Baltimore explained what it meant to live as equals before the law. Edward Crew, for example, wrote to his wife, Belinda, about seeing black men in military uniform: "We had also the pleasure on Sunday afternoon, of seeing the soldiers in the barracks, there are some hundreds of them, all colored." Richard Freeman explained how black men were lawmakers and ships' pilots, positions denied to them in Maryland: "You will here be in a country of equal laws, and have the satisfaction of seeing them administered in part by men of your own complexion . . . When we met the light boat in the river we had the satisfaction of taking the Pilot on board, who was a colored man." Edward T. Crew wrote: "We find no invidious distinction here, either in civil, social, or religious point of view, on account of color at least." Emigrants' testimony brought the shortcomings of free blacks' status in Baltimore into sharp relief.

Black Baltimoreans would continue to emigrate to Trinidad and Guiana, making them the targets of Northerners' ridicule. In January 1841, a Baltimore convention met at the Sharp Street Methodist Church to debate emigration, and they heard from at least one returnee. The meeting's conclusion was to encourage "our colored brethren who may be dissatisfied and discontented with their condition in their country, to accept the offers held out to them."[20] Emigration remained a viable alternative. At the same moment in New York, another convention resolved: "We consider emigration to the Island of Trinidad, as only second in its nature to colonization."[21] That is, emigration, in the minds of these Northern activists, was consistent with the aim of colonizationists who wished to rid the country of free people of color. Baltimoreans did not agree, and they organized their persons and their property for the journey to Trinidad and British Guiana.[22] In New York, commentators mocked them: "A party of forty or fifty colored persons left Baltimore last week for Trinidad, determined to make it their future residence. They had better have gone to Iowa, or staid [sic] at home."[23]

Even in Baltimore, emigration was the choice of only a few in the end. Most black Baltimoreans remained. Those who stayed knew that unjust laws required a response and that new tactics were in order. Writing under the pen name Amalgar, a local activist called for yet another emigration meeting, all the while lamenting Baltimore's loss of optimism: "There are many among us who cherish the fondest hope with a warmth of heart for the welfare of Maryland, and would sooner part with life itself than her soil and friendly white inhabitants." But there was no masking the depth of their degradation: "We are repeatedly threatened with laws too oppressive for any honest man to bear who has tasted the sweats [sic] of limited liberty." Those who remained assumed a heavy burden: "It behooves us, as a debt we owe to God and the millions of souls yet unborn to us, yea, our off-spring, to do all in our power to secure them their liberty in a land where reason has triumphed over prejudice . . . where none shall make us afraid or ashamed."[24]

Amalgar went to some lengths to explain why Baltimoreans would choose emigration, responding in part to criticism coming from New York. Black activists in the two cities were split on the issue and had sparred in the pages of the *Colored American*. From Baltimore, Nathaniel Peck and Thomas Price challenged New York's Charles Ray for his doubts about migrating to the British Caribbean: "We hope there will be relaxation of emigrants . . . for we can there enjoy that which law denies us here."[25] The word "here" is key to understanding this rift. The standing of Baltimoreans differed from that of New Yorkers. The former fought for citizenship as a shield against removal, while the latter were second-class citizens claiming voting rights. The New Yorkers fired back, accusing the Baltimoreans of having been bamboozled by Caribbean planters who had enticed them with fine meals and accommodations during a fact-finding mission. Ray labeled Peck and Price "simple-minded men [and] easy victims."[26] An ordinary difference of opinion was reasonable; reports from Trinidad and British Guiana fueled arguments for and against emigration. But this was no simple difference borne of the evidence.

African American political conventions had resumed in New York, and throughout the North, by 1840. The subjects of emigration and colonization were taken up, largely in the spirit of condemnation. The primary focus of these meetings was, however, political rights. They were laboratories for the development of full-fledged arguments for black citizenship. Meeting in Albany in 1840 and 1841 and then Schenectady in 1844 and Geneva in 1845, black New Yorkers asserted their rights as "native born citizens" and opposed all distinctions among state citizens "growing out of complexion."[27] Here they ridiculed what was arguably an irrational distinction between black and white New Yorkers in the state constitution. At the same time, the delegates painted themselves as like others born in the state, and objected to being ranked below "foreigners naturalized." Such discrimination, they declared, "oppressed those who fought and bled for their country's freedom, and thereby were entitled to the unrestricted enjoyment of its political institutions." Black New Yorkers grounded their claim to a right of citizens – the vote – in their labor and their military service.

Colonization was singled out for special condemnation in New York as a system "calculated to throw us into a state of restlessness . . . break up all those settled habits which would otherwise attach us to the soil, and . . . furnish our enemies with arguments to urge our removal from the land of our birth." God, they explained, intended that "here on this continent we are to remain, citizens of this republic."[28] Even in a state that granted African Americans a baseline degree of citizenship, activists guarded against the possibility that they might be removed from the state and from the nation. And an argument that was largely grounded in state citizenship was extended to encompass national citizenship as well.

The refrains "we are Americans" and "we are citizens" echoed in conference throughout the North.[29] Birthright figured importantly – delegates frequently characterized their status as that of native-born citizens. Conventions were an opportunity to convert white allies to this view. "We beg leave to submit some proofs which we think you will not hastily set side," remarked the authors of a Troy, New York, convention address. A history lesson followed. First there were the Articles of Confederation from which the qualifier "white" had been purposely omitted when providing for the privileges and immunities of citizens. In 1803, congressional deliberations over seamen's protections assumed "free persons of color" were protected like all seamen citizens. They proffered evidence of military service in the Revolutionary War, and the endorsement of lawmakers from Rhode Island, Pennsylvania, and New York confirmed the valor of black soldiers. Service during the War of 1812 was similarly invoked. For these activists, a potent mix of birthright, foundational texts, legislative deliberations, and military service both affirmed their citizenship and justified their entitlement to the franchise.[30]

These ideas echoed throughout the free states. At Pennsylvania conventions there was an added urgency. The end of the 1830s had brought two major defeats. The state's 1837–38 constitutional convention had disenfranchised black men, for the first time in Pennsylvania's history inserting the word "white" into voting provisions.[31] And in deciding the case of *Hobbs, et al. v. Fogg*, the state's high court had concluded that African Americans were neither "freemen" nor citizens under the state's constitutional scheme.[32] Delegates to Pennsylvania's black conventions pushed back, pressing for political rights. "If we are asked what evidence we bring to sustain our qualifications for citizenship, we will offer them certificates of our BIRTH and NATIVITY," declared activists gathered in the state capital of Harrisburg.[33] In New Jersey, activists sought to overturn a provision in the state constitution that limited the vote to white men, terming themselves citizens with a somewhat matter-of-fact air.[34] Connecticut activists met in 1849, declaring the vote was "OUR RIGHT, as native born MEN, Citizens of the great Republic, and members of the Commonwealth of Connecticut." Among their authorities was *State v. Crandall*.[35] In Michigan delegates to an 1843 Detroit convention declared themselves native-born citizens, invoking the state and federal constitutions, the Declaration of Independence, and black men's service in the Revolutionary War and the War of 1812.[36]

Baltimoreans, though they had been originators of such conventions, were not participants in the conventions of the early 1840s. The final year that Baltimore sent delegates to a national convention was 1835. That year delegates Nathanial Peck and Robert Cowley had represented the city, and the full convention had openly encouraged Marylanders to remain active. A communication from Baltimore's Phoenix Society was read during the proceedings, and the group was encouraged to appoint delegates to the national organization.[37] But when conventions resumed, Marylanders did not rejoin the movement. Some key activists had shifted their allegiances. Peck, for example, who represented Baltimore and served as a national convention vice president in 1835, was leading emigrants to the British Caribbean by 1840.

Differing circumstances created distance between New York and Baltimore. Maryland's legislature set in place harsh restrictions that likely influenced the content of the black politics in the state. Talk of emigration and colonization was encouraged. And free black people in possession of antislavery materials were subject to an especially harsh penalty: "Any free negro" was prohibited to "knowingly call for, etc., any abolition handbill, etc., having a tendency to create insurrection, etc., among the people of color." A conviction carried with it a sentence of ten to twenty years.[38] Regular lines of communication frayed. Restrictions on the circulation of abolitionist literature ensured that the Northern press did not reach black residents of Baltimore to the degree it once had. In the late 1820s New York's *Freedom's Journal* had multiple agents active in Baltimore. William Watkins had acted as an agent for Boston's *The Liberator* in 1831.[39] Things had changed by the time the *Colored American* was first published, in 1837. Its Baltimore agent was a Philadelphia minister, Stephen Gloucester, whose territory included Maryland, Pennsylvania, Delaware, and western New Jersey.[40] There is no sign that Gloucester actively solicited subscriptions in Baltimore. To do so would have entailed great risk to both Gloucester and his readers.

Local circumstances demanded local strategies. If George Hackett was to take up the helm of leadership from his father, it would not be by way of conventions calling for slavery's abolition or civil rights. He did find another way, however, and an 1844 encounter in the Baltimore courthouse suggests how. That summer Hackett was party to an assault case, a routine proceeding in a city where sailors, black and white, were regularly hauled before local authorities after a fight. Still, Hackett's first appearance in the Baltimore courthouse was highly unusual by the standards of the day. He was the complainant, not the defendant. Hackett charged a white man named John Pitts with assault. Between white men, such confrontations were routine and the charges typically dismissed. Not so in Hackett's case: "State v. John Pitts, charged with an assault and battery upon George Hackett, a colored man. Fined $1 and costs."[41] What had transpired we cannot say. Whatever it was, Hackett sought redress. He secured the assistance of a watchman or sheriff and charged Pitt with a criminal offense. Pitts was tried, found guilty, and then fined a customary $1 plus court costs.

Hackett had sworn out a complaint, testified against a white man, and then won a modest judgment. He had not accomplished this alone. Hackett enlisted the aid of a sheriff, then conferred with a clerk over the swearing out of a complaint, and finally followed the lead of the state's attorney in the courtroom. In the courthouse, blunt racism might be kept at bay long enough for a jury to find a white man guilty of assaulting an African American, he learned. This insight was one that Hackett would wield strategically in the years to come. Black Baltimoreans could engage with the local legal culture and, through its rituals and rules, secure modest but potent rights: to sue and be sued, to testify, and to be secure in their persons and their property.

Hackett's disagreement with Pitt introduced him to a scene that was central to the arbitration of race and rights in Baltimore: the city courthouse. It was at once a symbol of civic pride and grandeur, and a crowded, fraught venue that strained to contain the tensions that litigants carried with them. It was also a crossroads where working people and the gentry, African Americans and European immigrants, all crowded together in courtrooms, offices, and hallways. When they listened, courthouse visitors heard vivid tales of life in the city.

Lawmakers had always envisioned the city courthouse as an embodiment of state and municipal power. The 1773 courthouse stood on a bluff overlooking Jones Falls, the river that winds through Baltimore, giving the building prominence – it could be seen at a distance from all directions. Street-level observers encountered a whipping post and pillory outside the courthouse, signs of how legal authority was constructed, in part, through force. The court relied on its proximity to life on Baltimore's streets and an audience to achieve its intended effect.

Early nineteenth-century changes were fueled by new thinking about law and its place in a growing urban center. Baltimore's development into a commercial port fed the explosion of its legal culture. The city's population doubled between 1790 and 1800, and so did the demands on the courthouse. By 1806, the state had commissioned a new building for the Calvert Street site. This signified Baltimore's new status as the nation's third largest city, having surpassed in population Boston to the north and Charleston to the south. And it announced the dawn of a new era for the city's legal culture. The old, awkward brick structure was replaced with a five-story high building of brick and marble, made all the more imposing by the addition of Ionic columns and a domed cupola. The architect was George Milleman, described by one city chronicler as a "self-educated" man.[42] Had Milleman done the courthouse justice? One visitor questioned the architect's judgment, declaring that he had "placed the principal front of his building on the declivity of a steep hill in Lexington-street, and the end of the building . . . where the front certainly ought to be." Still, he conceded that the "interior arrangements are so spacious and commodious as to give it the reputation of being the most perfect courthouse in the United States."[43] The courthouse's exterior received a boost in 1814 when city leaders placed a battle monument in the adjacent square. Designed by local architect Maximilian Godefroy, Baltimore's tribute to local veterans of the War of 1812 was created to reflect the spirit of popular democracy.[44] When the thirty-nine-foot-high pedestal of a work titled *Baltimore* was finished in 1822, the new Monument Square amplified the courthouse's presence and further incorporated it into the city's civic culture.

In 1835 the courthouse was remade yet again, though not exactly by design. This time a fire preceded the transformation. The episode had been dramatic and nearly catastrophic. At 11:00 a.m. on a cool February morning, passersby noticed flames emanating from the courthouse cupola. The structure's height made it difficult for fire fighters to reach the blaze, and a few were injured in the battle. The courts, including the grand jury, were in session, but everyone escaped the danger. Nearly as important were the records, which were saved by fireproof rooms and the quick thinking of the clerk, who carried bundles of documents in his arms as he fled the burning structure. One newspaper lamented: "The court house was one of the best built and extensive, and noble buildings of its kind – the ornament and pride of our city. Its destruction is a great public loss."[45] Through restoration and renovation after the fire, lawmakers would take the opportunity to enhance the cultural importance of the courthouse to life in Baltimore City. A commission was appointed to oversee the repairs, and the city and state paid generously to rebuild and improve its hall of justice.[46]

Inside the courthouse, African Americans were regulars. Often they were the subjects of criminal proceedings. In 1850, for example, 578 African Americans were convicted of criminal charges in Baltimore, representing nearly 25 percent of all convictions in the jurisdiction that year.[47] These cases considered a broad range of offenses: unpaid debts, breaches of the peace, assault and battery, bastardy, aiding runaways, and the selling of liquor on Sunday. And as the cases entered the courthouse, so too did the social worlds of those involved. Stories of commercial transactions that led to unmet debts, disagreements in homes and in public places that led to physical confrontations, intimate relations that led to the births of children, antislavery politics that led to the sheltering of fugitives, and leisure time activities and the accompanying consumption of alcohol all made their way into the building's hallways, offices, and courtrooms.[48]

The courthouse was a public place where Baltimore's public gathered. Although its placement on Monument Square, with its grand approach and long vantage point, set it apart from the cityscape, at the same time it was a scene for the enactment of civic rituals, ensuring that the courthouse was more than a distant hall of justice. It was a central figure in Baltimore's cultural landscape. On an ordinary day, the space teemed with foot traffic, carts, and the vans that transported prisoners to the penitentiary. Hucksters plied their goods while various sorts of speechifying typically drew modest crowds of a hundred people. Monument Square was the site for so-called town meetings, political conventions, and pageants. To venture there with a grievance or a bid for status was to take a place on Baltimore's main stage.

Some courthouse rituals were less than laudatory in the eyes of free black Baltimoreans. There were, for example, those that played out at the courthouse door. Court-ordered auctions of property and people were conducted in that liminal space between the bustle of the city streets and the cool grandeur of the courtroom. The steady cadence of the auctioneer's call punctuated such occasions. Confiscated houses, lots, and household goods were sold to the highest bidder. So were free African Americans – those who had been convicted and sentenced to be sold out of the state for a term of years.[49] They often stood alongside enslaved men and women, as executors disposed of those said to be property in persons and the state disposed of those found to be fugitives.[50] Even for casual passersby, these Monument Square scenes – of judges on the political stump and African Americans on the auction block – suggested how legal culture was intimately intertwined with life in Baltimore City.

Though deeply embedded in the city, the courthouse was never simply a local place. The people who passed through its doors ensured that its work was tied to a broader culture of race and rights. It was about a hundred miles from Baltimore to the US Supreme Court in Washington, DC. But the legal claims of free black men like Baltimore's Cornelius Thompson narrowed the distance.[51] If asked how his travel permit came to bear the signature of Roger Brooke Taney, Thompson was ready to explain. In July 1845 Thompson was preparing to leave Maryland in search of work at one of the region's summer resorts. Virginia's nearby natural springs were a popular destination for Baltimore's elite, who enjoyed the lively sociability and curative effects of the region's spas. Attorney George Brown, later mayor of Baltimore, wrote to his law partner Frederick Brune about his time at White Sulphur Springs, in what is today West Virginia. Brown was in the company of his sister Clara, who was seeking out the "healing waters" of the place. He described to Brune how lines of professional life and sociability crossed during summers at the spas. Gathered were some "900 people," including men from the city's merchant and legal elite, including lawyers Orville Horwitz and S. Teackle Wallis.[52] This same resort was the summer vacation place of Roger Taney and his family throughout the 1850s.

These "watering places" offered work to free black men and women, who served meals, provided entertainment, and performed housekeeping duties for plantation and city dwellers who took refuge in the hotels, cottages, and guest houses during the hottest months. Before heading off to take up this seasonal work, Thompson had one required stop: the Baltimore City courthouse. He knew that, generally, state law barred free African Americans from reentering Maryland once they had crossed the state line. Thompson also knew that a travel permit could shield him against kidnappers.[53] He would have to secure a permit at the courthouse if he hoped to avoid a troubled fate.

Thompson's trek from his home on Tyson Street to the courthouse was short, fifteen minutes on foot along crowded streets and alleys to Monument Square. Perhaps he had his application folded in a breast pocket or tucked in a satchel.[54] Thompson's application bore three signatures, that of Chief Justice Taney, his wife, Anne P. C. Taney, and their son-in-law, J. Mason Campbell. As he handed his application to Orphan's Court clerk David Perine, Perine may have paused knowingly.[55] He knew Taney's signature well; when the chief justice was away from Baltimore, Perine managed his business affairs. Perine was also familiar with Thompson's purpose. During the summer of 1845 alone, he issued nine such travel permits to free black men pursuing work at the region's resorts.[56] Thompson left the courthouse, permit in hand, having joined the ranks of the many other free black men and women who, after adding the courthouse to their itinerary, had permission to travel granted to them by the court.

It was not the first time that Thompson had sought Taney's alliance in a courthouse matter. He had first turned to him more than a decade earlier, in 1832, when, as a slave, he arranged to purchase his own freedom. Thompson had struck a bargain with Taney's former Frederick County neighbor Daniel Hughes: his freedom in exchange for $450. But Thompson had only $150 in hand. He hoped that Taney – then US attorney general – would lend both money and legal advice. Taney obliged. First, he wrote to Hughes's agent to say he knew Thompson, who was "a good boy" (although Thompson was nearly thirty years old). Taney proposed to pay the balance due of $300 by check in exchange for a bill of sale. He intended to "at once execute a deed of manumission." But Taney was clear that this was a business transaction. He and Thompson had arrived at an understanding: "Cornelius and I will agree on the time he is to serve," meaning that Thompson would compensate Taney for his freedom by serving a term of years.[57] Taney then brought to bear his lawyer's expertise. Better to avoid Maryland's local courthouses, he advised. State law prohibited Thompson's manumission under the circumstances.[58] There was a way around Maryland law, Taney advised, directing that matter should be formalized in the District of Columbia.[59] As a result of their arrangement, Thompson won his freedom papers and Taney gained a bound servant. It was a relationship that allowed for negotiation and exchange in a way that approached collaboration.[60]

By the summer of 1845, Thompson planned to travel. When he approached Taney about signing a travel permit application, the two men had long been allied, and layers of familiarity, exchange, and experience underlay their bargain. But it was an uneven alliance that rested on fragile agreements and conflicts that brewed just below the surface. They reached an accord about the travel permit, and at first glance, the permit appears to reflect a convergence of interests: Thompson's in finding more lucrative employment, and Taney's in ensuring good service for elite patrons in Virginia's resorts. And in light of their long-standing alliance, Thompson's access to the Taney family was affirmed. For Taney, his dealings with Thompson reinforced his self-asserted image as a benevolent figure in the lives of free African Americans.[61] The document papered over fault lines between the two men. There is much to suggest that Thompson and Taney differed over what a travel permit meant. Did the permit suggest that Thompson held a right or a privilege?

Taney's views are most easily examined. His correspondence and opinions, published and unpublished, place Thompson's travel permit in an illuminating context. Since 1841, Taney had been working out his ideas about a constitutionally derived right to travel between the individual states. What of men like Cornelius Thompson? Taney recognized the right of free white citizens to traverse the country, but free black people were a different category. Thompson might secure a travel permit in the local courthouse. Indeed, Taney might aid him in such a proceeding. Still, in the chief justice's view, Thompson's permit represented a privilege rather than a right, one that could be revoked, violated, or otherwise impaired by the state at will.

Thompson's perspective is more difficult to unearth. Only from the records of those things that he did is it possible to draw conclusions about how he thought about them. Did Thompson understand his travel permit to be a right or a privilege? Surely he hoped it was more akin to a right. Adorned with distinguished endorsements and a judicial imprimatur, his permit was intended to stave off aggressors, including would-be kidnappers and profit seekers. Thompson expected the terms of the permit to be unassailable, shielding him from imprisonment, fines, and sale into servitude, even if such protections existed only for the permit's duration. In this expectation, Thompson lived like a man who possessed rights – rights he was prepared to secure in the local courthouse. This was consistent with the other ways that Thompson used law to demonstrate his belonging in Baltimore. In another aspect of his life, Thompson was a vestryman at the St. James Protestant Episcopal Church, a black-led congregation, charged with taking care of the congregation and its property, including a modest church building on the corner of North and Saratoga Streets.[62] Thompson was also part of Baltimore's associational economy and its networks of debt and credit. In 1849 when a man named Henry Gibson sought insolvency relief, Thompson served as a court-appointed trustee, collecting and distributing Gibson's assets on behalf of the court. Thompson had been at the 1852 black emigration convention, where he joined in with the delegates who called into question the failure of Maryland's new constitution to recognize the citizenship of black Marylanders. Thompson was a modest property holder, and in 1855, after his death, his family would depend on the court's register of wills to administer his estate. Even if an explicit declaration of Thompson's rights was not forthcoming from lawmakers, he nonetheless used the local courthouse to exercise the rights to travel, own property, and sue and be sued.

When lawmakers adopted black laws, they did so in an effort to control and confine the lives of free black Marylanders. Some saw people of color as indolent burdens on the state. Others believed that free African Americans would inspire uprisings among enslaved people. In combination with colonization schemes, black laws pressured some black Baltimoreans to abandon their homes and the state. Others stayed and remained subject to the laws' requirements. When they entered the courthouse, what transpired was not at all what lawmakers had intended. Black petitioners looked more like rights-bearing people than the degraded subjects they were intended to be. They took part in courthouse culture. They secured the support of leading white men. They navigated the clerk's office and the courtroom. They assembled the endorsements of lawyers and judges into an authority that ensured they would live, in small but important ways, unmolested. On the city's streets, with court-issued papers in their pockets and pouches, black Baltimoreans looked more and more like persons with rights.

5

Between the Constitution and the Discipline of the Church

Making Congregants Citizens

Baltimore's Bethel Church was four years into a heated dispute over money, leadership, and styles of worship by the spring of 1849.[1] On a Thursday afternoon in late February, courtroom tensions boiled over during a church trial when a trustee charged with misuse of church funds was found guilty. Wielding a bag of nails, church member Serena Richfield, whose husband, Aaron, was among those accused, attacked the Reverend Darius Stokes. Stokes escaped serious injury, although his brother Robert suffered a fractured skull and the minister in charge, Daniel Payne, was also assaulted. Just days later, a supporter of Stokes and Payne wrote to a local newspaper explaining what had transpired. The assault on Payne was unwarranted, his supporter wrote; the minister had brought much-needed reform to the congregation. Stokes, "a respectful, obedient, honest drayman," was also unjustly singled out. His opponents had tried "with all their ingenuity" to "dislodge" Stokes, but he held his ground, "resting with one hand upon the Constitution and with the other upon the Discipline of the Church."[2] Grounded in this foundation, his advocate explained, Stokes had held fast against an assault on the integrity of both his person and the church.

Stokes was a leader in the city's oldest black Methodist congregation. In the late 1840s Bethel was consumed by "a terrible Church trouble" that grew out of attempts to curb "extravagances in worship" and transfer property from one congregation to another.[3] The trouble, which some said was led by lay leader George Hackett, brought the congregation into the city courthouse on numerous occasions. A trustee faction was charged with misappropriating church funds. Members were accused of disturbing a religious meeting and, in more than one instance, assault and battery. Deeds and indentures were scrutinized. The letter of the church constitution was invoked. Before the trouble was over, injunctions had been issued, fines levied, and members expelled. The Reverend Stokes, after having his horses poisoned under suspicious circumstances and

THE PRESENTATION
of a Gold Snuff Box to the Rev. H. T. Beckenrage
in Bethel Church by Rev Darius Stokes in behalf of the colored people of Baltimore as a gift of gratitude.   A.B.Dec.r 18.th 1845

FIGURE 5.1 Baltimore's Bethel AME Church. Church communities were important sites for the exchange of legal knowledge and the development of courthouse skills, whether acquired through the wranglings of incorporation, defending church property, or handling disputes over power and governance. Baltimore's Bethel AME Church, depicted here, spent much of the 1850s managing its affairs in the city courthouse. Image courtesy of the Library of Congress.

his wife "threatened and abused," left Baltimore to take charge of a new congregation in faraway San Francisco. The affairs of Baltimore's most prominent African American church were managed in the street, in the sanctuary, and in the local courthouse.

The fracas in Bethel Church might be dismissed as mere excess until one recalls that, second only to commerce, antebellum Baltimore was built on the institutionalization of religious life.[4] For African Americans, no other institution rivaled the churches; they were the pillars of black culture. Tied to varied denominations – Methodist, Baptist, Episcopalian, and Presbyterian – the city's churches were spiritual havens in which antislavery and civil rights messages were companions to the Gospels. They also offered material sustenance through their mutual aid and benevolent societies. And they hosted most of the city's schools for black children.

Their founding had been hard-won. Black Baltimoreans rejected the second-class status that had characterized their treatment in white-led congregations and undertook to establish their own institutions.[5] The state took notice. Generally, Maryland imposed strict regulations on African American religious gatherings.[6] Black laws tightly constrained opportunities to assemble and worship independently.[7] Not so in Baltimore, however. There, exceptions made for black congregations became custom and left such religious gatherings unmolested and at liberty to manage their own affairs.

Black churches occupied prominent turf in the city, from Montgomery Street in the southwest to Spring Street in the northwest.[8] On Sundays, the sight of African American worshipers making their way along Baltimore's streets told a story that white churchgoers could not help but notice. For example, walking across Saratoga Street on their way to Saint John's Roman Catholic, Saint Paul's Protestant Episcopal, Third Baptist, or the Friends meetinghouse, white churchgoers would have been in the company of African Americans headed to the Colored Presbyterian, Saint James Protestant Episcopal, or Bethel Church. Heading up and down Sharp Street near Lombard, those going to the white First Baptist or Saint Peter's Protestant Episcopal would have made their way to services alongside African American members of the Sharp Street African Methodist Episcopal Church.[9] Black churches decorated the city's landscape and served as signs of African American ambition, pride, and permanence.

This chapter examines how black church leaders did indeed work between the Constitution and the law of the church. Legal acumen was constructed in religious tribunals, where church law and ritual set the terms for judging wrong-doing and meting out punishment. Church disagreements also came before local judges, introducing congregants to the strictures of civil and criminal proceedings. In these ways, legal consciousness was developed in communal settings, becoming deeply embedded in the daily lives of black Baltimoreans.[10] There were in all these instances pressing questions about the right of assembly. Who could regulate gatherings of black Christians, and by what terms? Such occasions also spoke to belonging: as congregations purchased lots and buildings, they became property owners whose rights included protecting their interests by being sued and suing others. These were fragile and often risky circumstances for communities that were always financially strapped. Whether in the act of incorporating their churches, or defending a church building from foreclosure or walking along the city's streets on their way to worship, black Christians inhabited the rights of citizens.

Some churches emerged out of bold bids for autonomy as black Christians broke away from white-led congregations to forge their own identities. Baltimore's Zion Church was established through the efforts of a small cadre of men: a hod carrier, a wood sawyer, a drayman, and a laborer.[11] These working people joined together in their sense of community and commitment to establish a new center of worship for black Baltimoreans. The church's origins also lay in the law. Beginning in 1802, Maryland law provided for the incorporation of Christian congregations. The change aimed to eliminate the necessity to directly petition the legislature. Passed at a time when state lawmakers were expressly enacting laws that deprived black Marylanders of political rights, including the right to vote, the rules for incorporating churches applied to "all quiet and inoffensive Christian societies in this state, without any exception."[12] The act provided guidelines related to the civil administration of churches, but expressly drew a line forbidding the state to abridge or affect "the rights of conscience or private judgment, or in the least to alter or change the religious constitution or government of any church, congregation or society, so far as respects, or in anywise concerns, doctrine, discipline or worship." Black congregations would press courts to give precision to this line as they brought their disputes and church law into the local courthouse.

Any religious incorporation largely was routine. And in the case of Zion Church, the documents themselves were overall formulaic. In 1842 the congregation's leaders set out the terms of its governance, interweaving the requirements of Methodist church law with the state's statutory requirements. Two witnesses, both justices of the peace, were on hand to formalize the incorporation. Still, there was something poignant about the moment when the church's leadership took pen in hand and executed the document.[13] The leaders numbered nine in total: Minister Jacob Moore and eight trustees. Moore was first to sign his name. Henry Ridgeway, a peddler on Baltimore's streets, was next.[14] The fact that Ridgeway, and after him four more of the nine trustees, signed with an X is only partially telling. Many of the men who founded and led Baltimore's churches were not literate or formally educated.[15]

Still, literacy was not a prerequisite when it came to understanding law. Years earlier, for example, Ridgeway had deployed a sophisticated legal maneuver when he placed a notice in the local *Baltimore Patriot* warning potential creditors not to "trust" his wife, Caroline: "I will not hold myself responsible for any debts contracted by her." Ridgeway knew how to use law – in this case, a legal notice – to manage both his marital affairs and his exposure to debt.[16] And when his fellow trustee Daniel Purnell was faced with a wife who had, as he put it, "left my bed and board without any provocation," he adopted Ridgeway's tactic. A notice titled "Caution" warned against harboring or trusting his wife, Matilda, and stated that Purnell would not pay her debts.[17] Legal strategies were thus shared among the men of Zion Church. And as they stood together to formalize the congregation, men like Ridgeway and Purnell expanded their legal acumen. It was through such scenes that black Baltimoreans learned how to use law to carve out rights.

In the summer of 1844 Zion Church leaders took a chance and purchased a small lot located on Spring Street priced at $350. The group had little cash on hand. They handed over just $5 as consideration. But their credit was sufficiently good that James Bush, a local carpenter and furniture dealer, entered into an indenture that imposed a lien on the site – a contract that entitled Bush to seize the property for nonpayment of the church's loan amount. Bush appears to have remained at some distance from the transaction; his attorney, Randle Moale, held a power of attorney and acted on Bush's behalf. The agreement provided that the trustees would repay their obligation to Bush in three installments.[18]

The formal execution of the indenture brought together again the original group of black Methodists, including eight trustees and the presiding minister, Jacob Moore. They stood with Bush's attorney and two witnesses, justices of the peace, one after the other inscribing his mark on the text. Only three of the men – Moore, George Stansbury, and Israel Prout – were sufficiently literate to sign their names. Perhaps one of those three also read the indenture document to the others. With that, they took possession of a plot of land intended as the site for a sanctuary and Sunday school in the northwest of Baltimore, on Spring Street near Jefferson.[19] The Colored Independent Wesleyan Methodist Church was born.

The congregation seems to have struggled financially from the outset. All black churches in Baltimore, at one time or another, faced troubles brought on by scarce resources. It was a city without a black philanthropic or capital class. Congregations were filled with working people who themselves struggled to remain solvent in the 1840s. The records also beg questions about the management of Zion's funds. The trustees were never called on to explain why, despite a congregation of hundreds and a Sunday school attended by many more, they made only sporadic payments toward Zion's mortgage debt. But other circumstances also seemed to undermine Zion Church. The first was the matter of competition. By 1842 Baltimore had twelve black churches, more than half of them affiliated with one or another Methodist sect. Baltimore's black Methodists had an array of choices when it came to selecting a house of worship. Perhaps the absence of a clear denominational affiliation hampered the congregation's fiscal security. The AME Zion Church, headquartered in New York, claimed the congregation as its own, while the congregation's chosen name misleadingly suggested the church was affiliated with the Wesleyan Methodists, largely a British denomination. In Baltimore, some of Zion's leaders developed ties to yet another group, the AME Church, but they would formalize those ties only after enduring the effects of the church's indebtedness. Zion Church was a congregation unsure about its institutional identity.

The county court records tell a bare-bones version of the story. Payments made toward Zion's mortgage debt were sporadic and far below the amount provided for in the indenture. After paying $75.00 in January 1845 and another $25.00 in October 1845, the trustees paid just $7.75 in December 1845. Meanwhile, interest accrued. The result was that by September 1846 the church still owed nearly $200 when James Bush stepped up to collect. Bush filed a complaint that was straightforward on its face: the trustees had defaulted on their loan obligation and Bush sought the sale of the Spring Street property. The proceeds would go toward paying the mortgage balance and related costs. Attorney George Whelan represented the trustees. Their answer was unremarkable. They did not take issue with Bush's claim and instead conceded their failure to pay. All that remained, it seemed, was to organize a sale of the property and settle the church's accounts. After a public auction and then a trustee's accounting, by March 1847 the matter was settled.

If the proceedings in the Baltimore County court suggest that the dissolution of Zion Church was a matter of efficient administration, proceedings in another part of the courthouse made the congregation's stresses more apparent. In July 1846, just weeks before Bush filed his complaint, Zion's minister, Jacob Moore, was arrested and charged with "creating a disturbance" at a church meeting. A local justice of the peace took a closer look and found the minister without fault, and Moore was discharged. The judge then demanded that each of Zion's trustees post a peace bond to guarantee his future good conduct. A local paper noted: "There is a church difficulty on hand which it is said will be settled before Baltimore county court."[20] Word was circulating about the prospect of Bush's case against the congregation. Zion's leadership fractured and tempers flared. Later that fall, the Baltimore criminal court indicted two men – William Johnson and Isaac Vincent – for assaulting Zion trustee Daniel Purnell. By then it was no secret that, as a local paper put it, "difficulties in the church" were being litigated in the courthouse.[21] Civil and criminal proceedings overlapped as the congregation faced the prospect of losing its sanctuary and school building. What may have appeared to the county court as a routine matter of debt recovery was wrenching to the congregation.

The timing of the confrontation between Johnson and Vincent, on the one side, and Purnell, on the other, suggests how tensions peaked as the church property was finally sold at auction. The fight erupted just two days after the court-ordered sale of Zion's sanctuary and school. On October 10, a court-appointed trustee publicly offered the lot and buildings to the highest bidder at the Baltimore Exchange. The sprawling Exchange building was the crossroads of Baltimore's commercial culture.[22] The sale had been in one sense inevitable; once the trustees admitted to the charges against them, it was only a matter of time before the property was sold to satisfy the debt. Still, emotions ran high. And the identity of the purchaser at auction may have especially enraged congregants. The highest bidder was none other than one of Baltimore's most notorious slave traders, James F. Purvis.[23] With a bid of $535, Purvis became the owner of the property and a party to the congregation's demise.[24]

Purvis's presence in Baltimore embodied the type of threat that free black Baltimoreans lived with as they went about building institutions. Predatory individuals moved in their midst. In the early 1830s Purvis had migrated to Baltimore from Washington, DC, first operating out of Sinner's Tammany Hall on Water Street and later opening his own Calvert Street office. Throughout the 1830s and into the mid-1840s, he regularly advertised in Baltimore, seeking to purchase large numbers of slaves whom he proposed to sell in the booming market of New Orleans. In ads titled "Cash in Market," he promised to pay the highest prices for slaves, especially those between the ages of twelve and twenty-five.[25] The city's slave trade had long been associated with the kidnapping of free African Americans. As slave prices rose further south, traders and other low-level opportunists preyed on free black people, seizing and then transporting them to the slave markets of cities like New Orleans.[26]

Purvis profited in multiple ways when he purchased the Zion Church property. In addition to the dollars he may have earned, Purvis gained in reputation as he worked to transform himself from disreputable slave trader to entrepreneurial gentleman. By this time he had stopped advertising for slaves. Instead, he appears in the records as a partner in a brickmaking enterprise and a real estate speculator. Free black people were no less integral to this new enterprise, however. As he had long speculated on their bodies, Purvis now speculated on their property and religious associations. The courthouse gave the Zion Church proceedings an ordered veneer that may have offered some consolation. But even their exercise of a right to defend their property against creditors did not deflect the loss that congregants experienced as their sanctuary and school became the property of Purvis. By 1849 Purvis was among the trustees of the newly proposed Baltimore Female College, and by the 1850s he sat on the board of managers at the city's House of Refuge, or poorhouse. His was a reputation gained at the expense of African Americans in more ways than one. In a cruel twist, after owning the church property for less than a year, Purvis sold it back to the city's black Methodists at a profit.[27]

Zion Church's leadership may have confronted difficult, even unresolvable financial difficulties, but nothing short of a formal foreclosure proceeding could deprive the congregation and its leadership of its church building and school. In cases such as these, black Baltimoreans developed their own legal acumen, and they hired experts – lawyers and justices of the peace – who contracted to serve as allies, for a fee. Nonetheless, legal rights did not account for all eventualities, and a property sale that promised to remedy a congregation's difficulties could turn out to be no remedy at all when the purchaser was not to be trusted. As in the case of Zion Church, legal proceedings could facilitate unjust, even perverse ends.

Disputes internal to churches did not always find their resolution by way of church law. But turning to the city's court was risky because it put in the hands of judges decisions about a congregation's future. Such was the case with Bethel Church, the city's most prosperous black congregation. Bethel's leaders hired lawyers, filed complaints, and otherwise exercised a right to sue and be sued. Although that capacity turned out to be a robust and versatile right, in Bethel's case it was also a risky tactic. The line that state lawmakers hoped would separate church affairs from state matters was not a bright one by the 1840s. When the local Chancery Court was asked to intervene in a dispute between warring factions of the congregation, black Methodists learned that despite the apparent wishes of the congregation, a court might interpret for itself the terms of the state statute, the articles of incorporation, and the church's own law, *The Doctrines and Discipline.*

Baltimore's Bethel Church was among the earliest of black Methodist groups to split from the Methodist Episcopal Church.[28] Daniel Coker led the Baltimore congregation starting in 1801, and in 1815 Coker's group left the city's white-led Sharp Street Church.[29] The experience in Baltimore paralleled those of churches in cities such as New York and Philadelphia. Black congregants lacked decision-making power in white-led congregations and were subject to segregation in the sanctuaries and church cemeteries. Bethel also was Baltimore's first black congregation to avail itself of the state laws of incorporation, and its engagement with that process suggests what a legally self-conscious congregation Bethel was from the outset.[30] Between 1816 and 1820, Bethel's leaders filed no less than three times with the clerk of the court as they worked to get the terms of their congregation formalized through articles of incorporation. In April 1816, five trustees and Minister Daniel Coker filed a first act of incorporation that established Bethel as freestanding and independent.

It was a bold move in a period during which most black congregations were still tied to white leadership and oversight. Not so at Bethel, where the trustees were, by the terms of the founding document, "descendants of Africans" and free. Bethel's leaders had more in mind, however. Discussions about establishing an independent black denomination, one that would join Bethel with congregations in New York, Philadelphia, and other cities, were already underway. Hence, the articles of incorporation were carefully drawn, anticipating how church law would come to play an important role in the legal life of the congregation. Reserved for what was termed a "convention of colored ministers and lay members" was the power to "alter and amend such parts of this constitution as they may think require alteration or amendment."[31] By 1819 the new denomination, the African Methodist Episcopal Church, had been established, with Bethel among its founding congregations. The trustees then amended the articles of incorporation to reflect this new governance structure: spiritual matters would be regulated by denomination-wide conventions. Male members over the age of twenty-one whose names were formally recorded could vote to further amend the constitution. Important authority was being ceded to the denomination and local governance was tightened by the keeping of formal membership rolls.[32]

Questions about Bethel Church's governing documents persisted into the next year, 1820. The congregation had been debating how to express its governance through the terms of its constitution, a creature of the state, and its *Doctrines and Discipline*, the terms of which were set by the denominational conference. The trustees explained: "Doubts have arisen as to the true construction of the constitution of 1816 and its amendments. It has been thought advisable rather to make a new compact than attempt further amendments of the old one." An expanded board of trustees, fourteen lay leaders, and Minister David Smith appeared before two justices of the peace to execute a third constitution. Among this group was George Hackett's father, Charles. The source of church law now included a published text, "the book entitled the doctrines and discipline of the African Methodist Episcopal Church" authored by, among others, Bethel's former minister, Daniel Coker. The number of trustees was expanded to nine, including the minister.[33] Trustees were required to be free men of African descent, age twenty-five or older, who had been church members for at least two years. The constitution made provisions for elections and the control of church property.[34] Law was taken seriously as a foundational dimension of Bethel Church, and the expanding leadership carefully crafted a scheme in which the laws of the state and those of the church were in harmony.

While state law encouraged Bethel Church's independent incorporation, it nonetheless regulated African American religious assemblies. Formal regulation began in 1806 when the state legislature authorized local constables to arrest free African Americans at "noisy or suspicious meetings," including religious gatherings.[35] Over the subsequent decades lawmakers openly decried large gatherings of African Americans, charging that they would lead to "dissipation and riot." But it was not until 1831, after the Nat Turner rebellion in Southampton County, Virginia, that state lawmakers acted. All African Americans were forbidden from assembling or attending religious meetings unless the gathering was led by a licensed white clergyman or other respectable white person. Under this scheme religious gatherings would continue, but they were envisioned as happening under close supervision, requiring that white people be present until the close of the meeting and constables break up unsupervised gatherings.[36] In this respect, Maryland's restrictions resembled those in other slaveholding states.

The city of Baltimore, however, remained an exception to the state's general laws. Custom regulated religious assemblies in Baltimore, and the mayor's office went so far as to issue permits that could be presented should a constable or sheriff seek to interfere.[37] Black Baltimoreans were permitted to hold independent services, with written leave of a white preacher. Lawmakers drew a distinction between religious gatherings, which were generally tolerated, and secret society meetings, which were deemed felonies. For the latter, participants could be fined, sold into service, or, in the case of repeated convictions, sold for a life term of slavery. By 1845, religious gatherings were restricted to houses of worship in Baltimore, making camp meetings and other outdoor gatherings illegal. Still, the city hosted large-scale religious gatherings, including AME conferences. In 1847 Baltimore had at least thirteen black congregations, including ten Methodist groups.[38]

Bethel Church had its own share of disputes, none more prolonged than the case of *Bethel Church v. Carmack*. One starting point for this case was the 1845 appointment of the new minister in charge, Daniel Payne, a man who would go on to serve as bishop in 1852.[39] Payne's journey to Baltimore was circuitous. As a young man in 1835, he had been pressed to leave his native Charleston when local authorities forced the closing of his school. He migrated to Gettysburg, Pennsylvania, and attended a Lutheran seminary. A brief stint pastoring a congregation in Troy, New York, followed. On moving then to Philadelphia, Payne joined the AME Church in 1840. He arrived in Baltimore five years later as an ambitious minister committed to a reform agenda that was at odds with Bethel's existing culture. Payne aspired to purge enthusiastic styles of worship – folk rituals, songs, and dances. In their place, he sought to impose a restrained style of worship that relied on "order and decorum," an educated clergy, and scripted organ music. Payne later recalled these years in his 1888 memoir as a deeply unsettled time.[40] He clashed with Bethel's lay leadership over his efforts to "modify extravagances in worship" and to grant independence to one of Bethel's local missionary congregations, Ebenezer Church. Church law and custom generally set the terms of these disputes and Payne prevailed in both instances.

Payne's reflections on his years at Bethel Church were bitter. Years after departing from Baltimore, he declined efforts to bring him back, even after being reassured that his reform efforts and stern leadership style were "supported by civil and ecclesiastical law."[41] Payne certainly knew that affairs at Bethel Church were governed simultaneously by the law of the church and that of the state because this juridical equation had been tested during Payne's last year in Baltimore. For Bethel's leadership, the two approaches to adjudicating church differences coexisted awkwardly.

The trouble in Bethel Church began even prior to Payne's arrival in 1845, when Bethel Church took up a regular collection to raise funds for a new church building. On his arrival, Payne sought to speed up this effort and secured the assistance of another local AME minister, Darius Stokes. Their campaign met with success. By December 1848 the amount in the building fund had reached nearly $3,000. But as it grew, animosities surfaced. Two factions developed among the nine trustees; five, led by a lay member named Joel Carmack, refused to grant the remaining four trustees access to the funds or present the church account books for review. Stokes and three others responded, issuing demands for access to Bethel's financial records by the terms of church law.[42] Soon Carmack presented the church's books, papers, receipts, and vouchers, but still he refused to give over the bank book. At an impasse, Stokes and the other complaining trustees turned to the civil law and the local courthouse for assistance. Their bill of complaint alleged that the five offending trustees had disregarded and defied "all the requisitions and resolutions" demanded of them and were thus "faithless to their duty and in fraud of their trust."[43] The court acted quickly, granting the complainants an injunction that barred Carmack and the other defendants from interfering with church affairs.

The defendants responded, accusing the complainants of another sort of wrongdoing. They admitted to a small accounting difference of $319, which they insisted could be explained. The charge of financial mismanagement was, they asserted, cover for an effort to take control of the congregation. The complainants, it was charged, had no genuine concern about the use of church monies and instead aimed to exclude the defendants "from any participation in the affairs of the corporation" and to "confer on the persons promoting this suit all the powers of the said corporation." The case was in essence a power grab, one that aimed to displace the defendants from their leadership of Bethel. Hearing this, the court left the injunction in place and set a hearing for five weeks later, in March.

During this pause in the proceedings, Bethel Church was in the hands of Stokes and the other complainants. In late February, they convened a church tribunal. A public trial was held in the Bethel sanctuary.[44] Carmack and the other defendants were accused of appropriating "for their own use money collected for the benefit of the Church."[45] What local newspapers termed a "melee" broke out. A "general fray" ensued, the one described at the outset of this chapter, which ended only when the city watch arrived. Five men were charged with disturbing a religious meeting, and two women were arrested for assaulting and beating Darius Stokes, his brother, and the Reverend Payne. For the second time in as many months, Bethel's congregants and lay leaders found themselves presenting grievances to a state tribunal. Once in court, the dispute only escalated. Supporters of the accused attended the sentencing and were no more deferential to the authority of the state court than they had been to the ecclesiastical one. Some took up a collection to pay the fines levied by the court. Another remarked that "he was sorry for one thing – that it was Stokes that was not killed; or in other words, that the woman did not give him half enough."[46]

Bethel's disputes moved to the pages of the local newspaper in the days that followed. The court of public opinion demanded attention, as news reports deemed the confrontation at Bethel Church "disgraceful."[47] Carmack and his allies took out a paid notice that explained their arrest as nothing more than a ploy to open the way for layman George Hackett and "his colleagues" to assume leadership of Bethel. Carmack defended himself and his associates as "honorable men . . . whose character for honesty and sobriety can stand a scrutinizing test."[48] Writing for the opposition was "H.," – likely George Hackett – an ally of Stokes and Payne. He defended the ministers' characters. The dispute, he suggested, went as far back as a disagreement between Stokes and Bethel's trustees in 1846, when the trustees had apparently refused to settle an account with Stokes. Instead, they had brought suit against him. Stokes prevailed at trial and was awarded nine dollars. But the trustees appealed the case to a higher court, where it was still pending two years later. Hackett made clear his purpose: "We submit this statement of facts to the public, and leave it to them to judge upon whom their censure ought to fall." There was indeed yet a third tribunal of consequence, and that was Baltimore's general public, which might pass its own judgment.[49]

Subsequent filings made clear what was at stake. At the heart of the case were questions about who controlled the "temporal matters" of the church. What body was authorized to act on behalf of the church in state courts? Both sides asked Maryland's Chancery Court to reach its own finding, even though the same questions had already been vetted by a church tribunal, in a criminal hearing, and in the newspapers.[50] Church law remained key. Bethel's constitution empowered nine trustees, one of whom was the minister in charge, to manage the business affairs. Yet in this dispute, the trustees themselves were divided. Three trustees, along with a number of laymen, had brought suit on behalf of the congregation. But they did not constitute a majority of the trustees. Five trustees were named as defendants. Did they constitute a majority such that they could justly determine church finances and exercise control over its assets?

And what of the congregation? Did it have any standing independent of the trustees in the matter? By early March the complainants thought they might, and they organized two meetings during which the matters pending in *Bethel Church v. Carmack* were put to the church membership. George Hackett's entire family was present: his parents, Charles and Charlotte, and his daughter, Henrietta. The result was a four-foot long petition with nearly three hundred signatories, said to have been appointed by the congregation as a whole for the purpose of endorsing a series of resolutions. They condemned Carmack and the other defendants: "$1,000 could not pay us for the misery they have done . . . Neither could a life time of repentance . . . ever efface . . . the stain which they have brought upon [the church]."[51] The body then did away with the existing corporate seal – in essence the official signature of the congregation – and authorized the pastor to commission a new one for his exclusive use. The congregation's petition captures the details of a dramatic scene: a public gathering at which hundreds of congregants, men and women, lined up to approve the litigation already under way. Their authority was nowhere provided for, not in church law nor in the law of the state. Still, on March 9 the complainants filed what came to be labeled "Exhibit A": a lengthy document that evidenced a collective church ritual intended to shape the outcome in a civil proceeding.

Was the congregation empowered to authorize the suit and collectively testify on its merits? Chancellor John Johnson of the Chancery Court concluded it was not. Only the trustees could act on behalf of Bethel. The three trustee complainants were, however, the correct parties. Their number constituted a majority of a quorum and thus their decision to bring suit would be honored by the court. In contrast, the five trustee defendants had been sued in their individual capacities, rather than as representatives of the church, and the charges against them would go forward.[52] Convening a mass assembly likely galvanized the church community as a whole. Hundreds of worshipers became parties to the dispute and collectively condemned the defendant trustees, much in the way the church tribunal had done months before. Still, the congregation's resolutions were deemed irrelevant to the Chancery Court proceedings. They were instead represented by a small quorum of trustees, and without standing as a body to challenge the mismanagement of church funds under the terms of Bethel Church's constitution and its laws, *The Doctrines and Discipline.*

The image of Darius Stokes "resting with one hand upon the Constitution and with the other upon the Discipline of the Church" was less a metaphor than a literal reflection of how Bethel Church managed a serious and prolonged dispute. Church law as expressed in Bethel's constitution and denominational law, *The Doctrines and Discipline*, provided one framework for resolving who controlled church finances and under what terms. A church tribunal had been convened to try offending trustees, who faced formal findings of wrongdoing and the threat of expulsion. The laws of the state of Maryland were no less significant. State statutes that punished the disruption of religious assemblies and assault regulated the inner workings of Bethel's sanctuary and brought congregants face to face before state authorities to testify in the local courthouse about conduct within the sanctuary. Baltimore's Chancery Court assumed authority over the allocation of church decision making. Trustees might act on behalf of the congregation as a whole, it found, if they came together in sufficient numbers. But they might be liable in their individual capacities when they acted without the approval of the trustee board. Congregants, in the state's view, were without standing to influence a dispute among trustees. Still, their collective denunciations might influence how contests over church authority played out in the day-to-day life of the church.

Where the story of *Bethel Church v. Carmack* ended is difficult to say. One end point was the court's decision of June 1851, in which the standing or authority of the three trustees to bring a case against five fellow trustees was upheld.[53] The case then languished until at least 1857, when it was abandoned by all concerned. There is however another end point, one that follows the lives of the key protagonists. Their stories reveal how civil authority and church authority worked in tandem. In June 1850, Baltimore's AME Quarterly Conference – the body that governed the city's local congregations – ordered Darius Stokes to give up his position as chief steward of Bethel Church. Shortly thereafter Stokes was suspended for six months after he held a "bush meeting" without authorization.[54] Congregants also continued to take leadership disputes with Stokes into their own hands. During the summer of 1852, church members Lucy Riggs and Ann Hughes were charged with assaulting Stokes's wife. Stokes himself was again assaulted in the Bethel sanctuary, and his assailant, James Brown, was charged with inciting a riot.[55] Later that year, in November, Stokes's twelve drayman's horses died, it was said, by a "foul means . . . by malicious persons."[56] By late 1853 Stokes was living in San Francisco, where he resumed his work as an AME preacher.[57] Hackett also faced challenges to his leadership, as was the case in March 1852 when Mary Taylor, the wife of a Bethel Church sexton, attacked Hackett in front of the sanctuary.[58] Hackett too abandoned Bethel Church, and by 1865 he was serving as presiding elder Baltimore's Ebenezer AME Church.[59] The dispute that became *Bethel Church v. Carmack* continued to reverberate. Intimate confrontations that played out in Baltimore's courthouse would continue to play a role in rearranging black Methodist leadership.

Baptist churches, like their Methodist counterparts, navigated between secular and church law. Baptist churches also came together before lawyers and justices of the peace before worshipers could come together for a Sunday service. The subject matter of sermons and the style of music to be played were secondary matters. First, Maryland law insisted, a church must be incorporated and establish governance structures. By church law, Baptist congregations enjoyed more autonomy than did their Methodist counterparts because decision making was carried out locally, rather than by centralized associations. Church members, for example, elected their own ministers. Even so, black Baptist congregations remained financially and culturally linked to white-led associations such as, in Baltimore, the Maryland Baptist Union Association.

Baltimore's black Baptists faced some of the same tensions experienced by Methodists. Church communities grew in size, factions emerged among the leadership, and the establishment of new congregations was fraught and sometimes deceit-laden. Baptists tussled over control of church buildings, and new congregations were born out of a painful and legally complex set of contests. Turning to the local courthouse and seeking the intervention of a judge became routine.

Baltimore's First Baptist Church was founded out of happenstance.[60] In 1812 the city's white-led First Baptist Church on Sharp Street opened a school. Its intent was to educate white adults, but when African American men and women began to vastly outnumber the white pupils, the mission was changed. At the end of that year, 160 African American students made up the core of Baltimore's first black Baptist congregation, and for the next twenty-five years the congregation remained an informal though vibrant community. How things changed is a matter of some debate. Was the congregation formalized at the behest of white Baptist activist William Crane, or was it the former slave and Baptist preacher Moses Clayton who took the initiative? Both Crane and Clayton arrived in Baltimore in 1837 from Norfolk, Virginia. By late that winter, five members of the African American First Baptist Church, along with the Reverend Moses Clayton, were before two justices of the peace, formalizing their incorporation.[61]

But first Clayton had called together his congregants to settle on the terms of their union. The male members over the age of twenty-one met and elected a board of trustees. They established the voting rights of congregants: only men over the age of twenty-one and "free from the charge of any breach of morals" would vote. Only free men could hold leadership slots. A majority of the members – a term that appears to have included women (the term "voters" was crossed out in the text) – would choose the minister. On March 14, the trustees and Clayton himself executed the articles of incorporation.[62]

The formalities were typically carried out, with First Baptist's leaders asserting their ownership and control of the congregation by signing their names or otherwise making their marks. A closer look at the incorporation document reveals an important omission. At no point did this group of black Baptists acknowledge or make reference to white Baptists or suggest that their governance was tied to a broader polity or rule of laws. This autonomy is striking when contrasted with that of Bethel Church, for example, where leaders went to some lengths to formalize their deference to the denomination and its laws. Most striking, the well-known Baptist leader William Crane was nowhere to be seen in this founding moment. Whether he was excluded or just out of sight on the margins of the scene is difficult to say.

It is clear, however, that the First Baptist Church remained closely tied to the city's white Baptists. The latter had organized in 1836, the Maryland Union Baptist Association. Black Baptists had not been included at the outset, but in 1841, when Clayton and his congregation requested admission, they were welcomed.[63] By 1844 the "colored church on Lewis street, Baltimore," was among the fifteen congregations that made up the association.[64]

Moses Clayton came to First Baptist with his own experience. Clayton was born enslaved in Virginia's Tidewater region in 1783.[65] Had he been manumitted or had purchased his own freedom, the record does not say. But without question, his early life included time spent in a local courthouse. Clayton carried the evidence of this on his person, in the form of "free papers" for himself and wife and her two daughters.[66] By the time he arrived in Baltimore in 1836, he was literate and possessed a preacher's gift for public speaking.[67] Clayton immediately set out to formalize the city's black Baptist community. There were negotiations with white Baptist leaders like William Crane, but it was Clayton who oversaw the steps necessary to formalize the community.

Clayton is remembered as a builder. He constructed a small church for his flock on Baltimore's Lewis Street. He was as responsible as any black minister for making visible the commitment that many African Americans had to living out their lives in Baltimore. And still, Clayton had doubts. When it was proposed that black Baltimoreans migrate to British Guiana or Trinidad, the Baptist leader lent his support to the public debate.[68] Emigration schemes captured the aspirations of black congregations, and their ministers facilitated extended debates about the relative merits of life in the United States versus that in black-led republics elsewhere in the world.

By 1849, First Baptist was experiencing what might be termed growing pains. There was talk about the need for a second black Baptist congregation in Baltimore. But the situation devolved into one of deception and deceit. Before there was open debate or outright litigation, signs suggested that control over the congregation was in flux. Keys to the sanctuary and the church's account books passed from hand to hand. Assemblies were called, evidencing varied capacities to attract and perhaps sway a majority of voters. Soon such internal wrangling proved inadequate. No resolution was in sight. The question of who controlled the First Baptist sanctuary was brought before Baltimore's Chancery Court.

In 1850 two competing factions were in contention in First Baptist. Moses Clayton had resigned from his post as founding minster, and in his place stood John Carey, who brought with him a new roster of trustees. We do not know whether it was Clayton or Carey who first proposed forming a second congregation. Clayton may have resigned in anticipation of establishing a new congregation; witnesses said that it was Carey who approached the city's white Baptist leadership to secure its approval for a new church. What is sure is that by 1851, the two men and their factions were openly at odds. Their point of contention was the church's debt: How much was it, and how should it be satisfied? The trustees had entered into an indenture in 1841 that had yet to be satisfied. Carey recommended the sale of the Lewis Street church. Clayton disagreed and, according to a witness, asserted that Carey and his cohort "ought to be whipped if they allowed it to be sold." Another faction proposed taking stock of the debt and then paying it down at the rate of fifty dollars per month. The question was put to the congregation on more than one occasion.

By the time the parties came before the court, Clayton had been reelected minister and his trustees, too, had been reinstated. But this formality had not stopped Carey and his allies from selling the building. In November 1851, three months prior to the filing of Clayton's suit, the building had been sold to a Benjamin Brown for $240. Brown was a former trustee and Carey ally. Clayton's complaint alleged fraud. Brown, he asserted, had conspired with Carey and the other trustee defendants to deprive Clayton and those loyal to him "from worshipping there and from enjoying their *religious and legal* rights and privileges" (emphasis added). Clayton's attorney, Orville Horwitz, was experienced in church matters. He had also represented Bethel's leadership in its case. Clayton prevailed; Carey and his trustees were enjoined from everything but worshiping "as other members or persons" and prevented from further interfering with Clayton's use and occupancy of the building "for the worship of God."[69] Carey was unrepentant, and within weeks Clayton was back before the court seeking an amendment to the order that would prevent Carey from locking him out of the sanctuary. The court agreed, but it was a short-lived victory. By April the court had dissolved the injunction. There was no evidence, Judge Frick concluded, that Clayton and the other complainants were being excluded from worship services at First Baptist. (He left the other question about current leadership, the sale of the sanctuary, and fraud for a trial on the merits.)[70] Fifteen months later the Maryland Court of Appeals would agree.[71]

Had Carey and his allies defrauded the Clayton faction? Perhaps. Not long after the case settled, Carey organized a new congregation, Union Baptist Church. And Union Baptist would take over legal ownership of the First Baptist property, purchasing it for $240.50 and thereby winning Brown a profit of just

50 cents.[72] Either Brown had been overtaken by a sense of benevolence and given the property back to his former church, or he and Carey had indeed colluded against Clayton, successfully winning control of the building by way of a fraudulent sale. This would have to be enough to satisfy Carey and his faction. Moses Clayton persisted and reopened First Baptist in a new building on Thompson Street.

William Crane, the white Baptist lay leader, frequently inserted himself into the workings of black Baptist congregations. Some characterized him as a patron. He viewed himself as a benefactor. His interference may have been the price churchgoers paid for his support in the building of black congregations. It was evident, however, that Crane's presence equaled white meddling in black church affairs, or worse. In 1847 Crane repeated the scenario that he had enacted with Clayton a decade before. Crane invited a former slave from Virginia, Noah Davis, to Baltimore, where Davis set up a new Baptist congregation in a small meeting room. In the following year, 1848, it was Davis, it is said, who formally established the Second Baptist Church. Now there was competition in Baltimore for black Baptist congregants, and that contest was being facilitated if not fueled by white church leaders.[73]

Two points in this story suggest how ties to white Baptists continued to trouble black Baptist congregations. The first point is about structure. Davis, unlike his counterparts Clayton and Carey, had an interracial board of trustees that was dominated by the six of its nine members who were white. Nothing in the law prevented this. The articles of incorporation of black Baptist congregations did not restrict leadership to men of African descent, as was the case for black Methodists. Had either Clayton or Carey faced pressure to have white men on their boards? It is not possible to say. But Davis's case suggests that white Baptist leaders in some cases were eager to control black congregations and nothing in either church or state law prevented that.

The second point is about the complexities of property ownership. In the early 1850s Davis and Crane collaborated on the construction of a new church building for Second Baptist. It was an ambitious proposal that included a large sanctuary that would seat more than a thousand worshipers and, upstairs, meeting rooms and a school. Crane's sense of benevolence took on grand proportions as he financed the construction, at a cost of $8,600. The congregation was, however, responsible for repaying the debt on Crane's vision. By the time the sanctuary opened, questions and the crushing nature of the obligation led Crane to make a public disclosure. He had retained ownership of the church building and had never passed the title to Davis and the congregation. In addition, Crane had originally planned to rent out the upstairs meeting rooms at a profit, a scheme that failed for lack of clientele. Crane's heavy-handed alliance with Second Baptist left the congregation with no sanctuary and a debilitating debt. The contest between Clayton and Carey had been fraught and underhanded, but they had managed to sustain two congregations in the wake of their litigation. Davis, on the other hand, never challenged Crane, and the result was fatal for his congregation.[74]

Law mixed with spiritual fervor in the creation of religious communities in black Baltimore. When disputes arose, congregations variously wielded the law of the church and that of the state. Law was in one sense where all black congregations began, and free black religious leaders took great care in crafting their founding documents to delineate the relationship between their church, the state, and their white benefactors in the church's day-to-day governance. In some instances courts came to serve as distant arbiters on fine points of leadership and authority. At other points, judges became unwitting actors in scenes of pitched disagreement and deception. As church cases made their sojourn through Maryland's courts, the limits of the state's capacity to interpret the letter of church law were exposed.

Differences over church finances and leadership shed light on how free African Americans made citizenship-like claims. The capacity to incorporate their associations and then exercise the right to sue and be sued in the state's courts wove free black Baltimoreans into the fabric of the city. And the presence of their church buildings and the sight of their bodies on their way to worship served to sharply counter proposals for the colonization or banishment of African Americans from Maryland. The presence of black church members in the courthouse, as complainants and defendants, reflected how they exercised what would come to be recognized as one of citizenship's hallmark civil rights: the right to protect their persons and property before the law.[75]

6

By Virtue of Unjust Laws

Black Laws as the Performance of Rights

"We are Americans, having a birthright citizenship," wrote Martin Delany. The year was 1852 when Delany set out his ideas in *The Condition, Elevation, Emigration, and Destiny of the Colored People of the United States*.[1] Delany's reputation as a journalist and antislavery orator was well set. In this, the first of his six books, he shifted from chronicle to analysis before ending with polemic, mixing feelings of contempt and despair with pride. Free black Americans had reached remarkable heights in education, commerce, politics, and the arts, he acknowledged, despite a rising tide of racism. Delany concluded that the time had come for African Americans to leave the United States, marking the emergence of a new emigration movement. Still, Delany made plain what he was walking away from: citizenship.

Delany explained African American belonging in cultural and historical terms: "Our common country is the United States. Here were we born, here raised and educated; here are the scenes of childhood; the pleasant associations of our school going days; the loved enjoyments of our domestic and fireside relations, and the sacred graves of our departed fathers and mothers." The United States was home in an affective sense, Delany recognized. Further, free black Americans had demonstrated their belonging through labor and military service. Delany recounted for readers the many African American contributions to the nation, its security, and its prosperity.[2]

Law was central to Delaney's construction of citizenship. Nothing less than birthright guaranteed to black Americans their place: "We are Americans," he declared, by virtue of "having a birthright citizenship – natural claims upon the country – claims common to all others of our fellow citizens – natural rights." Why, then, emigration? Delany explained how the rights of African Americans could "by virtue of unjust laws, be obstructed, but never can be annulled." Black laws, in this view, were at odds with a natural-law claim to birthright. Delany's list of such "unjust laws" was long. State black laws regulated

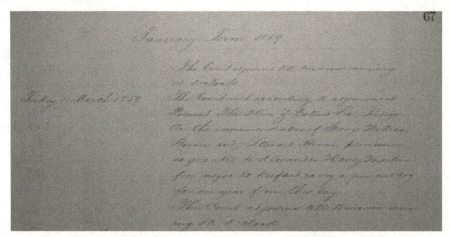

FIGURE 6.1 Gun Permit Application. Black Baltimoreans were among those who carried guns in a city whose political culture was often riven with violence. They also carried court-issued gun licenses, a sign of inequality and evidence of a right won with the cooperation of lawyers and judges. Image courtesy of the Maryland State Archives.

labor, associational life, travel, and commerce. Troubling on their face, these statutes also had an unspoken aim, in Delany's view: the removal of free black Americans from the United States. Provided for in the text of state black laws were conditions so adverse that free black people, it was hoped, would leave their individual states and perhaps even leave the United States entirely. Delany railed against lawmakers who plotted the excision of free African Americans. The right to remain, to stay put, was Delany's foremost claim.[3]

Birthright citizenship was a fully formed idea by the early 1850s. Even men who opposed Delany's emigration scheme, such as those who met at the 1853 Colored National Convention in Rochester, New York, mirrored his thinking. Frederick Douglass headed a committee at the convention that wielded citizenship as a weapon against black laws and removal in its address "to the people of the United States." The address positioned black Americans "not as aliens nor as exiles" but as "American citizens asserting their rights on their own native soil." "We would, first of all, be understood to range ourselves no lower among our fellow-countrymen than is implied in the high appellation of '*citizen.*'" This was an expressly legal claim: "By birth, we are American citizens; by the principles of the Declaration of Independence, we are American citizens; by the meaning of the United States Constitution, we are American citizens." Supporting authorities, such as the delegates to New York's 1821 Constitutional Convention, were invoked. The language of the Constitution was examined to explain that "white" did not restrict the guarantee of privileges and immunities to citizens. Pronouncements connected to Missouri's 1821 admission as a state were reprinted, evidence that some members of Congress believed themselves bound to recognize free people of color as citizens. An 1814 proclamation from then Major General Andrew Jackson was quoted for its suggestion that the free colored inhabitants of Louisiana were "fellow-citizens" to their white counterparts. William Yates's 1838 treatise likely helped the committee set out its evidence. And their conclusion was unequivocal.[4]

The delegates objected to laws "limiting the aspirations of colored men, as against white men." Such black laws must be repealed, they urged. White men needed no protection from competition, and black men were entitled to honorably pursue "life, liberty and happiness." The convention aimed to see "wicked and oppressive law become dead letters upon the page of our statute books; societies for our removal become extinct."[5] Such laws were antirepublican and unconstitutional, they argued, and aimed at not simply the regulation of everyday life. Instead, they constituted a grander scheme to "down us and drive us into exile!"[6]

This chapter examines the confrontations that Maryland's black laws provoked for free people of color in Baltimore. While their terms were wide ranging, a closer look at the city's criminal docket shows how infrequently such laws were enforced. Laws requiring travel permits and gun licenses are two of the more striking examples. Both mobility and the possession of firearms had material significance – they enabled self-sufficiency and self-protection. They were also linked to emerging discussions about what rights the Constitution might protect: abolitionists argued that the Second Amendment extended to free people of color a right to bear arms, and the Supreme Court was beginning to provide for a right to interstate travel. In Baltimore, free people of color were regarded as an exception in the sense that they required court permission to inhabit such rights. But they did gain the rights to travel across state lines and carry firearms. Along the way, they made lawyers and judges into accomplices whose own reputations turned on the ability of free black people to comport themselves like rights-bearing people.

Black Baltimoreans were not represented at the 1853 national "colored" convention. Nevertheless, little of what unfolded in New York would have surprised them. Closer to home, in Annapolis and Baltimore, other conventions – some led by black men and some by their white counterparts – continued wrestling with how to define their status. State lawmakers asked how a new constitution should define their relationship to its protections. Activists clashed over the old question of whether they should submit to colonization, embrace emigration, or simply stay where they were. Baltimore put to the test ideas debated in New York's national convention, and the proving ground for citizenship was not a meeting hall. Baltimore's black men and women brought their questions to the local courthouse. What they did there, securing travel permits and gun licenses, carried a double meaning. The state might regulate its African American residents, but such regulations could be turned into assertions of rights.

This chapter reconsiders the significance of license and permit applications. Black laws that required court permission to travel or own firearms were not

widely enforced in Baltimore. Still, black men and women presented themselves to the local courts, asking for approval. If there was little fear of apprehension or punishment, why did they take the trouble? One answer lies in
the degree to which permits and licenses were also symbolic, transforming
travel outside of the state and the possession of a gun into the exercise of
rights approved and enforceable by the city's judges. The everyday means by
which black Baltimoreans secured their persons and their possessions were
also performances of belonging, endorsed by the recommendations of white
lawyers and the orders of white judges. By 1851 the backdrop for these acts
was a new state constitution that had failed, despite its framers' efforts, to
fix the status of free black Marylanders. In the face of legal indecision and
uncertainty, those who traveled or owned a gun might very well have a right
to do so.

The drafting of a new state constitution in 1850 was an opportunity. The
convention, the first in eighty years, was an occasion for breaking the silence
around the status of free African Americans. Maryland had been governing
free black people by way of legislative edicts passed over many decades. As
delegates gathered in Annapolis, many of them were eager to fix the status
of free black people. Weeks were devoted to long and probing deliberations.
On some issues, slavery among them, there was easy agreement. The state's
elite lawmakers agreed to protect slavery as an institution and ensure that it
remained unmolested by the legislature. The result was an absolute bar against
abolition in Maryland, guaranteeing the future of slavery.[7]

On free people of color, the tenor could not have differed more. There was a
brief, early agreement. Few questioned the proposed terms of article 1, section
1, which reserved the right to vote to "free white male persons of twenty-one
years of age." This provision was carried over from the prior constitution.[8] This
turned out to be the only easy meeting of the minds. Slavery was inviolable,
and free black men could not vote. But beyond that, when delegates were asked
what other rights, if any, free African Americans might be guaranteed, or when
asked if they might be citizens, discord reigned.

Such questions first arose indirectly during a debate over a proposed guarantee of security to "freemen" in their persons and their property. The term
"freemen" was ambiguous. Did it include only free white men, or did it include
free men of color? Opposition to the term coalesced around the view that
nothing in the constitution should impair the legislature's right to remove free
people of color from the state, at will. To promise protection of the property
and persons of free black men was to compromise the right to remove them, it
was said. The parameters of a debate were set.

In the exchanges that followed are signs of how salient the designation
"citizen" could be. Some delegates proposed substituting the word "citizen" for
"freeman," urging that such language would exclude free African Americans
from such protections. Free black people were patently noncitizens, in this
view. Others argued that no such amendment was necessary because free black

people were already understood to be mere denizens – in other words, somewhere between a natural-born citizen and an alien and, in Maryland, always subject to the state's police power of removal. Some advocated that it was imprudent to place free men of color outside the "pale of legal protection," while others urged that the convention could invoke its "right" to "violate the rights of the colored people" only if such persons first conducted themselves unpeaceably.[9] William Blackistone, former speaker of the State Assembly, insisted that free black people must necessarily enjoy some rights: Once "a human being, native, or foreigner, white or black, bond or free, sets his foot upon our soil, he is under the protection of the laws of the State." Blackistone conceded that he would be willing to remove free people of color to Liberia, where they "would have rights which will not be given to them here." But short of that, he insisted, free African Americans should be secure in their persons and property.[10]

Freemen. Denizens. Human beings. These were among the various characterizations of free black Marylanders at the convention. Most lawmakers struggled with locating a middle ground, asking what sorts of rights might be guaranteed to African Americans. The final text of the constitution guaranteed to "free men" security in their property and persons, while at the same time allowing the legislature to pass "all such laws for the government, regulation and disposition of the free colored population . . . as they may deem necessary."[11] No mere denizens, free African Americans might be accorded protections for their persons and property, but the legislature had the discretion to supersede such rights.

In the face of this fumbled opportunity, the convention's Committee on the Free Negro Population determined to arrive at some substantive provisions. The committee's charge was explicit: To submit "some prospective plan, looking to the riddance of this State, of the free negro and mulatto population thereof, and their colonization in Africa."[12] Its first effort was a statistical report. The state's free black population had increased by 1,000 percent since 1790, from just over 8,000 to more than 73,000 people in 1850. But the most important numbers were those that explained the relative rates of population growth for free black versus white Marylanders: "The free negro population, given the rate of progression, must, in a few years, exceed the white population in eleven counties of the state."[13] What did such numbers say? To the committee, they quantified the growth of a population that burdened the state with its passivity, lack of ambition, and complacency. The committee's recommendations aimed at ridding Maryland of such people "reared in all the vices, ignorance, wants and degradations, characterizing a class of our population called free, but in reality the veriest slaves on earth."[14]

Here was a rationale for doing what the delegates as a whole had failed to do: enact policies that would ensure the removal of free people of color from Maryland, a position borne of radical colonizationist thought. The committee's proposal came in the form of four additional articles proposed for inclusion in the final constitution. The first clause authorized legislation for the "governance" and "removal" of free people of color, and further directed that a registration requirement be imposed. Here, lawmakers laid the groundwork for a scheme that countered the voluntary quality that generally characterized colonization. All free black people in Maryland would be on notice that they could be forcibly removed from the state, as was expressly authorized by law, no due process required. They would be called on to facilitate their own removal by registering their presence with the state. The second clause declared free people of color barred from holding "real property," and that any such conveyances would be "null and void."[15] Here lawmakers sought to negate a long-standing strategy by which free black Baltimoreans had asserted ties to the state, homeownership. As for black churches, their titles, too, would be annulled, undercutting the center of associational life and the autonomy that grew out of owning church sanctuaries and schools.

Proposal three voided manumissions if former slaves failed to leave the state within thirty days of gaining their freedom. This offense, which previously had been punished only by a fine, would lead to reenslavement. The fourth proposed article would bar any free person of color from entering the state. This was envisioned as an absolute bar, and here the committee's intentions were explicit. No longer would the movement of free blacks into or out of the state be permitted – not pursuant to a court-ordered permit, nor in the company of whites, nor for those headed to Liberia by way of Baltimore's port.[16]

The committee's proposals were consistent with its mandate. Still, they went nowhere. The chair, Eastern Shore slaveholder Curtis Jacobs, never persuaded delegates to consider his report.[17] Instead, deliberations were delayed by a vote of the delegates as a whole.[18] Not only were delegates unable to fix the general status of free black people, they ignored a committee report on the matter and effectively left the question in the hands of the legislature. After months of deliberation, Maryland's lawmakers had gotten no closer to settling the question of free black people and their status. Competing ideas and interests had scuttled consensus. More important, they exposed how divided were the minds of white lawmakers. The 1851 constitution introduced more questions than answers.

Baltimore's free black activists were watching, and in response to the new constitution, they called a Free Colored People's Convention of their own. They were disheartened. Black laws had long been used to pressure them to leave the state. Now lawmakers had again openly advocated their forced removal. There was little consolation in lawmakers' failure to either arrive at a consensus or set forth transparent terms for removal. The legislature clearly retained the general discretion to enact laws it deemed appropriate and also held a constitutionally sanctioned right to remove free black people from the state. Black Baltimoreans responded with a well-established practice among free black activists; a meeting that brought together sixty-one black leaders from throughout the state. Commentators such as Frederick Douglass expressed surprise that such a meeting could be held in a slave state at all. Still, ministers, teachers, barbers, and carters came together to reconsider colonization in Liberia and to make recommendations to the state's free black residents.[19]

A circular announcing the meeting put colonization and emigration up front, inviting delegates to "take into serious consideration our present condition and future prospects in this country, and contrast them with the inducements and prospects opened to us in Liberia, or any other country."[20] Silence in the state constitution of 1776 had left room for black Marylanders to negotiate their status. The constitution of 1851, Chairman John Walker explained, did not recognize them at all.[21] Walker set the tone by reminding delegates how their legal status had deteriorated over the years. Black Marylanders in 1852 lived in the same state their fathers had lived in, he explained. But they did not live under the same constitution.[22]

Walker recognized the influence of colonization in the 1850–51 constitution. For example, delegate William Blackistone had measured free black people's rights in the United States against those they could expect to enjoy in Liberia, promoting the colonizationist view. Maryland's legislature had always extended financial support to colonization, unlike Congress. By 1850 the state had expended nearly $300,000 to encourage and facilitate the out-migration of African Americans. Just over a thousand individuals had emigrated, while many thousands of others were witness to the black families who passed through Baltimore en route to Liberia. In 1852, interest was renewed.[23] This was because, as Blackistone suggested, Liberia promised a robust citizenship, pledging to make each black Marylander "a free man" who could exercise "all the functions of a free republican government [and hold] an honorable position."[24] Lawyer John H. B. Latrobe had drafted the colony's constitution, guaranteeing to black migrants the rights to bear arms, to trial by jury, to security in persons and property, to due process of law, to testify and confront witnesses in court, to own real property, and to make and enforce contracts.[25] In contrast, the prospects in Maryland remained dim. While colonization generally had been the target of African American disdain, black Maryland's leaders once again reconsidered the prospect of making their lives over for the better.[26]

A meeting to discuss colonization was highly provocative. Before the convention completed its first day, delegates were confronted by what the *Sun* newspaper described as several hundred "evil disposed and riotous" individuals. Protestors assailed delegates as they entered the hall, while others gained entry and disrupted the proceedings. By the day's end, some delegates so feared for their safety that they abandoned the convention. The local press credited the city police with reprimanding the "outsiders" and "rowdies" and preventing a general melee.[27] Such violence was not new in Baltimore, as black Baltimoreans were often the targets of mob violence. But this confrontation was distinct. The outsiders and rowdies set on disrupting the proceedings were

African Americans themselves. Talk of colonization led the city's free black activists to confront one another in meeting halls and in the streets.[28]

The 1852 convention was exceptional, and not simply for the violence that it generated. It was still true that black-led conventions were rare in Baltimore. And while the convention had attracted press attention well beyond the city, that coverage likely exaggerated the significance of the clash. The local courthouse remained the main stage for confrontations over race and rights. Black laws – those acts that broadly defined what it meant to be a free black person – drew free people of color to clerks' offices and judges' courtrooms most days of the week. Most despised the black laws that originated in Annapolis, where legislators hammered out their compromises. Most often spearheaded by the slaveholder-dominated Committee on the Free Colored Population, proposals for black laws failed in the legislature as often as they succeeded, with lawmakers breaking down along geopolitical lines: Baltimore representatives were frequently at odds with men from the state's south and the Eastern Shore. Those laws that passed reflected concessions on both sides. At the same time, they papered over the same differences that had troubled the 1850–51 constitutional convention. There was no agreement about how to regard black Marylanders before the law.

Through permits and licenses, the law's power was being redistributed to a degree that many working people, white as well as black, recognized. Such documents embodied more than a contract or privilege and by the end of the eighteenth century had come to be viewed as personal property by those who held them, or at least that was the case in Massachusetts.[29] In Baltimore it was also true, and workers drew on the language of rights when opposing authorities who revoked or restricted the transfer of licenses. Black law-derived permits and licenses might be viewed in the same way. The legal authority of white men was also affirmed. Those who provided recommendations reinforced their standing before the court as individuals with high reputations and discerning capacities that could undergird a judicial determination. For judges, the authorization of permits was an imposition of their legal judgment on the social world. All parties to a permit or license expected that, on the city's streets, their agreements would be respected and deferred to. There are no signs that they were not.[30]

Big questions framed small permit transactions. Was there a right to interstate travel in the 1850s, and if so, for whom? This question occupied the thinking of courts high and low, as individual states sought to regulate who could enter their territory and under what terms. At the heart of these deliberations were the puzzles posed by free African Americans. Congress in 1821 had debated Missouri's attempt to bar free black migrants by the terms of its founding constitution. By the 1850s, the question was before the United States Supreme Court, linked to its efforts to define Congress's authority pursuant to the commerce clause. Could a state regulate interstate migration, or was that power reserved exclusively for Congress?

In the nation's high court, a right to interstate travel was emerging. As early as 1841, in *Groves v. Slaughter*, the Supreme Court asked whether individual states could regulate the interstate travel of free African Americans but left the question open.[31] The issue of free black travel again undergirded the court's thinking in the 1849 *Passenger Cases*.[32] Reviewing the constitutionality of Boston's poor law and New York's quarantine law, the companion cases linked the jurisprudence of interstate commerce, free black Americans, and the right to travel.[33] The initial articulation of a constitutionally guaranteed right to interstate travel was contained in Roger Taney's dissent: "For all the great purposes for which the Federal government was formed, we are one people, with one common country. We are all citizens of the United States; and, as members of the same community, must have the right to pass and repass through every part of it without interruption, as freely as in our own States."[34]

Free black people were, however, an exception. Taney's use of the term "citizen" was a sign that the right to travel was qualified. Indeed, not one of the seven justices who wrote in the *Passenger Cases* argued for an unfettered right to travel. Instead, they offered a litany of those excepted from said right: Convicts, felons, vagabonds, paupers, the infirm, and slaves. No justice objected to the exclusion of free African Americans and the curtailment of their right to travel. In Taney's view, no scheme, be it a state regulation, an act of Congress, or an international treaty, could permit "Great Britain to ship her paupers to Massachusetts, or send her free blacks from the West Indies into the Southern States or into Ohio, in contravention of their local laws."[35] Essential to the development of the court's reasoning was the threat that the movement of free black Americans was said to pose.[36]

In the local courthouse, free black men and women posed another version of this question. If there was a right to travel, how might they act on it? The answer was to make an appearance before the city's criminal court. The courthouse atmosphere also presented a challenge to asserting a right to travel. Notorious, for example, was the courtroom of Judge Henry Stump, the sole judge to preside over the city's criminal court after his election in 1851. Later, in 1860, Stump would be removed for being drunk and sleeping on the bench.[37] Until then, it was Stump's careless regard for free black people that drew criticism from the state's court of appeals. In 1859 Thomas Watkins had been convicted of larceny.[38] Stump's sentence exceeded permissible guidelines and directed that Watkins be sold out of the state. The high court overturned the sentence, noting with concern that the court record had been improperly tampered with in an attempt to shield Stump from rebuke.[39] But even with his conviction overturned, Watkins had to use a writ of habeas corpus against the warden of the city jail to secure his liberty. He avoided Stump during this last matter, filing the petition with circuit court judge Z. Collins Lee.[40] Neither success nor the promise of success awaited black litigants in the Baltimore City courthouse.

Entering Stump's courtroom, Baltimore's free black permit seekers must have steeled themselves for the possibility that their dignity would be challenged. Still they went to court, with their seriousness of purpose awkwardly juxtaposed against a legal culture that did not always regard them with respect. They carried their petitions, slim formulaic documents that reveal the rhythms of their lives and the scope of their ambitions. Permitted travel took people to Virginia's spas for work. It took them to New York and Philadelphia, where family awaited them. Some travelers anticipated journeys that would begin at the port. They were bound for Trinidad, Haiti, and Liberia but took care to ensure their right to return should their ventures fail. Travel permit petitions were built on carefully cultivated networks. Applicants held in their hands endorsements from white Baltimoreans who vouched for their respectability and the worthiness of their journeys. Reputations were traded, black and white people alike claiming qualities that would impress a judge. Charity Govan and William Henry Calhoun both chose June 26, 1854, as the day to submit their travel permit applications. It was not a day of particular note in Baltimore. In the city's livestock market, cattle prices continued to decline while hogs were plentiful.[41] The Baltimore Board of Health reported that city's health was overall "very good," although it cautioned that infant mortality was on the rise.[42] Plans were well under way for the city's annual Fourth of July parade.[43] The city council considered matters ranging from fire company petitions and road construction to the erection of a footbridge.[44] A local paper deemed weather the "engrossing topic of conversation." Unseasonable temperatures led to the hottest days in nearly two years.[45]

Early that summer morning, Calhoun and Govan were among those making their way along the city's busy streets, and it is likely they did not stand out in the crowds. A visitor from England, Alfred Pairpoint, remarked, in unflattering terms, on the many people of color he observed on Baltimore's streets, from the wharf to the markets. At work and at leisure, their ubiquitous presence was a contrast to what he had observed in New York and Boston.[46] Govan and Calhoun headed to the courthouse; their purpose, to obtain permits for the right to travel. Calhoun likely began the day at his home on Arch Street in Baltimore's densely populated Fourteenth Ward, where he lived with his wife, Mary, and their nine children. The forty-eight-year-old was a member of the city's small class of skilled African American workers, having operated as a blacksmith since at least 1848.[47] Govan traveled from the opposite side of the city, the west side's Fifth Ward, with another woman named Charity Govan Johnson, likely a relative.[48] Govan was also a skilled artisan, with a reputation for producing fine gilt objects.[49]

Just as they were ordinary figures on the city's streets, the presence of Govan and Calhoun in the courthouse would not have given most Baltimoreans pause. They were among scores of Baltimoreans taking part in the court's formal proceedings. The docket that day included a dispute over the opening of a city street, Cecil Alley, and the grand jury had just returned an indictment in a case of wrongful death. Nearly twenty criminal defendants would be called to answer to various charges, including larceny, intent to commit rape, and murder.[50] Govan and Calhoun were to have their applications for permission to leave the state heard by Judge Stump.[51]

The terms of an 1844 statute drew them to the courthouse. The statute required those free black Marylanders intending to leave the state to secure the court's permission if they planned to return. Specifically, if intending to leave the state for more than thirty days and later seek reentry, free black Marylanders were required to secure a travel permit from the criminal court.[52] The law was a double-edged sword. It conferred legal standing while also distinguishing free blacks entering the state as different from and indeed inferior. Newcomers were discouraged from coming to the state, and long-time residents found their mobility restricted. In both cases, those who entered Maryland without leave of court were subject to arrest, fine, or sale into servitude.[53] The statute also required an applicant to provide the written endorsement of "three respectable white persons, known to be such by the judge or judges of said court."[54]

While the obstacles they faced were formidable, the court record suggests that both Govan and Calhoun were summarily granted the permits they sought. Each must have stood before Judge Stump and stated the purpose of his or her travel, although these details the clerk failed to record. Govan spoke for herself and her companion; perhaps she was traveling to visit family, a reason typically offered by permit seekers. Calhoun proposed to travel alone; perhaps he sought work, another commonly proffered rationale.[55] In these cases only the clerk's notes have survived. But among the loose permits sheets from 1845, we see the range of reasons permit seekers gave for traveling outside of Maryland. Robert Murray was a musician who planned to work in the resorts of White Sulphur Springs, Virginia. John Jones wished to visit "his family residing in Gettysburg, Pennsylvania." Julia Prout was headed to New York "to attend to her husband who [was] sick in that city." Harriet Adams also sought a permit to go to New York, where she would "see her sister & and brother." Ann Boyer was on her way to visit "her husband a cooper by trade who is now working in Pennsylvania near Chesnut Street." Thomas Watkins's application was more unusual. He received a permit to leave Maryland "for the purpose of preaching & lecturing on religious & temperance to his own color."[56]

Obtaining a travel permit rested on negotiations that produced the necessary endorsements. What sorts of relationships did free African Americans have with white men such that they would stand together before the court? Permits from the late 1840s evidence the important role that employers played in supporting black permit and license seekers. Often applications were expressly endorsed with phrases that underscored the employer-employee context for the application. These were negotiations that turned on familiarity and a delicate dependency. Employers served as patrons whose support of a permit application was both a reward for loyalty and a promise of protection. Exploiting such patronage relationships appears to have been one strategy by which free black men and women secured the permits and licenses they needed.

By the 1850s, this picture had changed. The permits granted to Govan and Calhoun reveal how patronage and paternalism had been replaced with contractual arrangements, and employers displaced by lawyers, clerks, and justices of the peace. Baltimore was a city without African American lawyers.[57] Lawyering was a livelihood for white men, one that occasionally meant some white lawyers stood up for the interests of free blacks. The same men were just as likely to promote the enforcement of black laws or property rights in persons, should the opportunity arise.[58]

Charity Govan chose her supporters from among the city's mature political leaders. Among them were brothers David and John Stewart, who had long practiced law in Baltimore. David Stewart had served in both the state legislature and the US Senate in the late 1830s and early 1840s and was well known to the court, but not only as a legislator and practitioner. Stewart had long accepted fees for work done on behalf of African American clients, and the Stewarts worked as brokers for enslaved people who sought manumission by way of self-purchase.[59] James Buchanan also signed on Govan's behalf. He was a justice of the peace who was by statute authorized to accept a fee for such a service.[60] What Govan paid her endorsers we cannot say. But it was enough to elicit an agreement from these courthouse regulars.

William Calhoun's references included two of men – George William Brown and Hugh Lennox Bond – who are remembered as important political allies to free people of color. Brown's reputation stemmed from his successful defeat of proposed black laws. In 1842 he thwarted the consensus at a Maryland slaveholders' convention that would have imposed new, more stringent laws on free blacks.[61] Hugh Lennox Bond was a twenty-four-year-old lawyer and Know-Nothing Party activist. His signature on Calhoun's application was a modest gesture of alliance. But in the post–Civil War era, Bond would, as a state court judge and Radical Republican, be an advocate for the equal citizenship of black Marylanders. He became a celebrated supporter of black suffrage, and from the bench operated as an ally to those black Marylanders making rights claims. For example, Bond declared the state's indenture contracts unconstitutional, a move that buttressed African American claims for familial autonomy in the years after the Civil War.[62] Attorney William Talbott, whose firm was located near the courthouse, provided Calhoun's third and final signature. He does not appear to have wholly shared Brown's and Bond's views about free people of color, but he was not uninterested, serving on the board of the Maryland State Colonization Society.[63] Would he have preferred that Calhoun leave the state permanently? That seems likely. But Talbott also saw value in encouraging free people of color, while in the state, to live pursuant to the law.[64]

Govan and Calhoun presented the requisite recommendations, which in both cases were signed by members of the bar. Without remark, the court granted each the right to leave the state and later return. Of their travels little more is known. Calhoun returned to Baltimore and resumed his work as a blacksmith.[65] Govan also came home to Baltimore, settling back into the same Aisquith Street house where she remained until her death in 1878.[66]

Rights were not, for Govan and Calhoun, edicts set out in governing documents or high court pronouncements. They were not claimed by way of speeches from a podium or letters penned to an editor. Instead, they were secured through more ordinary acts. They used their cultural knowledge and skills to gain the "enforcement of potentially favorable laws."[67] All parties to the proceedings expected their travel permits to function with the force of a right. Govan and Calhoun expected citizens and constables to defer to the permit terms. Their white supporters signed their names expecting that they would carry weight with the court and give the permits authority. Judge Stump expected his orders would be obeyed should the permit holders find themselves questioned. And judges and juries, in Maryland and beyond, were expected to honor the right of men and women like Calhoun and Govan to move between states.

The case of barber Thomas Harvey suggests how the letter of the law did not determine the right to travel. The men who stopped him hoped to profit from Harvey's circumstances: he was subject to $50 per week penalty for every week he was out of the state and one-half of any fine collected was to be paid directly to those who had turned him over to authorities. The total fine of $600 would bring destitution to the Harvey family, and Harvey himself faced the prospect of being sold into slavery. The case was heard by a Baltimore jury. Supporting witnesses described Harvey as an "inoffensive, industrious and very worthy colored man." Harvey, whose family had remained in Baltimore, had traveled to Philadelphia "chiefly on account of his health," newspapers report.[68]

What happened next would have disappointed lawmakers in Annapolis, but it suggests how rights were created locally. The presiding magistrate dismissed the case "for want of jurisdiction," ruling that only courts (and by inference not magistrates) could decide such cases. The magistrate denied his own authority and dismissed the charges. Harvey endured an ordeal – arrest, a trial, and the threat of punishment – that reinforced the value of a permit. But his exoneration showed that Baltimore's officials were prepared to bend the law. Harvey remained in Baltimore, and could be found years later still operating his barbershop on Hanover Street.[69]

Officials in Baltimore were not the only ones in Maryland who concluded that the act of traveling could give rise to a right to travel. Pardon petitions evidence the tension between the provisions of state law and how local officials thought travel should be regarded. To some, a scheme that interfered with the need of black people to travel presented an imbalance that could be adjusted. Richard Grason, state's attorney in northern Cecil County, saw more than his share of such disputes. His jurisdiction bordered on the state of Delaware, and free black travelers were especially at risk when crossing into Maryland from a neighboring state. Grason twice petitioned the governor, asking that a black man and a black woman who had reentered without travel permits be excused from prosecution. He argued that the circumstances of both travelers should be deemed outside the law, citing the worthy purposes of their trips, the support expressed for them by local white citizens, and their respectable characters.[70] An attorney and the son of a former governor, nothing about the politically ambitious Grason suggested he was especially allied with free black people. In fact, he would go on to actively support the Confederacy during the Civil War.[71] Still, his sense that a black law that inhibited travel invited disorder in his county served as an opening into which free African Americans in Cecil County and in Baltimore stepped. Permit requirements were compatible and even extended protection to their travel for work, family, and health, and later their return to Maryland.

Gun ownership was no less fraught than travel. Again, black-law license requirements made black Baltimoreans an exception to the city's general rule. The rule for firearms was that there was no rule: guns in Baltimore were plentiful, frequently used, and oftentimes essential tools in the work of politics. But black Baltimoreans had to request permission from the Circuit Court to own firearms. Like those seeking travel permits, they were required to secure the signatures of three "respectable" white references – very often, lawyers. Finally, they appeared before Judge Z. Collins Lee, who, in open court, inquired about each applicant's reputation, purpose, and general suitability for gun ownership. Once successful, gun license applicants returned to their neighborhoods with the right to own a gun, a license authorized by the court, and a story to tell.

Practice in Baltimore diverged from general law and custom by putting guns in the hands of African Americans. Black gun ownership generally was restricted throughout the South, owing to varying concerns. The prospect of gun ownership raised expectations that free black men would participate in Southern state militias, something long barred by law. In contrast, black militia service had caught on in the North. Between 1848 and 1860, at least twenty independent black militia companies had been formed in New York, Ohio, Massachusetts, Rhode Island, Pennsylvania, and what was known as Canada West, now Ontario. Nevertheless, the companies were controversial. In 1850 Canada's black militia was disbanded. In Ohio, a state constitutional convention in 1850–51 became embroiled in a debate about whether to strike the word "white" from provisions related to military service. Massachusetts was home to the most sustained support for black militias. There, free African American leaders maintained independent militia organizations throughout the 1850s.[72] The questions they presented resurfaced time and again before Maryland lawmakers, first in a constitutional convention and then in petitions to the legislature. Baltimoreans watched this and, as William Watkins put it, asked: "We have colored lawyers, physicians, and teachers; why not colored soldiers?"[73]

Legal analysts allied with the abolitionist movement saw a clear relationship between gun ownership and rights. Legal commentators like Joel Tiffany interpreted the US Constitution's Second Amendment as providing for just such a right. Tiffany was a lawyer and reporter for the New York Supreme Court who came of age in antislavery Ohio.[74] It is not clear how widely his ideas circulated; if they did so it was only clandestinely. His was a seditious view and it would have been folly or worse to invoke Tiffany in a Baltimore courtroom.

Free black gun owners were more often said to pose a threat, that of lending assistance to slaves seeking freedom. Just seventy-five miles to the north and east, the 1851 "battle for liberty" in Christiana, Pennsylvania, suggested just that. The incident began when a Baltimore slaveholder, Edward Gorsuch, set out with a posse and federal marshals to recapture fugitive slaves who had escaped from his wheat farm. Two slaves had taken refuge in Pennsylvania at the Lancaster County farm of William Parker, a free African American. Parker was an abolitionist, a member of the local black self-protection society, and a gun owner. Gorsuch's band confronted Parker and his allies: "One hundred to one hundred and fifty armed blacks all of whom are free except three . . . and there was considerable firing of guns and other fire arms."[75] The result was grave. Gorsuch was dead, and armed African Americans had repelled those who claimed property in their persons.[76] News from Christiana filled Baltimore's papers. Commentators decried the killing of a slaveholder and lamented the hostility that Pennsylvanians held for Marylanders. Six thousand Baltimoreans gathered in Monument Square for an "indignation meeting" during which they vilified those who had abused the constitutional rights of Southern slaveholders.[77]

Marylanders watched closely the proceedings that followed. Thirty-eight men, black and white, were indicted for treason. But only one was tried, and that trial provocatively demonstrated how the courtroom was a space for the arbitration of wrongdoing and the assertion of citizenship. Castner Hanway had been among the men who helped Parker defend his farm and the slaves sought by Gorsuch. The courtroom proceedings were, for Maryland's attorney general Robert J. Brent, a world turned upside down. Free black men received courteous if not preferred treatment, and were "admitted through the Marshal's office into the Court room, when crowds of white citizens were kept outside of the door." A black witness, key to the prosecution, declined to testify and confessed that he had not been present during the incident. The attorney general explained that the black men present appeared to orchestrate their presence in an effort to confuse and perplex witnesses: "These negroes were seen sitting in a row supported on each side by white females . . . [E]ach of the negroes appeared with a new 'comfort' around their necks, their hair carefully parted and their clothing in every respect alike, so as to present an uniform appearance, to the eye, as far as possible."[78] The right to defend themselves, invoked by Parker and his comrades in the streets, extended into the courtroom, where their legal claims were supplemented by performances of belonging and respectability. A capacity to bear arms, and use them, was one linchpin in that right.

In Baltimore, although guns symbolized a capacity for self-defense, they were also used in hunting, and it was not unremarkable for free black people to exercise that privilege. In the antebellum South generally, conducting "a hunt" was one embodiment of white supremacy. Slaveholders organized this leisure activity and included slaves in the hope of engendering a sense of awe for white mastery. Those enslaved people who gained the possibility of hunting alone redefined the ritual's purpose. For them, game and fowl became key sources of food, items for trade, and independence.[79] Southern elites decried allowing blacks access to hunting deer, pheasants, or trout, as that led to greater autonomy.[80] In mid-nineteenth-century Maryland, hunting and fishing were no longer practices governed by the right of citizens to use public land. Indeed, heavy regulations were the order of the day by the 1850s. Still, the possibility that black men could own guns and dogs, and use them to hunt, troubled the meanings of race and freedom.[81]

Self-defense. Self-sufficiency. Gun ownership spoke clearly about how some black Baltimoreans may have appeared to the city's white residents. Permits were routinely granted, with no commentary in the court records or the local newspapers about concerns or fears. Statutory restrictions on black gun ownership enacted in Annapolis never suppressed black gun ownership and never led to prosecutions for illicit, unlicensed gun possession. Striking are the many instances in which black Baltimoreans were charged with using a gun in the commission of a crime without being punished for failing to secure a license to own the weapon. Daniel Hunt fired a pistol at Robert Murray with the intent to kill.[82] Frank Weeks attempted to shoot Alexander Jackson, "snapping the weapon in his face."[83] Dennis Watkins shot Hiram Young through the arm.[84] William Keys assaulted his wife, Mary, and shot her, intending to kill.[85] These free African Americans possessed guns and used them in the commission of crimes. Still, they were never charged with having failed to secure a license. Gun ownership was not a right as prescribed in the constitution or a statute, but it also was not a wrong.

Some license seekers come into view enough in the records for us to explore the meaning of such court-issued documents. Samuel Hardy and Nathan Bowers left traces of their purpose, returning to the courthouse year after year to renew their gun licenses. Their court appearances appear routine in the clerk's minutes. They appeared together, one after the other standing before Judge Lee.[86] The men were longtime residents of Baltimore. Forty-one-year-old Bowers was a carter and a resident of Baltimore's Twelfth Ward, where he lived with his wife, Anna, a seamstress, and their five children.[87] Hardy was another "free man of color," and was married with four children.[88] Both men made their living as a carters, and Hardy appears to have been the older and more experienced of the two.[89] Each man appeared with references from white men in hand. Attorneys Richard Battee and John Ing recommended that both Bowers and Hardy be granted permission "to keep and carry a gun for one year." The clerk's notes offer a summary: Permission was granted and with that, the court adjourned. Bowers and Hardy left the courthouse having successfully extended their right to carry a gun.[90]

Also among the petitioners was Alexander Martin, who sought licenses to own a gun and a dog. These documents would equip Martin to leave the city limits to hunt the deer and fowl that inhabited Baltimore's environs. Martin was a thirty-year-old porter who lived with his parents. His father was a modestly prosperous bookkeeper and church activist who had participated in the era's African American religious conventions.[91] Martin was recommended by two local attorneys – George Williams Brown, who had also been a reference for William Henry Calhoun's travel permit, and Stewart Brown, a twenty-five-year-old lawyer. The clerk's docket concludes: "Permission is granted to Alexander Henry Martin a free negro to keep and carry a gun and dog for one year."[92]

Men like Bowers, Hardy, and Martin also sought to own guns as a logical response to Baltimore City's violent climate. Bowers likely had in mind that just a few years earlier, in the summer of 1854, he had been the victim of an assault and beating at the hands of a white ship's pilot, Joseph Hebb.[93] And in 1856 he had managed to fend off an attack by two black men. More generally, a wave of violence that often included the brandishing and discharging of guns swept through Baltimore in the 1850s. Historians have explained this violence as largely tied to the Know-Nothing Party, which promoted the organization of political clubs with names like the Rough Skins and the Blood Tubs and wreaked havoc on public places and private homes. A corrupt and ineffectual police force added to the danger on the city's streets, particularly in the evenings. Election days were especially deadly. In 1856, court business was halted altogether when the mayhem associated with an election day caused city authorities to shut down the courthouse.[94] By the day's end, 8 people had been killed and 250 wounded.[95]

The desire among free black men to own guns for their own security was a value widely shared in Baltimore. They did not have to maintain their guns clandestinely at home, and they even used them without fear of reprisal. However, concern that the state law could be invoked may have been one reason such men sought gun licenses. Although local discretion was exercised by the authorities in Baltimore, a change of climate or turn of events could have led constables and watchmen to enforce licensing requirements, leaving only those who had secured court permission safe from prosecution. Also, there was likely some status associated with license holding. Brandishing a gun along with a license may have distinguished men like Bowers, Hardy, and Martin as respectable neighbors and legally savvy community members.

The most important effect of securing a gun license was how that license, once in hand, could take on rights-like qualities as an absolute claim to carry a gun.[96] For free African Americans, the license had a potent authority attached to it: that of its three white references and Judge Lee and the Superior Court. The document rested on the reputations and the authority of white men. To display or otherwise advertise a license foregrounded more than the mere fact of gun ownership. It also advertised the holder's capacity to secure alliances with white men, navigate the courthouse maze, and then stand up to the scrutiny of Judge Lee. There is no way to tell how this knowledge may have functioned on Baltimore's streets. It is also difficult to envision a scenario in which a license might have been refused or disregarded. To do so would have been to challenge the court as well as the free African American license holder. What constable, watchman, or sheriff was prepared to directly question that legally crafted alliance? A free black man who carried his license and his gun might just have appeared like a man who had a right to do so.

A puzzle emerges from these examples. Unlicensed gun owners faced no formal charges connected with gun possession, even when charged with using a firearm during an assault or attempt to kill. There was little threat of being punished. So why did some men take the trouble to procure a license? Perhaps the value was symbolic as well as material; the courtroom scenes in which licenses were issued suggest this was significant The Superior Court was a theater for the enactment of more than one performance of citizenship. Naturalizations were explicitly such acts. Immigrant men and women appeared before Judge Lee to renounce their prior allegiances – to a king, an emperor, or a state. They took an essential step toward becoming United States citizens by declaring their intent to naturalize, and then became immediately eligible to vote in local elections. Black men could approach citizenship only indirectly. They could not naturalize, nor could they vote. They could, however, participate in the courtroom. Gun permit applications in hand, they stood before the court in the same place that those seeking naturalization occupied. Looking on was a crowd of lawyers, clerks, and spectators. And they came away with their own piece of a citizen's bundle of rights, the right to own a firearm.[97]

Permit and license requirements were intended by lawmakers to be a burdensome scheme that curtailed the liberties of free black people and discouraged them from remaining in the state. For some, this was sufficient reason to leave Maryland and migrate north, west, or across the Atlantic to Liberia. For most, black-law requirements represented an opportunity to study both the text of the law and legal culture. How one regarded the black laws depended on one's understanding of how they were enforced and by whom. Some may have derived confidence from the knowledge that certain laws, such as gun license requirements, went unenforced. However, when enforcement was uneven or episodic, as in the case of travel permits, greater resources were required to avoid prosecution and penalties. Still, for all license and permit seekers the courthouse was a place of opportunity. Free black people used black-law proceedings to develop their legal acumen, collaborate with white allies, assert their claims in a public setting, and alter their standing in the city's streets and alleys. However, assembling a bundle of rights, rights that many associated with citizenship, was an incremental and unsure endeavor. Removal still threatened, even as rights claims aimed to keep it at bay.

Black laws remained much reviled by African Americans. The expansion of their subject matter and their reach reflected lawmakers' fears of the threats that free African Americans were said to pose. Some hoped that stringent black laws would cause free black men and women to abandon the United States. This was a circumstance worthy of lament, especially as restrictions on the economic, social, and political lives of black Americans fueled the perception that they were not citizens at all. Gamaliel Bailey, a white antislavery commentator and newspaper editor, decried how the deprivations brought about by black laws were also denials of citizenship:

What are the facts? The free negro . . . is denied every privilege of citizenship. He cannot hold an office. He cannot vote. He cannot testify in court, or sit on a jury, and is therefore at the mercy of every knave with a white skin. A free negro cannot keep a gun; he cannot go out at night, without a pass from a white person who may have the charity to assume the office of a master. He cannot go out of his neighborhood without carrying free papers, on pain of being arrested and sent to prison. He cannot move from State to State, in the South, under any circumstances, without forfeiting his freedom. This and more is the law.[98]

But Baltimoreans knew otherwise – at least in part. Political rights eluded the city's black men and women. Still, they could keep guns. They could also travel, even from state to state. If citizenship was a bundle of rights, as Bailey suggested, then black Baltimoreans were in possession of some part of that bundle. Bailey's purpose had been to blame Southern lawmakers for keeping free black Americans in "ignorance and disgrace." He warned that such laws prevented free black people from training for "political freedom," while making Southerners despots no better than those of "Russia, Austria, or Turkey." Black Baltimoreans likely took issue with Bailey's characterization of them as ignorant and disgraced. As they traveled with a permit or carried a licensed gun, they were that much closer to citizenship.

7

To Sue and Be Sued

Courthouse Claims and the Contours of Citizenship

The first chapter of Charles Dickens's novel *Bleak House* greeted readers of *Frederick Douglass' Paper* in April 1852. Douglass had in mind building a readership and keeping his weekly afloat, and the English novelist was at the height of his popularity. Dickens was a friend of the antislavery cause and attracted a like-minded readership. Some among Douglass's subscribers questioned giving over the paper's pages to a work of fiction.[1] Undeterred, Douglass remained committed to the project and, over the course of twenty months in 1852 and 1853, serialized the whole of Dickens's novel.[2] Why would black Baltimoreans have wanted to read *Bleak House*? Some might have been drawn to the novel by Douglass's endorsement. Others would likely have remembered Dickens's 1842 visit to the city and his subsequent critique of slavery in Baltimore, published in *American Notes*.[3]

Through Dickens, readers of Douglass's weekly were introduced to a satirical view of problems well known to free black Americans: debt and apprenticeship. Dickens's story made plain the necessity and the excesses of credit in the nineteenth century, extending humorous sympathy to those who found themselves beyond their means while warning against those who would see in the losses of others an opportunity for their own gain. Though set in London, the novel resonated with the lived experience of free black Americans, for whom credit and debt were foundations of the associational economy of which they were a part. Dickens never dwelt long on the high end of elite law-making. Instead, he wrote from his experience as a legal clerk, giving *Bleak House* an intimate and textured quality borrowed from the nitty-gritty details of courtrooms, chambers, and lawyers' offices. In his fictional telling, few fared well in a world swirling with uncertainty and avarice, and the novel underscored how those who incurred debt were vulnerable not only to creditors. Indentures also threatened. Children whose families had little means or otherwise fell on hard times would be put to labor, as apprentices whose true

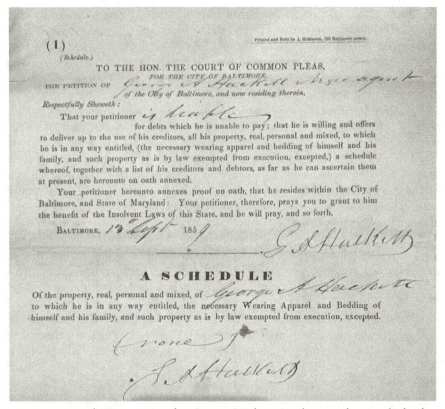

FIGURE 7.1 Insolvency petition for George Hackett. Insolvency often marked a low point in the lives of black laborers, craftsmen, and entrepreneurs. Debt-relief proceedings rested on a right to sue and be sued, and then went further by subverting the usual prohibitions against black petitioners' authority over white parties. Image courtesy of the Maryland State Archives.

compensation was little more than sustenance. They were vulnerable most of all, in Dickens's view, to a legal system that put its own interests above all else. Petitions for debt relief and challenges to apprenticeship contracts provide a paper trail that traces another reason free black Baltimoreans entered the courthouse. These proceedings had less of the discriminatory premise that travel permits and gun license applications had. Insolvency petitions and writs of habeas corpus were tools with which African Americans could bring formal grievances against whites to the courthouse. They testified against white parties, even though state law prohibited it. They even served as court-appointed trustees. In these actions, they exercised the right to sue and be sued. The result could be the extinguishment of a debt and the restoration of a reputation; it might be the canceling of an indenture and the return of a child to family control. Black Baltimoreans used law to their own ends. Still, justice was elusive. Rights were not the only stakes in these proceedings. One might sue or be sued, or act to protect one's property, person, and family. But the outcomes of such proceedings were not guaranteed. Disappointment often followed the triumph of a proceeding well prosecuted.

In Baltimore, *Bleak House* dramas – of credit, debt, and apprenticeship, laced together by subterfuge and intrigue – were well known.[4] Their setting was the office of the Commission for Insolvent Debtors.[5] In 1854 Maryland standardized what had been for half a century an unstable and confusing system of debt relief. The state regularized its patchwork of general and private laws, replacing an act of 1805 and its fifty-one amendments with a consolidated statute. The result was a modern scheme that favored the forgiveness of debtors rather than the satisfaction of creditors. It imposed no residency requirements on those seeking forgiveness for what they owed. Nor did it require that creditors consent to the discharge of debts.[6] Coupled with the terms of the 1851 state constitution, which abolished imprisonment for debt, Maryland's approach to insolvency relief extended benefits even to small debtors.[7]

Debtors in Maryland had new recourse, but in Baltimore their fates passed through the hands of one man, Commissioner Edward Palmer. Palmer had originally been appointed to his post in 1838 by then Democratic governor William Grason. Palmer spent more than twenty-five years, 1838 through 1864, on Baltimore's Commission for Insolvent Debtors.[8] In 1854 the city's three-person commission was replaced with just one official, and that March Palmer was reappointed to the post by the Court of Common Pleas.[9] He personally reviewed and affixed his signature to every "schedule," or petition, filed during his time on the commission.

Black Baltimoreans navigated the intimate exchanges of credit and debt that were the fabric of Baltimore's networks of transportation, trade, and commerce. This scene was deemed risky because many remembered a time when imprisonment for debt – said to be a trampling upon citizenship – was extensive.[10] Whether they were carters, draymen, mariners, or laborers, they did not merely work. They were also knitted into financial relationships that crossed lines of color and class. Debt relief kept the economy and relationships working, providing a remedy to support household solvency and reputational health in the leanest times. Baltimore's small class of black entrepreneurs and business owners saw more than their share of fiscal ups and downs. They accumulated debts and also extended credit to others. And when, in the ordinary course of business, those who owed them failed, so did they. Questions then arose about how to protect the stability of a household and restore a reputation in order to undertake whatever new scheme was on the horizon. Insolvency petitions became one strategy. In a cross-racial economy some creditors were bound to be white men and women. Many black petitioners who came before the commission pushed the limits of generally held proscriptions on their legal capacity, giving testimony against the interests of white creditors and serving as court-appointed trustees. Even when black men had to testify, the proceedings went forward, often securing the discharge of debts.

George Hackett's insolvency petition reflected ambition and disappointment. His coal enterprise had failed, and in 1859 Hackett became one among many dozens of insolvent Baltimoreans. In 1857, a market panic had littered the city with men no longer able to meet even modest obligations. They, like Hackett, made their way to the courthouse and before the commissioner for insolvent debtors. Their accountings – to the court, to trustees, and to creditors – told stories of a belonging that was fragmented and frail. But debt relief knew no color in its formal terms, and black men were able to expand upon their roles in the courthouse while they also grappled with the despair of hard economic times.

"Insolvency" and "bankruptcy" were terms woven through the rhetoric of black activists like Hackett. The terms sometimes carried a moral valence, serving as metaphors for the condition of slaveholders' hearts and minds. However, there was a material quality to these ideas. Economic failure for planters left enslaved families pulled apart and facing sale. Sometimes insolvency was said to be a form of vengeance visited on those who persisted in dealing in persons said to be property. These ideas mixed with lived memory in Baltimore City, thanks to the 1834 failure of the Bank of the Maryland. That collapse had presaged subsequent bank failures and the financial crisis of 1837. Closer to home, the Bank of Maryland's failure reached into the lives of ordinary Baltimoreans, whose faith in the bank was destroyed along with their savings. The city convulsed when depositors learned the full extent of their losses. In the 1935 Baltimore bank riot, angry citizens targeted the home of lawyer and bank director Reverdy Johnson, near the courthouse on Monument Square.[11]

Many of the rights debated in political conventions and in the press were embodied in petitions for debt relief. The right to contract was affirmed as black Baltimoreans sought to collect on or be relieved of obligations incurred in the city's economic marketplace. They exercised standing in the city's courts by securing orders that provided for the discharge of debts. Even at the end of the decade, with the rhetoric of *Dred Scott* declaring them noncitizens, black Marylanders extracted from the state's Act for the Relief of Insolvent Debtors the sorts of rights that the 1866 Civil Rights Act later aimed to guarantee.[12]

For Hackett, petitioning for debt relief was but one episode in a lifetime spent constructing a public identity that mixed entrepreneurship with civic leadership. Hackett began his young adult life as a seaman, stable operator, and coal digger.[13] By 1850, at the age of forty-one, he had built his own business, as a coal agent for city residents and skilled artisans. He supported his wife, Mary, and three children.[14] Hackett's reputation was built on his relative wealth and benevolence. At his funeral services in 1870, Bishop John Mifflin Brown of the AME Church would chronicle Hackett's long history of activism in the church, fraternal orders, and black politics, noting that his "money was spent and whole life given in a good cause."[15] This dimension of his reputation had been hard-won, however. Hackett's insolvency petition paints a picture of a man simultaneously ambitious for and humbled by the possibility of commercial success.[16]

Debt relief petitions typically reflect some underlying events in the life of the petitioner. This was the case for Hackett, who reported a downturn in his business in the months prior to his filing in the fall of 1859. The now forty-nine-year-old businessman appeared before Commissioner Palmer, signing his name to the paperwork rather than marking it with an X, as many applicants did. Hackett was also marked as being an African American or, in the lexicon of Commissioner Palmer, a "Negro." This designation appears both in the commission's docket book and on the petition itself, all of which was recorded by Palmer.[17]

Hackett was not alone when he first appeared before Palmer. Documents related to the appointment of a provisional trustee fill out the scene that unfolded that day. Hackett was in the company of at least three men. There were the two who had agreed to serve as trustees in the case, city constable Daniel Weaver and a John H. Marriott, who posted a $200 bond. Notably, Hackett himself did not contribute to the bond, as was frequently the case with black petitioners. Palmer appointed Weaver provisional trustee on the spot. A third man, William Scott, served as a witness to the trustee appointment. We know little about these men and how they came to appear with Hackett before the commission. Their presence suggests a series of pre-appearance negotiations by which Hackett secured the alliances of others.

Hackett's networks of debt and credit, constituted through his work as a coal agent, are the most vivid details recorded in the case file. His petition shows that Hackett exercised, in an everyday sense, the right to contract. Every petitioner was required to provide such details, usually in the form of a name and a dollar amount, and the debts that Hackett reported owed to him totaled nearly $1,400. Hackett was a creditor who had extended goods and services to individuals in amounts that ranged from $6, due from a William Carpenter, to $757, owed by farmer John A. Lloyd. How might an individual with such extensive assets come to file for debt relief? Hackett noted in his petition that the "above debts are entirely worthless and cannot be collected."[18] He had extended credit to twelve individuals and one company, all of whom were unable to meet their obligations.

Hackett was, of course, also a debtor, and his list of those who had extended him credit included eleven individuals and "sundry small debts."

His outstanding obligations totaled $925 (considerably less than was owed him). This list fills out the picture of Hackett's financial network. There were "Mr. Beatty," a blacksmith, and a Mr. Ridgley; Hackett owed each of them $20. There were also James McCracken, the carter, who was owed $50, and Mr. Klinefelter, a forwarding merchant, who was owed $250. Hackett's network of credit and debt and his contractual relations extended into Baltimore's economy of black and white farmers, skilled artisans, entrepreneurs, and capitalists.[19]

Until his insolvency petition in 1859, Hackett appears to have been in good standing in his professional circle. When pressed, he offered a more elaborate explanation for his financial woes, an explanation that went to repairing and sustaining his business reputation. Hackett's answers to interrogatories – written questions – reveal more about his situation.[20] His responses came in the form of a sworn statement in which he said he had not, for example, made "enough to pay his expenses and that he became aware of his insolvency some months before his application." He denied any suggestion that his bankruptcy was premeditated or otherwise an outgrowth of long-standing fiscal mismanagement. To underscore the direness of his circumstance, Hackett reported that in the months prior to his filing he had received "for his services, [as little as] five to ten dollars per week." Nearly all of Hackett's assets were held in those uncollectible debts. He reported to the court that he had little else, "no property, besides . . . the equity . . . in his household furniture."

Hackett's answers were studied responses to a lawyer's questions. They ensured that he could not be charged with having "conveyed, concealed or disposed of his property to defraud or delay his creditors," a finding that could lead to the denial of his petition.[21] His responses kept some details secret. For example, nowhere did Hackett explain to the court that in December 1856, seven tons of coal had been stolen from his holdings. Perhaps that case had been too hotly contested – witnesses had appeared on both sides. A man named Charles Parsons was found guilty and sentenced to three and a half years in the penitentiary.[22] Instead Hackett's answers went to sustaining or repairing his reputation generally as a businessperson. He hoped they would even ensure his ability to contract and be extended credit in the same circles.

His sworn statement, intended to defeat the objections of white creditors, went unremarked upon. Hackett had in substance testified against the interest of whites, something that Maryland law generally barred free black litigants from doing. The state's insolvency act made no exception for this sort of circumstance. Hackett was so effective in his petition that his word ultimately discouraged objections to the discharge of his debts. The Trenton Coal and Railroad Company withdrew its challenge to Hackett's petition, and the court granted the petition. Hackett's debts were forgiven.

Debt relief proceedings treated some black debtors as peers to their white counterparts. Their right to make contracts and then enforce them by way of legal proceedings was affirmed. In a sense, every black insolvency petition that listed a white creditor was an instance in which black men gave testimony against the interests of white men. Some insolvent black petitioners, like Hackett, had the opportunity to give direct evidence against white creditors, at least to the degree that they could provide testimony in support of the legal forgiveness of their debts. These moments may not have been remarked upon, but it is unlikely that they went unnoticed.

The typical insolvency petition brought by an African American in the 1850s was decided on less evidence than that in George Hackett's case. While we have the names and some bare facts about the more than one hundred black insolvency petitioners in the 1850s, few of the names are found in other sources. Many debtors were transients, at least with respect to legal culture. Their petitions have a fleeting quality, one that suggests a courthouse visit was made out of pressing expediency rather than a plan for long-term stability. Still, even those who made only a brief appearance before Commissioner Palmer were marked by the experience. Palmer used his authority and his pen to arbitrate the legal identity of black petitioners, working against a legislative scheme that had left race out of the debt-relief equation. Each was recorded as "Negro."

State law made no distinction between black and white Marylanders for purposes of administering debt relief.[23] Black petitioners initiated filings in Palmer's office, on average, ten times per year between 1850 and 1860. Their petitions were distinct only in that their total average debt was lower than that of white debtors, with an average reported amount of just under $60.[24] The majority of black petitioners were laborers, men with small debts, although a number of skilled workers, seamen, and carters were among them. Missing are the professional men – bankers, small proprietors, and clerks – who appear on the lists of white petitioners. The profiles of black debtors reflect the overall economic standing of the city's African American community. They were poorer and more likely to work at the bottom of the labor market.

Typical was the 1857 petition of "Col'd Waiter" James H. Jones, who appeared before Palmer in April of that year, just weeks after the *Dred Scott* decision was reported. Jones declared that he owned no property and owed $160 to three creditors. Cooper Peter Logue and Magistrate Basil Root posted a bond of $100, and Logue was appointed trustee. There the formal proceedings ended, except for a September 1857 notation of "Discharge refused" by Commissioner Edward Palmer. Palmer explained: "Petitioner having failed to make his appearances hath not complied with the terms and conditions of the aforesaid law and that a discharge hath not been granted."[25] Jones asserted his having made contracts. He initiated a suit. Was his filing a stop-gap measure? Did he settle his debts out of court?

Insolvency petitions reveal the part that black men played in Baltimore's associational economy. Historian Tony Freyer has described how such local networks of credit and debt operated in antebellum cities such as Baltimore.[26] Cash was in short supply, and credit extended across a broad network of city dwellers in which many individuals both borrowed from and loaned to others with whom they were associated by family, community, and commerce. These were relationships built on familiarity and trust between creditor and debtor. Through their insolvency filings we see how black men were both creditors and debtors, though more often the latter. Insolvency, Freyer explains, was a mechanism by which state lawmakers bolstered the local associational economy. Generally, the proceedings favored debtors.

Less clear is the degree to which insolvency provided sustained economic stability to black workers. Their petitions were declined or "refused" at a high rate, in just over 50 percent of cases, meaning that often they did not receive the full benefits that insolvency promised. Court records are not explicit about why so many petitions were refused. The commissioner used a standardized form to issue such orders. In some instances, the petitioners never returned to finalize their accounting. These same men are not easily found in other sources, such as city directories and census returns. They are less visible and perhaps more transient than other debtors. Insolvency proceedings could allow a debtor to remedy an immediate problem, alleviating pressure from creditors just long enough to regroup and relocate. By the time many petitions were denied, the debtor could have left the jurisdiction.

A remarkable feature of these many debt-relief files is the care that Commissioner Palmer took to mark each black applicant as "colored" or "Negro." Palmer was not the first official to handle an insolvency petition. Typically, prospective applicants consulted first with a justice of the peace, who aided in completion of the paperwork. This was especially true for black applicants, the majority of whom were unable to read or write, as evidenced by their X marks in place of a signature. When they arrived at Palmer's office, they did so with a completed petition in hand. The commissioner's role was to review the filing, confirm it was in order, and shepherd it though court review. In the case of African American petitioners, Palmer took care to amend each and every filing: by his hand he inserted a color term in each record. The relevant statute made no distinctions between black and white debtors. Still, for Palmer the distinction was so germane that he took the trouble to mark the files of black petitioners as such, though he never maintained two dockets or filing systems, one for black and another for white petitioners.

It is common to find black litigants indicated as such in the court records of the 1850s. Other agencies, such as the federal census bureau, marked residents by race; in 1850, the possibilities for the census were B for black, M for mulatto, and W for white.[27] City directories distinguished between black and white Baltimoreans to such a degree that African Americans were listed in a separate section marked "Colored Householders." Back in the courthouse, most records were marked in precisely this way as well, and in some proceedings such designations were related to the substance of the underlying cases. For example, the enforcement of black laws applied only to African American Baltimoreans. Criminal laws provided for distinct punishments for those African Americans convicted of crimes. Slaves had no standing to bring many sorts of proceedings in state courts; they were marked as slaves in court records. Free black men and women declared themselves people of color in court proceedings, rebutting the presumption that they were enslaved.

In insolvency proceedings the role of trustee posed another possibility for the authority black people might exercise. David Pratt's petition for insolvency relief stretched those limits in the fall of 1856. He was a caulker by trade, a "Negro" by designation of the commissioner, and he lived with his wife, Jane, and their six children.[28] Pratt's East Avenue neighbors included the Reverends John Fortie and Moses Clayton, notables in the city's black activist community.[29] Pratt reported owning no property and had no debts owed to him. His own arrears were not modest. They totaled $358, including $44 owed to grocer and dry good dealer Robert Craig, $63 to clothier Asbury Jarrett, and $30 to a Doctor William Baltzell.[30] Likely, these men had extended credit to Pratt for goods and services. In January 1857, the court discharged Pratt's debts without comment.[31]

More remarkable in David Pratt's case was how the color line drawn by Commissioner Palmer was crossed when an African American trustee was appointed to oversee the case. The record of this appointment was made on a preprinted form that was typically employed in the designation of trustees. The bond was reported to have been for the sum of $5, paid by Joseph A. Pratt and David Boston. Pratt signed with his name; Boston, by his mark, an X. Attorney Benjamin Horwitz witnessed the document and Commissioner Edward Palmer cosigned the form. We do not know any more about Boston, but it was Joseph Pratt who was appointed a trustee by the court. Pratt was the petitioner's son and was himself African American.

Joseph Pratt was assigned a role ordinarily reserved for white men. The appointment of a trustee was among the most critical dimensions of an insolvency proceeding. Private citizens had only recently become eligible to serve as insolvency trustees. The privilege had initially been reserved for sheriffs.[32] Such individuals executed their duties on behalf of the state and were charged with serving for the benefit of the creditors. A trustee was bound "with surety for the faithful performance of his trust" and was entitled to control all the debtor's property, as well as his "rights and claims," which "shall vest in the said trustee." Trustees remained under the control and supervision of the court for the duration of their appointment and were subject to removal for misconduct.[33] Serving in this capacity, Joseph Pratt stood in the shoes of the court rather than those of his father. The younger Pratt occupied a status well above that of any ordinary litigant. His authority derived from a court appointment, he served in a fiduciary relationship to the debtor and his creditors, and he remained an agent of the state for the duration of the proceeding. Nothing in state law precluded Pratt, as an African American, from serving as trustee. Still, a marginal note written in pencil on the "Trustee's Bond" form suggests that there may have been a question. Just adjacent to the signature of the witness, attorney Benjamin Horwitz, is a sloppily scrawled marginal note that reads "who will be trustee if required." During this insolvency proceeding, the white lawyer, Horwitz, stood by ready to step into the black trustee's shoes.[34]

The discharge of debts could be at best bittersweet. Such was the case for Jonathan Trusty, who filed his initial petition at the end of what was an otherwise ordinary week in the Baltimore City courthouse. It had begun with the continued trial of "a case in equity," *Cook v. Gheislen*, before Judge Marshall of the Superior Court, and a criminal court indictment for murder in *State v. Dale*. By the week's end, juries had rendered a verdict in favor of the plaintiff in an action of debt on a foreign judgment and sent Susan McDowell to the almshouse for being a lunatic and pauper. The day after Trusty's initial appearance before the Commission of Insolvent Debtors, the local paper reported: "Nothing done in the court yesterday."[35]

Trusty's case file suggests otherwise. Judge William Marshall's bench may have been idle that day. Still, in the nearby office of the Commission for Insolvent Debtors, Jonathan Trusty appeared before Edward Palmer, a petition in hand that listed $133.87½ owed to thirty-six creditors. Trusty petitioned for the extinguishment of his debts pursuant to the state's 1854 Act for the Relief of Insolvent Debtors. This was, however, far more than a ministerial encounter. Commissioner Palmer made sure to note that Trusty was black, carefully adding to the caption that already read "Jonathan Trusty" the phrase "Col'd Stevedore." Palmer was noting his observation and signaled that, as a black man, this party was somehow unlike many others.[36]

Trusty was a fifty-five-year-old dockworker who lived with his wife, eight children, and one grandchild. He signed his name to the petition. The structure of his debts was not typical, though. He listed a great many creditors, and his indebtedness to any one creditor did not exceed $11.00. Most of the obligations Trusty enumerated were small, even when measured against other African American debtors in this period. The average amount owed was just under $3.72. Initially Trusty reported that he had no assets other than his personal household belongings.[37]

Sometime subsequent to his initial filing, Trusty returned to the commissioner's office. He needed to amend his petition. Trusty corrected his initial schedule to state that he indeed did own property relevant to the proceeding: "One small house on Bethel Street." Trusty's home was, in the phrasing of the petition, "subject to sale" to satisfy his debts. The court-appointed provisional trustee moved quickly to seize the house and land. Ads were placed in two local newspapers, as the statute required, one published in the "German language" and the other the *Sun*. Subsequently, at the behest of Benjamin Horwitz, who was named permanent trustee in the case, the auction was set for the afternoon of January 14, just six weeks after the initial filing. Things appeared to be moving very quickly.[38]

The details of Trusty's case evidence an unusual set of circumstances. The relatively small amounts involved in each of his debts raise questions about why Trusty might have filed a debt relief petition at all. Among his creditors, for example, was a "Mr. A Kateman" to whom Trusty reported owing 87½ cents, less than one dollar. Trusty's creditors were an organized group that acted in concert during the proceeding. Thirteen of them petitioned the court to have Horwitz appointed permanent trustee. Trusty's creditors were also more proactive than most, working together in a proceeding in which the individual stakes were very low.

No detail of Trusty's case is more arresting than the sale of his Bethel Street home, described in an auction notice as "a two-story and attic Brick Dwelling, with a Back Building." The notice appears to have had the desired effect. Horwitz reported to the court that the premises sold for the sum of $460 cash, and that after satisfying all encumbrances there remained $146 to be paid out to Trusty's creditors, a sum that ensured his creditors would be made whole. Left to the imagination is the scene that Saturday afternoon on Bethel Street. Horwitz reported that a Frederick Konig was the "highest bidder," but the record does not say whether others had vied for the property or if the Trusty family was present. The conclusion was far from a triumph. Jonathan Trusty had restored some fraction of his reputation. He had been relieved from his contractual debts. But those lofty accomplishments likely felt hollow, as Trusty had reached them but lost his family home.

For men like Hackett, Pratt, and Trusty, the struggle for rights was one waged with the weapons that were legal papers. Insolvency Commissioner Edward Palmer discerned this, striking out with his pen to define the status of black petitioners. Each racialized marking functioned to distinguish and contain the legal agency of African Americans in his part of the courthouse. James Jones, as best can be discerned, used his insolvency petition to fend off especially aggressive creditors, buying himself and his family enough time to either pay their obligations another way or leave the jurisdiction. More prosperous men, like Hackett and Pratt, used paper and the authority of the court to the most complex ends of all. To make their way in Baltimore's associational economy, they needed to be sure of their ability to receive and extend credit. They wanted to project confidence that they could enforce contractual obligations when the need arose. Insolvency proceedings were one component in their strategies for well-being and stability. Through them, they might have debts forgiven. They might also push aside race-based restrictions on their courthouse capacities. Paper was their weapon throughout. Aided by justices of the peace and even Commissioner Palmer, insolvency petitioners pressed through the negotiations that completing complex forms and finalizing the forgiveness of debt required. Like many nineteenth-century Americans, they managed to brush away the stigma that falling short on obligations entailed. Debt, even that which could not be satisfied, provided an entrée into the rituals of rights.

Property in household goods was easier to defend than were the children of black Baltimoreans. The city's free black people might sometimes testify against the interests of white parties and serve as court-appointed trustees. But in Baltimore's Orphan's Court, where African American families challenged the terms and sometimes the very fact of their children's indenture or apprenticeship contracts, parents and "next friends" – court-recognized legal guardians – were too often disappointed. State law opened the door to white Marylanders who aimed to control and exploit the labor of black children. Some were farmers, looking to rebuild a bound labor force in a region where slavery was economically less viable. Others were merchants and small urban manufacturers who promised training in a trade in exchange for exploiting the labor of young black Baltimoreans. Still others were speculators who bought and sold the indentures of black boys and girls on an open market.

Apprenticeship's viability relied on the state's intervention into such relationships, as measured by the Orphan's Court records. Contracts were initiated (especially in the case of children said to be orphans), extended (when a young apprentice was said to have breached his or her obligations), and traded (as farmers, merchants, and manufacturers navigated their shifting labor needs to meet the ebb and flow of the local economy). The Orphan's Court also served as a forum for aggrieved free black families. They might be formally present when their children were apprenticed, lending their approval to arrangements regrettably necessary in a world in which education and training for black children were limited. Black families also became parties to the court's apprenticeship proceedings when such arrangements went wrong, which they often did.[39]

Apprenticeship was one mechanism by which black families were regulated, especially in the realm of parent-child relationships. It also emerged as a site in which black families asserted autonomy and authority over their children. If the state appeared never to reject an opportunity to arbitrate such disputes, it did more than merely buttress the interests of white indenture holders. The state, as embodied in the Orphan's Court judge, allowed for the possibility that black parents might exercise supremacy over their children. The case of *Owings v. Williams* illuminates the outlines of such a confrontation. In June 1855 the Baltimore City Orphan's Court summoned a Mrs. Williams, demanding that she "show cause" (that is, formally present her objections) to the indenture of her son, Henry. A farmer, Caleb Owings, sought to take legal custody of young Henry and put him to work.[40] Mrs. Williams did not appear, but laborer Ebenezer Gibbs did.[41] The record does not reflect what Gibbs told the court. Did he object to the substance of Owings's terms? Or did he explain that Henry was already otherwise employed, or at school? Court records reflect that Gibbs appeared before the court as Henry's "next friend" and evidence was "adduced." After considering the information before it, the court dismissed Owings's petition. Henry was free to return to his mother and his community.[42]

Apprenticeship proceedings were structured such that black parents, neighbors, and so-called next friends could speak on behalf of young people. Did this extend then into the capacity to control the children's lives and labor? Not in every case. The ability to sue – using the writ of habeas corpus and the opportunity to testify – may have approached the rights of citizens. The same was not true, however, for the right to ensure the proper, correct, or contractually provided-for regard for a young apprentice. A distressing range of allegations surfaced as indentures underwent court scrutiny. In *Rollins v. Anderson Brothers*, Edward Rollins complained about events that followed the apprenticeship of his fourteen-year-old nephew, John, to local merchants John and George Anderson. Rollins explained that his brother Jesse had, some thirty months earlier, agreed to place young John under the care and in the employ of the Andersons. But they had breached the terms of the contract by removing the youth beyond the city limits and transferring his indenture without the required approval of the court. John's family was alarmed. They could not locate the boy, "although diligent search and inquiry has been made." Rollins demanded that the Andersons answer for their conduct and present the body of his nephew, filing a writ of habeas corpus.[43] The record does not offer much in the way of details. Weeks later the court dismissed Rollins's claim, recording nothing about the fate of John. Perhaps his disappointed family continued their search unaided by the court.

The Rollins case is a story about the limits of rights. Edward Rollins indeed enjoyed a capacity to sue and to testify, in that he could openly and formally challenge the white Anderson brothers and their relationship to his nephew. There is no reason to think that the proceedings were irregular or otherwise predestined in their outcome. And still, being in possession of such rights did not guarantee Rollins a just outcome. Clearly he sought the alteration if not the rescission of John's indenture arrangement. More literally he demanded to know the whereabouts of John and to regain custody of the child. In this respect he was wholly thwarted. We would be mistaken to overstate the significance of the right to sue when such rights were never a guarantee of substantive justice.

The writ of habeas corpus proved to be a tool by which black apprentices, and their families and friends, could bring those said to be wrongdoers into the courthouse. Their testimony alone, through what began as an ex parte, or one-sided, claim, gave their words the force of law. The court not only permitted black witnesses in these proceedings but also regarded their assertions as true, at least for the purpose of compelling the appearance of indenture holders. Charles Snell, for example, noted in city directories as a laborer, objected to the indenture of his young daughter, seven years old.[44] Whether she had been held beyond the agreed upon time or subjected to mistreatment, Snell, assisted by counsel, took out a writ of habeas corpus at the city's Circuit Court. The challenge was a formidable one. Snell's daughter was held to labor by the mother of police officer James Maddox.[45] The local paper notes only that the case was postponed. But by 1860 a census enumerator counted among those living in Snell's household his daughter Mary, then age twelve.[46] By court order, perhaps along with some negotiation, Snell had successfully pressed his claim.

Many disputes over apprenticeship were like that of Charles Snell, singular confrontations with an indenture holder on one side and the apprentice on another. In other cases, apprentices were caught in more deliberate webs. For Michael Moan, an Irish immigrant and nightman, apprenticeship was at the heart of a scheme that was entrepreneurial and nearly predatory. Moan bought and sold apprenticeship contracts, pressed claims for the full value of his investment, and appeared repeatedly at the center of disputes with apprentices, their families, and next friends. He leveled law and custom with cutting sophistication, making him a formidable adversary. Still, he was not immune to the challenges that black Baltimoreans put up, although they stretched the limits of their legal capacity to do so, nearly meeting Moan as equals.

Nothing in what we know about Michael Moan suggests that he had any formal legal training. He arrived in Baltimore along with dozens of Irish immigrants, identifying himself as a laborer.[47] This modest claim had likely satisfied port officials when Moan looked to sail from Liverpool to Baltimore. But there was, from the outset of his journey, nothing ordinary about Moan. He carried with him, for example, a "large double-case Gold Horizontal Watch, with plain gold chain, made by H. Storey, London," engraved "M. O. Moan" on the case.[48] Whether a sign of his wealth or his aspirations, or a souvenir of more prosperous times, the gold watch in his pocket likely made Moan stand out from the ordinary passengers. Perhaps because of this, even before departing from England, Moan got a taste of what it was like to oversee a young charge, Sarah McKenna, who was placed in his care for the voyage to Baltimore – a turn of events that may have given Moan the idea there was profit to be made from such vulnerable young workers. McKenna later charged that Moan had stolen from her. According to a notice she placed in a newspaper, McKenna had been "a lone female" who was put in Moan's care, only to have him take charge of her goods and "rifle" through them.[49]

Moan and McKenna were late arrivals among the thousands who disembarked in Baltimore during the middle decades of the nineteenth century. The arrival of Irish and German migrants did as much to change the city as did the growth of the free black population. Between 1815 and 1845 approximately 850,000 Irish men, women, and children crossed the Atlantic.[50] Over the course of the 1830s, at least 55,000 entered the United States at Baltimore, while during the 1840s and 1850s as many as 170,000 immigrants arrived in Maryland; 100,000 in the 1850s alone.[51] Germans, pressured by crop failures and political unrest, made up half of all immigrants to the United States by

1854.[52] Ship manifests recorded the pace of this migration to Baltimore. In 1839, for example, fifty-seven ships made the journey from Bremen to Baltimore, more than one per week, on average. From England and Ireland, twenty-one ships arrived in Baltimore, carrying nearly 4,000 Irish passengers, in the first half of 1849.[53]

Such large numbers might suggest that Moan's 1840 arrival on the *Ellen Brooks* should have been routine.[54] Such was not the case. On reaching Baltimore his ship was immediately held in quarantine by local officials, who suspected smallpox was aboard. They were right. A total of nineteen people were transferred to a nearby hospital in the days that followed.[55] Local residents were anxious to get the others off the ship. The paper noted that, with many passengers compelled to remain on board pursuant to the quarantine, "there was a good deal of excitement among their friends on shore . . . because they were not allowed to visit the ship."[56] One group went so far as to force its way on board. Knives were drawn and a Doctor Martin, the city health officer, was injured. The group managed to carry two passengers ashore.

Submitted well after the chaos of the quarantine, the charge that Moan had stolen McKenna's modest possessions introduces an important feature of Moan's nearly thirty years in Baltimore: He never avoided controversy. McKenna leveled her accusation in November 1840, five months after the two disembarked in Baltimore. Moan's response to McKenna's charge conveys how quickly he adapted to the city's legal culture. He explained that the ship's health officer, Doctor Martin, had taken charge of all the passengers' belongings, adding: "I, for one, sued him and received $31.37½ for what I lost." All this played out in the pages of the daily *Sun* through advertisements paid for by Moan and McKenna. More than dollars and cents, reputations were at stake. Moan went the extra mile, swearing to his statement before a justice of the peace and annexing the statement of a third passenger, who testified that McKenna was indebted to Moan.[57] Less than six months in the city, Moan was swearing out statements before a justice of the peace, bringing suit in the city court for damages, and mixing legal and public statements to enhance his position.[58]

The rights or wrongs of Moan's disputes are largely lost. They generally survive only as slim newspaper notices that suggest he was a magnet for controversy and not shy about appearing before a judge. In one instance, his pastor at Saint Patrick's Church "certified" that Moan had not caused the ejection of a lay leader from his post.[59] Thomas Davis brought suit against Moan for malicious prosecution.[60] Moan warned the public "not to receive a Promissory Note drawn by me in favor of D. Levering," for he had not received value for it, he wrote for readers of the *Sun*.[61] Moan was a witness when heirs challenged the validity of Rachel Colvin's will; he deemed her "exceedingly frugal but of sound mind."[62] During the trial of John Clagett for murder, Moan testified that he had observed the accused killer at a cattle show "shaking a pistol in his hand . . . pale and crazy looking." Moan explained he had not wanted to cross Clagett and simply "got out of the way."[63] In a long string of cases, Moan appealed the minor findings of local justices of the peace.[64] What might be termed a courthouse "regular," Moan was a known figure whose familiarity with court personnel and procedure was likely unrivaled in Baltimore.

By the early 1850s, Moan reported to city directory editors that he was employed as a nightman, or privy cleaner; it is also known that he kept cows at his Eden Street residence.[65] And it is in records from the same decade that his connections to various African Americans become evident. Perhaps it was the work of a nightman that led Moan to begin trading in black apprentices. The job was perceived by many to be "dirty and disgusting" work that was also unhealthy.[66] While the precise organization of this work in Baltimore is not clear, it is likely that a master nightman like Moan used teams of laborers to do the hands-on work of clearing privy pits and cesspools.[67]

Moan had complicated and even out-of-the-ordinary relationships with African American workers. The example of young Benjamin Hill hints at how lines could be blurred. Moan found himself in jail in the summer of 1850. With him was a "colored boy," Benjamin Hill. The two had been arrested for assaulting and beating John Butler and his wife. When their bonds were not immediately posted, the two were jailed. Had Moan and Hill been accomplices? The fragmentary record suggests yes. And this was not the end of their relationship, although their circumstances diverged.[68] Hill would be arrested a number of times in subsequent years. He was finally sold by the Criminal Court in 1854, in punishment for his alleged wrongdoings. At that point Moan intervened, but not to extricate Hill. Instead, Moan secured an order that required the sheriff of Baltimore County to pay Moan the net proceeds of Hill's sale as a slave convict.[69] Moan and Hill's relationship transgressed the boundaries of master and slave, but the law extended to Moan a set of rules from which only he was positioned to benefit.

Other indenture cases had this same quality. Vulnerable apprentices or "term slaves" appear to have been relatively passive, even absent, as parties like Moan and the local courts determined who owned them and by what terms. Moan sold the indenture contract of Michael Dorsey to James Johnson, for example, after holding it for just shy of one year. How much he profited, the court record does not say. Dorsey was subsequently convicted of larceny – for stealing a watch – and sentenced to two years and six months in the penitentiary. Johnson was surely disappointed, as he applied to extend Dorsey's term of service to compensate for his lost labor time. Dorsey never had a say, however, in the sale of his contract to Johnson or in Johnson's application to further bind him to labor. There is no sign that the court ever heard his point of view directly. Still, the judge held against Johnson's request, leaving him to appeal to a higher court.[70]

Such complicated chains of ownership suggest that Moan knew how to skirt the trouble and expense associated with reluctant and resistant apprentices, and he likely profited from such maneuvers. In 1855 Moan purchased the indenture contract of William Jones, a boy of twelve who was to serve until the age of twenty-four, for more than $300. Moan explained the complex path that had brought Jones to this point. He was made "free and discharged from service and servitude in accordance with an 1832 deed of manumission" from John Berry. "Free" was a qualified term, of course; Berry then apprenticed young Jones to Bernard Campbell in 1833. Moan acquired Jones's contract from Campbell and said he had encountered "trouble" with the young man that he described as stealing. Moan appeared before the Orphan's Court seeking to extend Jones's term of service, swearing that his apprentice was in the "habit of running away [and causing] much trouble and expense." The court assented, extending Jones's contract until 1867 and authorizing Moan to sell the young man "within or without the state." These were stock terms that accompanied most extensions of indenture contracts; the holder won the court's permission to sell his apprentices. And this Moan quickly did. He passed off the trouble to another Baltimorean, J. A. Lynch. Perhaps Lynch knew of Jones's history, or the final price reflected the risk. In any case, it was not long at all before Lynch echoed Moan's complaints. Lynch's 1856 newspaper ad read: "Last Monday week, my servant William Jones about 16 years old [ran away]. He was last heard from in this city . . . formerly the property of Michael Moan."[71]

His success in proceedings such as those involving Michael Dorsey and William Jones may have emboldened Moan. He appeared to trade in apprenticeship contracts, unfettered by whatever opposition the young apprentices themselves would have set out had they been present. Some were perhaps more fortunate, at least to the degree that they were represented by court guardians or next friends who aimed to match Moan move for move in the courthouse. They were empowered by law to bring Moan before a judge and to compel him to account for their friends and loved ones.

Henrietta Right had been apprenticed at the age of six to Charles Kuster. The terms of her indenture were typical of those approved for black children in Baltimore's Orphan's Court. Henrietta was reported to be "unemployed and without means sufficient for her maintenance or support." Her apprenticeship would enable her to "learn some trade or useful business." In return for Henrietta's being bound to serve until age eighteen, Kuster pledged to "teach or cause her to be taught plain sewing and housework and to supply her with suitable clothing and maintenance." Henrietta was to receive the "customary freedom dues," and Kuster also promised she would be "taught to read during her apprenticeship or in lieu thereof [he would] give her the sum of seventy dollars."[72]

Kuster died in 1849 and his estate transferred Henrietta's indenture to a William Hackett.[73] When Hackett died shortly thereafter, Michael Moan entered the picture.[74] It seems that Henrietta worked in Moan's household. At least she spent her days proximate enough to Moan that she was subject to regular beatings. Henrietta's next friend, Maria Johnson, swore out a writ of habeas corpus that brought Moan before the Orphan's Court. Johnson demanded that Moan account for his treatment of Right, declaring that "she has been most cruelly treated; that she has been dreadfully beaten and has been in fear of her life; that said Moan does not take that care of her or treat her as he should an apprentice." Johnson called for the outright termination of the contract that bound Right to Moan, explaining: "He is not [a] fit or proper person to have the care of your petitioner."

Johnson surfaces too briefly for us to determine who she was to Right, other than the apprentice's next friend. Johnson did go so far as to consult with a local attorney, though, William C. N. Carr.[75] In this she evidenced her own legal savvy. Moan was a formidable opponent, even in the face of brutality charges. In his answer to the court, he denied Right's allegations, explaining that he had "never treated said petitioner in a cruel manner and . . . [had] treated her in a proper manner," disciplining Right only "when she deserved it for gross bad conduct."[76]

The court was faced with competing testimony: that of Right, a young black apprentice, versus Moan, the white businessman and property owner. Moan might have taken the position that his words should irrefutably counter those of Right. He might have invoked the state law barring blacks' testimony against whites' interests, thus depriving Right's allegations of any weight unless she could produce a white witness prepared to reiterate them. But Moan did neither of those things. Instead, he worked just out of the court's sight in an end run. Moan went to see a local magistrate and, through another ex parte action, "had the girl bound to him." This did not make the allegations disappear, but it did have the effect of derailing the proceeding by depriving the court of jurisdiction. Without authority to further hear the case, the challenge concluded with a direction that the matter be "taken to the Orphan's Court."[77] There is no sign that it was.

Families and friends of apprentices continued to confront Moan. In summer 1855, Isabella Jolly secured a writ of habeas corpus from the city's Circuit Court. Jolly's aim was to secure the custody of a young girl, Mary Ann, whom she had raised like a daughter. She told the court her story. About twelve years earlier, Mary Ann had come to live with Isabella, a widow, as a child who was in a "helpless and destitute condition." The older woman had been like a "parent and in health and sickness provided for said child whatever was necessary for its comfort." Isabella knew her authority with respect to Mary Ann was informal. Thus, while she demanded that Michael Moan show cause for his detention of Mary Ann, she also asked the court to make her the girl's indenture holder, binding Mary Ann to Isabella by law.[78]

The writ was issued. Isabella Jolly's sworn statement had enough force to bring Moan before the court. It did not, however, secure his deference. Moan did not produce Mary Ann. Nor did he admit to having her in his custody. The girl had "run away," he explained, sometime after the proceeding had begun. Moan's time to present Mary Ann to the court was extended, and he took advantage of what was a familiar tactic. He told the court that Mary Ann had been bound to him by her mother, who was someone other than Isabella. Then he produced an indenture, a document which could be reviewed only by the Orphan's Court. As in the Right case, the Jolly challenge against Moan was dismissed.[79]

Their capacity to sue brought Baltimore's black apprentices into the local courthouse. The testimony of black children and their next friends carried important weight in that place. And allegations of wrongdoing on the part of an indenture holder triggered the court's authority on behalf of black claimants. Black witnesses swore to instances of cruelty, mismanagement, and subterfuge. But if disputes over indenture arrangements invited black claimants to stretch the limits of their rights, they did not lead to the sort of substantive justice that most surely hoped for.

In more cases than not, especially when facing off against savvy indenture holders, black apprentices were out-matched. The same procedural maneuvers that enabled them to use the writ of habeas corpus to great effect enabled their opponents to escape scrutiny. These were likely disappointing and discouraging scenarios. The capacity to sue and be sued might elevate one to a status on par with citizens, but no outcome was guaranteed, and black children continued to disappear and to be bought and sold in Baltimore, even if this was accomplished through rules of procedure.

Among the lessons of Dickens's *Bleak House* were those about the nature of legal culture. Power in the novel was enacted through the wielding of paper and documents, rather than by way of the fist or the lash. As literary scholar Suzanne Daly explains, through documents that were "created, sanctioned, or appropriated as evidence by legal authorities," legal culture exercised "the power to derange or destroy, legally and bloodlessly."[80]

This framing of the courthouse as a site of contestation is in one sense ordinary. By definition, much of what occupied clerks, judges, and juries were disputes, disagreements, and differences to be resolved. Power was not, however, delineated only through the outcomes of cases. The courthouse was saturated with the performance of authority. Even novice litigants would have recognized power as animating the place, from the deployment of specialized knowledge and language to the arrangement of space: wells and benches, boxes and stands. Power was constructed by where people were placed and from what place they spoke. Sartorial difference underscored social differences that took on heightened significance in the courthouse: well-cut clothes contrasted with the crude fabric of a laborer's well-worn pants. Some men spoke, while others determined who could speak, and when. There were those who wrote, making real the proceedings by making a record of what transpired. The demeanor of the courthouse regular – confident and at ease – contrasted with the guarded movements of those who were new and often had the most to lose during any given court session.[81]

Contests waged in the courthouse began with weapons of pen and ink and the production of documents in collaboration with a clerk or another courthouse functionary. These scenes were shielded from the public gaze, conducted in second-floor offices. The register of wills recorded and safeguarded estate-related records, the sheriff took complaints, the county commissioners heard applications on public safety matters, and the clerk of the court recorded real property proceedings and issued licenses for matters ranging from marriage and the ownership of firearms to the sale of liquor and the owning of dogs. These proceedings did not broadcast their power. Still, as black Baltimoreans initiated their own claims, they found a court that was quietly accommodating.

8

Confronting *Dred Scott*

Seeing Citizenship from Baltimore City

Hezekiah Grice looked back from 1859 to explain his history for the readers of *Anglo-African Magazine*. Invoking the *Dred Scott* case, Grice explained how the meaning of that 1857 Supreme Court decision expanded in the months and years that followed. In his telling, *Dred Scott* did not stand only for a single decision of the nation's high court. The phrase "Dred Scott" was shorthand for a broader struggle over race and rights, one in which black Americans claimed to be citizens of the United States. One beginning of that struggle was the effort by Grice and Baltimore's Legal Rights Association in the early 1830s to win citizenship. They had been disappointed, but Grice's questions about birthright remained alive. Then, in 1857, two of Baltimore's most distinguished lawyers, Reverdy Johnson and Roger Taney, took the occasion of *Dred Scott v. Sandford* to answer Grice's questions: No, they asserted, free people of color were not citizens and they could not look to the Constitution for protection. Rather than settling the question, *Dred Scott* stood for a controversy that showed no sign of abating.

Citizenship was both the push and the pull that led free black men like Grice to take up a different life in Haiti. They believed colonization schemes and black laws in the United States were designed to press them into exile. Some suspected that these measures might soon take on a compulsory tenor. Haitian authorities, in contrast, welcomed them to a black republic that had thrown off slavery and guaranteed citizenship. Grice's encounters with attorneys William Wirt, Horace Binney, and John Sergeant had been decisive. Something in Grice's questions had been too provocative, too up-ending, or too thorny to allow for an answer, though he never speculated publicly about what their silence meant. Perhaps they were reluctant to risk their reputations in the interests of black Americans. The question of black citizenship may have been too incendiary. The political undoing of the Cherokee people's legal victories may have tempered their ambitions. Their silence left open a door through which others

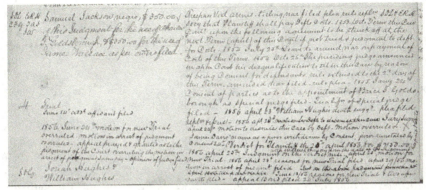

FIGURE 8.1 Docket entries for *Hughes v. Jackson*. This crowded court docket records the years of litigation that led to the decision in *Hughes v. Jackson*, a case that began when one neighbor seized the family of another as slaves. Maryland's high court rejected the logic of *Dred Scott* and affirmed the right of Samuel Jackson, a free black man, to sue in the state's courts. Justice eluded him, however, when three of his children remained enslaved until abolition in Maryland in 1864. Image courtesy of the Maryland State Archives.

might make the case for black citizenship, but Grice did not look back with gratitude. In branding the experience his *"Dred Scott* case," Grice placed men like Wirt, Binney, and Sergeant in the same category as Roger Taney. If the phrase conveyed a lament, it also leveled an indictment.[1]

Dred Scott was, of course, more than metaphor. In the months leading up to the March 1857 US Supreme Court decision, newspapers stirred the interest of Baltimoreans by reporting details of the arguments, predictions about the outcome, and more.[2] For those grappling with questions about race and citizenship, a ruling from Washington might be a critical piece of the puzzle. But there were many instances that demanded analysis in the weeks leading up to a final resolution of *Scott v. Sandford*. Race and rights continued to be arbitrated by the individual states, not abated by the imminence of a high court ruling. In Arkansas, a bill proposed the removal of all free people of color from the state.[3] In Mississippi, the legislature passed a law prohibiting African Americans from preaching.[4] North Carolina lawmakers considered bills that would remove black residents from the state and admit black testimony in cases where persons are tried for "exciting insurrection."[5] Wisconsin legislators contemplated prohibiting "negroes, mulattoes, Indians and black persons" from being witnesses in that state's courts.[6] Other examples suggested that local black activists influenced such deliberations. In Providence, Rhode Island, there was a black-led movement to abolish separate schools for black children.[7] In Sacramento, California, a black convention was called to demand the lifting of a ban on black testimony against white men.[8]

Baltimoreans saw the legal distinction between free people of color and slaves further muddied in a dispute over the 1850 Fugitive Slave Act. The case was brought by a Baltimore attorney and former clerk of the city court, William Gatchell.⁹ Gatchell's son had encountered a man in Philadelphia whom the younger Gatchell believed was owned by his father.¹⁰ Philadelphia police apprehended the man, who went by the name Henry Tiffney, and whom the Gatchells said was a fugitive slave from Baltimore named Michael Brown. Gatchell swore out a claim in Baltimore, before Judge Giles in the federal district court.¹¹ During a two-day hearing before a federally appointed slave commissioner, a crowd of black residents sought to attend but was barred from the proceedings.¹² Tiffney's friends and neighbors did testify, swearing that he had lived among them in Philadelphia for six years.¹³ The court nonetheless ordered Tiffney to return with Gatchell to Baltimore. In Philadelphia, outrage over the case lingered, leading to at least one public meeting during which black activists reviewed the proceedings.¹⁴

The precariousness of the lives of black seamen was evident to all those who observed their troubles. Their ill-defined status meant that their fates would be determined in contests involving local officials, diplomatic authorities, and ships' captains. For example, when a British bark, the *Billow*, stopped over in Baltimore on its way further south, its captain, anticipating the restrictions imposed in Southern ports by Negro seamen's acts, inquired about protecting his black sailors when they were in Norfolk. He was advised that "the men could go ashore during the day, but, if on shore at night, must have a written pass."¹⁵ Later, at liberty in Norfolk, two of the ship's black sailors, William Carter and John Powell, were arrested for being absent from their vessel without leave; the mayor ordered that they be whipped. The ship's captain intervened and brokered a compromise: The men would pay the city's costs and then be charged with desertion and face penalties back on board the *Billow*. But the British consul in Norfolk balked, stressing that the men were British subjects not subject to local law. The mayor's determination, he said, was "contrary to the comity of nations, contrary to the laws of Virginia and contrary to common sense." Commentators disagreed. Editors of the *Norfolk Argus* concluded that "the Mayor in this case is in strict conformity with State Sovereignty, the maintenance of which is absolutely necessary for the preservation of the rights of the Slaveholding States."¹⁶ The *Baltimore American* sided with the consul's position: "Mr. James is sustained by the *Richmond Examiner* and will doubtless be by the Virginia lawyers generally." Whatever the correctness of a given legal position, the *American* offered practical advice for black sailors: "The moral of the matter is, however, give black seamen a written pass in Norfolk."¹⁷

The work of Maryland's colonization society added to a tense climate for Baltimore's free black population. In February 1857 the American Colonization Society met for its fortieth annual convention. While the national colonization movement had ebbed in influence, such was not the case in Maryland – and it showed. As a first order of business, the meeting elected Baltimore's John H. B. Latrobe its president.[18] Latrobe was no figurehead. His ascendancy to the organization's helm reflected the role that Marylanders played in enabling a major project: the construction of the packet *Mary Caroline Stevens*, fully equipped to transport black emigrants to Liberia. Predominant on the colonization society's 1857 agenda was conveying appreciations to those who had supported that undertaking to the sum of $40,000. The supporters were Marylanders through and through. John Stevens of Talbot County, Maryland, had donated $36,000 by way of a bequest, and the ship was named for his daughter. Thanks went to Latrobe, Elisha Whittlesey, and James Hall, trustees of the Stevens estate. The lawyer Frederick Brune, partner of George Williams Brown, and businessman Thomas Wilson had supported the purchase of equipment for the vessel.[19] And Doctor James Hall, agent of the Maryland State Colonization Society, had overseen the building of the *Stevens*. Two hundred nineteen African Americans had been aboard the packet's inaugural journey in November 1856. For those who remained in Baltimore, the robust support for the project was a reminder that colonization sentiment in their state was alive and thriving.

In Baltimore, the *Dred Scott* case was big news. The city's daily newspaper, the *Sun*, chronicled the legal wrangling generated by the freedom claims of Dred Scott and his wife and daughters. Commentators parsed the arguments for signs of how Roger Taney's court would rule. And when the final decision came down, Baltimoreans quickly learned that the court had invalidated the Missouri Compromise, making possible the extension of slavery into federal territories. They also learned that the Scott family had no standing, as black people, to bring a suit in federal court. On balance, the rights and expectations of slaveholders expanded, while the freedom claims of enslaved people collapsed.

For Baltimore's free black community, no dimension of the case was more salient than that which declared no black person – enslaved or free – was a citizen of the United States. Chief Justice Taney concluded that only those who had been citizens of the individual states at the time of the Constitution's adoption could be citizens of the United States. To reach this decision, he set forth his own view of history. Taney found no evidence that black people had been state citizens in 1787. They generally could not vote, hold public office, or sit on juries, he explained. He declared that in the eighteenth century, black people had had no rights that whites were bound to respect – or at least they had no rights that could be enforced through the federal courts. Taney pointed out that article 3 of the Constitution restricted the jurisdiction of federal courts to specific types of cases. Dred Scott and his family had asserted their right to bring suit there by virtue of diversity jurisdiction: When citizens of two different states had a dispute, they could bring it before a federal court rather than before one or the other state's court. Scott and the respondent, John Sandford, were of different states, and therefore federal jurisdiction, Scott asserted, was proper. But the word "citizen" proved to be what might keep Scott and all black Americans out of federal court. Not being citizens of the United States, black people were barred from bringing suit in federal court under the Constitution's diversity-of-citizenship provision. Not only were Scott and his family barred from bringing a federal suit, so were all black Americans.

What black Baltimoreans thought about the decision in the weeks and months that followed is not easy to recover. Absent are speeches, memorials, or tracts giving evidence of their reactions. A closer look at the pages of the *Sun* suggests some of the information they may have had. From the paper they would have learned that the Supreme Court was threatening their status, a blow to those who maintained that they had rights, including the right to be free from removal. They likely recognized a shift in emphasis in the *Sun* after *Dred Scott*. Once a paper that avoided the subject of slavery, its pages included robust coverage of the subject in the wake of the decision. Those black Baltimoreans who turned to the paper for details about how the decision might affect them would have found alarming answers.[20]

The *Sun* was widely admired for its editorial vision and skilled reporting. Editor Arunah Abell was a career newspaperman who brought to Baltimore years of experience from having established penny presses in New York and Philadelphia.[21] In the 1850s the paper was recognized for its pioneering, quick, and cooperative news gathering that linked Washington, Baltimore, Philadelphia, and New York. Innovative use of the magnetic telegraph further extended its reach west to Ohio and Kentucky. The paper reached some 30,000 readers each day.[22] Coverage of the courts and of Washington were the paper's signature features.[23] James Lawrenson, a Post Office clerk, wrote as the paper's Washington correspondent between 1837 and the Civil War.[24] The *Sun*'s coverage was timely, detailed, wide-ranging in perspective, and rarely partisan or commercial in its leanings.

Another Washington correspondent, Elias Kingman, took the lead in bringing news about *Dred Scott* to Baltimore. He set the paper's tone when recounting the scene as Roger Taney read his opinion: "It was listened to with profound interest, and will be everywhere respected for its wisdom, and acquiesced in as the decision of the constitutional tribunal."[25] Only days after the court's finding was released, the *Sun* went out of its way to declare that "the decision, we are glad to say, seems to be welcomed in most quarters." Although the paper did acknowledge there were critics, they were said to be without reason and downright lawless: "There are indiscreet and suicidal ravings among some of those who know no law except that of their own violent self-will and passions."[26] The *Sun* also encouraged "the patriotic and conservative masses at the north [to] receive this judgment as the law of the land and govern their conduct accordingly."[27] Much of this early commentary was boosterism, revealing little more than how the paper hoped the decision would be received.

In Baltimore there was an added reason to follow the *Sun*'s coverage of *Dred Scott*. The paper served as a showcase for the city's legal prowess. Representing

John Sandford before the Supreme Court was the team of Henry Geyer and Reverdy Johnson. Baltimore had long been Johnson's home, even when his professional life took him to Washington. As the nation's foremost constitutional lawyer, he brought prestige to any case he took.[28] He served as a US senator and an attorney general, and he was a slaveholder at least until 1840.[29] Johnson was a friend to Roger Taney, and historians have shown how his legal acumen and intimate esteem shaped Taney's ideas.[30]

Chief Justice Taney himself loomed larger than any figure in the construction of Baltimore's reputation.[31] Taney began his career practicing in Maryland and then served as a state legislator and attorney general.[32] Throughout his years in Washington, Taney remained a keenly followed and highly regarded figure.[33] He spent extended time in his family home just footsteps from Baltimore's courthouse, and sat on the United States Circuit Court for the District of Maryland. Despite the demands of the high court, he occasionally led public gatherings, including bar proceedings.[34] His large oil portrait hung in the city's Bar Library, thus presiding in the courthouse even when the chief justice was himself absent.[35] The *Sun* had long fueled Reverdy and Taney's distinction through its coverage, and the men's involvement with *Dred Scott* provided another opportunity to enhance the city's image.

As the *Sun* underscored the roles of these greatly admired Baltimoreans, it also explained the case's implications for the city's free black community. For lay readers, the paper acted as an interpreter. One editorial set out the "main propositions of constitutional law," two of which delimited the status of black Americans. In a city where African Americans lived awkwardly between slavery and freedom and were embroiled in debates about their legal status, the *Sun* left little question about what it believed the case meant as it outlined those propositions:

1. That no negro, whether he be descendant of ancestors who were slaves when the constitution was adopted or of ancestors who were free at that time, or whether he be the descendant of free negroes who came into any State of the United States after the constitution was adopted can, even though he be born within the limits of a free State, be recognized by the law as a citizen of the United States.

2. That any of the State of this confederacy may, if they see proper, confer upon a free negro the rights of citizenship within that particular State, either by the provision of their organic law or by direct enactment: but the free negro upon whom this right is conferred does not for that reason become a citizen of the United States; nor is he entitled to the benefit of those classes in the constitution which apply to those who are both citizens of a State and citizens of the United States. He cannot sue in any of the courts of the United States, nor is he entitled to claim, if he enters a State other than his own, the privileges and immunities that are there

enjoyed by those who are not only citizens of that State but also citizens of the United States.[36]

The paper's tone was authoritative, suggesting that the court's reasoning was sound and unassailable. Thereafter, claims to black citizenship were subject to open derision in its pages. One May 1857 commentary critiqued the political visibility of Northern men like Charles Remond and Frederick Douglass. In it the *Sun*'s editors remarked on "the impossibility of recognizing negroes as citizens arising from their offence to the olfactories of the white race."[37] It was an old joke, but one that took on new significance in the wake of *Dred Scott*.

Owing to such partisanship in the *Sun*'s coverage, Baltimoreans would have to read beyond their local daily to encounter criticism of *Dred Scott*. Stinging were reports on those federal district courts that limited the opinion's effect.[38] The dissenting opinions from the Supreme Court decision were taking on the force of law. The United States Circuit Court for Indiana, for example, held that "a negro of the African race born in the United States . . . is a citizen of the United States . . . and entitled as such to sue in its courts."[39] Justice John McLean had been a dissenter in the decision at the Supreme Court.[40] Then in July 1857, while sitting on the federal Circuit Court for Illinois, he limited the scope of *Dred Scott* in the case of *Mitchell v. Lamar*. Joseph Mitchell, a free African American from Illinois, brought a suit against Charles Lamar, a white resident of Wisconsin.[41] Lamar had assaulted Mitchell, who sustained significant injuries and thus sought damages.[42] Did the federal court have jurisdiction? McLean thought it did and reasoned that Mitchell, a free black man not descended from slaves, was a citizen in that he was "a freeman, who has a permanent domicile in a State, being subject to its laws in acquiring and holding property, in the payment of taxes, and in the distribution of his estate among creditors, or to his heirs on his decease."[43] McLean conceded that Mitchell did not enjoy rights equivalent to those of white men. However, "it is not necessary for a man to be an elector in order to enable him to sue in a Federal Court," McLean reasoned.[44] "Such a man is a citizen, so as to enable him to sue, as I think, in the Federal Courts."[45] The debate over African American citizenship continued.

State court judges in Maine and Ohio outright refused to incorporate *Dred Scott* into their determinations.[46] In Ohio, one court confronted the question when called on to interpret the phrase "citizen of the United States" as set forth in its state constitution.[47] Distinguishing Justice Taney's opinion as limited to descendants of slaves, the court declined to hold that a free man of mixed racial descent could never be considered a citizen.[48] In Maine, by the request of the legislature, the justices of that state's high court interpreted a key provision of the state constitution which provided in pertinent part that "[e]very male citizen of the United States, of the age of twenty-one years and upwards . . . shall be an elector for governor, senators and representatives in the town or plantation where his residence is so established."[49] The question for the court was whether free men of color could serve as electors under this provision. While the law imposed no explicit barrier to enfranchisement based on race, the court admitted that a strict application of *Dred Scott* would mean the qualification "citizen of the United States" necessarily excluded free African Americans.[50] Yet, Maine's Supreme Court rejected such an interpretation, writing: "We are of the opinion that our constitution does not discriminate between the different races of people which constitute the inhabitants of our state; but that the term, 'citizens of the United States,' as used in that instrument, applies as well to free colored persons of African descent as to persons descended from white ancestors."[51] Thus, at least in some non-slaveholding states, courts declined to afford *Dred Scott* binding weight, even when United States citizenship was expressly at issue.

At least one Southern state, Mississippi, ultimately deemed *Dred Scott's* reasoning consistent with state law.[52] Still, the state's high court appeared to be of two minds. In the spring of 1858 the court held in *Shaw v. Brown* that a free African American had standing to sue in pursuit of his claims as an heir.[53] Writing for the majority, Justice Alexander Handy explained:

But negroes born in the United States, and free by the laws of the State in which they reside, are in a different condition from aliens. They are natives, and not aliens. Though not *citizens* of the State in which they reside, within the meaning of the Constitution of the United States, they are *inhabitants* and *subjects* of the State, owing allegiance to it, and entitled to protection by its laws and those of the United States; for by the common law, and the law of nations, all persons born within the dominion of the sovereign are his natural born subjects, and owe allegiance to him, and obedience to the laws, and are entitled to protection.[54]

The court acknowledged *Dred Scott* as establishing African Americans as "a subordinate and inferior class of beings" but did not go the next step and deem them without standing to pursue their claims in the State of Mississippi.[55] However, when confronted with a similar set of facts the following spring, the court embraced *Dred Scott* and deemed free black people *"alien strangers*, of an inferior class, incapable of comity, with which our government has no commercial, social, or diplomatic intercourse."[56] Justice William Harris wrote for the majority while Justice Handy, who had written for the majority in *Shaw* just one year earlier, dissented.[57]

By fall 1858, Roger Taney was uncomfortably aware that his reasoning on the matter of black citizenship was being called into question.[58] The ordinarily taciturn Taney wrote to his confidante David Perine to ask: "Have you read the opinion of the court in this case of Scott v. Sanford? I hope you find it all right."[59] Vexed by the "abuse that [had] been lavished" on him, the chief justice took time out to privately pen a supplemental opinion to *Dred Scott*.[60] It focused on one matter alone: black citizenship at the time of the Constitution's ratification.[61] Taney thanked his son-in-law and confidante, attorney J. Mason Campbell, for approving of his "supplement." The chief justice had hoped to

publish it "while the question is still exciting attention," but "judicial propriety" demanded the he wait for a relevant case to come before the court.
Publishing in pamphlet form was also out of the question: "I do not feel willing
to write a defense of one of my judicial opinions," Taney explained. The aging
jurist suggested that its publication would come only after his death – "My
executors must in some form or other bring it before the public" – which is
indeed what would happen.[62]

As he had in *Dred Scott*, Taney in his supplement relied on historical analysis
to show that African Americans had enjoyed no rights from 1689, as British
colonial subjects, through 1787, when the Constitution was ratified.[63] The
opinion was no mere exercise in argumentation. Taney explained that he stood
ready, should the court's docket present him with another opportunity, to clarify
and to persuade: "If the questions come before the Court again in my lifetime, it
will save the trouble of again investigating and annexing the proofs."[64]

Taney scoffed at all commentary "adverse" to his published opinion.
Generally, he deemed a reply not worthwhile, asserting that his critics based
their views on mere "misrepresentations and perversions." Still, the chief
justice could not refrain from launching a thinly veiled rebuttal to Horace
Gray's 1857 pamphlet, *A Legal Review of the Case of Dred Scott*. Gray was
the reporter of decisions for the Massachusetts Supreme Judicial Court, and
would be appointed to the Supreme Judicial Court of Massachusetts in 1864
and the United States Supreme Court in 1881.[65] Gray's analysis of the opinions
in *Dred Scott* led him to conclude: "The court have [*sic*] not, and could not
have, consistently with sound principles, decided that a free negro could
not be a citizen of the United States."[66] Gray challenged Taney in doctrinal
terms, but then went further to question Taney's character. The chief justice's
opinion, according to Gray, was "by no means the ablest or soundest of the
opinions" in the case. Its "tone and manner of reasoning, as well as in the
positions which it assumes" were "unworthy of the reputation of [Taney] that
great magistrate."[67] Taney replied that Gray's volume was "a disingenuous
perversion and misrepresentation of . . . what the Court has decided."[68] Taney
concluded his supplemental opinion on this point, urging that that those "in
search of truth . . . will read the opinion." Thus, he said, he would not "waste
time and throw away arguments" on commentators such as Gray.[69] Contrary
to his stated indifference, Taney's tone and the lengthy supplement suggest
that he was all too cognizant of how *Dred Scott* was being called into serious
question by well-informed analysts.

In a formalistic sense, there was no reason to expect a change in Maryland's
doctrine in response to a ruling that applied only to federal courts. Still, the
Supreme Court's determination invited questions about how other courts –
federal and state – would incorporate its conclusions into their deliberations.
The Taney Court decision may have simply been the latest volley in an ongoing
debate over race and citizenship. Or it may have set in motion a series of
changes that could reach into local venues.

In Baltimore, free African Americans did comment on how they saw the case, if only by way of their actions. They continued to bring disputes to court, much as they had before *Dred Scott*. They did not appear in the city's federal courts, but they never had. At least since 1850, black Baltimoreans had not used the federal courts to make claims. While Taney's opinion appeared to formally bar them, it was a symbolic barrier. Nothing changed for them after 1857.[70] The same was true in the city's local courts. There, black Baltimoreans continued their business as usual. They kept up their steady presence in the local courthouse. That their names and the charges against them continued to be marked in the pages of the city's criminal court docket is of little surprise. Still, there is no evidence in those records that after *Dred Scott* free black people in Baltimore were more likely to be arrested. Nor were they any more likely to be convicted of a crime.

Their court presence was unremarkable, at least to the eyes of the *Sun*'s correspondents. Nothing struck them as out of order when African Americans initiated proceedings just as they had for years. James Jones filed for insolvency relief for his debts, secured with the sworn support of local magistrate Basil Root and police officer Peter Logue.[71] Joseph Crawford and Edwin Scott challenged their detentions as a deserter from a vessel and a fugitive slave, respectively, using the writ of habeas corpus.[72] Black church leaders continued to wrangle over ownership of property and church governance.[73] Confidence appears to have been high that *Dred Scott* would have no effect.

It took nearly a year for the question to reach Maryland in the case of *Hughes v. Jackson*. Baltimoreans watched from the sidelines as two free black men from Dorchester County battled over whether they had the right to bring suit in the state's courts. The Maryland Court of Appeals, the state's high court, would be asked to determine whether the logic of *Dred Scott* – which might be extended to bar free black Marylanders from state as well as federal court – should become the law of the state. No formal rule required the state court to adopt the Supreme Court's reasoning in *Dred Scott*. While the Taney court was the highest authority on the access to federal courts, Maryland's high court had exclusive authority courts in the state. Thus, in 1858, when the lawyers for Hughes argued that free black people should be prohibited from suing in Maryland, it was an open question. Once again, the state stood at a major crossroads in its regulation of free black Americans.

Hughes v. Jackson did not pose a wholly new question. Prior cases had examined the extent to which free black Marylanders possessed rights in the state's courts. The Maryland Court of Appeals had from time to time been asked to determine the degree to which black laws, for example, might conflict with constitutional precepts. Under the leadership of Chief Justice John Carroll Legrand from 1851 to 1861, the court's conclusions were murky. Free African Americans could sue and be sued in Maryland, but actual rulings did not unqualifiedly affirm this view. The 1855 case of *Jason v. Henderson*, for example, asked whether a free person could recover damages for being unlawfully detained as a slave. The court said yes, as a general matter. Still, Jason could not recover from Henderson based on the facts because Henderson had not detained Jason "wantonly, and without color of title," but had acted in good faith in that he "supposed the negro to be the property of the estate he represented, and there appears a show of title for such a claim."[74] This sort of affirmation was but a partial victory for a litigant like Jason: He had a right to sue, but his claim failed.

These types of outcomes continued even after *Dred Scott* was decided. Free black people appeared before the state's highest court; they were never categorically excluded. The Maryland Court of Appeals issued rulings that may have pleased advocates for free black rights, but still disappointed the actual litigants. In December 1857, nine months after *Dred Scott*, the case of *Atwell v. Miller* probed the rights of free people of color in Maryland. The question in the case had been posed initially in a Baltimore trial court: Were free African Americans barred from giving testimony against the interests of white persons?[75] A 1717 state law governed the question: "No Negro or Mulatto Slave, Free Negro, or Mulatto born of a White Woman, during the Time of Servitude by law, shall be received as Evidence in any Cause wherein any Christian White Person is concerned."[76] The petitioner in *Atwell* nevertheless attempted to introduce the declarations of a free black man, Asbury Johns, at trial. The lower court had refused his testimony categorically, relying on the early eighteenth-century statute.

Before the court of appeals, the appellant urged that Johns's testimony should have been admitted. To resolve the question, the court might have relied on the 1717 law, but it did not. Instead, Chief Justice Legrand ruled that the defendants had not established the relevance of Johns's testimony – he was not a principal or agent such that his declarations had bearing on the case. Had his testimony been relevant, might Johns have been able to testify? Legrand did not close off this possibility, remarking: "This view relieves us from all necessity of inquiring, whether the color of the party, whose declarations were proposed to be given in evidence, could have a legal bearing on the question in any event."[77] The court declined to decide on the right of Johns to give evidence and left a door open. Perhaps, under another set of facts, a man of color might be permitted to give testimony against the interests of a white party, notwithstanding the terms of the 1717 law. Local tribunals were left with a bit more discretion than the trial judge in *Atwell* had been willing to exercise.

Six months later, in *Hughes v. Jackson*, the state's high court confronted *Dred Scott* head on. Free black litigants forced the Maryland Court of Appeals to consider the degree to which the state might adopt the logic of the Supreme Court. What rights, if any, did free people of color possess in Maryland's legal culture? Could they bring suit, or were they by virtue of their color barred from lodging complaints? In Baltimore, questions of race and rights had long simmered in the local courthouse. In Dorchester County, they boiled over.

Dorchester County sat on Maryland's Eastern Shore, a portion of the state where slaveholding remained extensive and proslavery politics dominated.[78] Between 1850 and 1860 the Eastern Shore's free black population grew by 14 percent, and many landholders in the region depended on free black laborers.[79] Still, the area's proximity to the free states generated tensions. Rumors of impending slave insurrections and rising numbers of escaped slaves generated a tense solidarity among slaveholders. Harriet Tubman carried out her clandestine raids in Dorchester County, freeing slaves from the county's farms. The escape of the Dover Eight, aided by Tubman, had rocked the county courthouse. Former slave Sam Green was arrested for aiding the group and was prosecuted for possessing a copy of Harriet Beecher Stowe's *Uncle Tom's Cabin*.[80] Local slaveholders organized around their concerns about the free black population, which was said to corrupt and demoralize slaves, making men like Hughes and Jackson a troublesome presence.[81]

Hughes v. Jackson grew out of years of stop-and-start litigation between William Hughes and Samuel Jackson that began in 1842 when Hughes purchased two slaves. Hughes was a free black farmer and landowner who managed his property with the help of four sons: Denwood, William, Josiah, and Robert.[82] He had never before been a slaveholder, though it would not have been out of the ordinary for a farmer like Hughes to hire enslaved people seasonally or for specialized tasks. This changed in the summer of 1842, when he paid Catherine Ray $280 for a woman and her infant daughter.[83] Hughes bargained to hold a temporary title to this "certain Mulatto woman named Mary Teackle and her infant child named Lilly." He agreed that the mother and daughter would be held only for a term of years, after which they would be free. The arrangement was set to begin on August 15, 1840, and terminate eleven years later, in 1851.[84]

Samuel Jackson's version of the bargain between Hughes and Ray included details nowhere recorded in the deed. Yes, Hughes had purchased Mary and Lilly, but Hughes had done so on Jackson's behalf. Mary Teackle was Jackson's wife. Hughes had permitted the Jackson family to live together in Dorchester County while Jackson paid Hughes for the freedom of Mary and Lilly over time. Jackson later explained that he had, from the outset of the agreement, been in "possession" of Mary and Lilly. Together they had made a home.[85]

For nearly ten years the bargain between Hughes and Jackson was an agreeable one, it seems. There were no outward signs of discord. Samuel and Mary's family grew to include four children: Lilly, the eldest, was followed by siblings Theodore, Dennis, and Ellen.[86] They rented a home from Hughes. Then, sometime in 1850, shy of the end of Mary's and Lilly's terms as slaves, William Hughes died. His sons Josiah and Denwood, as executors, were charged with distributing the elder Hughes's estate. Jackson and the Hughes brothers were soon at odds.[87] Was Jackson's family the property of William Hughes's estate? The parties did not agree. Samuel Jackson, feeling their liberty under threat, gathered his wife and children in an effort to escape the reach of the Hughes family. They got as far as the town of Cambridge but were thwarted in their attempts to board a ship to cross the Chesapeake Bay to the Western Shore. Denwood Hughes intercepted the family, seizing Mary and her children.[88] It was a vexed circumstance that would take more than a decade to resolve, during which time a local trial court, the state's court of appeals, and a constitutional convention would all weigh in. Questions about slavery and freedom were most pressing for the Jackson family. Still, their claims would turn, in part, on whether Samuel Jackson, as a free black man, had a right to sue in Maryland's courts. This was Maryland's *Dred Scott*.

The Hughes's intent soon became evident: the Jackson family was an asset. The brothers sold the Jacksons' three youngest children – Ellen, eight; Dennis, seven; and Theodore, four – to a prominent and prosperous white farmer, Alward Johnson, for $460.[89] Johnson purchased the children for cash pursuant to a bill of sale and deed that declared them to be the property of widow Mary Ann Hughes and slaves "for life." Johnson's purchase agreement also provided for the children's eventual manumission: Ellen after eighteen years, Dennis after twenty-four years, and Theodore after twenty-seven years. There was, perhaps, some small comfort for Samuel and Mary Jackson in knowing that their children would not be taken far. Johnson's farm was also in Dorchester County.

Samuel Jackson wasted little time before heading to the Dorchester County courthouse. He hired a lawyer and initiated a string of lawsuits aimed at regaining custody of his family and punishing the Hughes brothers. First were five freedom suits filed in April 1851, just weeks after the children's sale to Alward Johnson. Jackson filed these petitions as the so-called next friend of his wife and four children. Second, filed in October 1851, was a claim against Josiah and William Hughes for trespass. Jackson sought damages for the Hughes brothers' unlawful detention of his family. Third, Jackson brought suit against Denwood and Josiah Hughes as executors of the estate of William Hughes, also in October 1851. The specific nature of this claim the court record does not indicate. Fourth and finally, one year later in October 1852 Jackson filed suit against Denwood and Josiah Hughes and Alward Johnson. Again the specific charges are not recorded. These complaints might appear scattershot, but it is more likely that neither Jackson nor his lawyer knew precisely what sort of framework the court was likely to adopt for resolving such a dispute. In this they were not wrong. Very quickly two of the four proceedings came to a conclusion. The freedom suits were marked "off" the court calendar by October 1852, while the case against the Hughes brothers as executors of their father's estate was settled: "Discontinued and Judgment for Defendant Costs." Samuel Jackson paid $19.53⅔ for his trouble.[90]

What followed over the next years was muddled, at least when viewed from the vantage point of the court's docket books. Perhaps a combination of failed attempts at settlement combined with shifts in local political appointments kept the parties from getting to the merits. Hughes and Jackson appeared to be nearing a settlement in the trespass case in the spring of 1852. By the fall of 1853, with no settlement in sight, the court sounded impatient when it noted that if the case was not tried the following spring, it would enter a judgment for the defendants. Another year had passed when a newly appointed trial judge announced that he would disqualify himself; he had been counsel for the Hugheses earlier in the proceeding. A new "special judge" was finally appointed in January 1855. In the spring of 1856, Jackson's lawyers made one more push. A jury was sworn in April and on the twenty-fifth of that month it found in favor of Jackson. The Hugheses were to pay him $750 plus interest and costs for their trespass on his family. When the case was over Mary and Lilly were granted their liberty, although the three younger children remained in the hands of Alward Johnson.[91]

Samuel Jackson had managed to defeat the Hughes brothers by persuading a jury that he had been wronged. His strongest evidence was likely the array of white witnesses who testified on his behalf. Jackson drew from Dorchester County's associational networks to build his case.[92] Among his witnesses was a Hughes family neighbor, farmer William Corkran. Jackson relied on slaveholders, including the brothers Polish and Banaman Mills. And at least one woman testified, Eliza Hicks, a widow who owned her own farm, which was run by her children and black laborers. The general climate suggested that free black men and women in Dorchester County were subject to increasing scrutiny, including in the courthouse. But a modest laborer like Samuel Jackson could still call on the reputations and authority of local whites to substantiate his claim. They knew enough about the bargain between Jackson and Hughes to make them reliable and relevant witnesses. Throughout the proceedings, no one – no lawyer, no witness, no jury member, no judge – questioned Jackson's right to bring suit.

Jackson's victory at trial might have ended the matter, but Josiah Hughes appealed the trial court's ruling to the Maryland Court of Appeals, transforming Samuel Jackson's grievances from a local matter into an occasion for testing the reach of *Dred Scott*. Hughes's objections were partly routine. He sought to overturn the verdict or otherwise have it set aside based on technical defects.[93] For example, Jackson had failed to indicate in his initial pleadings that he was a "free" negro, inviting the presumption that he was a slave and thus incapable of bringing suit.[94] Hughes also asserted a novel position. He argued that the Supreme Court's logic in *Dred Scott* should decide the matter. The Hughes family attorney, Elias Griswold, asserted that Samuel Jackson (and, by curious implication, his own client), as a free black Marylander, was without standing before the state court, as Dred Scott had been before the federal court.[95] No black person, Griswold urged, enslaved or free, had standing to sue in the state. Jackson's case, he concluded, must be dismissed.

Hughes provided Maryland's high court its first opportunity to consider the implications of *Dred Scott*. Griswold suggested that, in Maryland, legal remedies for Jackson were out of reach. His argument was not tightly woven.[96] Griswold did not rely on specific citizenship language in the Maryland state constitution. Nor did he insist that there was any necessary relationship between federal citizenship, which had been Taney's subject, and the state citizenship that might have been relevant in the *Jackson* case. Instead, Griswold made a vague but cunning cultural-legal argument that might have allowed the court to bend toward the interests of white supremacy.[97] He referred to the "opinion of Chief Justice Taney in *Dred Scott*" to support the view that if Jackson was without standing to sue, the court itself was without jurisdiction. Then, without elaboration, Griswold declared that if no law extended civil rights to black Marylanders, "the plaintiff in this case had no right to sue."[98]

Jackson's attorneys, James Wallace and Charles Goldsborough, confronted the problem of *Dred Scott* directly, arguing that Maryland should take a distinct position on the question of African Americans' standing to sue and be sued. Their argument relied on an alternative view of history. Since the latter decades of the eighteenth century, Jackson's attorneys explained, African Americans "going at large and acting as free" had been viewed as free men.[99] They had, when the Constitution was ratified, given evidence in court and performed other acts, such as voting, that only subsequently had been reserved to white men. The free African American occupied an "anomalous position, having more rights than a stranger, yet not the same as an heir. He can sue and be sued in our courts, hold property and enjoy the fullest protection of our laws."[100] Jackson's counsel carefully distinguished the United States citizenship that was the subject of *Dred Scott* from citizenship in the state of Maryland, arguing that even if Jackson was disqualified under the federal Constitution, "he might still be a citizen of a State, and as such a free man."[101]

Hughes presented a matter of first impression for the Maryland Court of Appeals, while also positioning state court judges to assess Taney's ideas. Had Maryland's high court adopted the chief justice's views on race and rights, it would have been little surprise.[102] Legrand surely understood Taney's position. The two had a great deal in common. Both were raised in slaveholding households.[103] Both had practiced law in Baltimore before entering public service.[104] Taney had served as Maryland's attorney general, and Legrand had held the office of secretary of state.[105] The two were also active lay leaders in the city's Catholic Church.[106] Both men were moderate proslavery voices whose ideas reflected a paternalism that was characteristic of Maryland's pro-colonization white elites.[107]

On the rights of black people in legal culture, however, Legrand and Taney parted ways. Despite his general admiration for Taney and their shared cultural sensibilities, Legrand rejected the chief justice's reasoning and unequivocally refused to extend *Dred Scott* into the state of Maryland.[108] Samuel Jackson was entitled to bring suit in the state's courts, explained Legrand writing for the court.[109] In Maryland, there were only two instances in which black people were presumed, by their color, to stand apart from white Americans in legal culture. Blackness barred African Americans from testifying as witnesses against white people, and in freedom suits blackness raised the rebuttable presumption that they were slaves.[110] Otherwise, black Marylanders enjoyed a broad right to sue and be sued.[111] The court addressed the relevance of *Dred Scott* through Taney's own approach – a history of race and rights. "From the earliest history of the colony," Legrand explained, "free negroes have been allowed to sue in our courts and to hold property, both real and personal, and at one time, they having the necessary qualifications, were permitted to exercise the elective franchise."[112] In Justice Legrand's view, race had never served as an absolute bar to rights in Maryland. This was consistent, he said, with the state's interests: "To deny to them the right of suing and being sued, would be in point of fact to deprive them of the means of defending their possessions, and this, too, without subserving any good purpose . . . Neither the policy of our law, nor the well-being of this part of our population, demands the principle of exclusion contended for by the appellant."[113]

Legrand looked ahead and suggested that "so long as free negroes remain in our midst a wholesome system induces incentives to thrift and respectability, and none more effective could be suggested than the protection of their earnings."[114] Maryland's high court rejected Taney's view of both the history and the status of free black Americans. Legrand laid out for black Marylanders a bundle of rights.[115] It was an imperfect, partial, but still potent bundle of rights: to sue and be sued, to hold property real and personal, to defend possessions and earnings, and in some cases to vote.[116] Justice Legrand concluded by affirming the lower court judgment, entitling Samuel Jackson to his $750.

Court decisions – event those decided by high courts, like *Hughes v. Jackson* – did not settle matters in Baltimore. If George Hackett had followed that case, his attention did not linger. In the state capital, the same radical colonization that had inspired Octavius Taney nearly thirty year earlier was being revived. Maryland was caught up in an "anti-free Negro" wave that was sweeping much of the South. Lawmakers in Annapolis renewed efforts to set in place some of the most restrictive black laws the state had ever contemplated. Curtis Jacobs, head of the failed effort to regulate free black Marylanders in the 1851 state constitution, led the campaign as chair of the Committee on the Colored Population. The proposed legislation resurrected old ideas, including prohibiting manumission, imposing a registration requirement, and developing plans for the removal of all free black Marylanders from the state.

Jacobs shared with the Maryland Hall of Delegates a history of race and rights that supported his radical colonizationist position. He demanded, for example, atonement for the "horrid murder" of Edward Gorsuch at Christiana. Enslaved people had been "happy and contented . . . before our free negroes had become so numerous," he claimed. "This government," Jacobs explained, "was made exclusively for the benefit of the white population." Free black people were at the root of slave uprisings, from "the bloody massacre of the whites by the slaves on the Island of Hayti" to the "sad event at Harper's Ferry [when] John Brown so foolishly supposed the slaves of Virginia were . . . anxious to be free."[117]

Jacobs insisted that, by law, white Marylanders had the "right to re-enslave our free negro population." He then recounted the state's history of black laws from 1831 to 1858, which demonstrated that the freedom of black Marylanders was "only nominal and sheer mockery, and that it in no sense confers any of the attributes or rights of citizenship." He reviewed the support for colonization, which dated back to the 1830s. He drew on the decision in *Dred Scott*, promoting it while never remarking on *Hughes v. Jackson*. Finally, he acknowledged that manumission was the prerogative of slaveholders, but said such acts merely transferred ownership to the state, which could dispose of nominally freed people as it deemed fit.[118]

The Jacobs bill set off alarms in black Baltimore. The *Sun* employed understatement when it commented that the bill's "novelty, if nothing else, will no doubt attract considerable interest and elicit no little comment and discussion."[119] A writer to the *Weekly Anglo-African* was more direct: "The Maryland bill far excels any I have seen for severity. The idea of selling convicts, old persons, etc., as well as our church property, is very severe."[120] No number of claims enacted in the everyday sense would guarantee defeat of the proposed legislation. Hackett rethought the strategy that had guided Baltimore's black community through the preceding decades. It was, he concluded, time to organize on a grander scale, bringing the sentiments of black Baltimoreans together with those of their white allies.[121] Petitions were drawn up calling for defeat of the legislation, and hundreds came out to affix their signatures. Dissent came from many corners, including in news commentary. Southern Maryland's *Somerset Union* remarked: "We fear that his (Mr. Jacobs') zeal for the cause he has overshot the mark, and that his ultra position is better calculated to retard than advance the end which he, in common with the large majority of citizens in this part of Maryland, desires to see consummated."[122]

Hackett left Baltimore, petitions in hand, for a visit to the state capital of Annapolis. There, he confronted Curtis Jacobs, and at least one chronicler reports that two had a brief brawl on the statehouse lawn. The story of their encounter, told by librarian and book collector Daniel Murray, survives in Murray's handwritten notes. Murray planned to publish an encyclopedia of black history, but it never came to fruition.[123] His draft entries appear to have been compiled out of published works, interviews, and his own personal recollections. Murray was also a Baltimorean, born in 1852, which meant he would have been old enough to have met Hackett and his family. He recorded this version of the confrontation in Annapolis between Hackett and Jacobs:

[Hackett] at once got up a petition to urge the Legislature to reject the monstrous proposition of Mr. Jacobs, which was freely signed by both white and colored residents of Balto. and to Annapolis Mr. Hackett carried it. He proceeded to the door of the

Legislative Chamber, and his presence being made known to Mr. Jacobs he at once confronted Mr. Hackett and with violent gestures inquired, how dare he a negro bring a petition to the Legislature in opposition to a bill proposed by a white member? And without more ado lurches a blow at Mr. Hackett, who having with him a stout cane belaboured Mr. Jacobs good and hard ere they were separate.[124]

Murray's story is likely at least partly apocryphal. It is more probable that the two met to debate the matter. When Hackett was through at the capital, the Jacobs bill had been so modified that it could be regarded as watered down, a credit to Hackett's organizing efforts and the support of white allies. Hackett had once again cloaked himself in the garb of one who had an unqualified right to do so.

Like many legislative victories, the outcome of the Jacobs bill struggle did not warrant celebration. Hackett and the thousands who had joined him on paper had succeeded in petitioning the legislature, but it was a qualified success. It was another chapter in what black Baltimoreans like Hezekiah Grice termed their "Dred Scott," the struggle over race and rights that Grice and his Legal Rights Association marked as beginning in the 1830s. It stood for a Supreme Court case that had symbolic meaning but little material effect. Roger Taney's reasoning was tested in many states, Maryland among them, and many jurists avoided its most strict application, finding black Americans to hold rights in a qualified sense. The Maryland Court of Appeals rejected the view that the state should bar free black men and women from its halls of justice. Chief Justice John Carroll Legrand affirmed a set of rights that were not equivalent to citizenship but did include the right to sue and be sued. This possibility alone had long given free black Marylanders an opening through which to construct their well-being and belonging.

Conclusion

Rehearsals for Reconstruction: New Citizens in a New Era

"Even in *Baltimore* colored men have rights that white men are bound to respect." The *Dred Scott* decision was not far from the mind of surgeon Alexander T. Augusta when, in late spring 1863, he reflected on a series of troubled confrontations in Baltimore. His morning had begun with a group of "roughs" threatening him as he sat aboard a Philadelphia-bound train in his Union officer's uniform. Augusta fled the car, but the assault continued on the street with a severe blow to his face that drew blood. By midafternoon Augusta was back in his train seat, headed north in the company of fellow officers, white men who vowed to protect him at the risk of their own lives. Augusta would look back on the day with satisfaction, relating that some of his assailants had "been tried and sent to Fort McHenry."[1] Augusta was keenly aware that the sight of his uniformed black body traversing the city streets would draw attention. Still, he claimed his place, and on that afternoon his hard-won status was affirmed.

Behind the wit that Augusta displayed as he inverted Justice Taney's infamous words was an important truth. Despite persistent assertions to the contrary, Baltimore's free black residents had long lived as rights-bearing people who cobbled together a strain of belonging that looked like citizenship. By 1863 the muted, indirect, and often implied rights claims that characterized the antebellum years were being eclipsed by bold manifestations of black citizenship. Amid war and on the cusp of Reconstruction, long-constrained aspirations were being unleashed. When Augusta donned his uniform and walked through Baltimore's streets, he displayed an unfettered belonging that had not been possible before the war, loosening the constraints of colonization, black laws, and *Dred Scott*.

The start of the Civil War marked a new chapter in the story of race and rights in Baltimore City. It brought renewed opportunity for black men to perform their belonging and to conduct themselves like citizens, first and

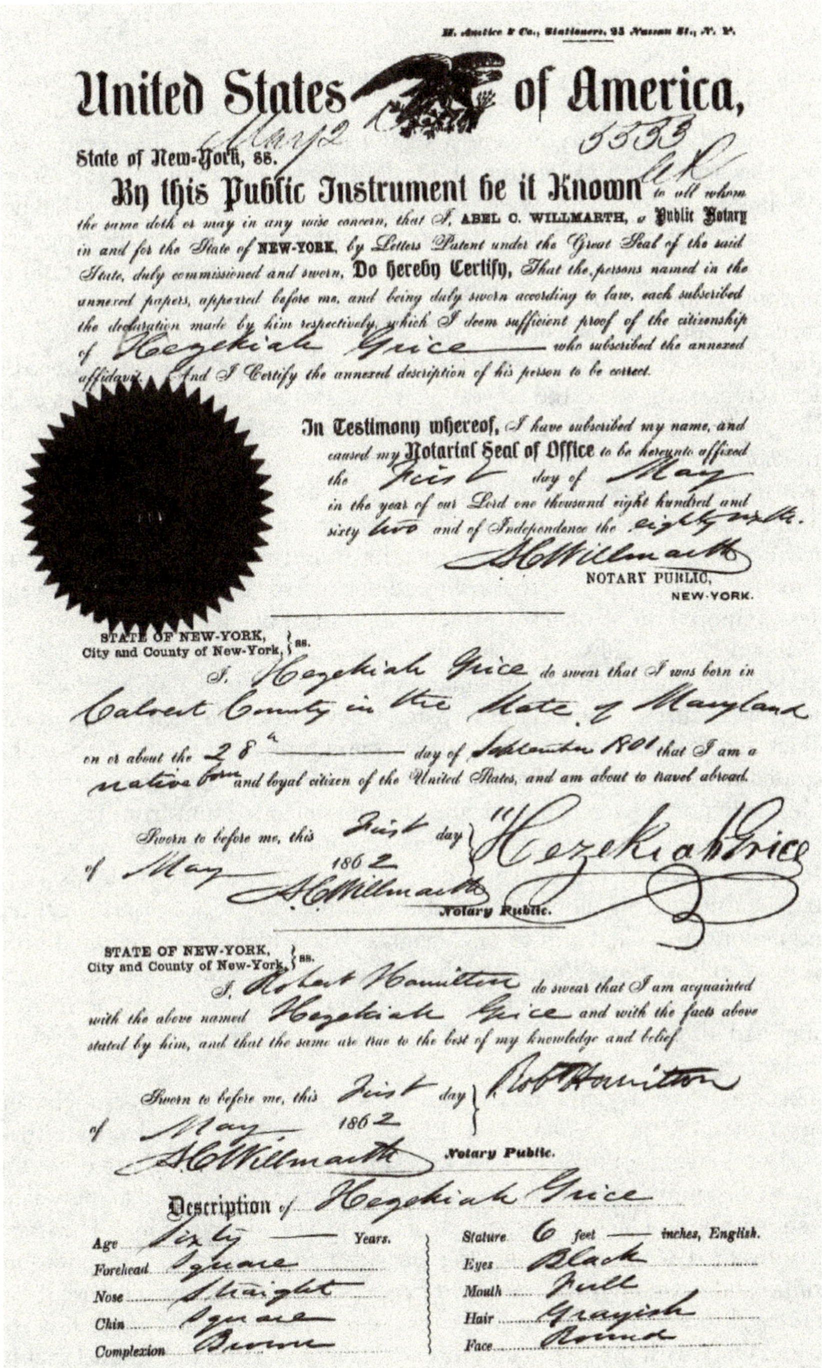

H. Ansilce & Co., Stationers, 93 Nassau St., N. Y.

United States of America,

May 2 5553

State of New-York, ss.

By this Public Instrument be it Known to all whom the same doth or may in any wise concern, that I, ABEL C. WILLMARTH, a Public Notary in and for the State of NEW-YORK, by Letters Patent under the Great Seal of the said State, duly commissioned and sworn, Do hereby Certify, That the persons named in the annexed papers, appeared before me, and being duly sworn according to law, each subscribed the declaration made by him respectively, which I deem sufficient proof of the citizenship of Hezekiah Grice who subscribed the annexed affidavit. And I Certify the annexed description of his person to be correct.

In Testimony whereof, I have subscribed my name, and caused my Notarial Seal of Office to be hereunto affixed the First day of May in the year of our Lord one thousand eight hundred and sixty two and of Independence the eighty sixth.

A. C. Willmarth
NOTARY PUBLIC,
NEW-YORK.

STATE OF NEW-YORK, City and County of New-York, } ss.

I, Hezekiah Grice do swear that I was born in Calvert County in the State of Maryland on or about the 28th day of September 1801 that I am a native born and loyal citizen of the United States, and am about to travel abroad.

Sworn to before me, this First day of May 1862 } Hezekiah Grice

A. C. Willmarth
Notary Public.

STATE OF NEW-YORK, City and County of New-York, } ss.

I, Robert Hamilton do swear that I am acquainted with the above named Hezekiah Grice and with the facts above stated by him, and that the same are true to the best of my knowledge and belief.

Sworn to before me, this First day of May 1862 } Robt Hamilton

A. C. Willmarth
Notary Public.

Description of Hezekiah Grice

Age	Sixty Years.	Stature	6 feet — inches, English.
Forehead	Square	Eyes	Black
Nose	Straight	Mouth	Full
Chin	Square	Hair	Grayish
Complexion	Brown	Face	Round

FIGURE C.1 Passport application, Hezekiah Grice. The Civil War and Reconstruction amplified the claims that black Baltimoreans had long put forth about their rights as citizens. Hezekiah Grice, disappointed about the outcome of his Legal Rights Association work, had abandoned the United States for Haiti in the 1830s, only to return to secure a passport in 1862. Image courtesy of the National Archives and Records Administration.

foremost through military service. Thousands of men from Baltimore and the surrounding county enlisted as soon as the Union army lifted the color bar. They also watched as their city became a stage for the testing of the Constitution. From the arrest and detention of local officials, including Mayor George W. Williams, to the standoff between Abraham Lincoln and Roger Taney in *Ex parte Merryman*, all Baltimoreans were students of law as the exigencies of war changed the terms on which everyone would come to understand the Constitution and its force in the state. Even the great writ of habeas corpus, it turned out, could be suspended.[2]

Ideas about citizenship were beginning to reflect the view long espoused by black activists. In 1862, the newest United States attorney general was called on to give his opinion about the capacity of black men to pilot ships along the nation's coast. It was no secret that the answer to this question lay, as it long had, in whether black men were viewed as citizens of the United States. President Lincoln's attorney general, Edward Bates, broke with his predecessors William Wirt and Roger Taney.[3] Free people of color were citizens of the United States, offered Bates in an opinion that reviewed debates of the preceding forty years. Bates composed the strongest treatise in support of black citizenship since that of William Yates, published twenty-five years earlier.

Alexander Augusta was emblematic of a generation of Baltimore activists whose lives reflected their claim to place. They had made their lives and their politics in a city that offered few platforms and little reassurance. Augusta had migrated from Norfolk to Baltimore as a young man. There, he married and set his sights on a career in medicine. Racism excluded him from US medical schools and so he joined the stream of northbound migrants to Canada, where he earned a degree from the University of Toronto. With the outbreak of the war, Augusta and his family returned to Baltimore. A series of army officers' commissions propelled him to new heights. His achievements reflected broad and ultimately sweeping national changes in the equation of race and rights. They also carried special meaning for Baltimore's black activists, so many of whom had also come and gone, only to return to the city to press their claims to belonging.

Changes to Maryland law contributed to Reconstruction-era changes, though they did not define them. Exempted, as a loyal border state, from President Lincoln's Emancipation Proclamation, Maryland charted its own path to becoming a postslavery society. Lawmakers haltingly approached questions about black rights, much as they had always done. The state's Constitutional Convention of 1864 provided for immediate, unconditional abolition, although with 30 percent of delegates opposing the measure. Long-standing disputes like *Hughes v. Jackson* came to a final and more just conclusion. Only with the state's abolition of slavery in 1864 did Samuel Jackson and his wife Mary regain custody of their three youngest children. In 1864 the family was reunited.

Many black laws remained in place, while others were reformed only piece-meal. The in-migration of black people was still prohibited in 1865, although penalties were lessened. Black criminals could be whipped or imprisoned but no longer sold as slaves. An effort to free all persons imprisoned under laws related to slavery lost to a tie vote. The legislature inaugurated statewide public education, but no provisions were made for black pupils.[4] Prohibitions against interracial marriage were struck down, and the marriages of former slaves were recognized by law. Yet, other restrictions were left in place, including the punishment for spreading incendiary matter among black Marylanders. The courthouse remained unreconstructed to an important degree: long-standing limits on black testimony against white parties remained in place. Still, by 1870 political rights were being restored, with black voters participating in local elections that spring.[5]

Black Baltimoreans matched lawmakers' muddled actions with their own characteristically bold assertions of citizenship, steps ahead of statutes and constitutions. For some, asserting citizenship was a quiet journey. This was true for Hezekiah Grice, who decades earlier had emigrated to Haiti, despairing of what was possible in Baltimore. In 1862, Grice was one step ahead of state and federal lawmakers when he appeared in New York City to apply for a US passport.[6] Grice had maintained ties to the United States; his job managing public works for the Haitian government brought him back to New York regularly.[7] He headed to the office of Notary Public Abel Willmarth and testified to his birth in Calvert County, Maryland, in 1802. His friend, *Anglo-African Magazine* editor Robert Hamilton, came along and swore that Grice had been born in the United States. The resulting document was, finally, evidence of his citizenship. Grice had an answer to the question he had posed to lawyers and black convention goers decades before.

More often, however, citizenship was expressed in loud voices. With George Hackett in the lead, black men, firearms, and military service converged on Baltimore's streets. The earliest postwar confrontations between black and white Baltimoreans arose when newly discharged African American soldiers returned to the city. Bearing government-issued firearms, they were confronted by local officials who sought to deprive them of those badges of citizenship. In 1865 black Marylanders were still refused admission to the state militia – the issue came up in the state legislature but no action was taken. They thus began to form their own organizations. They secured equipment – muskets purchased from the US Army – established armories, adopted uniforms, and paraded through city streets. The Butler Guard was among them, first appearing as an honor guard for a public celebration sponsored by Bethel AME Church. The captain of the Butler Guard was George Hackett. In this new role, Hackett also would lead a contingent of "Baltimore's colored citizens" in Abraham Lincoln's Washington, DC, funeral procession. He was in the company of Nathan Bowers, who served as the Butler Guard's first sergeant. Bowers had long carried his gun and a court-issued permit. But publicly bearing arms as part of a collective was possible in Baltimore only after the war.[8] And doing so in a militia named for Union general Benjamin Butler made the political significance of such an act clear.

The local courthouse remained a site for rights claims, and in light of a new constitution that provided for slavery's abolition, it was possible to challenge black laws, such as those that imposed apprenticeships. Apprenticeship remained a fraught practice, as local courts continued to arbitrate the relationships between black children, their parents, and indenture holders. Little changed in the Orphan's Court. But now black parents began to use the writ of habeas corpus in an unorthodox way, bringing their grievances to the criminal court. There, Judge Henry Stump had been unseated, and in his place was the Radical Republican Hugh Lennox Bond, who as a young lawyer had been an ally to free black license and permit seekers. Even though Bond's court did not have jurisdiction, he began to hear challenges to apprenticeship arrangements. He then went a step further. Bond voided individual apprenticeship contracts and went on to also declare all such agreements unconstitutional. When the state's new constitution of 1864 abolished slavery, he reasoned, it also extinguished all legal distinctions between the races. As a result, Bond concluded, the state's apprenticeship laws, which differentiated between black and white children, were void. It was not long before the state legislature agreed.[9]

Educator and rights activist William Watkins did not live long enough to join in the transformations of the Reconstruction era. In 1852 Watkins had abandoned the city he loved for Canada, despairing that equal citizenship was forever out of reach. He died there in 1858. Still, his early work as a teacher and advocate for public education was remade in the postwar period. A new generation of education activists took up where Watkins had left off, beginning in 1865 with calls for local officials to support black schools.[10] Reconstruction's statewide reforms included the establishment of public education. Funding did not, at the start, extend to black children, but when it eventually did, black residents' tax dollars were earmarked for this purpose. In Baltimore, the issue was not a new one. African American taxpayers had petitioned since the 1830s for the return of their tax dollars. Only when their children had access to the city's schools, parents argued, should they have to contribute to the expense.[11]

Baltimore's Reconstruction agenda included the building of new institutions: schools. Awkward alliances with white civic leaders required careful negotiations, much as the building of black churches had before the war. Schools demanded unprecedented resources, and the modest tax dollars of black Baltimoreans were not enough to build an entire system. Support came from local philanthropists, with Judge Hugh Lennox Bond at the fore. His Baltimore Association for the Moral and Educational Improvement of the Colored People collected funds from black and white donors, the city council, and Northern benefactors, and opened twenty-five schools during its first year. Bond loaned his reputation to the cause and built national donor networks that sustained it. By 1867 the federal Freedmen's Bureau assumed much of the responsibility for the association's schools. Still, Bond toured the state, expanding enthusiasm and support for black children's education. By the summer of that year, Baltimore's council was calling for the establishment of a far-reaching system of public schools for the city's black children.[12]

Alliances across the color line remained fraught, and in Baltimore few white champions of black rights were pure of heart. Bond's personal correspondence reveals his complicated ideas about black Baltimoreans. He abhorred the crude racial inequality embodied in black laws and their vestiges. At the same time, he openly doubted the intellectual capacities of black Americans and twisted their aspirations into cruel ridicule.[13] Did black activists know of Bond's racist ideas? Perhaps they did, although if he revealed them in a courtroom or meeting hall, they escaped the written record. Publicly, black commentators expressed only admiration for Bond. Whatever his private attitudes, he was lauded as a zealous ally for advocating for black suffrage in Maryland and afterward, as a federal judge, for presiding over South Carolina's Ku Klux Klan trials in 1870.[14]

No single event better captures how Reconstruction gave license to the ambitions of black Baltimoreans than the founding of the city's first black newspaper, the *Lyceum Observer*, in 1863. Black print culture had played an important role in the city's political culture of the 1820s, with men like Hezekiah Grice and Charles Hackett serving as agents for *Freedom's Journal*. Baltimore had nurtured antislavery journalists, including William Lloyd Garrison, through the pages of the *Genius of Universal Emancipation*. William Watkins had written about the city's political and cultural concerns as "A Colored Baltimorean" in the *Genius of Universal Emancipation* and the *Liberator*. Still, the city had never been home to a publication operated by black editors for a black readership. And with good reason. State law made it a crime to publish material that might incite free black Marylanders. But in 1863 that changed, as a band of young men organized to publish a chronicle of black ideas and black activism.

"Maryland! My Maryland!" was the title of William Matthews's contribution to the *Observer*'s first issue.[15] It was a biting rebuke to the proslavery and pro-Confederate factions in the state. "Maryland! My Maryland!" had been the title of a secessionist anthem. With his parody, Matthews turned the very notion of Maryland on its head; by 1863 he saw the changes that were under way and credited black Marylanders with fomenting them: "Those men of color, who, in the consciousness of their manhood, have leaped from the dark recesses of ignorance, and with their hands wrote their names in unperishable [sic] letters of renown upon the apex of Fame's rugged mount . . . those veterans who manfully stood at their post where the first of the enemy was hottest, have been Marylanders!" Matthews's list of black Marylanders was impressive. The state had been a crucible that formed many of the era's best and most influential thinkers: Frederick Douglass, Henry Highland Garnet, Benjamin Banneker, William Douglass, and William James Watkins.

Among the names of Maryland's illustrious "men of color" was that of one woman: "Francis Ellen Watkins Harper, a fluent writer and poetess of no mean attainments." Harper had been raised in Baltimore by her uncle, William Watkins, and had taught school in the city before migrating north.[16] Her reputation was as a poet, an antislavery orator, and an organizer who had effectively recruited black troops for the Union. Watkins's repertoire was wide-ranging, and her force derived from her capacity to wield allegory and sentiment interlaced with anecdote and personal reflection. She also understood something about law, and wove natural-law principles and the text of the Constitution into her prose:

Slavery is mean, because it tramples on the feeble and weak. A man comes with his affidavits from the South and hurries before a commissioner; upon that evidence ex parte and alone he hitches me to the car of slavery and trails my womanhood in the dust. I stand at the threshold of the Supreme Court and ask for justice, simple justice. Upon my tortured heart is thrown the mocking words, "You are a negro; you have no rights which white men are bound to respect." . . . When I come here to ask for justice, men tell me "We have no higher law than the Constitution."[17]

The awkward inclusion of Watkins Harper here is no accident. She was among the women who were transforming black public culture – in her case, to such an extent that it was nearly impossible for Matthews to take stock of Baltimore's impact on the struggle for citizenship without including this most talented daughter. But Matthews's inability to find more precise language – leaving Watkins Harper listed among "men of color" – suggests that early Reconstruction marked a turning point. Much if not most of the antebellum era's citizenship debate was premised in deep assumptions about its gendered nature. Never did a claim surface that suggested womanhood precluded citizenship. Still, the struggle proceeded in large part without any engagement with the problem that gender posed for understanding and arbitrating rights. The early debate about citizenship largely assumed it to be a problem between and about men.

Watkins Harper and her generation of black women activists threatened this assumption and signaled the ways in which questions of race and rights would take on a deliberately intersectional quality in the post–Civil War era. Indeed, when debating the terms of the Fifteenth Amendment's voting rights protections, it was Watkins Harper who argued, "We are all bound up together in one great bundle of humanity." She inaugurated a new framework for understanding citizenship, one that extended beyond birthright to incorporate black women's perspective. Their vantage point, as what she termed the "weakest and most feeble," made black women the measure of law's ambition and its capacity to arbitrate justice.

In 1870, Baltimore's Monument Square was the site for a national celebration of the Fifteenth Amendment's ratification. The Fourteenth Amendment was already in place and with its guarantee of birthright citizenship, the threat of radical colonization – removal – fell away. In its place, though, arose thorny questions about political and civil rights. Black Baltimoreans came out to see one of that city's most distinguished sons, Frederick Douglass, preside over a ceremony that boldly celebrated a constitutional revolution that put African Americans, both formerly enslaved and free, on a new footing before the law.

George Hackett did not attend that gathering. He had died just months before. His funeral had been a grand public occasion that recognized the remarkable array of Hackett's distinctions. His contributions to public culture – through leadership in churches, fraternal orders, and benevolent associations – were lauded. His entrepreneurial skills were remembered. The last of his ventures was the founding of the black-owned Chesapeake Railway, Marine and Dry Dock Company, which employed hundreds at its facility in Fells Point.[18] He had been a man devoted to family. And unbeknown to Hackett, his stepdaughter Henrietta Vinton Davis would in her adult life be a key leader of the Garvey Movement, a fitting manifestation of Hackett's legacy.[19]

Law attended Hackett in death, much as it had during each phase of his life. He wrote a last will and testament in 1869; likely he knew he was ill. Hackett carefully provided for his wife and three daughters. He directed the sale of properties, the establishment of annuities, and made express provisions for the long-term security of his children and grandchildren. In this he had assistance. A will of such complexity required an expert hand. And the confidence that its terms would be carried out required a trusted one. Hackett turned in those last weeks of his life to a man he knew well, Theophilous Horwitz. The Horwitz brothers – Theophilous, Orville, and Benjamin – were well known to many black Baltimoreans. The three had signed permit applications and served as trustees in insolvency proceedings. Orville Horwitz had long been an attorney to the congregation at Bethel Church.

The courthouse had been many things to Hackett: a site for righting wrongs and protecting interests; a scene for the performance of rights and citizenship. It also had been, it seems, a place for forging relationships. After many years, George Hackett trusted Horwitz enough to place his family's future in the lawyer's hands. And likely he paid the usual fee.

Epilogue

Monuments to Men

Today Baltimore's courthouse sits in the very place that all the city's courthouses have occupied. As far back as the era of the American Revolution, law and the social world have collided in that exact location. The modest courthouse of Roger Taney's era remained standing until the end of the nineteenth century. Its proceedings, however, were transformed by the Civil War and emancipation, when new state and federal constitutions rewrote the fundamental terms of race and law. Black Baltimoreans continued to steadily stream to that building off Monument Square, but with new claims at their disposal.

The courthouse was once again changed with the rise of Jim Crow. A place for the enactment of interracial democracy became a battleground, testing the power of the Reconstruction era's civil rights acts. By the 1890s the antebellum past was being razed. A new building with a grand scale and even grander pretensions replaced the nineteenth century's modest structure. This edifice did not easily welcome rights claims. But nearby, a new icon of legal culture was born. He was a man who spoke to issues of race and law with all the force and conviction that had characterized Roger Taney, though with another valence altogether. Thurgood Marshall was born in Baltimore in 1908, and in his hometown's courthouse he advocated a new order – desegregation – cutting his teeth, honing his skills, and laying the groundwork for a radical reordering of the relationship of race to rights.

It would be another seventy-five years before Thurgood Marshall would wholly remake the courthouse as artifact of memory. In 1985, the 1890s' edifice to Jim Crow justice was renamed. Its rededication as the Clarence M. Mitchell, Jr. Courthouse was a powerful gesture of both remembering and forgetting. Mitchell was a peer to Marshall and had served as lobbyist for the National Association for the Advancement of Colored People (NAACP) for nearly thirty years. Bearing his name, the courthouse became both a tribute to and an emblem of the civil rights era's vision of race and justice. But what did

FIGURE E.1 Former site of Chief Justice Roger B. Taney monument. In 2017 Chief Justice Roger B. Taney's figure was removed from many of its pedestals in Maryland amid challenges to the pro-Confederate and pro-white supremacy views he was said to stand for. Local residents remade this site in Baltimore's Mount Vernon neighborhood by placing an empty chair where the Taney figure once sat. The city's other monuments to Taney, two of which are in the local courthouse, have remained. Image courtesy of Martha S. Jones.

the same gesture erase? Is it possible to see through Mitchell's name to a past less sanguine?

These days, I follow the daily goings-on in Baltimore with a special eye on the courthouse. Commentators most often lament its dilapidated state – leaks, vermin, and crumbling plaster. Hardly a gleaming monument to civil rights, but a monument nonetheless. On my first visit to the courthouse, I was in a hurry. I was headed to the Bar Library of Baltimore, to review bound volumes of nineteenth-century treatises and court opinions. I spied the sole public entrance, on Monument Square, then mounted the steps, already anticipating the metal detectors and security pat down. Almost inside, I heard a curious call. It wasn't my name. The voice wasn't one I knew. Still, it was oddly familiar – familiar enough that I paused just a moment to glance back. It was auction day.

The organized, determined actions of creditors still animate proceedings at the Baltimore courthouse. And those creditors still appear to be aiming to gain possession of the only assets held by many African American families, their homes. Since January 2008, when Baltimore charged Wells Fargo Bank with predatory lending, the story of how banks have targeted the city's minority communities with unfair lending practices has become well known. Maryland's attorney general leveled charges against illegal "foreclosure practices, including the 'robo-signing' of affidavits and other required documents." The state's high court echoed the attorney general's concerns, issuing an "emergency" rule that explicitly "allows circuit courts to appoint independent lawyers to review fore-closure documents for problems."[1]

The mortgage crisis that began in 2008 continues to play out on the steps of the city courthouse. On that fall afternoon, heeding Joseph Roach's admon-ition that scholars should spend more time in the streets, I stopped to watch.[2] The drama had begun offstage, with notices published in local newspapers and on the internet. Now, on the noticed day and time, the auctioneer had positioned himself at the top of the steps. At his feet at were red milk crates filled with files. He cradled a clipboard stacked with documents. He shuffled the paperwork and conferred quietly with another man. It was the sheriff. At some moments there was a small crowd gathered. Other times, there were only an interested few. Now I understood his purpose, even if I could not make out his exact words. I heard the auctioneer's staccato words strung together in a distinct cadence. Then a pause signaled the single-word refrain and his open palm slapped the clipboard: "Sold." Homes are for sale on the courthouse steps. Insolvent debtors – today, as defaulted mortgage holders – can watch as their homes are sold to the highest bidder. Underlying this scene are rights, including the right to make contracts and to sue and be sued. In this haunting performance, the city courthouse is again, as it was in the nineteenth century, a stage for complex dramas of race and law.

Inside the courthouse, I headed upstairs. I knew I was on Roger Taney's turf. Both Taney's home and the federal courthouse, where he sat on the US Circuit Court, were just one block from Monument Square.

It still is possible to walk Taney's streets, but only with a good dose of imagin-ation. Some of the place names have changed, and the layout has too. Not the slightest of those changes is, of course, the courthouse itself. The buildings of Taney's era were long ago razed, including the former Masonic Hall where he presided over the federal Circuit Court. Where once stood the Taney home, on the northeast corner of Saint Paul and Lexington Streets, is today the Courtside Building, erected in 1918 as the Wolf Building, housing a law firm of the same name. Perhaps the only vista that remains the same as in Taney's era is that of the column of the war memorial that marks Monument Square.

What is there left of Taney, and of an era in which courthouse auctions disposed of the bodies as well as the homes of black Americans? Visit the Baltimore courthouse and you will be struck by how it embraces and honors its history. A courtroom space on the building's first floor was set aside in 1984 as a museum, governed by the Baltimore Courthouse and Law Museum Foundation. Each weekday between noon and one, visitors can study the history of the courthouse and the city's legal culture. Volunteer attorneys serve as docents. The courthouse also boasts of its prominent portraiture. Nearly every courtroom and many corridors are appointed with the oil likenesses of the city's legal luminaries from across more than two centuries.

On my first visit, I prowled the courthouse halls and courtrooms looking for traces of its early nineteenth-century history. I would have to make my way to the top floor, methodically combing through the building, before I would find him. Taney might not mind that visitors need to ascend to the building's uppermost floors to encounter his memory. Floors six and seven include vaulted ceilings and a domed roof that today, after renovations in the 1950s did away with the structure's ground-floor atrium, are some of the building's grandest features. And there, Taney still presides in the building as a figure accorded prominence and respect. I had heard tell of the Baltimore Bar Library well before I finally visited the courthouse's sixth floor.

The city's lawyers had banded together in 1840 to create the library, which had its first home in the courthouse that stood in this location from 1808 to 1895. Commentators complained about its cramped, poorly appointed rooms, but it was a shared meeting place for the city's legal elite and made resources such as case reporters and legal treatises more broadly available. The library overlooked Taney's home, it was said, though not by design. For historians today, the library holds tremendous allure because it is intact. The library's collection from the nineteenth century has been preserved, set aside in a "historical" section, and researchers can browse the stacks much as nineteenth-century local attorneys once did. Some lawyers donated their personal libraries to the institution at the end of their career. Their book labels and handwritten names are scattered throughout the collection. Here I hoped to see the antebellum world from the perspective of the city's practitioners.[3]

I had not expected to find Taney there (even though I would have welcomed the discovery of his books). But as I pushed open the library doors, there he was, the first to greet me even before the staff had time to rise from their desks. Taney's portrait is an imposing one. Completed during his lifetime by the artist Miner Kilbourne Kellogg, it depicts the chief justice at rest in an armchair, quill in one hand and paper under the other. A case reporter on the table just within reach, Taney is set in an elegant frame of silk drapes, classical columns, and heavy oak furniture. He gazes beyond the frame in studied concentration.

How should historians of race and law interpret the Bar Library, as an archive? I was welcomed there. As a member of the guild, the director assured me, lest I had forgotten, I am an honorary member of the library. I admired the ornate vaulted ceilings, long and wide reading tables, and green-shaded reading lamps. There was not a computer terminal in sight. I was invited to visit the "Moose Room" in which is prominently displayed the head of said moose. There is a story to go with it, about competing law firms and a bet: the winner got the head. Then I made my way back to the historical room, and I had the run of the place. I rummaged and rifled in the open stacks with no one peering over my shoulder. I began to piece together the libraries of men I had read about in the courthouse archives. Is there anything more alluring than having free rein in an archive, the run of the stacks, and the sort of privacy that lets you just sit right there on the floor and read?

But the portrait of Taney haunted me. I avoided taking it in when I stepped out to make a phone call or get something to eat. I could not reconcile how, despite the gracious accommodation that was extended to me, I wasn't sure I belonged. Or did I mean my research topic did not belong? Could I discover here a history of race and law that sought to displace Roger Taney with Cornelius Thompson or George Hackett, one that sought to displace *Dred Scott* with deliberations in the local courthouse? What part of my work was intended to grapple with this scene? What tools did I have that might permit me to explain how I expected to dethrone Taney in the very place in which he still presided?

My last stop on that day was a courtroom at the other end of the hall. It was the city's Circuit Court, a largely commercial, big-money part of the courthouse. It is the grandest courtroom in the building, with a domed ceiling inscribed with the names of the city's legal forebears. I craned my neck searching for it: there was Taney, his name emblazoned in plaster. I had expected I might find him here. And I took a seat at the back, thinking I would quietly observe and reflect on all I had seen that day. But it was, as I said, a court set aside for resolving commercial disputes, with a trial under way. And while it is a public space, it is not unusual for the court to wonder about who visitors might be. Mostly, in my experience, they want to be mindful about reporters.

Judge Wanda Heard eyeballed me from the bench and then beckoned her clerk, whispering in his ear. He made his way over to me and asked my business. I am a historian, I explained, writing a history of the early courthouse. I was just there to observe, I said, and handed over my card. Some minutes passed before Judge Heard paused the proceedings just long enough to go off the record and speak directly to me: "Wait for the break. I'd like to talk with you." It didn't come as an order exactly, but I knew I needed to stay. And I did. It turned out that Heard herself is deeply interested in the courthouse and its history. I explained my project, and she presented me with a brief written history of her courtroom. The marble, I learned, had come from the Vatican quarry. We talked about the courthouse museum, the portraiture, and the library.

I explained more about my history of race and rights. We mentioned Taney, and Heard, who is African American, chuckled, pointing to his name up above her head on the ridge of the courtroom's dome. I didn't tell her about the awkwardness that the chief justice's portrait had generated in me. It turns out I didn't have to.

"My courtroom is haunted," said Judge Heard. Now, I am no believer in ghosts, but she is a judge and I was a researcher looking for clues. There had been, over the years, a series of inexplicable incidents in her courtroom, Heard explained. She had experienced them, and so had her clerks. Members of the bar were ready to confirm that something was not right, up there on the sixth floor. Some sort of spirit or force or energy was making itself felt. Broken glass and cold chills were examples of what regulars called the courtroom's ghost. It was, Judge Heard believed, Roger Taney. The chief justice, whose name and likeness were so prominently on display, was unsettled. "He might have a little bit of a problem with me presiding," Heard once told a reporter for the *Sun*.[4] Her ancestors, she explained, had been slaves.

We do not need to be believers in ghosts to appreciate Judge Heard's story. Whether discomfort with her presence is felt by the dead or also by the living, her story underscores the degree to which questions haunt a black woman, the descendant of slaves, when she presides in the Baltimore courthouse. Those who challenge her authority may be spirits from the past; they may be twenty-first-century men and women. What is certain is how race still animates that place where the city's courthouse has sat for more than two centuries. Justice Taney, be he ghost or icon, remains a force in Baltimore even today.

Notes

PREFACE

1   Alfred Kelly terms this "law office history," which refers to the "selection of data favorable to the position being advanced without regard to or concern for contradictory data or proper evaluation of the relevance of the data proffered." Alfred H. Kelly, "Clio and the Court: An Illicit Love Affair," *Supreme Court Review* 1965 (1965): 119–58, 122.

2   On everyday public interest law practice, see Kris Shepard, *Rationing Justice: Poverty Lawyers and Poor People in the Deep South* (Baton Rouge: Louisiana State University Press, 2007). See also Nisha Agarwal and Jocelyn Simonson, "Thinking Like a Public Interest Lawyer: Theory, Practice, and Pedagogy," *NYU Review of Law and Social Change* 34 (2010): 455–98. On the power dynamics that shape legal services practice, see Mark Kessler, "Legal Mobilization for Social Reform: Power and the Politics of Agenda Setting," *Law & Society Review* 24, no. 1 (1990): 121–43. On the conditions of legal practice during the 1980s, see Ginny Looney, "Biting the Budget at Legal Services," *Southern Changes* 4, nos. 4–5 (1983): 257–84. For a discussion of MFY Legal Services, for which I worked, see Noel A. Cazenave, "Ironies of Urban Reform: Professional Turf Battles in the Planning of the Mobilization for Youth Program Precursor to the War on Poverty," *Journal of Urban History* 26, no. 1 (1999): 22–43. Kevin Olson explains citizenship in the context of the community-action model of legal services as the capacity for self-governance, in "Constructing Citizens," *Journal of Politics* 70, no. 1 (2008): 40–53. On the early history of Mobilization for Youth, see Tamar W. Carroll, *Mobilizing New York: AIDS, Antipoverty, and Feminist Activism* (Chapel Hill: University of North Carolina Press, 2015).

3   Dave Cowan and Emma Hitchings, "'Pretty Boring Stuff': District Judges and Housing Possession Proceedings," *Social & Legal Studies* 16, no. 3 (2007): 363–82.

4   Tony Alfieri further complicates this aspect of "poverty" law practice by foregrounding the divergences between the interests of poor people and their lawyers. Anthony V. Alfieri, "Reconstructive Poverty Law Practice: Learning Lessons of Client Narrative," *Yale Law Journal* 100, no. 6 (April 1991): 2107–47.

5   On the ethical dilemmas produced when lawyers' interests diverge from those of their clients, see Derrick Bell, "Serving Two Masters: Integration Ideals and Client Interests in School Desegregation Litigation," *Yale Law Journal* 85, no. 3 (July 1976): 470–516.

6   On the nexus of housing organizing and housing court litigation, see Roberta Gold, *When Tenants Claimed the City: The Struggle for Citizenship in New York City Housing* (Urbana: University of Illinois Press, 2014).

7   For a depiction of the Civil Court building, including the Housing Court, see the discussion of Judge Margaret Taylor in Milner S. Ball, *The Word and the Law* (Chicago: University of Chicago Press, 1993), 24–38.

8   On gentrification in Manhattan, see Kathe Newman and Elvin K. Wyly, "The Right to Stay Put, Revisited: Gentrification and the Resistance to Displacement in New York City," *Urban Studies* 43, nos. 1–4 (2006): 23–57, and Neil Smith and James Defilippis, "The Reassertion of Economics: 1990s Gentrification in the Lower East Side," *International Journal of Urban & Regional Research* 23, no. 4 (1999): 638–53. On the deinstitutionalization of people with mental illness, see Richard Warner, "Deinstitutionalization: How Did We Get Where We Are?" *Journal of Social Issues* 45, no. 3 (1989): 17–30, and Gerald N. Grob, "Deinstitutionalization: The Illusion of Policy," *Journal of Policy History* 9, no. 1 (1997): 48–73.

9   For a discussion of the New York City Housing Court generally, see "Symposium: The New York City Housing Court in the 21st Century: Can It Better Address the Problems Before It?" special issue, *Cardozo Public Law, Policy and Ethics* 3 (January 2006); Russell Engler, "And Justice for All – Including the Unrepresented Poor: Revisiting the Roles of the Judges, Mediators, and Clerks," *Fordham Law Review* 67 (April 1999): 1987–2068; Laura K. Abel and David S. Udell, "Judicial Independence: If You Gag the Lawyers, Do You Choke the Courts? Some Implications for Judges When Funding Restrictions Curb Advocacy by Lawyers on Behalf of the Poor," *Fordham Urban Law Journal* 29 (February 2002): 873–906; and Harvey Gee, "Is a 'Hearing Officer' Really a Judge? The Presumed Role of 'Judges' in the Unconstitutional New York Housing Court," *New York City Law Review* 5 (Summer 2002): 1. I benefited greatly from the discussions I had during the 2013 conference New York City's Housing Court at 40: Controversies, Challenges, and Prospects for Its Future, held in New York at the New York City Bar. My thanks to the Honorable Michelle D. Schreiber for including me among the participants.

10 On Five Points, see Tyler Anbinder, *Five Points: The 19th-Century New York City Neighborhood That Invented Tap Dance, Stole Elections, and Became the World's Most Notorious Slum* (New York: Free Press, 2001), and James W. Cook, "Dancing across the Color Line," *Common-Place* 4, no. 1 (October 2003), www .common-place.org. Charles Dickens, *American Notes for General Circulation* (New York: Harper & Bros., 1842), 32–38. See also Rebecca Yamin, ed., *Tales of Five Points: Working-Class Life in Nineteenth-Century New York*, 7 vols. (Washington, DC: General Services Administration, 2002). For a discussion of approaches to writing the history of Five Points, see Alan Mayne, "Tall Tales But True? New York's 'Five Points' Slum," *Journal of Urban History* 33, no. 22 (January 2007): 320–31.

11 For an overview of conditions at The Tombs, see Timothy J. Gilfoyle, "'America's Greatest Criminal Barracks': The Tombs and the Experience of Criminal Justice

in New York City, 1838–1897," *Journal of Urban History* 29, no. 5 (2003): 525–54. Max Page offers a contrast to New York's Tombs by way of the development of Philadelphia's nineteenth-century courthouse, in "From 'Miserable Dens' to the 'Marble Monster': Historical Memory and the Design of Courthouses in Nineteenth-Century Philadelphia," *Pennsylvania Magazine of History and Biography* 119, no. 4 (1995): 299–343.

12 On New York's court reform, see Barry Mahoney, "The Administration of Justice and Court Reform," *Proceedings of the Academy of Political Science* 31, no. 3 (1974): 58–72.

13 For an especially vivid depiction of the Housing Court in Brooklyn, see Clyde Haberman, "For Housing: Civil Court, Chaos Part," *New York Times*, May 30, 1997; Jan Hoffman, "Chaos Presides in New York Housing Courts," *New York Times*, December 28, 1994.

14 Charlotte Libov, "In Security Move, More Metal Detectors Are Placed in Courts," *New York Times*, December 1, 1985. George A. Davidson offers a more sanguine look at the modern courthouse in his essay, "The Lawyer's Perspective: Celebrating the Courthouse," *The Green Bag: An Entertaining Journal of Law* 11 (Winter 2008): 159–70. Davidson's essay was reprinted from the 2006 book *Celebrating the Courthouse: A Guide for Architects, Their Clients, and the Public*, edited by Steven Sanders (New York: Norton, 2006): 168–76.

15 Joseph Roach, *Cities of the Dead: Circum-Atlantic Performance* (New York: Columbia University Press, 1996), xii.

16 Ibid.

INTRODUCTION

1 Later treatises addressed, in part, the status of free African Americans. For example, Thomas R. R. Cobb's *An Inquiry into the Law of Negro Slavery* (Philadelphia: T. & J. W. Johnson; Savannah: W. Thorne Williams, 1858) included a final chapter on "The effect of manumission and the status of free persons of color," 312. Also on the rights of former slaves, see Joel Tiffany, *A Treatise on the Unconstitutionality of American Slavery* (Cleveland: J. Calyer, 1849); Samuel Nott, *Slavery, and the Remedy, or, Principles and Suggestions for a Remedial Code*, 3rd ed. (Boston: Crocker and Brewster, 1856); and John Codman Hurd, *The Law of Freedom and Bondage in the United States* (Boston: Little, Brown; New York: Van Nostrand, 1858). Other treatises were limited to the subject of slavery. Jacob D. Wheeler, *A Practical Treatise on the Law of Slavery* (New York: Allan Pollock; New Orleans: Benjamin Levy, 1837); George M. Stroud, *A Sketch of the Laws Relating to Slavery in the Several States of the United States of America* (Philadelphia: Kimber and Sharpless, 1827), with one brief mention of free "negroes"; and William Goodell, *Views of American Constitutional Law: In Its Bearing upon American Slavery* (Utica, NY: Jackson & Chaplin, 1844).

2 William Yates, *Rights of Colored Men to Suffrage, Citizenship and Trial by Jury: Being a Book of Facts, Arguments and Authorities, Historical Notices and Sketches of Debates – With Notes* (Philadelphia: Merrihew and Gunn, 1838).

3 "Items: The Troy Press," *American* (New York), August 10, 1832.

4   Yates was a delegate to an 1835 New York State antislavery convention, as reported by the *Liberator*. "To the Friends of Immediate Emancipation in the State of New York," *Liberator*, October 3, 1835. He was a member of the three-person delegation from Troy.

5   Yates's report on his work with free people of color in Delaware has survived and is published in Harold B. Hancock, "William Yates' Letter of 1837: Slavery, and Colored People in Delaware," *Delaware History* 14 (1971): 205–16. Yates previewed this work in the *Colored American*. "Letter from William Yates, Esq.: Slavery and Colored People in Delaware," August 12, 1837, and August 19, 1837.

6   I use the terms "free African American" and "free black" and "free people of color" interchangeably throughout this chapter, mostly out of a writerly interest in keeping the prose fresh. I do recognize how interpretations of "black" versus "African American" may differ, with the former being a broader term that would also encompass African-descended people from Africa, the Caribbean, and South America. The term "free" may also give some readers pause, especially when reading about Baltimore. Some historians have concluded that in Maryland many African Americans lived by way of a quasi-freedom, even as they were in another sense claimed as property. "Free" is intended to indicate a legal status and to suggest how Baltimore's black community was shrouded by the same questions that African Americans in post-slavery Northern states confronted. These terms should not be understood as referring to essential differences, including those of biology or genetics. Race was in the nineteenth century, as it is today, a social construction. For readability, I have not adopted cumbersome phrasings such as "people believed to be black." Still, my use of racial terms should not be mistaken for the promotion of what Karen and Barbara Fields have termed racecraft. Karen E. Fields and Barbara J. Fields, *Racecraft: The Soul of Inequality in American Life* (London: Verso, 2012).

7   A. W. B. Simpson, "The Rise and Fall of the Legal Treatise: Legal Principles and the Forms of Legal Literature," *University of Chicago Law Review* 48 (Summer 1981): 633–34.

8   James Kent, *Commentaries on American Law, in Four Volumes* (New York: O. Halsted, 1826–30), and Joseph Story, *Commentaries on the Constitution of the United States . . . in Three Volumes* (Boston: Hilliard, Gray, 1833).

9   Simpson, "The Rise and Fall of the Legal Treatise," 670–72.

10 On networks of legal publishing (which were distinct from those of the abolitionist print culture), see M. H. Hoeflich, *Legal Publishing in Antebellum America* (New York: Cambridge University Press, 2010), and Erwin C. Surrency, *A History of American Law Publishing* (Dobbs Ferry, NY: Oceana Publications, 1990).

11 His publisher, Merrihew and Gunn, printed African American-authored, antislavery, and religious texts. *Philadelphia National Enquirer*, March 15 and March 29, 1838; *The Colored American*, March 3, March 15, March 22, April 5, and April 19, 1838. Also see *Emancipator* (New York), May 24, 1838. ("For sale at the Anti-Slavery Office, 143 Nassau-street. Price *twenty-five cents*.")

12 On African American print culture generally, see Joanna Brooks, "The Early American Public Sphere and the Emergence of a Black Print Culture," *William and Mary Quarterly* 62, no. 1 (January 2005): 67–92. On abolitionist print culture and law generally, see Jeannine Marie DeLombard, *Slavery on Trial: Law, Abolitionism, and Print Culture* (Chapel Hill: University of North Carolina Press, 2007).

13 Yates, *Rights of Colored Men*, iv.

14 Ibid., 71.

15 Ibid., iii. In 1855, African American historian William Cooper Nell would publish his *The Colored Patriots of the American Revolution, with Sketches of Several Distinguished Colored Persons: To Which Is Added a Brief Survey of the Condition and Prospects of Colored Americans* (Boston: Robert F. Wallcut, 1855), which embraced Yates's strategy by documenting black military service during the War for Independence.

16 Yates, *Rights of Colored Men*, 47, 48–52.

17 Suffrage, Yates observed, was neither universal nor absolute. White women and children, he pointed out, did not vote; still, they were deemed citizens. Ibid., 48.

18 Ibid., 6.

19 Ibid., 15, 36.

20 Ibid., 38. A decade later Joel Tiffany would argue that slaves were also citizens. Joel Tiffany, *A Treatise on the Unconstitutionality of American Slavery* (Cleveland: J. Calyer, 1849).

21 Yates, *Rights of Colored Men*, 54–75.

22 In an 1854 comment on the denial of passports to free African Americans, Rev. Amos Beman referred readers to Yates in support of the view that free black people were citizens of the United States. Rev. A. G. Beman, "Letter from Rev. A. G. Beman," *Frederick Douglass' Paper*, September 15, 1854. Preceding Thomas Sidney, Yates spoke about the "legal disabilities of the colored man" to New York's black leadership in October 1838. "Public Meeting of the Political Association," *Colored American*, October 20, 1838. "Origen," visiting Gettysburg, Pennsylvania, reported having "deposited in the hands of the Secretary of the Mental and Moral Improvement Society" Yates's book. "For the Colored American. To the Church and Congregation at T[roy]. Letter V.," *Colored American*, October 20, 1838. Black activist Theodore S. Wright quoted from Yates's book in a speech to the New York State Anti-Slavery Society in September 1837. "Is There No Eye to Pity," *Colored American*, January 20, 1838. The *Colored American* and the *Emancipator* published excerpts from Yates's book in the winter of 1838, in anticipation of its publication. "Wm. Yates, Esq.," *Colored American*, January 13, 1838. "Unequal Laws," *Colored American*, January 13, 1838 (reprinted from the *Elevator*).

23 In his final letter to the *Colored American*, published in May 1840, Yates reported on new antikidnapping legislation passed by New York's legislature. "New York," *Colored American*, May 30, 1840. The *Colored American* reported that Yates and his wife, Martha, lost an "infant" daughter in May 1840. "Died," *Colored American*, May 2, 1840. Yates's services to the American Anti-Slavery Society appeared to have been "discontinued" in fall 1838. "More Practical Measures," *Colored American*, October 27, 1838.

24 "An Act to Protect All Persons in the United States in the Civil Rights, and Furnish the Means of Their Vindication," 14 Stat. 27–30 (1866). Hereafter, Civil Rights Act of 1866. US Constitution, amendment 14, section 1 (1868).

25 Civil Rights Act of 1866.

26 Copies of Yates's treatise are noted in the *Catalogue of the New-York State Library: 1855* (Albany, NY: Charles Van Benthuysen, 1856), 824, and the *Catalogue*

of the Library of the Massachusetts Historical Society, vol. 2: *M–Z* (Boston: John Wilson and Son, 1855), 645.

27 Janette Hoston Harris, "Woodson and Wesley: A Partnership in Building the Association for the Study of Afro-American Life and History," *Journal of Negro History* 83, no. 2 (Spring 1998): 109–19, and Benjamin Quarles, "Charles Harris Wesley," *Proceedings of the American Antiquarian Society* 97, no. 2 (October 1987): 275–79.

28 Charles H. Wesley, "Creating and Maintaining an Historical Tradition," *Journal of Negro History* 49, no. 1 (January 1964): 13–33, quotation on 13.

29 Ibid., 21–33. R[obert] B. Lewis, *Light and Truth: Collected from the Bible and Ancient and Modern History, Containing the Universal History of the Colored and the Indian Race, from the Creation of the World to the Present Time* (Boston: Committee of Colored Gentlemen, 1836). James W. C. Pennington, *Text Book of the Origin and History of the Colored People* (Hartford, CT: L. Skinner, 1841). William C. Nell, *Services of Colored Men, in the Wars of 1776 and 1812* (Boston: Prentiss & Sawyer, 1851). William Wells Brown, *The Black Man: His Antecedents, His Genius, and His Achievements* (New York: Thomas Hamilton; Boston: R. F. W. Wallcut, 1863).

30 John L. Myers, "American Antislavery Society Agents and the Free Negro, 1833–1838," *Journal of Negro History* 52, no. 3 (July 1967): 200–19. "American Anti-Slavery Society, and the Free Colored People," *Colored American,* May 20, 1837. "Circular Letter . . . to the Free Colored Citizens of the United States," *Weekly Advocate,* February 18, 1837.

31 Myers was not, however, wholly consistent in his placement of Yates. He also reported that Yates had been "installed as pastor on January 8, 1836, of the Charleston Union Presbytery." Meyers, "American Antislavery Society," 206. This was an error. William Black Yates, to whom this fact referred, was for all his adult life a Presbyterian minister in Charleston, not the author of *Rights of Colored Men.* Alfred Nevin, *Encyclopædia of the Presbyterian Church in the United States of America* (Philadelphia: Presbyterian Encyclopaedia Publishing, 1884), 1051.

32 Harold B. Hancock, "William Yates' Letter of 1837: Slavery, and Colored People in Delaware," *Delaware History* 14 (1971), 205–16 (citing Myers).

33 For example, Yates served on a committee devoted to "the interests of our free colored brethren," along with six African American agents, for the American Anti-Slavery Society in 1838. "Encouraging to Our Heart," *Colored American,* June 2, 1838, 59; Wm. Yates, "For the *Colored American.* Philadelphia. June 6, 1837," *Colored American,* June 10, 1837; and Wm. Yates, "For the *Colored American.* Philadelphia, June 19, 1837," *Colored American,* July 1, 1837. Yates hosted the Colored American's Charles Ray at Troy's Seamen's Bethel Church. "Correspondence. Letter from Our General Agent," *Colored American,* September 2, 1837. And Ray drew on Yates's forthcoming book when he wrote: "Some say, let the colored people leave the country! We reply NO, BRETHREN. We would rather die a thousand deaths, in honestly and legally contending for our rights, in this our native country." "Disabilities of Colored People," *Colored American,* September 30, 1837. In the same issue, Yates provided to editor Cornish a short article on "legal disabilities." "Brother Cornish," *Colored American,* September 30, 1837.

34 Wm. Yates, "For the *Colored American*. Brother Cornish," *Colored American*, June 24, 1837. Origen, "To the Church and Congregation at T," *Colored American*, October 20, 1838; "Rights of Colored Men to Suffrage, Citizenship, Etc.," *Colored American*, April 19, 1838; "Right of Suffrage," *Colored American*, March 22, 1838; "A Subterfuge, or an Apology for Oppression," *Colored American*, March 22, 1838; "Yates' Rights of Colored Men," *Colored American*, March 22, 1838; "The Ohio Memorial," *Colored American*, March 22, 1838; "New and Important Publications," *Colored American*, March 15, 1838; "Important Publication," *Colored American*, March 3, 1838; and "Encouraging to Our Heart," *Colored American*, June 2, 1838.

35 "Public Meeting of the Political Association," *Colored American*, October 20, 1838.

36 Contrast this with the usage of the term "our," as in "our prospects" and "our brethren," by black activist Charles Reason as secretary to the "New York Association for the Political Elevation and Improvement of the People of Color," where Yates was in attendance. "Public Meeting of the Political Association," *Colored American*, October 20, 1838. The call for a related meeting, issued by black activists Patrick Henry Reason, Patrick A. Bell, and John J. Zuille, termed the organizers "we" and spoke of "our rights." "Public Meeting of the Political Association," *Colored American*, October 12, 1839.

37 George B. Anderson, *Landmarks of Rensselaer County, New York* (Syracuse, NY: D. Mason & Co., 1897), 343.

38 "More Practical Measures," *Colored American*, October 27, 1838, and "Fifth Annual Meeting of the American Anti-Slavery Society," *Liberator*, May 18, 1838.

39 Wm. Yates, "Letter from Wm. Yates, Esqr.: Brother Cornish," *Colored American*, January 27, 1838, and Wm. Yates, Esq., "Unequal Laws," *Colored American*, January 13, 1838.

40 "Public Meeting of the Political Association," *Colored American*, October 20, 1838; and "Legal Disabilities of Colored People," *Colored American*, January 13, 1838.

41 Charles Ray, editor of the *Colored American*, made a last note, reporting that Yates and his wife, Maria, had lost an infant daughter: "We sympathize with our worthy friends." "Died," *Colored American*, May 2, 1840. Yates appears to have withdrawn from antislavery activism in 1840. "New-York Legislation," *National Anti-Slavery Standard* (New York), June 18, 1840. In that same year he was noted as working as a coal agent in Albany, New York. "Coal by the Canal," *Albany Argus*, July 14, 1840. Yates and his wife, "Mariah," appear in the 1850 census from Albany, New York, where he is listed as a coal dealer. "William Yates," Dwelling No. 649, Family No. 1283, Schedule I, 6th Ward, Albany, New York, Seventh Census of the United States, 1850, NARA.

42 Amigo, "William Wells Brown's Book," *Pacific Appeal* (San Francisco, CA,) May 30, 1863.

43 On African American public culture in San Francisco generally, see J. William Snorgrass, "The Black Press in the San Francisco Bay Area, 1856–1900," *California History* 60, no. 4 (1981–82): 306–17; Delilah L. Beasley, *The Negro Trailblazers of California* (New York: G. K. Hall, 1997; 1919); and Rudolph M. Lapp, *Blacks in Gold Rush California* (New Haven, CT: Yale University Press, 1977).

44 On the experience of black Americans working in Washington's official venues in a somewhat different time, see Kate Masur, "Patronage and Protest in Kate Brown's Washington," *Journal of American History* 99, no. 4 (March 2013), 1047–71.

45 The manumission of William Yates was recorded on May 15, 1841. His wife, Emeliner Yates, and her children were manumitted just over two years later, on August 19, 1843. The freedom certificates for Yates and his family are cataloged in Dorothy S. Provine, *District of Columbia Free Negro Registers, 1821–1861* (Bowie, MD: Heritage Books, 1996), 403, 441.

46 "Colored Men of California. No. V. Mr. Wm. H. Yates," *Pacific Appeal*, August 1, 1863.

47 Douglas H. Daniels, *Pioneer Urbanites: A Social and Cultural History of Black San Francisco* (Philadelphia: Temple University Press, 1980), and Lapp, *Blacks in Gold Rush California*. On Yates and his daughter Frances, see Eric Gardner, *Jennie Carter: A Black Journalist of the Early West* (Jackson: University Press of Mississippi, 2007), 49n1.

48 Lapp, *Blacks in Gold Rush California*, 99.

49 William J. Novak, "The Legal Transformation of Citizenship in Nineteenth-Century America," in *The Democratic Experiment: New Directions in American Political History*, ed. Meg Jacobs, William J. Novak, and Julian E. Zelizer (Princeton, NJ: Princeton University Press, 2003), 85–119.

50 The literature on *Dred Scott* is voluminous, much of it aiming to evaluate the court decision. Vincent Hopkins's 1951 *Dred Scott's Case* centered on a defense of Roger Taney and concluded that he had been an evenhanded, restrained jurist. In the more than half a century that followed, scholars revisited these questions while remaining close to the text of the case and its prominent actors. Taney has been closely scrutinized, from Don Fehrenbacher, who pointed to his pro-Southern bias, to Mark Graber's vision of a disciplined judge whose views were consistent with those of the framers. Don E. Fehrenbacher, *The Dred Scott Case, Its Significance in American Law and Politics* (New York: Oxford University Press, 1978); Mark A. Graber, *Dred Scott and the Problem of Constitutional Evil* (New York: Cambridge University Press, 2006). Austin Allen has tried to reconcile Taney's record, explaining that his decision sought to protect both slavery and the rights of corporations. Austin Allen, *Origins of the 'Dred Scott' Case: Jacksonian Jurisprudence and the Supreme Court, 1837–1857* (Athens: University of Georgia Press, 2006). Perspectives on Taney-court dissenters John McLean and Benjamin Curtis provided a counterpoint to Taney's conclusions. Justin Buckley Dyer, "Lincolnian Natural Right, Dred Scott, and the Jurisprudence of John McLean," *Polity* 41, nos. 1–4 (January 2008): 63–85, and Lucas E. Morel, "The 'Dred Scott' Dissents: McLean, Curtis, Lincoln, and the Public Mind," *Journal of Supreme Court History* 32, no. 22 (2007): 133–51.

51 Lisa Crooms-Robinson, "The United States Constitution and the Struggle for African American Citizenship: An Overview," in *The Oxford Handbook of African American Citizenship*, ed. Henry Louis Gates Jr. et al. (New York: Oxford University Press, 2012), 519–20.

52 In this study I "pivot the center," meaning that I remain throughout rooted in the perspectives of people of African descent while asking how they were engaged with broader contexts and influences. In the history of law, this requires studying lawyers, jurists, and other litigants along with free people of color. Elsa Barkley

Brown, "African-American Women's Quilting: A Framework for Conceptualizing and Teaching African-American Women's History," *Signs: Journal of Women in Culture and Society* 14 (1989): 921–29.

53 This approach is indebted to work on popular constitutionalism, which has drawn the attention of legal historians to alternative realms of constitutional interpretation. Richard A. Primus, "The Riddle of Hiram Revels," *Harvard Law Review* 119, no. 6 (April 2006): 1680–734; Keith E. Whittington, *Constitutional Construction: Divided Power and Constitutional Meaning* (Cambridge, MA: Harvard University Press, 1999); Larry D. Kramer, *The People Themselves: Popular Constitutionalism and Judicial Review* (New York: Oxford University Press, 2004); and Rogers M. Smith, "The Inherent Deceptiveness of Constitutional Discourse: A Diagnosis and Prescription," *Nomos* 40 (1998): 215–54. On popular constitutionalism and underenforcement of law in a twenty-first-century example, see Ernest A. Young, "Popular Constitutionalism and the Underenforcement Problem: The Case of the National Healthcare Law," *Law and Contemporary Problems* 75, no. 3 (2012); 157–201.

54 Hendrik Hartog, "The Constitution of Aspiration and 'The Rights That Belong to Us All,'" *Journal of American History* 74, no. 3 (December 1987): 1013–34.

55 On legal consciousness, see ibid. and Michael Grossberg, *A Judgment for Solomon: The d'Hauteville Case and Legal Experience in Antebellum America* (New York: Cambridge University Press, 1996).

56 Walter Johnson, "On Agency," *Journal of Social History* 37, no. 1 (Fall 2003): 113–24.

57 For an illuminating discussion of the rights debates between critical legal studies and critical race studies scholars, see Patricia J. Williams, "The Pain of Word Bondage," in *The Alchemy of Race and Rights* (Cambridge, MA: Harvard University Press, 1991), 146–65.

58 Corfield v. Coryell, 4 Wash. Cir. Rep. 371. Today reported at 6 Fed. Cas. 546, no. 3,3230 C.C.E.D.Pa. 1823.

59 On this distinction, see Hendrik Hartog, "Pigs and Positivism," *Wisconsin Law Review* 4 (August 1985): 899–935.

60 On antebellum free-black politics, see Patrick Rael, *Black Identity and Black Protest in the Antebellum North* (Chapel Hill: University of North Carolina Press, 2002), and Martha S. Jones, *All Bound Up Together: The Woman Question in African American Public Culture* (Chapel Hill: University of North Carolina Press, 2007). On the political culture of enslaved people, see Steven Hahn, *A Nation under Our Feet: Black Political Struggles in the Rural South from Slavery to the Great Migration* (Cambridge, MA: Harvard University Press, 2004).

61 Bonnie Honig, *Democracy and the Foreigner* (Princeton, NJ: Princeton University Press, 2001), 98–106. On free African Americans as foreigners, see Kunal M. Parker, "Making Blacks Foreigners: The Legal Construction of Former Slaves in Post-Revolutionary Massachusetts," *Utah Law Review* 2001 (2001): 75–124, and Kunal M. Parker, *Making Foreigners: Immigration and Citizenship Law in America, 1600–2000* (New York: Cambridge University Press, 2015).

62 Hartog, "The Constitution of Aspiration."

63 Martha S. Jones, "Leave of Court: African-American Legal Claims Making in the Era of Dred Scott v. Sandford," in *Contested Democracy: Politics, Ideology, and Race in American History*, ed. Manisha Sinha and Penny Von Eschen (New York: Columbia University Press, 2007), 54–74.

64 Reynolds v. United States, 98 U.S. 145 (1879).

65 Ira Berlin's *Slaves Without Masters* remains an essential touchstone for any study of free African Americans in the antebellum South. Ira Berlin, *Slaves without Masters: The Free Negro in the Antebellum South* (New York: Pantheon, 1975). This study departs from Berlin's view, arguing that free African Americans were not reduced to slave-like status by black laws and colonization. Instead, in Baltimore they constructed rights and a citizenship-like status. An extensive literature documents the social history of free people of color in Baltimore. See Seth Rockman, *Scraping By: Wage Labor, Slavery, and Survival in Early Baltimore* (Baltimore: Johns Hopkins University Press, 2008); Christopher Phillips, *Freedom's Port: The African American Community of Baltimore, 1790–1860* (Urbana: University of Illinois Press, 1997); T. Stephen Whitman, *The Price of Freedom: Slavery and Freedom in Baltimore and Early National Maryland* (New York: Routledge, 1999); James Martin Wright, *The Free Negro in Maryland, 1632–1860* (New York: Columbia University Press, 1921); and Frank Towers, *The Urban South and the Coming of the Civil War* (Charlottesville: University of Virginia Press, 2004).

66 For works that take this approach to the study of race and law, see Ariela J. Gross, *Double Character: Slavery and Mastery in the Antebellum Southern Courtroom* (Princeton, NJ: Princeton University Press, 2000); Laura F. Edwards, *The People and Their Peace: Legal Culture and the Transformation of Inequality in the Post-Revolutionary South* (Chapel Hill: University of North Carolina Press, 2009); Dylan Penningroth, *The Claims of Kinfolk: Africa American Property and Community in the Nineteenth-Century South* (Chapel Hill: University of North Carolina Press, 2003); Christopher Waldrep, *Roots of Disorder: Race and Criminal Justice in the American South, 1817–80* (Urbana: University of Illinois Press, 1998); Melvin Patrick Ely, *Israel on the Appomattox: A Southern Experiment in Black from the 1790s through the Civil War* (New York: Knopf, 2004); Kirt Von Daacke, *Freedom Has a Face: Race, Identity, and Community in Jefferson's Virginia* (Charlottesville: University of Virginia Press, 2012); and Ted Maris-Wolf, *Family Bonds: Free Blacks and Re-enslavement Law in Antebellum Virginia* (Chapel Hill: University of North Carolina Press, 2015). See also Rebecca J. Scott, "Paper Thin: Freedom and Re-enslavement in the Diaspora of the Haitian Revolution," *Law and History Review* 29, no. 4 (2011): 1061–87.

67 On Maryland as the middle ground, see Robert J. Brugger, *Maryland: A Middle Temperament, 1634–1980* (Baltimore: Johns Hopkins University Press and Maryland Historical Society, 1988), and Barbara Jeanne Fields, *Slavery and Freedom on the Middle Ground: Maryland during the Nineteenth Century* (New Haven, CT: Yale University Press, 1987).

68 Steven Hahn, *The Political Worlds of Slavery and Freedom* (Cambridge, MA: Harvard University Press, 2009).

69 For this view, and this book's general approach from its grounding in trial court records to weaving together legal history's cultural and intellectual threads, I am indebted to the pioneering work of Ariela Gross. For a defining discussion of these questions through a focus on slavery and law, see Ariela J. Gross, "Beyond Black and White: Cultural Approaches to Race and Slavery," *Columbia Law Review* 101, no. 3 (April 2001): 640–90.

1 BEING A NATIVE, AND FREE BORN

1 On the political rights of Baltimore's black revolutionary generation, see David S. Bogen, "The Maryland Context of 'Dred Scott': The Decline in the Legal Status of Maryland Free Blacks, 1776–1810," *American Journal of Legal History* 34, no. 4 (1990): 381–411, and David S. Bogen, "The Annapolis Poll Books of 1800 and 1804: African American Voting in the Early Republic," *Maryland Historical Magazine* 86, no. 1 (1991): 57–65.

2 Seth Rockman, *Scraping By: Wage Labor, Slavery, and Survival in Early Baltimore* (Baltimore: Johns Hopkins University Press, 2008), 45–56.

3 James A. Handy, *Scraps of African Methodist Episcopal History* (Philadelphia: A.M.E. Book Concern, [1902]), 14.

4 Richard R. Wright, *Centennial Encyclopaedia of the African Methodist Church* (Philadelphia: Book Concern of the A.M.E. Church, 1916), 68.

5 For an example of how local tribunals operated, see Eric Armstrong Dunbar, *A Fragile Freedom: African American Women and Emancipation in the Antebellum City* (New Haven, CT: Yale University Press, 2008), 51–52 and 62–69.

6 Handy, *Scraps of African Methodist Episcopal History*, 29–30. The AME Church's *Doctrines and Discipline* was published first in 1817; see *The Doctrines and Discipline of the African Methodist Episcopal Church* (Philadelphia: Richard Allen and Jacob Tapisco for the African Methodist Connection, 1817). On *Doctrines and Discipline*, see Richard S. Newman, *Freedom's Prophet: Bishop Richard Allen, the AME Church, and the Black Founding Fathers* (New York: New York University Press, 2008), 177–81.

7 On African American schooling in antebellum Baltimore, see Willa Young Banks, "A Contradiction in Antebellum Baltimore: A Competitive School for Girls of 'Color' within a Slave State," *Maryland Historical Magazine* 99, no. 2 (June 2004): 132–63; Bettye J. Gardner, "William Watkins: Antebellum Black Teacher and Writer," *Negro History Bulletin* 39, no. 6 (1976): 623–24; and Bettye Gardner, "Ante-bellum Black Education in Baltimore," *Maryland Historical Magazine* 71, no. 3 (1976): 360–66.

8 *Silas Marean and James J. Fisher vs. Charles Hackett* (mortgage foreclosure on lot on Friendship St.), July 27, 1832, C295-1285, Chancery Papers, 1815–51, Baltimore County Court, Maryland State Archives, Annapolis, MD (hereafter MSA). Wright, *Centennial Encyclopaedia*, 68.

9 On Samuel Cornish, see David E. Swift, *Black Prophets of Justice: Activist Clergy before the Civil War* (Baton Rouge: Louisiana State University Press, 1989), 19–46.

10 "Authorised Agents," *Freedom's Journal*, March 16, 1827.

11 "To Our Patrons," *Freedom's Journal*, March 16, 1827.

12 On black newspapers as legal primers in the twentieth century, see Joel E. Black, "A Theory of African-American Citizenship: Richard Westbrooks, the Great Migration, and the Chicago Defender's 'Legal Helps' Column," *Journal of Southern History* 46, no. 4 (Summer 2013): 869–915.

13 Barbara Jeanne Fields, *Slavery and Freedom on the Middle Ground: Maryland during the Nineteenth Century* (New Haven, CT: Yale University Press, 1987), 23–40, and Robert J. Brugger, *Maryland: A Middle Temperament, 1634–1980* (Baltimore: Johns Hopkins University Press and the Maryland Historical Society, 1988), 248–306.

14 For recent work that examines Baltimore, see Rockman, *Scraping By*, and Christopher Phillips, *Freedom's Port: The African American Community of Baltimore, 1790–1860* (Urbana and Chicago: University of Illinois Press, 1997). T. Stephen Whitman, *The Price of Freedom: Slavery and Freedom in Baltimore and Early National Maryland* (New York: Routledge, 1999). Mary P. Ryan, "Democracy Rising: The Monuments of Baltimore, 1809–1842," *Journal of Urban History* 36, no. 2 (2010): 127–50.

15 Rockman, *Scraping By*, 18. On Baltimore's commercial development, see Sherry H. Olson, *Baltimore, the Building of an American City* (Baltimore: Johns Hopkins University Press, 1980), and Gary Lawson Browne, *Baltimore in the Nation, 1789–1861* (Chapel Hill: University of North Carolina Press, 1980).

16 Browne, *Baltimore in the Nation*, 20.

17 Garrison would be detained in the Baltimore City jail after being convicted of libel for publishing a story about a Massachusetts merchant's involvement in the domestic slave trade. David K. Sullivan, "William Lloyd Garrison in Baltimore, 1829–1830," *Maryland Historical Magazine* 68, no. 1 (1973): 64–79. Garrison's letters from the Baltimore jail are published in William Lloyd Garrison, *The Letters of William Lloyd Garrison*, ed. Walter M. Merrill, vol. 1: *I Will Be Heard!* 1822–1835 (Cambridge, MA: Belknap Press of Harvard University Press, 1971).

18 Glenn O. Phillips, "Maryland and the Caribbean, 1634–1984: Some Highlights," *Maryland Historical Magazine* 83, no. 3 (1988): 199–214, and Paul G. E. Clemens, *The Atlantic Economy and Colonial Maryland's Eastern Shore: From Tobacco to Grain* (Ithaca, NY: Cornell University Press, 1980).

19 "Removal of Slaves to Hayti," *Freedom's Journal*, December 21, 1827; "American Colonization Society," *Freedom's Journal*, November 30, 1827; "Summary," *Freedom's Journal*, May 4, 1827.

20 "Union Seminary," *Freedom's Journal*, July 4, 1828. On the AME Church, see Carol V. R. George, *Segregated Sabbaths: Richard Allen and the Rise of Independent Black Churches: 1760–1840* (New York: Oxford University Press, 1973); Richard S. Newman, *Freedom's Prophet: Bishop Richard Allen, the AME Church, and the Black Founding Fathers* (New York: New York University Press, 2009); and Martha S. Jones, *All Bound Up Together: The Woman Question in African American Public Culture, 1830–1900* (Chapel Hill: University of North Carolina Press, 2007).

21 On New York's gradual emancipation, see David N. Gellman, *Emancipating New York: The Politics of Slavery and Freedom, 1777–1827* (Baton Rouge: Louisiana State University Press, 2006).

22 On free black political culture in New York and Philadelphia, see Leslie M. Harris, *In the Shadow of Slavery: African Americans in New York City, 1626–1863* (Chicago: University of Chicago Press, 2003); Julie Winch, *A Gentleman of Color: The Life of James Forten* (New York: Oxford University Press, 2002); Shane White, *Somewhat More Independent: The End of Slavery in New York City, 1770–1810* (Athens: University of Georgia Press, 1991).

23 James T. Campbell, *Songs of Zion: The African Methodist Episcopal Church in the United States and South Africa* (New York: Oxford University Press, 1995), 35, and Reginald F. Hildebrand, *The Times Were Strange and Stirring: Methodist Preachers and the Crisis of Emancipation* (Durham, NC: Duke University Press, 1995), 2.

24 On slavery's expansion south and west, see Adam Rothman, *Slave Country: American Expansion and the Origins of the Deep South* (Cambridge, MA: Harvard University Press, 2007), 171–210, and Walter Johnson, *River of Dark Dreams: Slavery and Empire in the Cotton Kingdom* (Cambridge, MA: Harvard University Press, 2013), 404.

25 Steven Deyle, *Carry Me Back: The Domestic Slave Trade in American Life* (New York: Oxford University Press, 2005).

26 "Trade in Negroes," *Niles' Weekly Register*, July 19, 1817.

27 Maryland Act of 1780, chapter 8 (imposes 500 pound tax on slaves brought from outside of the state), and Maryland Act of 1783, chapter 23 (bars import of slaves into Maryland). See also Maryland Act of 1809, chapter 138 (penalties for captains or masters who bring black people into Maryland with the intent to sell them within the state). Deyle, *Carry Me Back*, 52 (quoting Whitman, *Price of Freedom*, 78).

28 "Grand Jury Room," *American and Commercial Daily Advertiser*, October 29, 1816. On the far-reaching extent of kidnapping in Baltimore after 1800, see Leroy Graham, *Baltimore: The Nineteenth Century Black Capital* (Washington, DC: University Press of America, 1982), 49–58, 60, 69–70. For one example of slaves kidnapped in Baltimore and sold in New Orleans, see Martha S. Jones, "The Case of *Jean Baptiste, un Créole de Saint-Domingue*: Narrating Slavery, Freedom, and the Haitian Revolution in Baltimore City," in *The American South and the Atlantic World*, ed. Brian Ward, Martin Bone, and William A. Link (Gainesville: University Press of Florida, 2013), 104–28.

29 The percentage in 1819 was 3.1. These numbers are likely very low, given that many free black seamen would have been absent from the city or living in boardinghouses and therefore excluded from the city directory. Phillips, *Freedom's Port*, 111.

30 Historian Julius Scott describes the port of Baltimore in 1793, with its relatively high percentage of black residents, receiving fifty-three ships over a two-week period, carrying a total of 500 people of color, all refugees from the revolution in Saint-Domingue. Julius S. Scott, "Afro-American Sailors and the International Communication Network: The Case of Newport Bowers," in *Jack Tar in History: Essays in the History of Maritime Life and Labour*, ed. Colin Howell and Richard Twomey (Fredericton, NB: Acadiensis Press, 1991), 37n52.

31 Jones, "The Case of *Jean Baptiste*."

32 Phillips, *Freedom's Port*, 60.

33 "To the Justice of the Peace and the Constables of Baltimore County and Particularly within This City," *Federal Gazette*, September 13, 1810.

34 Humanity, "Defence," *Federal Gazette*, September 13, 1810.

35 "To Our Patrons," *Freedom's Journal*, March 16, 1827.

36 "Proposals for Publishing the *Freedom's Journal*: As Education," *Freedom's Journal*, March 16, 1827.

37 *Freedom's Journal*, March 16, 1827. Historian Lamont D. Thomas describes this episode, including critical details about how the Cuffe brothers also had asserted their Native American identity to avoid tax obligations. Finally, Thomas explains, the Cuffes were excused only after paying the taxes due. Lamont D. Thomas, *Rise to Be a People: A Biography of Paul Cuffe* (Urbana: University of Illinois Press, 1986), 7–12.

38 James Sidbury, *Becoming African in America: Race and Nation in the Early Black Atlantic* (New York: Oxford University Press, 2007), 157–79.

39   "People of Color," *Freedom's Journal*, April 6, 1827.

40   "Hayti, No. III: From the Scrap-Book of Afracanus," *Freedom's Journal*, May 4, 1827, and, "Hayti No. V," *Freedom's Journal*, June 29, 1827.

41   "African Free Schools in the United States," *Freedom's Journal*, June 1, 1827.

42   "Liberia," *Freedom's Journal*, February 14, 1827.

43   S. B., "Colonization Society," *Freedom's Journal*, November 9, 1827.

44   "Travelling Scraps," *Freedom's Journal*, August 15, 1828.

45   Ibid.

46   By 1664 Maryland had introduced race or color terms into its laws. Jeffrey R. Brackett, *The Negro in Maryland: A Study of the Institution of Slavery* (Baltimore: Johns Hopkins University Press, 1889), 28–30.

47   Peter M. Bergman and Jean McCarroll, *The Negro in the Congressional Record, 1789–1801* (New York: Bergman Publishers, 1969), 41. Congress would authorize similar distinctions in anticipation of the 1800 census. Ibid., 276–77.

48   Ibid., 11, 29.

49   Ibid., 13–14, 42, 81; also 9 (1802), 26 (1803).

50   The Code Noir of 1685 regulated slavery in France's colonial empire. Malick W. Ghachem, *The Old Regime and the Haitian Revolution* (New York: Cambridge University Press, 2012), and Vernon V. Palmer, *Through the Codes Darkly: Slave Law and Civil Law in Louisiana* (Clark, NJ: Lawbook Exchange, 2012).

51   David S. Bogen, "The Maryland Context of 'Dred Scott': The Decline in the Legal Status of Maryland Free Blacks, 1776–1810," *American Journal of Legal History* 34, no. 4 (1990): 381–411. James M. Wright, *The Free Negro in Maryland, Columbia University Studies in the Social Sciences* 97 (New York: Columbia University, 1921), 1–319. Ira Berlin, *Slaves Without Masters: The Free Negro in the Antebellum South* (New York: Pantheon, 1975).

52   Bogen, "Maryland Context of 'Dred Scott.'"

53   State v. Fisher, 1 H&J 750 (Maryland, 1805). In the 1810 case of *Rusk v. Sowerwine* there was evidence that in other instances black witnesses were testifying against the interests of white parties, although in that case, a freedom suit, the court disallowed the testimony of a free black woman. Rusk v. Sowerwine, 3H&J 97 (Maryland, 1810).

54   Brackett, *Negro in Maryland*.

55   Ibid.; Bogen, "Maryland Context of 'Dred Scott.'"

56   "Restriction of Slavery," 16th Cong., 2d Sess., 37 Annals of Cong. 23 (November 22, 1820).

57   "Admission of Missouri," 16th Cong., 2d Sess., 37 Annals of Cong. 79–80 (December 9, 1820).

58   Ibid., 31–32 (December 4, 1820).

59   Ibid., 45–48 (December 7, 1820).

60   Ibid., 517–30 (December 7, 1820).

61   Ibid., 570 (December 8, 1820).

62   Ibid., 598 (December 11, 1820).

63   Ibid., 624 (December 12, 1820).

64   Enslaved people accounted for another 10,000 black people in New York. The state would not abolish slavery until 1827.

65   Nathaniel H. Carter, William L. Stone, and Marcus T. C. Gould, *Reports of the Proceedings and Debates of the Convention of 1821, Assembled for the*

Purpose of Amending the Constitution of the State of New York: Containing All the Official Documents, Relating to the Subject, and Other Valuable Matter (Albany: E. and E. Hosford, 1821). Paul J. Polgar, "'Whenever They Judge It Expedient': The Politics of Partisanship and Free Black Voting Rights in Early National New York," *American Nineteenth Century History* 12, no. 1 (March 2011): 1–23. Polgar argues that it was disagreement among New York's political factions, not race per se, that led to the state's nearly complete disfranchisement of black men in 1821.

66 James Kent, *Commentaries on American Law*, 8th ed. (New York: W. Kent, 1854), 281–82.

67 "Gilbert Horton," *Baltimore Gazette and Daily Advertiser*, October 2, 1826, and "Case of Horton," *Cabinet* (Schenectady, NY), October 4, 1826.

68 "City of Washington," *Freedom's Journal*, November 16, 1827.

69 On slavery in upstate New York, see Edgar J. McManus, *A History of Negro Slavery in New York* (Syracuse, NY: Syracuse University Press, 2001).

70 Girls were bound to serve until the age of twenty-five, boys until twenty-eight. "An Act for the Gradual Abolition of Slavery," March 29, 1799, in *Laws of the State of New-York, Passed at the Twenty-Second Meeting of the Legislature Begun . . . the Second Day of January, 1799* (Albany, 1799), 721–23.

71 The owner was States Dyckman. James Thomas Flexner, *States Dyckman: American Loyalist* (New York: Fordham University Press, 1992).

72 *Commercial Advertiser* (New York), August 23 and September 2, 1826.

73 *National Intelligencer*, August 1, 1826.

74 "Text," *Massachusetts Spy* (Worcester), August 16, 1826 (reprinted from the *Connecticut Herald*).

75 *Boston Traveler*, August 22, 1826 (reprinted from the *National Intelligencer*).

76 "Case of Gilbert Horton," *Commercial Advertiser* (New York), August 23, 1826.

77 "Case of Gilbert Horton," *New-York Daily Advertiser*, August 25, 1826.

78 "Case of Gilbert Horton," *Commercial Advertiser*. By 1828, Green was a justice of the peace in nearby Bedford, New York.

79 "Westchester County," *Commercial Advertiser* (New York), August 25, 1826. The USS *Macedonian* was a naval frigate that departed Norfolk, Virginia, on June 11, 1826, for a Pacific tour. James T. DeKay, *Chronicles of the Frigate Macedonian, 1809–1922* (New York: Norton, 1995).

80 *Baltimore Patriot*, August 29, 1826. In this report the men who visited Horton were not named.

81 "The Case of Gilbert Horton," *Commercial Advertiser*, September 2, 1826.

82 "The Case of Horton," *Commercial Advertiser* (New York) September 28, 1826.

83 *Daily National Intelligencer*, September 11, 1826. This notice about Horton's case was reprinted in the *Baltimore Patriot*, September 12, 1826.

84 "The Case of Horton," *Commercial Advertiser* (New York), September 10, 1826.

85 Bayard Tuckerman, *William Jay and the Constitutional Movement for the Abolition of Slavery* (New York: Dodd, Mead, 1894), 33–38. On slavery in the District of Columbia, see Stanley Harrold, *Subversives: Antislavery Community in Washington, D.C., 1828–1865* (Baton Rouge: Louisiana State University Press, 2003). See William Jay, *Miscellaneous Writings on Slavery* (Boston: J. P. Jewett & Co.; Cleveland: Jewett, Proctor, and Worthington, 1853). Stephen R. Budney, "William Jay (1789–1858)," in *Encyclopedia of Antislavery and Abolition*, vol.

2, ed. Peter Hinks and John McKivigan (Westport, CT: Greenwood Press, 2007), 383–85. See also Stephen Kantrowitz, *More Than Freedom: Citizenship in a White Republic, 1829–1889* (New York: Penguin, 2012).

86 "Laws of the District of Columbia," *Gales & Seaton's [Congressional] Register*, 19th Cong., 2nd Sess. (December 26, 1826), 555.

87 Ibid., 556. "Laws of the District of Columbia," *Daily National Intelligencer* (Washington, DC), December 27, 1826.

88 "Laws of the District of Columbia," *Gales & Seaton's Register*, 559.

89 Ibid., 565. "Free Persons of Color, House of Representatives, January 11, 1827," *Niles' Weekly Register*, January 27, 1827.

90 "Laws of the District of Columbia," *Gales & Seaton's Register*, 566. "Legislative Acts/Legal Proceedings," *Commercial Advertiser* (New York), December 30, 1826.

91 "Free Blacks in the District of Columbia," *Congressional Register*, January 11, 1827, 654. "Free Persons of Color," *Niles' Weekly Register*.

92 "Free Persons of Color in Washington," *Alexandria (VA) Gazette*, January 13, 1827.

93 Thank you to Kate Masur for sharing her work on the Gilbert Horton case. Kate Masur, "The Case of Gilbert Horton," in possession of author.

94 "City of Washington," *Freedom's Journal*, November 16, 1827.

95 At the time of William Jay's death in 1859, Frederick Douglass recalled in his eulogy for Jay the role the New York judge had played in Horton's case and as an advocate of free black citizenship. "Eulogy of the Late Hon. Wm. Jay." *Douglass' Monthly*, June 1859.

96 "Extracts from 'Reports of the Proceedings and Debates of the Convention of 1821 Assembled for the Purpose of Amending the Constitution of the State of New-York.' By N. S. Carter & W. L. Stone," *Liberator*, October 26, 1833, and "Facts Relative to Slavery in the District of Columbia," *Liberator*, May 24, 1834.

2 THREATS OF REMOVAL

1 Sarah Fanning, *Caribbean Crossing: African Americans and the Haitian Emigration Movement* (New York: New York University Press, 2015), 12–13.

2 Robt Prout, "Baltimore Emigration Society," *Genius of Universal Emancipation* (Baltimore), November 1824. On Boyer's scheme and Granville's mission, see Ousmane K. Power-Greene, *Against Wind and Tide: The African American Struggle against the Colonization Movement* (New York: New York University Press, 2014), 33–34, and Léon Dénius Pamphile, *Haitians and African Americans: A Heritage of Tragedy and Hope* (Gainesville: University of Florida Press, 2001), 42–45. Sara Fanning emphasizes that central to the Haitian project were ideas about law, specifically about the constitutional establishment of a black nation. Fanning, *Caribbean Crossing*.

3 A Colored Baltimorean [William Watkins], "For the Genius of Universal Emancipation," *Genius of Universal Emancipation* (Baltimore), March 3, 1827.

4 C. S. Smith, *A History of the African Methodist Episcopal Church* (Philadelphia: Book Concern of the AME Church, 1922), 15.

5 "Minutes and Proceedings of the First Annual Convention of the People of Color," *Liberator*, October 22, 1831. *Minutes and Proceedings of the Second Annual Convention, for the Improvement of the Free People of Color in These United*

States (Philadelphia: The Convention, 1832). *Minutes and Proceedings of the Third Annual Convention, for the Improvement of the Free People of Color in these United States* (New York: The Convention, 1833).

6 "Baltimore Emigration Society," *Genius of Universal Emancipation*, November 1824 (reprinted from the *American*, September 4, 1824).

7 On Raymond generally, see, T. Stephen Whitman, *The Price of Freedom: Slavery and Manumission in Baltimore and Early National Maryland* (Lexington: University Press of Kentucky, 1997), 141–56, and Paul K. Conkin, *Prophets of Prosperity: America's First Political Economists* (Bloomington: Indiana University Press, 1980), 77–107. Raymond is perhaps best remembered as an early American political economist. Donald E. Frey, "The Puritan Roots of Daniel Raymond's Economics," *History of Political Economy* 32, no. 3 (Fall 2000): 607–29.

8 Martha S. Jones, "The Case of *Jean Baptiste, un Créole de Saint-Domingue*: Narrating Slavery, Freedom, and the Haitian Revolution in Baltimore City," in *The American South and the Atlantic World*, ed. Brian Ward, Martin Bone, and William A. Link (Gainesville: University Press of Florida, 2013), 104–28.

9 "Abstract of the Proceedings of the Anti Slavery Society of Maryland," *Providence Gazette*, September 21, 1825. "Anti Slavery Society in Maryland," *Boston Recorder*, September 30, 1825, 159. "Anti-Slave Societies," *Enquirer* (Richmond, VA), October 7, 1825. "Manumission Societies," *Commercial Advertiser* (New York), October 23, 1826.

10 Raymond even edited Lundy's paper for a time in 1826, when the latter was on a mission to Haiti. The two disagreed about colonization but remained associates. Merton L. Dillon, *Benjamin Lundy and the Struggle for Negro Freedom* (Urbana: University of Illinois Press, 1966), 89, 99–100 (citing Herbert Aptheker, ed., *A Documentary History of the Negro People of the United States* (New York: Citadel Press, 1968): 100).

11 On Lundy and the Haitian emigration project, see Dillon, *Benjamin Lundy*, 87–103.

12 The phrase "borders of belonging" is borrowed from historian Barbara Welke, who explains the dynamics of nineteenth-century citizenship as having been shaped by the meanings or consequences of race, gender, and ability. For Welke, the history of citizenship turns on how belonging for some was "achieved through the subordination or exclusion of others." Barbara Young Welke, *Law and the Borders of Belonging in the Long Nineteenth Century United States* (New York: Cambridge University Press, 2010), 4–5.

13 On African American opposition to colonization, see Julie Winch, *A Gentleman of Color: The Life of James Forten* (New York: Oxford University Press, 2002), and Christopher Phillips, "The Dear Name of Home: Resistance to Colonization in Antebellum Baltimore," *Maryland Historical Magazine* 91, no. 2 (1996): 180–202.

14 William Watkins, "Address," *Genius of Universal Emancipation*, August 1825.

15 Robert Cowley, "Extracts from a Memorial from the Free People of Color to the Citizens of Baltimore," *The Speeches of Henry Clay, Delivered in the Congress of the United States* (Philadelphia: Carey & Lea, 1827), 336–38. The same memorial was first published as "Memorial of the Free People of Colour," *African Repository*, December 1, 1826; and "Memorial of the Free People of Colour," *Genius of Universal Emancipation*, December 16, 1826.

16 Cowley, "Extracts from a Memorial from the Free People of Color." Colored Baltimorean, "For the Genius of Universal Emancipation." Watkins's letter first appeared in the July 6, 1827, issue of *Freedom's Journal*. Bettye J. Gardner, "Opposition to Emigration: A Selected Letter of William Watkins (The Colored Baltimorean)," *Journal of Negro History* 67, no. 2 (1982): 155–58.

17 On the distinction between the emigration and colonization movements, see Power-Greene, *Against Wind and Tide*. Power-Greene suggests there were important links "between anticolonization agitation, blacks' quest for citizenship rights, and the social reform movements of the nineteenth century." Ibid., 13.

18 "An Act Relating to the People of Colour in This State," Maryland Law of 1831, chap. 281 (passed March 12, 1832). *The Ordinances of the Mayor and City Council of Baltimore* (Baltimore: John D. Toy, 1838), 385.

19 "Maryland in Liberia" had been established by the State Colonization Society in 1831. By 1850 the state had expended nearly $300,000 to encourage and facilitate the out-migration of African Americans. Just over 1,000 individuals had made the journey to Africa's west coast. Christopher Phillips, "The Dear Name of Home: Resistance to Colonization in Antebellum Baltimore," *Maryland Historical Magazine* 91, no. 2 (1996): 180–202; Penelope Campbell, *Maryland in Africa: The Maryland State Colonization Society, 1831–1857* (Urbana: University of Illinois Press, 1971); and Aaron Stopak, "The Maryland State Colonization Society: Independent State Action in the Colonization Movement," *Maryland Historical Magazine* 63, no. 3 (1968): 275–98. My understanding of colonization has been influenced by the work of Alex Lovit. See Alex Lovit, "'The Bounds of Habitation': The Geography of the American Colonization Society, 1816–1860," PhD diss., University of Michigan, 2011.

20 David Brion Davis, *The Problem of Slavery in the Age of Emancipation* (New York: Alfred A. Knopf, 2014). On colonization, see Lovit, "The Bounds of Habitation,"; Stopak, "Maryland State Colonization Society"; and Campbell, *Maryland in Africa*.

21 Douglass was married to Elizabeth Grice, daughter of Baltimore activist Hezekiah Grice, and he later became the first black man ordained as a minister in the Episcopal Church. He would spend most of his adult life leading Philadelphia's Saint Thomas African Church. George F. Bragg, "William Douglass," in *Men of Maryland* (Baltimore: Church Advocate Press, 1914), 47–53.

22 "Meeting of the Coloured People in Baltimore," *Genius of Universal Emancipation*, March 1831.

23 "The First Colored Convention," *Anglo-African Magazine*, October 1859.

24 One early historian of black Maryland explains that Grice was so closely allied with Garrison and Lundy that when the two were "mobbed" and run out of Baltimore for a time, Grice accompanied them, only to later return to the city. Bragg, *Men of Maryland*, 60.

25 Grice was a successor to Charles Hackett at *Freedom's Journal*. "Authorised Agents," *Freedom's Journal*, May 2, 1828.

26 James Sidbury, *Becoming African in America: Race and Nation in the Early Black Atlantic* (New York: Oxford University Press, 2007).

27 On at least two occasions Lundy took notice of Grice's work as a mapmaker. "Colony in Canada," *Genius of Universal Emancipation*, August 1830, and October 1830.

28 James Sidbury explains that Russwurm stayed with Grice after arriving in
    Baltimore from New York, on his way to Liberia. Sidbury, *Becoming African in
    America*. The two had known each other for some years, at least to the extent that
    Grice had been the Baltimore agent for Russwurm's newspaper, *Freedom's Journal*.
    Jacqueline Bacon, *Freedom's Journal: The First African American Newspaper*
    (Lanham, MD: Lexington Books, 2007), 260. Also on Russwurm, see Winston
    James, *The Struggles of John Brown Russwurm: The Life and Writings of a Pan-
    Africanist Pioneer, 1799–1851* (New York: New York University Press, 2010).

29 Sidbury, *Becoming African in America*; Juliet E. K. Walker, *History of Black
    Business in America: Capitalism, Race, Entrepreneurship* (Chapel Hill: University
    of North Carolina Press, 2009); Ira Berlin, *Slaves without Masters: The Free Negro
    in the Antebellum South* (New York: Pantheon, 1975). Grice's network extended
    beyond local circles: for example, he advised Boston's David Walker about his
    incendiary *Appeal to the Colored Citizens of the World* before its publication
    in 1829.

30 Bettye J. Gardner, "William Watkins: Antebellum Black Teacher and Writer,"
    Negro History Bulletin 39, no. 6 (1976): 623–24; Jacqueline Bacon, *Freedom's
    Journal*, 261. Watkins would, by the 1850s, change his view and migrate to
    Canada, following his niece, journalist Frances Ellen Watkins Harper. Frances Ellen
    Watkins Harper and Frances Smith Foster, *A Brighter Coming Day: A Frances
    Ellen Watkins Harper Reader* (New York, New York: Feminist Press, 1990).
    By the 1830s, Watkins would come to be known for his antislavery and anti-
    colonizationist politics. Bettye J. Gardner, "Opposition to Emigration, A Selected
    Letter of William Watkins (The Colored Baltimorean)," *Journal of Negro History*
    67, no. 2 (1982): 155–58.

31 Deaver also considered the prospect of emigration to Canada in the late 1820s.
    "Colony in Canada," *Genius of Universal Emancipation*, August 1830. Deaver
    appears in the 1822–23 and 1831 city directories as a rope maker. *The Baltimore
    Directory of 1822 & 1823* (Baltimore: R. J. Matchett, 1822), 74, and *Matchett's
    Baltimore Director, Corrected Up to June, 1831* ([Baltimore]: n.p., 1831), 102. The
    Friendship Society would later be incorporated by AME activists led by Richard
    Mason. *Journal of the Proceedings of the House of Delegates of the State of
    Maryland at a December Session Eighteen Hundred and Thirty Eight* (Annapolis,
    MD: By authority [J. Green, 1839]), 490, 766. Mason joined George Hackett and
    Cornelius Thompson in organizing the African American ceremony on the occasion
    of the death of black abolitionist, founding editor of *Freedom's Journal*, and emi-
    grant to Liberia John Russwurm. "Baltimore, February 28, 1852," *National Era*,
    April 1, 1852.

32 "For the Freedom's Journal," *Freedom's Journal*, July 27, 1827.

33 "The First Colored Convention," *Anglo-African Magazine*, October 1859.

34 Ibid. Historian Kyle Volk credits Grice and the Baltimore-based Legal Rights
    Association with laying a foundation for the challenges in the 1850s to New York's
    segregated streetcars, brought by that city's Legal Rights Association. Indeed,
    Grice maintained ties to his New York-based friends, including the family of
    Elizabeth Jennings, who was a petitioner in the city's first test case. Kyle G. Volk,
    Making Minorities and the Making of American Democracy (New York: Oxford
    University Press, 2014), 146–58. Volk explains the Legal Rights Association as
    "popular minority rights politics" through which black Americans contributed

to the nineteenth century's "theory and practice of democracy." Volk, *Making Minorities*, 2.

35 A Colored Baltimorean, "For the Genius of Universal Emancipation," *Genius of Universal Emancipation*, July 1831.

36 Ibid.

37 See, for example, Leon Litwack and August Meier, eds., *Black Leaders of the Nineteenth Century* (Urbana: University of Illinois Press, 1988), 17.

38 See, for example, Leslie M. Alexander, *African or American? Black Identity and Political Activism in New York City, 1784–1861* (Urbana: University of Illinois Press, 2008).

39 On the 1821 debates in Congress and in the New York state constitutional convention, see Chapter 1.

40 *Minutes and Proceedings of the First Annual Convention of the People of Colour, Held by Adjournments in the City of Philadelphia, from the Sixth to the Eleventh of June, Inclusive, 1831* (Philadelphia: Committee of Arrangements, 1831), 4–5.

41 Latrobe's diary of 1824 notes that he attended a meeting of Baltimore's Philomethean Society, during which he debated whether "was it politic to encourage the emigration of free blacks to Hayti." Entry of November 30, 1824, John H. B. Latrobe Diaries, 1824–40, MS 1677, Maryland Historical Society (MHS), Baltimore. Hereafter, Latrobe Diaries, MHS.

42 John H. B. Latrobe, *The Justices' Practice under the Laws of Maryland* (Baltimore: F. Lucas, 1826).

43 Entry of October 29, 1824, Latrobe Diaries, MHS. John E. Semmes was the first to write at length about Latrobe's early years as a lawyer, drawing in large part on the diaries. He did not mention Latrobe's work with African American clients. John E. Semmes, *John H. B. Latrobe and His Times, 1803–1891* (Baltimore: Norman, Remington, 1917).

44 Entry of December 7, 1824, Latrobe Diaries, MHS.

45 Entry of December 8, 1824, Latrobe Diaries, MHS.

46 "In 1827, the city's mayor Jacob Small ordered the night watch to arrest African Americans out past eleven o'clock at night who could not provide a pass from a white person. Three years later, Small was still complaining about the 'hords [*sic*] of colored persons . . . swarming' in the city. In response, he ordered free blacks home one hour earlier, at ten o'clock instead." Hilary J. Moss, *Schooling Citizens: The Struggle for African American Education in Antebellum America* (Chicago: University of Chicago Press, 2000), 90. Moss cites "Baltimore Justice!" *Freedom's Journal*, August 3, 1827, and Jacob Small, "Night Watch," *Baltimore Patriot and Mercantile Advertiser*, August 27, 1830.

47 "Baltimore Justice!"

48 "Watkins a colored man called to know whether the mayor's proclamation ordering the colored people to be taken up after 11 o'clock pm was constitutional." Entry of July 21, 1827. Latrobe Diaries, MHS.

49 Entry of July 23, 1827. Latrobe Diaries, MHS.

50 Entry of February 3, 1828. Latrobe Diaries, MHS. ("Received from Hezekiah Grice, on account. $5.00.")

51 "Wirt Wm. Counselor at law, 284 Baltimore E of Eutaw," *Matchett's Baltimore Director, Corrected Up to June 1831* (Baltimore: n.p., 1831), 398.

52 An 1831 city directory reports Wirt as a "counsellor at law" at 264 Baltimore, east of Eutaw, and Grice as a "dealer in ice," at Aisquith Street near Orleans. *Matchett's Baltimore Director,* 155. Wirt has not been the subject of a book-length study in more than 150 years. A brief biography can be found in Galen N. Thorp, "William Wirt," *Journal of Supreme Court History* 33, no. 3 (2008): 223–303.

53 William Wirt, *The Letters of a British Spy: Originally Published in the Virginia Argus, in August and September 1803* (Richmond: Samuel Pleasants Jr., 1803), and *The Rainbow; First Series: Originally Published in the Richmond Enquirer* (Richmond, VA: Ritchie & Worsley, 1804). Wirt would later publish *The Life and Character of Patrick Henry* (New York: McElrath, Bangs, 1833).

54 17 U.S. 316 (1819) and 22 U.S. 1 (1824). William Wirt, "Rights of Free Virginia Negroes," in *Official Opinions of the Attorneys General of the United States, Advising the President and Heads of Departments in Relation to Their Official Duties,* ed. Benjamin F. Hall (Washington, DC: Robert Farnham, 1852): 506–9.

55 Thorp, "William Wirt."

56 Wirt, "Rights of Free Virginia Negroes."

57 Ibid.

58 William Wirt, "Validity of the South Carolina Police Bill," in *Opinions of the Attorneys General of the United States,* 659–61. Subsequent to Wirt's ruling, Southern states began to impose "Negro seamen acts" that required black sailors remain confined aboard ship or in the local jail when in port. While Wirt disapproved of such laws as unconstitutional, courts took the opposite view and approved them. Philip M. Hamer, "Great Britain, the United States, and the Negro Seamen Acts, 1822–1848," *Journal of Southern History* 1, no. 1 (February 1935): 3–28, and Michael Schoeppner, "Legitimating Quarantine: Moral Contagions, the Commerce Clause, and the Limits of Gibbons v. Ogden," *Journal of Southern Legal History* 17, nos. 1/2 (2009): 81–120. On the strife that surrounded the important work of African American coastal pilots, see Maurice Melton, "African American Maritime Pilots in the South Atlantic Shipping Trade, 1640–1865," *Journal of the Georgia Association of Historians* 27 (2007/2008): 1–26.

59 Patent Act of 1793, Ch. 11, 1 Stat. 318 (Feb. 21, 1793). After 1800, a small opening was created for aliens who had been two years in residence in the United States. Act of April 17, 1800, Ch. 25, 2 Stat. 37 (1800).

60 "Thomas J. Jennings," *Anglo-African Magazine,* April 1859, 126–27.

61 Jennings is credited with being the first African American granted a United States patent. His Class III patent for "cloth, scouring" was granted in 1821. *Digest of Patents, Issued by the United States, from 1790 to January 1, 1839* (Washington, DC: Peter Force, 1840), 89.

62 William Wirt, "The Right of the Cherokees to Impose Taxes on Traders (April 2, 1824)," in *Opinions of the Attorneys General of the United States,* ed. Benjamin F. Hall (Washington: Robert Farnham, 1852), 645–53. Jill Norgren, "Lawyers and the Legal Business of the Cherokee Republic in Courts of the United States, 1829–1835," *Law and History Review* 10, no. 2 (Autumn 1992): 235–314.

63 30 U.S. 1 (1831) and 31 U.S. 515 (1832), respectively.

64 Norgren, "Lawyers and the Legal Business of the Cherokee Republic." Having negotiated a fee with the Cherokee, Wirt and his cocounsel, John Sergeant, were falsely derided for having charged the Cherokee $10,000. "Party Integrity," *Liberator,* January 28, 1832.

65 Historian Nicholas Guyatt looks at this period and concludes that there was more than an analogy at play. Between proponents of Indian removal and advocates of African American colonization ran a common thread: "benevolent colonization." In both cases, proponents sought a separation of the races to relieve their discomfort with sharing the nation with nonwhites, and through which, it was argued, nonwhites might demonstrate their capacity for "civilization" was equal to that of white Americans. Guyatt explains how some proponents of Indian removal argued that if native people were removed to unorganized western territories and established a colony, they might gain citizenship through the same territorial process that enfranchised white settlers. Nicholas Guyatt, "'The Outskirts of Our Happiness': Race and the Lure of Colonization in the Early Republic," *Journal of American History* 95, no. 4 (March 2009): 986–1011.

66 "A Voice from Baltimore," *Liberator*, April 2, 1831, 54. Garrison published this missive to evidence the degree to which free men and women of color rejected the logic of colonization.

67 "Report," *Liberator*, March 12, 1831, 42.

68 "An Address to the Citizens of New York," *Liberator*, February 12, 1831 (emphasis added). Garrison reprinted these remarks from an anti-colonization pamphlet, *Resolutions of the People of Color, at a Meeting Held on the 25th of January, 1831* (New York: n.p., 1831).

69 "Miscellaneous: The United States, The State of Georgia, and the Cherokees," *Liberator*, July 9, 1831; "Miscellaneous: Speech of Mr. Wirt in the Cherokee Case," *Liberator*, July 16, 1831.

70 Norgren, "Lawyers and the Legal Business of the Cherokee Republic."

71 "The First Colored Convention," 309.

72 John Tyson authored a biography of his uncle that was printed by none other than Benjamin Lundy. John Shoemaker Tyson, *Life of Elisha Tyson, The Philanthropist* (Baltimore: B. Lundy, 1825).

73 "The First Colored Convention," 309.

74 Evidence for this overview of Wirt's practice is from the William Wirt Papers, 1802–58, MSS46110, Library of Congress, Washington, DC.

75 "The First Colored Convention," 309.

76 Norgren, "Lawyers and the Legal Business of the Cherokee Republic."

77 "Minutes of the American Convention," *Freedom's Journal*, February 1, 1828 (reprint from the *Genius of Universal Emancipation*). "Horace Binney," *Proceedings of the American Academy of Arts and Sciences* 11 (May 1875–May 1876): 351–56. Horace Binney, *The Alienigenae of the United States under the Present Naturalization Laws* (Philadelphia: C. Sherman, 1853). Binney's expertise on questions of US citizenship would be established only decades later when he successfully advocated that the Senate recognize that children of citizens born outside of the United States were themselves citizens.

78 This body, at its 1828 meeting, endorsed colonization and called for the abolition of slavery in the District of Columbia. The Maryland delegates to the convention were Benjamin Lundy and Daniel Raymond. Peter Jay, Raymond, and Binney served as counselors to the convention. "Minutes, etc., of the American Convention," *Freedom's Journal*, February 1, 1828.

79 Historian Richard Newman explains that Richard Allen, head of Philadelphia's AME Church, wrote to his friend Daniel Coker indicating that "his lawyers were

great," and urging Coker to "relay this story as much as you can." It was one that likely made its way to activists in Baltimore. Newman, *Freedom's Prophet*, 166–69. Grice and Allen knew each other as far back as 1830, at least, when they collaborated on the first colored convention. Their association likely extended further back than that. Ibid., 269.

80 "The First Colored Convention."

81 Sergeant also opposed the admission of Missouri as a slave state, during a congressional debate. John Sergeant, "Speech on the Missouri Question, Delivered in the House of Representatives of the United States, on the Eighth and Ninth of February, 1820," in *Speeches of John Sergeant of Pennsylvania* (Philadelphia: E. L. Carey & A. Hart, 1832), 185–256. John Sergeant was trained in law and intermittently served in the Pennsylvania legislature and Congress between 1805 and 1821. He later became an effective advocate before the Supreme Court but declined a post to that bench in 1844. He ran for vice president, sharing the ticket with Henry Clay. Sargeant died in November 1852. "Obituary for 1852," *Evening Post* (New York), December 30, 1852. "The Late Honorable John Sergeant, of Philadelphia," *American Law Register* 1, no. 4 (February 1853): 193–98.

82 "The First Colored Convention."

83 "At an Annual Election of the Pennsylvania Abolition Society," *Freedom's Journal*, January 11, 1828. Historian Richard Newman explains how a formidable cadre of lawyers, including Sergeant, dominated the work of the Pennsylvania Abolition Society. Richard S. Newman, *The Transformation of American Abolitionism: Fighting Slavery in the Early Republic* (Chapel Hill: University of North Carolina Press, 2002).

84 William R. Leslie, "The Pennsylvania Fugitive Slave Act of 1826," *Journal of Southern History* 18, no. 4 (November 1952): 429–45, 430, citing Annals of Cong., 14th Cong., 1st Sess., 1068 (February 27, 1816). For the original resolution, see *Minutes of the Proceedings of the Fourteenth American Convention for Promoting the Abolition of Slavery, and Improving the Condition of the African Race*, assembled at Philadelphia (Philadelphia: W. Brown, 1816).

85 "The Mystery Revealed," *Enquirer* (Richmond, VA), November 3, 1826.

86 "The First Colored Convention."

87 The Turner revolt has been the subject of extensive and at times highly contested interpretation. For a more recent view of the case, see Patrick H. Breen, *The Land Shall Be Deluged in Blood: A New History of the Nat Turner Revolt* (Oxford: Oxford University Press, 2015), and David F. Allmendinger Jr., *Nat Turner and the Rising in Southampton County* (Baltimore: Johns Hopkins University Press, 2014). Turner's 1831 "confessions" were published. Nat Turner, *The Confessions of Nat Turner*, ed. Thomas R. Gray (Baltimore: Thomas R. Gray, 1831).

88 Letter, Anonymous to Editors of the Commercial, Chronicle, and Marylander, September 20, 1831, Item 434. Mayor's Correspondence, 1831, Baltimore City Archives, Baltimore (hereafter BCA). Addressed to editors of the city's newspapers, this letter was forwarded to the mayor with a note reading, "We have deemed it proper to send this communication to the Mayor."

89 Note, November 18, 1831, Item 462, Mayor's Correspondence, 1831, BCA.

90 Ezekiel Butler to Ben Thomas, September 21, 1831, Item 463, Mayor's Correspondence, 1831, BCA.

91 A Colored Baltimorean, "An Able Reply," *Liberator*, June 4, 1831.
92 Entry for January 16, 1831, *Journal of the Proceedings of the Senate of the State of Maryland* (Annapolis, MD: Wm. McNeir, 1831), 55.
93 Entry for January 16, 1831, in ibid., 55.
94 Entries for February 23, 1831, February 24, 1831, and March 2, 1831, in ibid., 191, 197, 245.
95 Maryland Laws of 1832, chap. 323, May 14, 1832.
96 H. Jefferson Powell, "Attorney General Taney and the South Carolina Police Bill," 5 Green Bag 2d (2001): 75–100.
97 *Minutes and Proceedings of the Second Annual Convention.*
98 Ibid.
99 In 1843 Grice was appointed director of public works in his adopted city. Leon D. Pamphile, *Haitians and African Americans: A Heritage of Tragedy and Hope* (Gainesville: University Press of Florida, 2001). Sara Fanning offers another context for Grice's migration to Haiti: the Haitian government's solicitation of black migrants from the United States and its increasing fears about a conflict between Haiti and France. On black migration to Haiti, see Sara Fanning, "The Early Roots of Black Nationalism: Northern African Americans' Invocations of Haiti in the Early Nineteenth Century," *Slavery and Abolition* 28, no. 1 (April 2007): 61–85, and Fanning, *Caribbean Crossing*.

3 ABOARD THE *CONSTITUTION*

1 A Colored Baltimorean [William Watkins], "For the Genius of Universal Emancipation," *Genius of Universal Emancipation*, July 1831 (published on July 4). More than twenty years later, in 1852, Frederick Douglass would deliver his oft-cited speech on the subject, "What to the Slave Is the Fourth of July?" in Rochester, New York. *Frederick Douglass: Selected Speeches and Writings*, ed. Philip S. Foner (Chicago: Lawrence Hill, 1999), 188–206. See James A. Colaisco, *Frederick Douglass and the Fourth of July* (New York: Palgrave Macmillan, 2006).
2 In this, Watkins espoused a brand of declarationism that antislavery thinkers, like Douglass, later adopted. Ken I. Kersch, "Beyond Originalism: Conservative Declarationism and Constitutional Redemption," *Maryland Law Review* 71 (2016): 229–82.
3 Colored Baltimorean, "For the Genius of Universal Emancipation," July 1831.
4 Ibid.
5 Bettye J. Gardner, "William Watkins: Antebellum Black Teacher and Anti-Slavery Writer," *Negro History Bulletin*, September/October 1976; Bettye J. Gardner, "Opposition to Emigration: A Selected Letter of William Watkins (The Colored Baltimorean)," *Journal of Negro History* 67, no. 2 (1982): 155–58; Bettye Gardner, "Ante-bellum Black Education in Baltimore," *Maryland Historical Magazine* 71, no. 3 (1976): 360–66. On antebellum black education generally, see Hilary J. Moss, *Schooling Citizens: The Struggle for African American Education in Antebellum America* (Chicago: University of Chicago Press, 2000).
6 William Watkins, *Address Delivered before the Moral Reform Society, in Philadelphia, August 8, 1836* (Philadelphia: Merrihew and Gunn, 1836).
7 Hackett's first wife, Mary Jane Gilliard, was the daughter of Nicholas Gilliard, one of Charles Hackett's lay colleagues in Bethel Church. Christopher Phillips,

Freedom's Port: The African American Community of Baltimore, 1790–1860 (Urbana: University of Illinois Press, 1997), 160.

8 "Considerable Excitement," *Sun*, June 20, 1837. ("Hackett was thrown into prison to await further examination.") "The Bloody Bones," *Sun*, June 21, 1837. ("He has been discharged guiltless; and it's no pleasant thing to add, that the poor fellow, who is a very worthy man, lost four or five horses in the flood.") "Rumors of Murder," *Liberator*, July 14, 1837.

9 W. Jeffrey Bolster, *Black Jacks: African American Seamen in the Age of Sail* (Cambridge, MA: Harvard University Press, 1998).

10 *Regulations, Circulars, Orders & Decisions, for the Guide of Officers of the Navy of the United States, Continued in Part and Issued since the Publication Authorized by the Navy Department in March, 1832* (Washington, DC: C. Alexander, 1851), 6.

11 On the protection certificates and the debates over black mariners generally, see Philip M. Hamer, "Great Britain, the United States, and the Negro Seamen Acts, 1822–1848," *Journal of Southern History* 1, no. 1 (February 1935): 3–28, and Michael Schoeppner, "Legitimating Quarantine: Moral Contagions, the Commerce Clause, and the Limits of Gibbons v. Ogden," *Journal of Southern Legal History* 17, nos. 1/2 (2009): 81–120. Nathan Perl-Rosenthal explains Seamen's Protection Certificates as part of an "unprecedented system for documenting and defending American citizenship . . . available to all American sailors, regardless of race or national origin," between 1796 and 1803. He notes that the language of the original 1796 legislation deliberately did not bar black seamen from acquiring certificates. Nathan Perl-Rosenthal, *Citizen Sailors: Becoming American in the Age of Revolution* (Cambridge, MA: Harvard University Press, 2015), 13, 183–90.

12 "Evidence Concerning the Effects of Immediate Emancipation," *Colored American*, June 3, 1837. "Resolutions Adopted by the A.A.A. Society," *Colored American*, June 10, 1837. "For the Colored American," *Colored American*, October 21, 1837.

13 "Good News: George Davison Released," *Colored American*, June 16, 1838. The pamphlet in question was Benjamin Lundy's *The War in Texas* (Philadelphia: Merrihew and Gunn, 1836).

14 "Ohio Memorial: Extract No. 5," *Colored American*, April 12, 1838. The pamphlet referred to was A. Wattles and A. Hopkins, *Memorial to the General Assembly of the State of Ohio* (Cincinnati: Pugh & Dodd, 1838), published with the support of the Ohio Anti-Slavery Society. See Ohio Anti-Slavery Society, *Report of the Third Anniversary of the Ohio Anti-Slavery Society, Held in Granville, Licking County, Ohio, on the 30th of May, 1838* (Cincinnati: Samuel A. Alley, 1838).

15 Historians of the twentieth century would come to compare more systematically the regimes of slavery and postslavery societies in the Americas. Still, Hackett's example suggests that such a comparison was already taking place as free black people in the United States surveyed the hemisphere for measures of their status and strategies for their activism. Frank Tannenbaum's *Slave and Citizen, the Negro in the Americas* remains the touchstone text on this question (New York: Knopf, 1946). Tannenbaum has been importantly revisited by historian Alejandro de la Fuente in "Slave Law and Claims-Making in Cuba: The Tannenbaum Debate Revisited," *Law and History Review* 22, no. 2 (Summer 2004), 339–69, and "From Slaves to Citizens? Tannenbaum and the Debates on Slavery, Emancipation, and Race Relations in Latin America," *International Labor & Working-Class History* 77, no. 1 (Spring 2010): 154–73.

16 On the USS *Constitution* generally, see Charles E. Brodine Jr., Michael J. Crawford, and Christine F. Hughes, *Interpreting Old Ironsides: An Illustrated Guide to USS Constitution* (Washington, DC: Naval Historical Center, Department of the Navy, 2007).

17 Alexander Claxton to Francis Sorrell, Norfolk, VA, March 24, 1839, Alexander Claxton Letters, Southern Historical Collection, University of North Carolina, Chapel Hill.

18 Ibid.

19 Communipaw [James McCune Smith], "Heads of the Colored People: No. 5: The Steward," *Frederick Douglass' Paper*, December 24, 1852.

20 Monthly Return of Officers and Crew of the U.S.S. *Constitution*, January 31, 1841, M1030, Logbooks and Journals of the USS Constitution 1798–1934, Logbooks of US Navy Ships ca. 1801–1940, Department of the Navy, Office of the Secretary (1798–09/1947), Record Group 24: Records of the Bureau of Naval Personnel 1798–2007, National Archives and Records Administration (NARA), Washington, DC. Hereafter cited as Logbooks and Journals of the USS Constitution, NARA.

21 Tyrone G. Martin, *A Most Fortunate Ship: A Narrative History of Old Ironsides* (Annapolis, MD: Naval Institute Press, 1997).

22 Historian Matthew Rafferty relies on federal circuit and district court records to recover the centrality of law to daily life aboard US merchant vessels in the half century before the Civil War. Matthew Rafferty, *The Republic Afloat: Law, Honor, and Citizenship in Maritime America* (Chicago: University of Chicago Press, 2013).

23 Henry James Mercier and William Gallop, *Life in a Man-of-War, or Scenes in "Old Ironsides" during Her Cruise in the Pacific, by a Fore-Top-Man* (Philadelphia: Lydia M. Bailey, 1841), 30. Sidney Kaplan explains that Herman Melville borrowed from Mercier's text when constructing his black characters. See Sidney Kaplan, "Herman Melville and the American National Sin: The Meaning of Benito Cereno," in *American Studies in Black and White: Selected Essays, 1949–1989* (Amherst: University of Massachusetts Press, 1996).

24 Mercier and Gallop, *Life in a Man-of-War*, 165–70.

25 Entries of December 12 and December 22, 1839, M1030, Logbooks and Journals of the USS Constitution, NARA.

26 *Rules, Regulations, and Instructions for the Naval Service of the United States* (Washington City: K. DeKrafft, 1818).

27 Lieutenant William H. Kennon, "Charges and Specification of Charles (William Bambury)," December 19, 1839; Lieutenant J. C. Rich, "Charge and Specification (James Morris)," December 20, 1839; Captain Daniel Turner to Commodore Alexander Claxton, December 20, 1839, Letterbook of Captain Daniel Turner, Record Group 45: Naval Records Collection of the Office of Naval Records and Library, NARA. (Hereafter cited as Letterbook of Captain Daniel Turner, NARA.)

28 Commodore Alexander Claxton to Captain Daniel Turner, December 22, 1839; Captain Daniel Turner to Lieutenant T. D. Shaw, December 25, 1839; Captain Daniel Turner to Lieutenant William Smith, December 25, 1839; Captain Daniel Turner to Flag Lieutenant Franklin Buchanan, December 25, 1839; Captain Daniel Turner, "Report of the Court of Inquiry," December 27, 1839, Letterbook of Captain Daniel Turner, NARA.

29 Mercier and Gallop, *Life in a Man-of-War*, 38. Brodine, Crawford, and Hughes, *Interpreting Old Ironsides*, 75.

30 Martin, *A Most Fortunate Ship*, 257.

31 David Turnbull, *Travels in the West: Cuba; with Notice of Porto Rico, and the Slave Trade* (London: Lorgman, Orme, Brown, Green, and Longmans, 1840), 198–202. Turnbull spent the years 1837–39 in the Caribbean.

32 Wm. A. Gibbs, "A Caution to Travelers in General," *Colored American*, October 21, 1837. Jane Landers notes that Gibbs himself had been briefly detained and interrogated in Matanzas, Cuba, and reported that he was a black carpenter from New York without a passport. Jane Landers, *Atlantic Creoles in the Age of Revolutions* (Cambridge, MA: Harvard University Press, 2011), 218–19 and 317n34.

33 Entry of July 4, 1839, M1030, Logbooks and Journals of the USS Constitution, NARA.

34 My thanks to Roseanne Adderley for introducing me to her work on the *Romney*. The bar against free black sailors in Havana had evolved over the 1830s. Legislation in 1832 excluded Jamaican freedmen, whom Cuban officials considered a "dangerous class." After emancipation in the British Caribbean, Cuba extended its prohibition against free blacks' access to port cities in 1837. Michele Reid-Vazquez, *The Year of the Lash: Free People of Color in Cuba and the Nineteenth-Century Atlantic World* (Athens: University of Georgia Press, 2011), 72–74. Franklin W. Knight, *Slave Society in Cuba during the Nineteenth Century* (Madison: University of Wisconsin – Madison, 1970), 96–97, citing Turnbull, *Travels in the West*, 70. Gibbs, "A Caution to Travelers in General." The *Romney* dispute would continue until 1839. Authorities in Madrid qualifiedly conceded admission of the black sailors into Havana in April 1839. Endless bickering followed. The British charged that the facilities allotted for the men's exercise were unsanitary. Locals complained that the black sailors were arrogant; it was found that the men were being lured into local homes with alcohol. Sailors were occasionally detained in Havana, and Spanish officials inspected the *Romney* to inventory men and equipment. By the fall of 1839, so much trouble was being generated that the British considered removing the ship from the port, but only in 1845 did they finally sell the hulk to the Spanish. David R. Murray, *Odious Commerce: Britain, Spain and the Abolition of the Cuban Slave Trade* (Cambridge, MA: Cambridge University Press, 1980), 114–27.

35 Entry of August 28, 1839, M1030, Logbooks and Journals of the USS Constitution, NARA. Martin, *A Most Fortunate Ship*, 258.

36 Entries of September 3 and September 4, 1839, M1030, Logbooks and Journals of the USS Constitution, NARA.

37 Entries of August 28, August 31, September 2, September 6, and September 7, 1839, M1030, Logbooks and Journals of the USS Constitution, NARA.

38 Mary C. Karasch, *Slave Life in Rio de Janeiro, 1808–1850* (Princeton, NJ: Princeton University Press, 1987), 338–42.

39 Herbert S. Klein and Francisco Vidal Luna, *Slavery in Brazil* (New York: Cambridge University Press, 2010), 290–92.

40 Captain Daniel Turner to Honorable, the Secretary of the Navy, March 7, 1841, "Letterbook of Captain Daniel Turner," NARA. The *Colored American* noted news of Claxton's death. "General Intelligence from the Pacific," *Colored American*, June 5, 1841.

41 Entry of March 3, 1841, M1030, Logbooks and Journals of the USS Constitution, NARA.

42 Mercier and Gallop, *Life in a Man-of-War*, 188–89. Captain Daniel Turner to Captain Isaac McKeever, March 13, 1841, Letterbook of Captain Daniel Turner, NARA.

43 Entry of March 3, 1841, M1030, Logbooks and Journals of the USS Constitution, NARA.

44 "Tuesday, 22. Arr. (at the Bar,) ship Ann, Brock, Pac. Ocean, with full cargo (2,400 bbls) sperm oil, to Jared Coffin," "Shipping News," *Nantucket* (MA) *Inquirer*, June 23, 1842.

45 Lloyd Pratt, "Speech, Print, and Reform on Nantucket," in *A History of the Book in America*, vol. 3: *The Industrial Book, 1840–1880*, ed. Scott E. Casper, Jeffrey D. Groves, Stephen W. Nissenbaum, and Michael Winship (Chapel Hill: University of North Carolina Press, 2009), 392–99. "Agents for this Paper," *Colored American*, September 25, 1841 (Nantucket, MA: E. J. Pompey).

46 "Meeting of Colored Citizens," *Colored American*, July 10, 1841.

47 "Maryland's Colonization Standing Boldly Out," *Colored American*, June 19, 1841 (emphasis in the original).

48 Ibid.

49 "A Call for a State Convention to Extend the Elective Franchise," *Colored American*, June 19, 1841. "Great Anti-Colonization Meeting in New York," *Colored American*, June 26, 1841.

4 THE CITY COURTHOUSE

 1 Baltimore's 1842 city directory lists George A. Hackett as a carter, seemingly in his parents' home on Gay Street near Aisquith. *Matchett's Baltimore Director, or Register of Householders* (Baltimore: Baltimore Director Office, 1842), 438.

 2 On the 1840 emigration to Trinidad, see Christopher Phillips, *Freedom's Port: The African American Community of Baltimore, 1790–1860* (Urbana: University of Illinois Press, 1997), 215–20.

 3 "Emancipation in the West Indies," *Colored American*, August 17, 1839. On the development of this scheme generally, see Madhavi Kale, *Fragments of Empire: Capital, Slavery, and Indian Indentured Labor in the British Caribbean* (Philadelphia: University of Pennsylvania Press, 2010), 44–48.

 4 "Description of the Island of Trinidad, and the Advantages to Be Derived from Emigration to That Colony," *Colored American*, August 31, 1839. This article was authored by a Mr. Burnley, the Trinidadian government agent.

 5 "Our Prospects," *Colored American*, September 14, 1839.

 6 "Emigration of Free Negroes," *Sun*, January 22, 1840.

 7 Maryland Laws of 1839, chap. 5.

 8 "From Our Correspondent, Annapolis," *Sun*, January 29, 1840.

 9 Phillips explains that on November 25, 1839, there was a meeting at Bethel Church to select delegates, at which Peck and Price were selected. Phillips, *Freedom's Port*, 190.

10 "To Emigrants to the British Island of Trinidad," *Sun*, April 3, 1840. "Notice to Emigrants to British Guiana," *Sun*, April 3, 1840.

11 "Trinidad," *Sun*, April 4, 1840.

12 "Public Meeting," *Sun*, April 15, 1840.

13 "The Return of the Agents from British Guiana and Trinidad," *Sun*, April 18, 1840.

14 *Report of Messrs. Peck and Price, Who Were Appointed at a Meeting of the Free Colored People of Baltimore, Held on the 25th November, 1839, Delegates to Visit British Guiana, and the Island of Trinidad* (Baltimore: Woods & Crane, 1840), 11.

15 "Colored Emigrants," *Sun*, April 14, 1840.

16 "For Trinidad," *Sun*, April 17, 1840.

17 "For Trinidad," *Sun*, May 8, 1840.

18 "Another Cargo," *Sun*, May 16, 1840.

19 The travel permits for emigrants from Baltimore to Trinidad are included among miscellaneous court records. Various Travel Permits, 1840, C1-90, Baltimore County, Baltimore County Court, Miscellaneous Court Papers, MSA.

20 Phillips, *Freedom's Port*, 194. "Pursuant to Notice," *Sun*, January 1, 1841.

21 "Returning of the Rev. Mr. Hunt to Newark, N.J.," *Colored American*, February 13, 1841 (reporting on a January 19, 1841, meeting).

22 As late as November 1841, emigrants were still reported to be sailing out from Baltimore for Trinidad. "Emigrants to Trinidad," *Sun*, November 18, 1841.

23 "For Trinidad," *Colored American*, December 4, 1841.

24 Amalgar, "Communication," *Sun*, February 4, 1841.

25 Peck and Thomas S. Price, "Counter Statement," *Colored American*, May 16, 1840.

26 "Messrs. Peck and Price," *Colored American*, November 7, 1840.

27 "Convention of the Colored Inhabitants of the State of New York, August 18–20, 1840," in Philip S. Foner and George E. Walker, eds., *Proceedings of the Black State Conventions, 1840–1865*, vol. 1 (Philadelphia: Temple University Press, 1979), 14–15.

28 Ibid.

29 "New York State Free Suffrage Convention, September 8, 1845," in Foner and Walker, *Proceedings of the Black State Conventions*, 1:39.

30 Ibid., 39–41.

31 *Proceedings and Debates of the Convention of the Commonwealth of Pennsylvania, to Propose Amendments to the Constitution, Commenced and Held at Harrisburg, on the Second Day of May, 1837*, 14 vols. (Harrisburg, PA: Packer, Barrett, and Parke, 1837–39).

32 Hobbs et al. v. Fogg, 6 Watts 553 (Penn. Supreme Court, 1837).

33 "Minutes of the State Convention of the Coloured Citizens of Pennsylvania, Convened at Harrisburg, December 13th and 14th, 1848," in Foner and Walker, *Proceedings of the Black State Conventions*, 1:131.

34 "Proceedings and Address of the Coloured Citizens of N.J. Convened at Trenton, August 21st and 22nd, 1849, for the Purpose of Taking the Initiatory Measures for Obtaining the Right of Suffrage in This Our Native State," in Philip S. Foner and George E. Walker, eds., *Proceedings of the Black State Conventions, 1840–1865*, vol. 2 (Philadelphia: Temple University Press, 1980), 4.

35 "Proceedings of the Connecticut State Convention, of Colored Men, Held at New Haven on the September 12th and 13th, 1849," in Foner and Walker, *Proceedings of the Black State Conventions*, 2:20, 26–28, 31.

36 "Minutes of the State Convention, of the Colored Citizens of the State of Michigan, Held in the City of Detroit on the 26th and 27th of October 1843, for the Purpose

of Considering Their Moral and Political Condition, as Citizens of the State," in Foner and Walker, *Proceedings of the Black State Conventions*, 1:181–97.

37 *Minutes of the Fifth Annual Convention for the Improvement of the Free People of Colour in the United States, held by Adjournments, in the Wesley Church, Philadelphia* (Philadelphia: William F. Gibbons, 1835), 6.

38 Maryland Laws of 1841, chap. 272, sections 1 and 2. *Index to the Law of Maryland: From the Year 1838 to the Year 1845, Inclusive* (Annapolis, MD: Riley & Davis, 1846.) This was a supplement to an 1835 law that barred any person from knowingly taking part in the preparation or circulation of printed or written materials having a tendency to create discontent among black Marylanders, or to stir them to insurrection. Jeffrey R. Brackett, *The Negro in Maryland: A Study of the Institution of Slavery* (Baltimore: Johns Hopkins University Press, 1889), 224–25.

39 "Agents for the Liberator," *Liberator*, March 4, 1831.

40 "Philadelphia Committee," *Colored American*, December 9, 1837.

41 "Baltimore City Court," *Sun*, August 5, 1844. The record is nearly silent about who John Pitts may have been. The following winter, a John Pitts was found guilty of having stolen a piece of red flannel valued at $6. "Balt. City Court," *Sun*, February 14, 1845.

42 John H. B. Latrobe and Fielding Lucas, *Picture of Baltimore, Containing a Description of All Objects of Interest in the City and Embellished with Views of the Principal Public Buildings* (Baltimore: F. Lucas Jr., 1832), 81–82. The selection of Milleman contrasted markedly with the possible choice of the distinguished architect Benjamin Latrobe, who was also in Baltimore, working on the construction of the Baltimore Basilica.

43 Silk Buckingham, *America*, 267–68.

44 Mary P. Ryan, "Democracy Rising: The Monuments of Baltimore, 1809–1842," *Journal of Urban History* 36, no. 2 (2010): 127–50.

45 "Worse and Worse," *Niles' Weekly Register*, February 14, 1835.

46 Court House Commissioners/Repairs, Administrative Records (1835–40), BRG 10, series 1, BCA. "An Act to Authorize the Repairing of the Court House of Baltimore County, and for Other Purposes," Maryland Laws of 1834, chap. 151 (passed, March 9, 1835). "A Supplement to an Act to Authorize the Repairing of the Court House of Baltimore County, and for Other Purposes, Passed at December Session," Maryland Laws of 1824, chap. 151, Maryland Laws of 1837, chap. 24 (January 30, 1838).

47 "Report to the City Council . . .," December 30, 1850, C2045-3, Baltimore City and County Jail, Proceedings of Visitors, MSA. African Americans were disproportionately represented, given that they made up just 17 percent of the city's overall population. With a criminal court that sat for four terms per year, this means that in an average of at least 175 proceedings per term, a black Baltimorean was the defendant.

48 Ibid. During its July term, the court held 54 jury trials and heard 300 "Saturday cases" (for assaults, rioting, etc.) over the course of thirty-nine working days. "Business of the Criminal Court," *Sun*, July 11, 1854.

49 "Sale of Convicts," *Sun*, July 3, 1858.

50 "Executor's Sale of a Negro Man," *Sun*, August 5, 1858.

51 *In re* Cornelius Thompson, July 31, 1845, Box 6, 1829–64, Certificates of Freedom, T629-1, Register of Wills, Baltimore City, MSA.

52 George W. Williams to Frederick Brune, July 27, 1858, 1853, F. W. Brune (1813–
    78), Incoming Letters, Box 5, Brune Family Correspondence, MS 2004, MHS.

53 Article 66, section 50, Immigration of Free Negroes, *The Maryland Code: Public
    General Laws and Public Local Laws, 1860* (Baltimore: John Murphy & Co.,
    1860), 458–60.

54 *In re* Cornelius Thompson.

55 Perine had been presented with a travel permit application endorsed by Taney
    before. Two weeks earlier, a Margaret Price had applied for leave to travel to visit
    her family in Pittsburgh. Both Roger and Anne Taney endorsed that application. *In
    re* Margaret Price, July 16, 1845, Box 6, 1829–64, Certificates of Freedom, T629-1,
    Baltimore City, Register of Wills, 1829–64, MSA.

56 *In re* Samuel Brown, June 23, 1845; *In re* Robert Murray, June 25, 1845; *In re*
    Erastus Briscoe, June 25, 1845; *In re* John Briscoe, June 25, 1845; *In re* James
    Anderson, June 25, 1845; *In re* Alfred Booth, July 2, 1845; *In re* Perry Thomas,
    July 9, 1845; *In re* Albert Hardy, July 19, 1845; and *In re* John B. Bailey, August 11,
    1845, Box 6, 1829–64, Certificates of Freedom, T629-1, Baltimore City, Register of
    Wills, 1829–64, MSA. Perine also accepted an application from Sarah Pelton dated
    June 4, 1845, indicating that Pelton expected to accompany Mr. and Mrs. Nelson
    Clarks "for their purpose of visiting some of the watering places." *In re* Sarah
    Pelton, June 4, 1845, ibid.

57 Taney had manumitted his own slaves years earlier, also demanding that some
    of them serve him for a term of years in exchange for their manumission. On
    Taney's manumission of his slaves, see Timothy S. Huebner, "Roger B. Taney and
    the Slavery Issue: Looking Beyond – and Before – Dred Scott," *Journal of American
    History* 97, no. 1 (June 2010): 17–38. Huebner notes that Taney's slaves then
    served him for a term of years as compensation for their liberty. Thompson appears
    to have met his obligation by working for Taney at least five years. He is referred
    to by name in one of Taney's letters to his son-in-law in June 1837. Roger B. Taney
    to J. Mason Campbell, June 2, 1837, Howard Papers, MSA.

58 Taney was likely suggesting this strategy in response to an 1831 state law that
    provided that slaves manumitted in Maryland should be referred to the Maryland
    Colonization Society and removed to Liberia. Should such freed persons refuse to
    be so removed, the society was authorized to remove them to a proper place where
    they would be willing to go and could to secure the assistance of the local sheriff if
    necessary. Maryland Laws of 1831, chap. 281. Historian Jeffrey R. Brackett notes
    that the law was not widely enforced, although Taney and Thompson would not
    have known that in 1832. Brackett, *The Negro in Maryland*, 165–66.

59 Roger B. Taney to William L. Beall, April 1832, and Taney to Beall, February 24,
    1831, Mary L. Urner Collection, MSC5818, MSA. Thompson's obituary notes that
    he "passed many years with the family of the Chief Justice, having accompanied
    him when he went to Washington as a member of the cabinet, and continued with
    him there the whole period of his stay." Baltimore *Sun*, April 16, 1855.

60 Taney references relying on Thompson to bring cigars from Baltimore to him in
    Washington in an 1837 letter to his son-in-law J. Mason Campbell. Roger B. Taney
    to J. Mason Campbell, January 2, 1837, Box 20, J. M. Campbell Papers, MS
    469, MHS.

61 Carl Brent Swisher, *Roger B. Taney* (New York: Macmillan, 1935), 518.

62 "Obituary of Cornelius Thompson," *Sun*, April 16, 1855. *Matchett's Baltimore Director, for 1849–50* (Baltimore: R. J. Matchett, 1849), 15.

5 BETWEEN THE CONSTITUTION AND THE DISCIPLINE OF THE CHURCH

1 The church was formally incorporated as Bethel African Methodist Episcopal Church, sometimes also referred to as Saratoga Street Bethel AME Church. This chapter adopts the commonly used moniker Bethel Church.

2 H., "A Card to the Public," *Sun*, March 2, 1849.

3 Bishop Daniel Alexander Payne, *Recollections of Seventy Years*, ed. C. S. Smith (Nashville, TN: Publishing House of the AME Sunday School Union, 1888), 92.

4 Historian Gary Browne explains that just twenty churches had gradually been established in Baltimore from the colonial period through 1815. Then, between 1816 and 1830, sixteen new congregations appeared. In addition, thirteen Bible, missionary, and tract societies sprang up in the 1820s that had not existed before. By 1830, religion, as defined institutionally, played a greater role in the life of the community than ever before. Gary Lawson Browne, *Baltimore in the Nation, 1789–1861* (Chapel Hill: University of North Carolina Press, 1980), 102.

5 Carol V. R. George, *Segregated Sabbaths: Richard Allen and the Rise of Independent Black Churches: 1760–1840* (New York: Oxford University Press, 1973), and Richard S. Newman, *Freedom's Prophet: Bishop Richard Allen, the AME Church, and the Black Founding Fathers* (New York: New York University Press, 2009).

6 Jeffrey R. Brackett, *The Negro in Maryland: A Study of the Institution of Slavery* (Baltimore: Johns Hopkins University, 1889).

7 Conditions in Baltimore add to our understanding of how independent black churches fared in Southern cities. In Charleston, Richmond, and Saint Louis, in contrast, they were subjected to expulsion or the close supervision of white authorities. Nicholas May, "Holy Rebellion: Religious Assembly Laws in Antebellum South Carolina and Virginia," *American Journal of Legal History* 49, no. 3 (July 2007): 237–56; and Ira Berlin, *Slaves without Masters: The Free Negro in the Antebellum South* (New York: Pantheon, 1975), 73. Berlin points out that while black Methodists failed to "penetrate much beyond Maryland," in Savannah three black Baptist congregations were in place by 1812. On free black churches in the South generally, see ibid., 70–78. Christopher Phillips, *Freedom's Port: The African American Community of Baltimore, 1790–1860* (Urbana: University of Illinois Press, 1997). On black laws see Stephen Middleton, *The Black Laws: Race and the Legal Process in Early Ohio* (Athens: Ohio University Press, 2005). Jeffrey Brackett chronicled Maryland's black laws in his 1899 study. Brackett, *The Negro in Maryland*.

8 Few of Baltimore's black churches have been the subjects of extended study, though church historians have chronicled their evolution. See, for example, George Freeman Bragg, *History of the Afro-American Group of the Episcopal Church* (Baltimore: Church Advocate Press, 1922); Mechal Sobel, *Trabelin' On: The Slave Journey to an Afro-Baptist Faith* (Princeton, NJ: Princeton University Press, 1988); A. Briscoe Koger, *Negro Baptists of Maryland* (Baltimore: n.p., 1946).

9 Such encounters were not always mutually respectful. From time to time there were complaints lodged against black congregations for the noise generated in and

outside of their sanctuaries. "Wholesale Arrest," *Sun*, August 24, 1857. "Rioting at a Fair," *Sun*, December 18, 1857. See also (on "obstructing the foot pavement") *Sun*, August 3 and October 12, 1858; August 9, 1859.

10 On legal consciousness, see Hendrik Hartog, "The Constitution of Aspiration and 'The Rights That Belong to Us All,'" *Journal of American History* 74, no. 3 (December 1987): 1013–34, and Michael Grossberg, *A Judgment for Solomon: The d'Hauteville Case and Legal Experience in Antebellum America* (New York: Cambridge University Press, 1996).

11 Incorporated as the Colored Independent Wesleyan Methodist Church, in this chapter I use its common name Zion Church when referring to the congregation.

12 "An ACT to Incorporate Certain Persons in Every Christian Church or Congregation in This State," Maryland Laws of 1802, chap. 111 (passed January 8, 1803).

13 "Incorporation of the First Colored Independent Wesleyan Methodist Society of the City of Baltimore," January 8, 1842, Liber TK 64/414, 134, CM143, Charter Records, Baltimore County Court, MSA.

14 *Matchett's Baltimore Director, or Register of Householders* (Baltimore: Baltimore Director Office, 1842), 460.

15 For an insightful perspective on the incorporation of African American churches in Philadelphia, see Sarah Barringer Gordon, "The African Supplement: Religion, Race, and Corporate Law in Early National America," *William and Mary Quarterly* 72, no. 3 (July 2015): 385–422.

16 "Notice," *Baltimore Patriot*, June 13, 1829. By 1850 Ridgeway had remarried and headed a household that included his second wife, Rebecca, and four children. "Henry Ridgeway," Dwelling No. 43, Family No. 58, Ward 15, Baltimore City, Maryland, Seventh Census of the United States, 1850, NARA.

17 "Caution," *Sun*, April 18, 1839. Purnell's wife may indeed have had cause to abandon him. Some months after warning creditors against Matilda, Purnell was arrested for being drunk and disorderly. "Watch Returns," *Sun*, December 9, 1839. Sometimes legal lessons came by way of criminal proceedings.

18 The installments were detailed as 116 dollars and 66⅔ cents, plus interest, payable on January 30 and July 30, 1845, and January 20, 1846. *James Bush v. Trustees*, September 14, 1846, Chancery Papers, C295-3433, C240, Baltimore County, Baltimore County Court, MSA.

19 Ibid.

20 "Further Examination," *Sun*, July 16, 1846.

21 "City Court," *Sun*, October 10, 1846.

22 J. Thomas Scharf, *History of Baltimore City and County* (Philadelphia: Louis H. Everts, 1881): 437–41.

23 Slave trading in Baltimore has been explored elsewhere through the example of Austin Woolfolk, who continued to trade in slaves after Purvis moved on to speculation in real estate. See William Calderhead, "The Role of the Professional Slave Trader in a Slave Economy: Austin Woolfolk, a Case Study," *Civil War History* 23 (September 1977): 195–211. On the border-state slave trade generally, also see William Calderhead, "How Extensive Was the Border State Slave Trade?" *Civil War History* 18 (March 1972): 42–55.

24 *James Bush v. Trustees*. "Sales at the Exchange," *Sun*, October 13, 1846.

25 See, for example, "Cash in Market," *Baltimore Patriot & Mercantile Advertiser*, November 26, 1831.

26 Jonathan B. Pritchett, "The Interregional Slave Trade and the Selection of Slaves for the New Orleans Market," *Journal of Interdisciplinary History* 28, no. 1 (Summer 1997): 57–85. Steven Deyle, *Carry Me Back: The Domestic Slave Trade in American Life* (New York: Oxford University Press, 2006).

27 "Baltimore Female College," *Sun*, February 28, 1849. "The House of Refuge," *Sun*, March 3, 1855.

28 Lawrence H. Mamiya, "A Social History of the Bethel African Methodist Episcopal Church in Baltimore: The House of God and the Struggle for Freedom," in *American Congregations*, vol. 1: *Portraits of Twelve Religious Communities*, ed. James P. Wind and James W. Lewis (Chicago: University of Chicago Press, 1994), 221–92.

29 A significant number of black congregants remained in the white-led church and eventually founded another separate congregation. J. Gordon Melton, "African American Methodism in the M.E. Tradition: The Case of Sharp Street (Baltimore)," *North Star: A Journal of African American Religious History* 8, no. 2 (January 2005).

30 Here, the emergence of black Methodism in Baltimore differs from that in border-state cities such as Saint Louis, Missouri. African American congregations did not emerge in Saint Louis until the church's 1844 schism over slavery. See Lucas P. Volkman, "Church Property Disputes, Religious Freedom, and the Ordeal of African American Methodists in Antebellum St. Louis: *Farrar v. Finney* (1855)," *Journal of Law & Religion* 27 (2011–12): 83–139.

31 "The Constitution of the African Methodist Bethel Church of the City of Baltimore," April 7, 1816, Liber WG 20/83, 21, Charter Records, Baltimore County Court, CM 143, MSA.

32 "Amendments to the Constitution of the African Methodist Bethel Society or Church in the City of Baltimore," July 19, 1819, Liber WG 24/33, 26–27, CM 143, Charter Records, Baltimore County Court, MSA.

33 Bethel's expanding leadership ranks reflected the burgeoning community it served. In the 1820s Baltimore was home to 10,300 free black people and 4,300 slaves. By 1850, the city's free black population would be just over 25,000. The expansion of the Bethel congregation reflected this change; its membership grew from 633 congregants in 1816 to 1,504 in 1853. M. Ray Della, Jr., "An Analysis of Baltimore's Population in the 1850's," *Maryland Historical Magazine* 68, no. 1 (March 1973): 20–35. Mamiya, "Social History of the Bethel AME Church."

34 "Incorporation of the African Methodist Bethel Church of the City of Baltimore," April 3, 1820, Liber WG 25/269, 27–29, Charter Records, Baltimore County Court, CM 143, MSA. *This Constitution or Incorporation Is an Extract from the Records of the State of Maryland: Printed by Order of the Bethel Church: Present Elder, The Rev. Edward Waters* (Baltimore: Woods and Crane, 1842).

35 Brackett, *The Negro in Maryland*, 199. This legislation followed a general decline in the circumstances of free black Marylanders that is most pointedly marked by their loss of the franchise in 1801. See David S. Bogen, "The Annapolis Poll Books of 1800 and 1804: African American Voting in the Early Republic," *Maryland Historical Magazine* 86, no. 1 (1991): 57–65, and David S. Bogen, "The Maryland

Context of 'Dred Scott': The Decline in the Legal Status of Maryland Free Blacks, 1776–1810," *American Journal of Legal History* 34, no. 4 (1990): 381–411.

36 Brackett, *The Negro in Maryland*, 200. "A Further Additional Supplement to the Act, Entitled, A Act Relating to the People of Colour of This State," Passed at December session, Maryland Laws of 1831, chap. 281, and Maryland Laws of 1834, chap. 160, *Ordinances of the Mayor and City Council of Baltimore* (Baltimore: John D. Toy, 1838), 462.

37 Brackett, *The Negro in Maryland*, 203–4. Maryland's laws generally paralleled those in South Carolina and Virginia. Nicholas May, "Holy Rebellion: Religious Assembly Laws in Antebellum South Carolina and Virginia," *American Journal of Legal History* 49, no. 3 (July 2007): 237–56.

38 Brackett, *The Negro in Maryland*, 206.

39 *African Methodist Bethel Church v. Joel P. Carmack, et al.*, No. 949, Equity Papers A, Miscellaneous, T53-10, 1857, Baltimore City Circuit Court, Baltimore City, MSA. African Methodist Bethel Church of the City of Baltimore, *The Constitution or Incorporation: Is an Extract from the Records of the State of Maryland* (Baltimore: Woods and Crane, 1842).

40 Bishop Daniel Alexander Payne, *Recollections of Seventy Years*, ed. C[harles] S[pencer] Smith (Nashville, TN: Publishing House of the AME Sunday School Union, 1888), 92. Historian Christopher Phillips explains how Bethel's membership roll indicates that a significant chasm erupted in its congregation during the winter of 1848–49 that led to the expulsion of leaders and laity for "rebellion," including the lay minister Nathaniel Peck and four class leaders. Phillips, *Freedom's Port*, 139. These same events are discussed by Barbara Jeanne Fields in *Slavery and Freedom on the Middle Ground: Maryland during the Nineteenth Century* (New Haven, CT: Yale University Press), 76–84.

41 Payne, *Recollections*, 94.

42 The complainants included Darius Stokes, William H. G. Brown, Alexander Murray, Henry Braddock, and George A. Hackett, as members of the AME Church. Bill of Complaint, December 19, 1848, *African Methodist Bethel Church v. Joel P. Carmack*, 1857, T53-10, Equity Papers A Miscellaneous, Circuit Court, Baltimore City, MSA.

43 Ibid.

44 James M. Campbell explains the operation of church-based tribunals in *Slavery on Trial: Race, Class, and Criminal Justice in Antebellum Richmond, Virginia* (Gainesville: University of Florida Press, 2007), 179–85. For a discussion of such tribunals in Philadelphia's Mother Bethel AME Church, see Erica Armstrong Dunbar, *A Fragile Freedom: African American Women and Emancipation in the Antebellum City* (New Haven, CT: Yale University Press, 2008).

45 "Melee in a Meeting House," *Sun*, March 2, 1849.

46 H., "A Card to the Public," *Sun*, March 2, 1849.

47 "Melee in a Meeting House."

48 Frederick Harris, Joel P. Carmack, Thomas Cook, and Aaron Richfield, "We, the Undersigned," *Sun*, February 28, 1849.

49 H., "A Card to the Public."

50 Whitman Ridgway explains how Baltimore's leaders "expressed their views through letters published in the commercial press." Whitman H. Ridgway, *Community*

Leadership in Maryland, 1790–1840: A Comparative Analysis of Power in Society (Chapel Hill: University of North Carolina Press, 1979), 76.

51 Complainants' Exhibit A (March 9, 1849), *African Methodist Bethel Church v. Joel P. Carmack*, 1857, T53-10, Equity Papers A Miscellaneous, Circuit Court, Baltimore City, MSA.

52 The African Methodist Bethel Church of the City of Baltimore v. Joel P. Carmack, et al., 2 Md. 143 (1849). The chancellor set the matter down for a trial. And his position on the defendant trustees softened. In November 1849, he dissolved the injunction that barred Carmack and the others from involvement in church matters. Chancellor John Johnson, "Order" (November 17, 1849), *African Methodist Bethel Church v. Joel P. Carmack*.

53 "Bethel Church Case of Baltimore," *Sun*, June 26, 1851.

54 James M. Wright, "The Free Negro in Maryland," in *Columbia University Studies in the Social Sciences*, Issue 97, ed. Faculty of Political Science, Columbia University (New York: Columbia University, 1921), 1–319, 234.

55 "Committed," *Sun*, July 20, 1852. "Inciting a Riot in Church," *Sun*, August 10, 1852.

56 "Fatality among Horses," *Sun*, November 5, 1852.

57 "Arrested for Receiving Stolen Property," *Sun*, October 18, 1865, and "The Case of Darius Stokes," *Sun*, October 21, 1856. Stokes would later sue his San Francisco church, seeking payment for a promissory note in a case not unlike his Maryland dispute over lumber charges. "Case of Haskell v. Cornish," *Sun*, April 1, 1859.

58 "Assault," *Sun*, March 19, 1852.

59 "Laying of a Church Corner-Stone," *Sun*, August 21, 1865.

60 This congregation was incorporated under the name Colored People's First Baptist Church in the City of Baltimore, referred to in this chapter as First Baptist.

61 "Incorporation of the Colored People's First Baptist Church in the City of Baltimore," Liber TK 57/158, 98–101, CM143/CR39175, Charter Records, Baltimore County Court, MSA. *Clayton and Coates, et al. v. John Carey, John Atkins, et al.*, 200.145.4; *John Atkins & others v. Moses M. Clayton, Josiah Coates & others*, 200.145.4.4; "Briefs," S37504, 1853, Court of Appeals; and *Moses M. Clayton, Josiah Coates & others v. John Carey, John Atkins & others*, in Docket, Court of Appeals, S412-5, December 1851–December 1854, MSA.

62 "Articles of Incorporation" (March 6 and March 14, 1837), *Clayton v. Carey* (Clayton v. Carey, 4 Md 26, [June 1853]), case no. 4, Briefs, S375-5, 1853, Court of Appeals, MSA.

63 [The Maryland Union Baptist Association], *Sun*, October 22, 1841.

64 "Maryland Union Baptist Association," *Sun*, November 12, 1844.

65 "$7,000 Raised at Moses Clayton Memorial Heritage Luncheon," *Baltimore Afro-American*, December 8, 1979.

66 In 1841 Clayton reported having lost his pocketbook, which contained his family's "free papers" as well as documents that evidenced his ordination in the church. "Lost in Washington City," *Sun*, September 18, 1841.

67 George F. Adams et al., *History of Baptist Churches in Maryland Connected with the Maryland Baptist Union Association* (Baltimore: J. F. Weishampel Jr., 1885), 87.

68 "The Return of the Agents from British Guiana and Trinidad," *Sun*, April 18, 1840. Clayton's church did not host this meeting; Bethel Church was the venue, perhaps

because it had a larger sanctuary. But Clayton participated in the program, providing "singing and praying."

69 "Complaint" (February 14, 1852), *Clayton v. Carey*, MSA.
70 " Injunction Dissolution" (April 20, 1852), in *Clayton v. Carey*, MSA.
71 "Opinion" (Legrand) (June 23, 1853), *Clayton v. Carey*, MSA.
72 A. Briscoe Koger, *Negro Baptists of Maryland* (Baltimore: A. B. Koger, 1946).
73 On Davis and Second Baptist, see ibid.; also Mechal Sobel, *Trabelin' On: The Slave Journey to an Afro-Baptist Faith* (Princeton, NJ: Princeton University Press, 1988).
74 Crane's speech at the opening of the new Second Colored Baptist sanctuary in 1855 is reprinted in Noah Davis, *A Narrative of the Life of Rev. Noah Davis, a Colored Man* (Baltimore: John F. Weishampel Jr., 1859).
75 On religious liberty in Maryland generally, see Kenneth Lasson, "Free Exercise in the Free State: Maryland's Role in Religious Liberty and the First Amendment," *Journal of Church and State* 31, no. 3 (1989): 419–49; and Kenneth Lasson, "Free Exercise in the Free State: Maryland's Role in the Development of First Amendment Jurisprudence," *University of Baltimore Law Review* 18 (Fall 1988): 81–109. See also Leonard Williams Levy, *The Establishment Clause: Religion and the First Amendment* (Chapel Hill: University of North Carolina Press, 1994); Mark Douglas McGarvie, *One Nation under Law: America's Early National Struggles to Separate Church and State* (DeKalb: Northern Illinois University Press, 2004); George Petrie, *Church and State in Early Maryland* (Baltimore: Johns Hopkins University Press, 1892).

6 BY VIRTUE OF UNJUST LAWS

1 Martin Robinson Delany, *The Condition, Elevation, Emigration, and Destiny of the Colored People of the United States* (Philadelphia: published by the author, 1852). On Delany and his text, see Robert S. Levine, *Martin Delany, Frederick Douglass, and the Politics of Representative Identity* (Chapel Hill: University of North Carolina Press, 1997), 58–98.
2 Delany, *Condition, Elevation, Emigration, and Destiny*, 49–66.
3 Delany's position with respect to rights reflects what Hendrik Hartog explains as a constitutional-rights consciousness based on a utopian vision – when African Americans are wronged there must be a remedy – and a theory of political legitimacy in which, to remain legitimate, the state must endorse such rights claims. Hendrik Hartog, "The Constitution of Aspiration and 'The Rights That Belong to Us All,' " *Journal of American History* 74, no. 3 (December 1987): 1013–34.
4 "Address of the Colored National Convention to the People of the United States," *Proceedings of the National Convention Held in Rochester on the 6th, 7th and 8th of July, 1853* (Rochester, NY: Frederick Douglass' Paper, 1853), 7–18.
5 "Address of the Colored National Convention to the People of the United States," *Proceedings of the National Convention held in Rochester on the 6th, 7th and 8th of July, 1853*, reprinted in *Minutes of the Proceedings of the National Conventions, 1830–1864*, ed. Howard H. Bell (New York: Arno Press and New York Times, 1969), 25.
6 Ibid., 16.

7   Article 3, section 43 of the 1851 constitution read, "The Legislature shall not pass any law abolishing the relation of master or slave, as it now exists in the state." *Debates and Proceedings of the Maryland Reform Convention to Revise the State Constitution: To Which Are Prefixed the Bill of Rights and Constitution Adopted,* 2 vols. (Annapolis, MD: William N'Neir, 1851), 1:8.

8   Ibid., 1:196. Prior to the adoption of the 1809 state constitution, free men of color had been eligible to vote and had exercised that in Maryland. See Bogen, "The Annapolis Poll Books of 1800 and 1804." Noteworthy here is that the right to vote was further qualified by citizenship, with eligible voters being limited to those individuals who were "at the time of the election a citizen of the United States." This provision tightly bound the rights of Maryland "residents" to their status as US citizens.

9   Ibid., 1:196.

10   Ibid., 1:259–60.

11   Ibid., 1:5.

12   Ibid., 2:220–23.

13   Ibid.

14   Ibid. The report included population numbers over time, net increases in population by county, ratios of black to white Marylanders, and number of manumissions.

15   Ibid.

16   Ibid.

17   Willa Banks, "Curtis Washington Jacobs: Architect of Absolute Black Enslavement, 1850–1864," *Maryland Historical Magazine* 104, no. 2 (Summer 2009): 120–43. Dustin Meeker, "Curtis W. Jacobs' Diary and Account Book, 1854–1866," *Maryland Historical Magazine* 106, no. 1 (Spring 2011): 135–35.

18   *Debates and Proceedings of the Maryland Reform Convention* 2:865–66. J. W. Harry, in a 1902 analysis of the convention generally, explains that the proceedings were unnecessarily protracted and, in the final weeks, chaotic. Harry concludes that the failure to consider Jacobs's report was tied to earlier debates over article 21, though his suggestion that the report's proposed amendments were redundant once article 21 had been amended appears unlikely. While changes to article 21 were intended to make possible the compulsory removal of free black people from the state, the committee report went more precisely to their rights while they remained in Maryland, and further introduced a ban on the ownership of real property, a subject that had never come up during the extensive debates over article 21. James Warner Harry, *The Maryland Constitution of 1851* (Baltimore: Johns Hopkins University Press, 1902).

19   The proceedings of this convention are reprinted in "A Typical Colonization Convention," *Journal of Negro History* 1 (June 1916): 318–38; "The Free Colored People's Convention," *Sun,* July 29, 1852; "Oppressive Legislation – Colonization," *National Era,* May 27, 1852; and Philip S. Foner and George E. Walker, eds., *Proceedings of the Black State Conventions, 1840–1865,* vol. 2 (Philadelphia: Temple University Press, 1980), 42–49.

20   "A Typical Colonization Convention," 322.

21   "A Typical Colonization Convention."

22   Ibid.

23   On the colonization movement in Maryland, see Christopher Phillips, "The Dear Name of Home: Resistance to Colonization in Antebellum Baltimore," *Maryland*

Historical Magazine 91, no. 2 (1996): 180–202; Penelope Campbell, *Maryland in Africa: The Maryland State Colonization Society, 1831–1857* (Urbana: University of Illinois Press, 1971); and Aaron Stopak, "The Maryland State Colonization Society: Independent State Action in the Colonization Movement," *Maryland Historical Magazine* 63, no. 3 (1968): 275–98. Alex Lovit, "'The Bounds of Habitation': The Geography of the American Colonization Society, 1816–1860," PhD diss., University of Michigan, 2011.

24 "A Typical Colonization Convention." Phillips, "The Dear Name of Home."

25 *Constitution and Laws of Maryland in Liberia with an Appendix of Precedents: Published by Authority of the Maryland State Colonization Society*, 2nd ed. (Baltimore: John D. Toy, 1847). On the Maryland State Colonization Society's Liberia colony generally, see Campbell, *Maryland in Africa*.

26 A Colored Canadian, "To the Editor," *Frederick Douglass' Paper*, August 26, 1853.

27 C. Christopher Brown, "Maryland's First Political Convention by and for Its Colored People," *Maryland Historical Magazine* 88, no. 3 (October 1993): 297–325.

28 This episode in Baltimore occurred alongside the broader emergence of an African American emigration movement in the United States. In the wake of the Fugitive Slave Act of 1850, many free black Americans doubted their future in the United States and organized around relocation to Africa, the Caribbean, and elsewhere. Floyd J. Miller, *The Search for a Black Nationality: Black Emigration and Colonization, 1787–1863* (Urbana: University of Illinois Press, 1975); Chris Dixon, *African America and Haiti: Emigration and Black Nationalism in the Nineteenth Century* (Westport, CT: Greenwood Press, 2000). Baltimore's emigration debates were linked through the city's connection to men such as William Watkins who, while living in the North, still wrote for the antislavery press under the moniker "The Colored Baltimorean." Bettye J. Gardner, "Opposition to Emigration: A Selected Letter of William Watkins (The Colored Baltimorean)," *Journal of Negro History* 67, no. 2 (1982): 155–58.

29 Hendrik Hartog, "The Public Law of a County Court: Judicial Government in Eighteenth Century Massachusetts," *American Journal of Legal History* 20, no. 4 (October 1976): 282–329, 291.

30 For these insights into the practice and the culture of licensing in Baltimore, I am deeply indebted to historian Robert Gamble, who generously shared his work on this subject. Robert J. Gamble, "Civic Economies: Commerce, Regulation, and Public Space in the Antebellum City," PhD diss., Johns Hopkins University, 2014.

31 Groves v. Slaughter, 40 U.S. 449 (1841).

32 Also in *Moore v. Illinois*, the court concluded that whatever restrictions the commerce clause might impose on the state, no act of the federal legislature could prohibit the individual states from exercising their police powers and sanctioning those who imported and harbored fugitives. This was consistent, the court explained, with the right of the individual states to impose regulations for the "restraint and punishment of crime, for the preservation of the health and morals of her citizens, and of the public peace." Among those who might be properly excluded pursuant to such legislation were fugitive slaves, paupers, criminals, and liberated slaves, otherwise known as free African Americans. Moore v. Illinois, 55 U.S. 13 (1852): 18, 11.

33   Smith v. Turner, 48 U.S. 283 (1849).

34   *Smith v. Turner*, 472. See Andrew C. Porter, "Comment: Toward a Constitutional
     Analysis of the Right to Intrastate Travel," *Northwestern University Law Review* 86,
     no. 3 (April 1992): 820–1169; Heather E. Reser, "Comment: Airline Terrorism: The
     Effect of Tightened Security on the Right to Travel," *Journal of Air Law and
     Commerce* 63, no 4 (May 1998): 819–49; Christopher S. Maynard, "Note: Nine-
     Headed Caesar: The Supreme Court's Thumbs-Up Approach to the Right to
     Travel," *Case Western Reserve Law Review* 51, no. 2 (December 2000): 297–352;
     Jason S. Alloy, "158-County Banishment in Georgia: Constitutional Implications
     under the State Constitutional and the Federal Right to Travel," *Georgia Law
     Review* 36 (Summer 2002): 1083–108.

35   *Smith v. Turner*, 647. In the instance of the *Passenger Cases*, readings of
     the decision were especially widespread. The text of the court's ruling was
     disseminated to an unprecedented extent when Congress ordered 10,000 copies
     of the decision be reprinted in pamphlet form, an innovation that facilitated
     wide reporting on the cases. "Opinions of the Judges of the Supreme Court of
     the United States in the Cases of 'Smith v. Turner' and 'Norris v. the City of
     Boston,'" *Southern Quarterly Review* 16, no. 32 (January 1850): 444–502.
     For one discussion of the significance for nineteenth-century legal culture of
     the wide dissemination of the case, see Alfred L. Brophy, "'A Revolution Which
     Seeks to Abolish Law, Must End Necessarily in Despotism': Louisa McCord
     and Antebellum Southern Legal Thought," *Cardozo Women's Law Journal* 5,
     no. 1 (1998): 33–77.

36   Regarding the relationship between ideas about European immigrants and
     African Americans, both enslaved and free, see Gerald L. Neuman, "The Lost
     Century of American Immigration Law (1776–1875)," *Columbia Law Review*
     93, no. 8 (December 1993): 1833–1901; Mary S. Bilder, "The Struggle over
     Immigration: : Indentured Servants, Slaves, and Articles of Commerce," *Missouri
     Law Review* 61, no. 4 (1996): 745–819; and Paul Brickner, "The *Passenger Cases*
     (1849): Justice John McLean's 'Cherished Policy' as the First of Three Phases
     of American Immigration Law," *Southwestern Journal of Law and Trade in the
     Americas* 10, no. 1 (2003–2004): 63–80. Another troubled nexus between free
     African Americans and travel surfaced in the 1850s around the matter of US
     passports. Craig Robertson, *The Passport in America: The History of a Document*
     (New York: Oxford University Press, 2010), and Elizabeth Anne Pryor, *Colored
     Travelers: Mobility and the Fight for Citizenship before the Civil War* (Chapel
     Hill: University of North Carolina Press, 2016).

37   On Stump's impeachment, see *Testimony in the Case of Judge Stump, before a Joint
     Committee of the Legislature* (Maryland General Assembly, Joint Committee of
     the Legislature, 1860).

38   "Local Matters [Arrest of Thomas Watkins]," *Sun*, January 5, 1859.

39   Watkins v. State of Maryland, 14 Md. 412 (1859).

40   *In re* Thomas M. Watkins, September 5, 1959, T219-2, MSA.

41   "Baltimore Cattle Market," *New York Daily Times*, June 27, 1854.

42   "Local Matters: Mortality of Baltimore," *Sun*, June 27, 1854.

43   "Local Matters: Fourth of July," *Sun*, June 27, 1854.

44   "Proceedings of the City Council," *Sun*, June 28, 1854, and "Local Matters: Effects
     of the Heat," *Sun*, June 29, 1854.

45 "Local Matters: The Weather," *Sun,* June 28, 1854.

46 Alfred Pairpoint, *Uncle Sam and His Country; or, Sketches of America, 1854–55–56* (London: Simpkin, Marshall, 1857), 219–24.

47 Baltimore's 1848 city directory reports Calhoun as a blacksmith; however, by 1858 he is reported working as a waiter. *Matchett's Baltimore Director, for 1847–8* (Baltimore: R. J. Matchett, 1847), 375, and, John W. Woods, *Woods' Baltimore Directory, for 1858–59* (Baltimore: John W. Woods, 1858), 445.

48 "Charity Govens," Dwelling No. 782, Family No. 960, Ward 5, Baltimore, Maryland, Seventh Census of the United States, 1850, NARA, and, Woods, *Woods' Baltimore Directory, for 1858–59,* 452.

49 Letter to the Editor, *Frederick Douglass' Paper,* August 26, 1853.

50 "Proceedings in the Courts," *Sun,* June 27, 1854.

51 Entry for June 26, 1854, Minutes, 1851–54, T483, Baltimore City, Criminal Court, MSA.

52 In 1844, the year the statute was enacted, the legislature limited the period during which free black residents could leave the state for more than thirty days to May through November. Jeffrey R. Brackett, *The Negro in Maryland: A Study of the Institution of Slavery* (Baltimore: Johns Hopkins University Press, 1889), 177, 179.

53 Since 1807 Maryland had barred the entry of free black people into the state. Ibid., 176.

54 Ibid., 177–83; *The Maryland Code: Public General Laws and Public Local Laws, 1860* (Baltimore: John Murphy & Co., 1860). In the early 1850s these strictures continued to be imposed. "Local Matters: Border Kidnapping," *Sun,* June 17, 1852. As discussed in Neuman, "The Lost Century of Immigration Law," numerous Southern states imposed similar restrictions on the movement of free black residents. Based on his review of the court records, Christopher Phillips reports that between 1832 and 1845, 1,430 free black Baltimoreans submitted travel permit applications; just over half, 55 percent, were men, and just over 27 percent signed with their signatures. Christopher Phillips, *Freedom's Port: The African American Community of Baltimore, 1790–1860* (Urbana: University of Illinois Press, 1997), 168. These statistics reflect only the surviving permit applications. For example, few applications for years after 1845 have survived.

55 Brackett, *The Negro in Maryland,* 175–83.

56 *In re* Robert Murray (June 28, 1845), *In re* John Jones (August 12, 1845), *In re* Julia Prout (July 15, 1845), *In re* Harriet Adams (July 9, 1845), *In re* Ann Boyer (June 9, 1845), and *In re* Thomas Watkins (June 6, 1845), Certificates of Freedom [*sic*], T629-1, 1829–64, Register of Wills, Baltimore City, MSA.

57 This contrasts with cities like Boston, where black lawyers were in practice. William Leonard, "Black and Irish Relations in Nineteenth Century Boston: The Interesting Case of Lawyer Robert Morris," *Historical Journal of Massachusetts* 37, no. 1 (Spring 2009): 64–85.

58 For a sense of this less ideological and more transactional relationship to black litigants, see Eric Foner's discussions of Abraham Lincoln's 1840s law practice in *The Fiery Trial: Abraham Lincoln and American Slavery* (New York: Norton, 2010), 46–51. Foner compares attorney Lincoln's relationships with free black litigants to that of Salmon Chase, whose legal work reflected his ideas about the rights of slaves and free black men and women. Ibid., 43–46.

59 T. Stephen Whitman, *The Price of Freedom: Slavery and Manumission in Baltimore and Early National Maryland* (Lexington: University Press of Kentucky, 1997), 126.

60 *Matchett's Baltimore Director*, 58. Clement Dorsey, *The General Public Statutory Law and Public Local Law of the State of Maryland, from the Year 1692 to 1839 Inclusive: With Annotations Thereto, and a Copious Index* (Baltimore: John D. Toy, 1840), 1530.

61 *The Bench and Bar of Maryland: A History, 1634–1901*, vol. 2 (New York: Lewis Publishing, 1901), 489–90. Brown discussed this episode in his 1887 memoir. George William Brown, *Baltimore and the Nineteenth of April, 1861: A Study of the War*, ed. Kevin C. Ruffner (Baltimore: Johns Hopkins University Press, 1887; 2001); Brackett, *The Negro in Maryland*, 242–46. Just a few years after signing Calhoun's application, Brown would be elected mayor of Baltimore.

62 Richard P. Fuke, "Hugh Lennox Bond and Radical Republican Ideology," *Journal of Southern History* 45, no. 4 (November 1979): 569–86. Bond was also among the leaders of the Baltimore Association for the Moral and Educational Improvement of the Colored People. Richard P. Fuke, "The Baltimore Association for the Moral and Educational Improvement of the Colored People, 1864–1870," *Maryland Historical Magazine* 66, no. 4 (Winter 1971): 369–404.

63 Phillips, *Freedom's Port*, 233. "George W. Brown," in *The Bench and Bar of Maryland*, 2:484–505. "The Maryland State Colonization Society," *Sun*, February 1, 1859.

64 Permit and license holders possessed rights to the extent that court proceedings provided them the "trump" over competing claims. Of course, such rights depended on a range of others for their guarantee, and they could be trumped in the future by a broader public interest. See Hartog, "The Constitution of Aspiration."

65 *Woods' Baltimore Directory, for 1858–59* (Baltimore: John W. Woods, 1858), 18, 445.

66 *Christian Recorder*, October 10, 1863. Charity Govan (October 28, 1878), S1483-1, 1875–80, Index 96, Baltimore City, Maryland Indexes (Death Record, BC, Index), MSA.

67 Alejandro de la Fuente, "Slave Law and Claims-Making in Cuba: The Tannenbaum Debate Revisited," *Law and History Review* 22 (Summer 2004): 339. Also on legal claims making, see Rebecca J. Scott, "Reclaiming Gregoria's Mule: The Meaning of Freedom in the Arimao and Caunao Valleys, Cienfuegos, Cuba, 1880–1899," *Past & Present* [Great Britain] 170 (2001): 181–216. Christopher Waldrep discovers freed people's legal agency in the immediate post-emancipation era in his examination of Black Code-created courts in Mississippi. Christopher Waldrep, "Substituting Law for the Lash: Emancipation and Legal Formalism in a Mississippi County Court," *Journal of American History* 82, no. 4 (March 1996): 1425–51.

68 "Local Matters: Interesting Question," *Sun*, January 4, 1856; "Local Matters: Magisterial Decision," *Sun*, January 5, 1856.

69 "Local Matters: Interesting Question"; "Local Matters: Magisterial Decision." In the 1860 census, Harvey is recorded as a thirty-year-old barber with a wife, Martha, daughter Ellen, seven, and another child, Charles Jackson, also age seven. "Thomas Harvey," Dwelling No. 2, Family No. 2, Ward 17, Baltimore City, Maryland, 1860 US Census, Population Schedule, NARA. In the 1860

City Directory, he is noted as a barber at 67 Hanover with home on Eutaw near Henrietta. *Woods' Baltimore City Directory* (Baltimore: John W. Woods, 1860), 440.

70 *In re* Nancy Johnson (October 8, 1856) and *In re* Peter Bostick (February 24, 1857), Pardon Papers, S1031-15, 1856, Secretary of State, State of Maryland, MSA. Bostick was pardoned by the governor and continued living in Cecil County until at least 1860. The fate of Nancy Johnson we do not know. "Peter Bostick," Dwelling 1306, Family No. 1396, District 2, County of Cecil, Maryland, 1860 U.S. Census, Population Schedule, NARA.

71 "Ex-Judge Richard Grason," *Maryland Journal*, September 23, 1893.

72 Charles Sumner, during the state's 1853 constitutional convention, defended a Massachusetts militia organized without "distinction of color or race." "On the Colored Militia," *Frederick Douglass' Paper*, July 15, 1853.

73 See, generally, Jeffrey R. Kerr-Ritchie, "Rehearsal for War: Black Militias in the Atlantic World," *Slavery and Abolition* 25, no. 1 (April 2005): 1–34, for an insightful overview of black militias. Watkins is quoted from his tract, *Our Rights as Men: An Address Delivered in Boston, before the Legislative Committee on the Militia, February 24, 1853* (Boston: Benjamin R. Roberts, 1853). Nicholas Johnson argues that in the antebellum decades there is evidence of a "budding culture of gun ownership and a commitment to self-defense" among enslaved and free black people. Johnson does not, however, consider cases in which guns were held by license. Nicholas Johnson, *Negroes and the Gun: The Black Tradition of Arms* (Amherst, NY: Prometheus Books, 2014). See also "Distinction by Color in a Bill for Classing the Militia, January 22, 1806, *Congressional Globe*," in Peter M. Bergman and Jean McCarroll, *The Negro in the Congressional Record*, vol. 3: *Seventh to Ninth Congress, 1801–1807* (New York: Bergman Publishers, 1969), 140.

74 Joel Tiffany, *A Treatise on the Unconstitutionality of American Slavery* (Cleveland: J. Calyer, 1849), 117–20. On Tiffany, see Paul Finkelman, ed., *Slavery and the Law* (Lanham, MD: Rowman & Littlefield, 2002); and Saul Cornell, "A New Paradigm for the Second Amendment," *Law and History Review* 22, no. 2 (Spring 2004): 161–67, 166.

75 Robert J. Brent, *Report of Attorney General Brent, to His Excellency, Gov. Lowe, in Relation to the Christiana Treason Trials, in the Circuit Court of the United States* (Annapolis: Thomas E. Martin, 1852), 13.

76 In the incident's wake, thirty-eight men, nearly all free African Americans, were indicted and charged with treason. Still, just one man, Castner Hanway, a local white miller and Parker's neighbor, stood trial. A Philadelphia jury acquitted him. Thomas P. Slaughter, *Bloody Dawn: The Christiana Riot and Racial Violence in the Antebellum North* (New York: Oxford, 1991); Ella Forbes, *But We Have No Country: The 1851 Christiana, Pennsylvania, Resistance* (Cherry Hill, NJ: Africana Homestead, 1998).

77 Jonathan Katz, *Resistance at Christiana: A Documentary Account* (New York: Thomas Y. Crowell Company, 1974), 157.

78 Brent, *Report of Attorney General Brent*, 4.

79 Nicolas W. Proctor, *Bathed in Blood: Hunting and Mastery in the Old South* (Charlottesville and London: University of Virginia Press, 2002), 3–4.

80 Scott E. Giltner, *Hunting and Fishing in the New South: Black Labor and White Leisure after the Civil War* (Baltimore: Johns Hopkins University Press, 2008),

1–5. See also Steven Hahn, "Hunting, Fishing, and Foraging: Common Rights and Class Relations in the Postbellum South," *Radical History Review* 26 (1982): 37–64.

81 The broader subject of arming enslaved people in the Americas is addressed in Christopher Leslie Brown and Philip D. Morgan, eds., *Arming Slaves: From Classical Times to the Modern Age* (New Haven, CT: Yale University Press, 2006).

82 *State v. Daniel Hunt* (negro) (January 25, 1859), Box 10, 1859, C1849-10, Criminal Docket, Criminal Court, Baltimore City, MSA, and *State v. Daniel Hunt* (col.) (No. 83, January Term 1859), C2057-13, City Criminal Docket, Jail, Baltimore City, MSA.

83 *State v. Frank Weeks* (December 10, 1858), Box 9, 1858, C1849-9, Criminal Docket, Criminal Court, Baltimore City, Maryland, MSA.

84 *State v. Dennis Watkins* (June 2, 1858), C2057-13, City Criminal Docket, Jail, Baltimore City, MSA.

85 *State v. William Keys* ("col'd") (January 11, 1859), C2057-13, City Criminal Docket, Jail, Baltimore City, MSA.

86 The Superior Court records reflect appearances by Bowers and Hardy in 1856, 1857, and 1858. Entry of November 16, 1856, C219-1, Minutes, 1851–57, Baltimore City Superior Court, MSA. The court's records reflect that an additional gun permit was granted in 1856. Entry of January 12, 1856, C219-1, Minutes, 1851–57, Baltimore City Superior Court, MSA. On Thursday, November 22, 1855, "Samuel Hardy, a free colored man was granted a license to keep and carry a gun." Entry of November 22, 1855, C219-1, Minutes, 1851–57, Baltimore City Superior Court, MSA. Zaccheus Collins Lee had served as US district attorney from 1848 to 1855, prior to taking the Superior Court bench. Edmund Jennings Lee, *Lee of Virginia, 1642–1892: Biographical and Genealogical Sketches* (Philadelphia: Edmund Jennings Lee, 1895), 466–67.

87 "Nathan Bowers," Dwelling No. 1159, Family No. 1334, Ward 12, Baltimore City, Maryland, 1860 US Federal Census, Population Schedule, NARA.

88 "Samuel Hardy," Dwelling No. 1180, Family No. 1502, Ward 17, Baltimore City, Maryland, 1860 US Federal Census, Population Schedule, NARA.

89 City directories report Hardy's trade as that of carter since at least 1842. *Matchett's Baltimore Director, or Register of Householders* (Baltimore: Baltimore Director Office, 1842), 439.

90 *In re* Samuel Handy (November 22, 1855), C219-1, Minutes, Superior Court, Baltimore City, MSA. *In re* Samuel Handy (November 22, 1855), 1851-56, C251-1, Rough Minutes, Superior Court, Baltimore City, MSA. *In re* Nathan Bowers and *In re* Samuel Handy (November 26, 1856), 1851-56, C251-1, Rough Minutes, Superior Court, Baltimore City, MSA. *In re* Nathan Brown [*sic*] and Samuel Hardy [*sic*] (September 18, 1858), C219-2, Minutes, 1858–62, Superior Court, Baltimore City, MSA. *In re* Nathan Bower [*sic*] and *In re* Samuel Hardy (September 18, 1858), 1851–56, C251-1, Rough Minutes, Superior Court, Baltimore City, MSA.

91 *In re* Alexander Henry Martin (March 11, 1859), C219-2, Minutes, 1858–62, Superior Court, Baltimore City, MSA. *In re* Alexander Henry Martin (March 11, 1859), 1851–56, C251-1, Rough Minutes, Superior Court, Baltimore City, MSA. "Alexander Martin," Dwelling 399, Family No. 441, 14th Ward, Baltimore City, 1860 US Federal Census, NARA. "Proceedings of the First Maryland State

Convention of the Colored Protestant Methodist Churches," *North Star*, November 23, 1849.

92 *In re* Alexander Henry Martin (March 11, 1859), C219-2, Minutes, 1858–62, Superior Court, Baltimore City, MSA. *In re* Alexander Henry Martin (March 11, 1859), 1851–56, C251-1, Rough Minutes, Superior Court, Baltimore City, MSA.

93 "For Court," *Sun*, June 23, 1854.

94 "Local Matters: The Election of Yesterday – The Governor and Mayor – Lawless Proceedings at the Polls," *Sun*, November 5, 1856; "Local Matters: Further Particulars of the Election Riots," *Sun*, November 6, 1856.

95 On Baltimore as "Mobtown," see Richard Chew, "The Origins of Mob Town: Social Division and Racial Conflict in the Baltimore Riots of 1812," *Maryland Historical Magazine* 104, no. 3 (2009): 272–301; Francis F. Beirne, *The Amiable Baltimoreans* (Baltimore: Johns Hopkins University Press, 1984); David Detzer, *Dissonance: The Turbulent Days between Fort Sumter and Bull Run* (New York: Houghton Mifflin Harcourt, 2007); Jessica I. Elfenbein, John R. Breihan, and Thomas L. Hollowak, *From Mobtown to Charm City: New Perspectives on Baltimore's Past* (Baltimore: Maryland Historical Society, 2002); and Paul A. Gilge, "The Baltimore Riots of 1812 and the Breakdown of the Anglo-American Mob Tradition," *Journal of Social History* 13, no. 4 (Summer 1980): 547–64.

96 William J. Novak, *The People's Welfare: Law and Regulation in Nineteenth-Century America* (Chapel Hill: University of North Carolina Press, 1996), 90–95.

97 Unlike in cases with African American litigants, the court clerk did not explicitly designate Europeans as such. Local newspapers did, on occasion, note litigants as "German" or "Irish," in much the same way they would note African Americans as "colored." "Proceedings in the Court," *Sun*, May 15, 1854.

98 "Free Negroes in Virginia," *National Era* (Washington, DC), August 31, 1854.

7 TO SUE AND BE SUED

1 "Could not the space occupied by Dickens' 'Bleak House' be better occupied?" queried James Dawes. Letter from James S. Dawes, *Frederick Douglass' Paper*, August 27, 1852.

2 Baltimoreans also could read *Bleak House* in the pages of *Harper's Magazine*, which advertised its installments in the *Baltimore Sun*. "In Advance!!! *Harper's Magazine* for May," *Sun*, April 26, 1852.

3 Charles Dickens, *American Notes for General Circulation* (London: Chapman and Hall, 1842).

4 For one example of how *Bleak House* was a touchstone for thinking about court reform in Baltimore, see "The New Land of Evidence," *Sun*, June 11, 1852.

5 In 1827 the US Supreme Court ruled that a state bankruptcy law, which operated prospectively, did not violate the US Constitution. Ogden v. Sanders, 25 U.S. 213 (1827). Five years later, in 1832, the court ruled that a Maryland debtor could not discharge a debt incurred in Louisiana in a Maryland state insolvency proceeding. Boyle v. Zacharie, 31 U.S. 635 (1832). After 1841, Congress left the matter of insolvency to the individual states. For an overview of federal bankruptcy legislation through 1867, see Elizabeth Lee Thompson, *The Reconstruction of Southern Debtors: Bankruptcy after the Civil War*

(Athens: University of Georgia Press, 2004). Thompson explains that Congress's 1841 act was in force just one year, and was not replaced until after the Civil War, in 1867. Ibid., 22. See also David A. Skeel Jr., *Debt's Dominion: A History of Bankruptcy Law in America* (Princeton, NJ: Princeton University Press, 2001).

6 For an overview of the changes in Maryland's insolvency laws during the first half of the nineteenth century, see Peter J. Coleman, *Debtors and Creditors in America: Insolvency, Imprisonment for Debt, and Bankruptcy, 1607–1900* (Madison: State Historical Society of Wisconsin, 1974), 162–78.

7 "An Act for the Relief of Insolvent Debtors," Maryland Laws of 1854, chap. 193 (enacted March 10, 1854.). Coleman, *Debtors and Creditors in America*, 162–78.

8 "Appointments by the Governor – Confirmed by the Senate," *Sun*, January 28, 1839; "Commissioner of Insolvent Debtors," *Sun*, March 13, 1854; and "Death of a Citizen," *Sun*, February 27, 1864. Palmer unsuccessfully ran for judge of the Orphan's Court in 1851. *Sun*, July 25, 1851.

9 "The Commissioner of Insolvent Debtors," *Sun*, March 14, 1854. There was a dispute over who was empowered to appoint the new commissioner, the court or the governor. "The Commissioner of Insolvent Debtors," *Sun*, March 13, 1854.

10 Beccaria, "Imprisonment for Debt," *Freedom's Journal*, October 31, 1828.

11 Robert E. Shalope, *The Baltimore Bank Riot: Political Upheaval in Antebellum Maryland* (Urbana: University of Illinois Press, 2009).

12 Historians have explored the general cultural-legal meanings of insolvency. Bruce H. Mann, *Republic of Debtors: Bankruptcy in the Age of American Independence* (Cambridge, MA: Harvard University Press, 2002). Scott Sandage foregrounds the character of the "loser" across US history, juxtaposing the "quest for success" against the "ordeal of failure," in *Born Losers: A History of Failure in America* (Cambridge, MA: Harvard University Press, 2005). See also Edward Balleisen, *Navigating Failure: Bankruptcy and Commercial Society in Antebellum America* (Chapel Hill: University of North Carolina Press, 2001), for a close examination of the records of the 1841 federal Bankruptcy Act.

13 Christopher Phillips, *Freedom's Port: The African American Community of Baltimore, 1790–1860* (Urbana: University of Illinois Press, 1997), 97.

14 "George Hackett," Dwelling No., 610, Family No. 674, 6th Ward, Baltimore, Seventh Census of the United States, 1850, NARA.

15 "The Late Geo. A. Hackett, Esq.," *Christian Recorder*, May 7, 1870.

16 The discussion of Hackett's petition is based on the record in *In re* George Hackett, Case. No. 1113, September 13, 1859, Court of Common Pleas, MSA.

17 *In re* George A. Hackett, Negro Agent (September 13, 1859), Case No. 1113, T515-28, Insolvency Papers, Court of Common Pleas, Baltimore City, MSA.

18 Ibid.

19 Historian Joanna Cohen suggests that these same transactions might be thought of as a manifestation of Hackett's right, as a citizen, "to purchase." Joanna Cohen, "'The Right to Purchase Is as Free as the Right to Sell': Defining Consumers as Citizens in the Auction-house Conflicts of the Early Republic," *Journal of the Early Republic* 30, no. 1 (Spring 2010): 25–62.

20 Benjamin Horwitz, attorney for the railroad company, prepared the interrogatories presented to Hackett. Horwitz is an intriguing figure who appears as an attorney, a trustee, and sometimes a witness in many African Americans' insolvency

filings of the late 1850s. He was the youngest of three brothers in Baltimore, all of whom were lawyers. His eldest brother, Orville, appears to have been the most distinguished of the three. J. Thomas Scharf, *History of Baltimore City and County* (Philadelphia: Louis H. Everts, 1881), 701–2.

21 "Act for the Relief of Insolvent Debtors," sections 7 and 8.

22 *State of Maryland v. Charles Parsons* (col'd), 1849, Criminal Docket, Criminal Court, Baltimore City, MSA.

23 This does not appear to be oversight, in any sense, by the state legislature. Indeed, on the same date that the state enacted its new Act for the Relief of Insolvent Debtors, it also explicitly distinguished the standing of black versus white Marylanders with the Act for the Better Protection of Slaveholders, which prohibited dealings with "any free negro or mulatto, or any negro or mulatto servant or slave" between sunset and sunrise. "An Act for the Better Protections of Slaveholders," Maryland Law of 1854, chap. 194 (March 10, 1854).

24 Records exist for 103 "colored" debtors between 1850 and 1860. They owed a total of $6,132. Only twelve debtors owed more than $100. Hackman Samuel Wilson reported the highest debt, at $1,215. *In re* Samuel Wilson (November 15, 1854), Box 5, T515-14, Insolvency Papers, Court of Common Pleas, Baltimore City, MSA. John Jones, a laborer, reported obligations totaling the lowest amount, $5. *In re* John Jones (June 19, 1851), Box 11, T515-9, 1852, Insolvency Papers, Court of Common Pleas, Baltimore City, MSA.

25 *In re* James H. Jones (April 22, 1857), Box 18, T515-21, Insolvency Papers, Court of Common Pleas, Baltimore City, Court of Common Pleas, MSA.

26 Tony A. Freyer, *Producers versus Capitalists: Constitutional Conflict in Antebellum America* (Charlottesville: University of Virginia Press, 1994).

27 On the history of race and the United States census see, Paul Schor, *Counting Americans: How the US Census Classified the Nation* (New York: Oxford University Press, 2017).

28 "David Pratt," Dwelling No. 740, Family No. 911, 5th Ward, Baltimore, Seventh Census of the United States, 1850, NARA. "David Pratt," Dwelling No. 39, Family No. 45, 5th Ward, Baltimore City, NARA. "Pratt, David," *Matchett's Baltimore Director, for 1855–56* (Baltimore: B. J. Matchett, 1855), 374.

29 "Fortie, Rev. John," *Matchett's Baltimore Director of 1855–56*, 360; "Clayton, Moses C.," ibid., 357.

30 For details on Pratt's creditors, see John W. Woods, *Woods' Baltimore Directory, for 1856–57* (Baltimore: John W. Woods, 1856), 15, 57, 135.

31 *In re* David Pratt, Case no. 561, October 1, 1856, Court of Common Pleas, MSA.

32 Coleman, *Debtors and Creditors in America*, 171.

33 "Act for the Relief of Insolvent Debtors," sections 2 and 11.

34 In at least two insolvency cases heard prior to Pratt's, African American men served as court-appointed trustees. Joshua Lucas was appointed trustee in the case of Wesley Thomas. *In re* Wesley Thomas (Negro Bricklayer) (July 26, 1853), Case No. 112, Box 7, T515-33, Insolvency Papers, Court of Common Pleas, Baltimore City, MSA. Thomas Nevitt was appointed trustee in connection with the petition of George Taylor. *In re* George Taylor (Negro Laborer) (September 22, 1852), Case No. 201, Box 7, T515-33, Insolvency Papers, Court of Common Pleas, Baltimore City, MSA.

35 "Proceedings of the Court," *Sun*, November 30, December 1, and December 3, 1853.

36 *In re* Jonathan Trusty (Negro Stevedore) (December 2, 1853), Case No. 172, Box 7, T515-33, Insolvency Papers, Court of Common Pleas, Baltimore City, MSA.

37 Ibid.

38 Ibid.

39 T600, Orphan's Court Docket, 1854–61, Register of Wills, Baltimore City, MSA; and T604, Orphan's Court Proceedings, 1851–70, Register of Wills, Baltimore City, MSA.

40 Owings was a courthouse regular owing to his repeated efforts to control the labor of black Baltimoreans, enslaved and free. Caleb D. Owings, "One Hundred Dollars Reward," *Sun*, October 15, 1849 (runaway Benjamin Marshall Hardy). *Caleb D. Owings v. Henry Williams* (a negro boy) (June 5, 1855), T600-2, 1855, Orphan's Court Docket, Register of Wills, Baltimore City, MSA. In *Owings v. Burgess*, Owings successfully petitioned to extend the term of service or sell out of state eighteen-year-old Elias Burgess. Owings subsequently sold Burgess to William Kriesmann. *William Kriesman v. Elias Burgess* (a negro boy) (June 27, 1855), T-621, Petitions, Orphan's Court, Register of Wills, Baltimore City, MSA. (January 9, 1855), T600-2, 1855, Orphan's Court Docket, Register of Wills, Baltimore City, MSA. *Owings v. Burgess*, T604-3, 1854–56, Orphan's Court Proceedings, Register of Wills, Baltimore City, MSA.

41 "Gibbs Ebenezer," *Matchett's Baltimore Director for 1855–56* (Baltimore: B. J. Matchett, [1855]), 125 (Laborer, 91 Bethel).

42 *Owings v. Williams* (a certain negro boy), T604-3, 1854–56, Orphan's Court Docket, Register of Wills, Baltimore City, MSA; and T600-2, 1855, Orphan's Court Proceedings, Register of Wills, Baltimore City, MSA.

43 On the writ of habeas corpus generally, see Paul D. Halliday, *Habeas Corpus: From England to Empire* (Cambridge, MA: Harvard University Press, 2010).

44 "Local Matters," *Sun*, April 13, 1854. "Snell, Charles," in R. J. Matchett, *Matchett's Baltimore Directory for 1851* (Baltimore: Richard J. Matchett, 1851), 337 (Laborer, 90 Orchard).

45 "Local Matters," *Sun*, April 13, 1854. *Matchett's Baltimore Directory for 1851*, 337. *Matchett's Baltimore Directory* for 1855–56, 414. *Woods' Baltimore City Directory Ending Year 1860* (Baltimore: John W. Woods, 1860), 454. *Woods' Baltimore Directory, for 1856–57* (Baltimore: John W. Woods, 1856), 319.

46 "Charles Snell," Dwelling No. 5071, Family No. 5295, 18th Ward, Baltimore City, 1860 US Federal Census, Population Schedule, NARA.

47 "Michael Moan," Ship Ellen Brooks (June 1, 1840), Baltimore. Passenger Lists of Vessels Arriving at Baltimore, 1820–81. NARA.

48 "Lost," *Sun*, December 22, 1840.

49 "To the Public," *Sun*, November 6, 1840.

50 D. Randall Beirne, "The Impact of Black Labor on European Immigration into Baltimore's Oldtown, 1790–1910," *Maryland Historical Magazine* 83, no. 4 (Winter 1988): 331–45. The pace of Irish immigration increased after the that country's 1846 potato famine.

51 Historian Seth Rockman recommends caution in relying on these numbers, pointing out that even official tallies from this period were certainly undercounts. Seth Rockman, *Scraping By: Wage Labor, Slavery, and Survival in Early Baltimore* (Baltimore: Johns Hopkins University Press, 2008), 285n36. Phillips, *Freedom's Port*, 195.

52 By 1870 Germans would outnumber Irish immigrants to Baltimore by a ratio of 5 to 2. Beirne, "Impact of Black Labor," 336.

53 Ibid., 336.

54 "Shipping Intelligence," *Pilot and Transcript*, May 28, 1840. The ship was reported to have landed at Baltimore on May 27; it remained in quarantine for two weeks, until June 10. "Shipping Intelligence," *Baltimore Pilot*, June 10, 1840. The trip from Liverpool was completed in just over seven weeks, as the ship cleared that port on April 14. "Liverpool," *Pilot and Transcript* (Baltimore), May 18, 1840.

55 "Summary of News," *Boston Recorder*, June 12, 1840.

56 "Police Intelligence," *Sun*, June 2, 1840.

57 "Liverpool, April, 1840," *Sun*, November 7, 1840.

58 "Caution to the Public," *Sun*, November 5, 1840.

59 "St. Patrick's Church," *Sun*, November 8, 1841.

60 "Local Matters," *Sun*, October 27, 1847.

61 "Notice," *Sun*, May 5, 1852.

62 "Proceedings of the Courts," *Sun*, February 6, 1855.

63 "Proceedings of the Courts, Criminal Court," *Sun*, December 5, 1857.

64 "John McBride vs. John and Michael Moan," *Sun*, January 26, 1853. "Benjamin Ringgold vs. Michael Moan," *Sun*, May 17, 1855. "Michael Moan vs. M. B. Cline," *Sun*, May 26, 1855. "Michael Moan vs. Patrick Nay," *Sun*, June 4, 1855. "William Leech vs. M. Moan," *Sun*, January 28, 1856. "Michael Moan vs. James Haggerty," *Sun*, May 24, 1856. "Thomas Kelley vs. Michael Moan," *Sun*, October 3, 1855.

65 *Matchett's Baltimore Director, for 1849–50* (Baltimore: R. J. Matchett, 1849), 277; R. J. Matchett, *Matchett's Baltimore Directory for 1851* (Baltimore: Richard J. Matchett, 1851), 191. *Matchett's Baltimore Director for 1853–54*, 217; *Matchett's Baltimore Director for 1855–56*, 237; *Woods' Baltimore Directory, for 1856–57*, 186. From time to time Moan published notices in the paper of cows straying from his property, sometimes offering a reward for their return. "Strayed," *Sun*, June 14, 1855; "Strayed," *Sun*, October 28, 1863.

66 "The Diseases of Nightmen," *Retrospect of the Medical Sciences* 5, no. 110 (November 5, 1842): 121 (reprinted from *Annales d'Hygiene Publique*, July 1842).

67 The privy system of New York City has received the most careful study of those in the nineteenth-century United States. Joan H. Geismar, "What Is Night Soil? Thoughts on an Urban Privy," *Historical Archaeology* 27, no. 2 (1993) 57–70.

68 "Local Matters," *Sun*, July 8, 1850.

69 "Benjamin Hill" (slave) (January 8, 1854), Entry 2298, C2057-11,1854–54, City Criminal Docket, Jail, Baltimore City, MSA. (Stealing an building flow valve worth $8. Released.) Entry for April 1, 1854, T483-1, Minutes, 1851–54, Baltimore City, Criminal Court, MSA.

70 "James Johnson to Michael Moan" (indenture) (March 1, 1851), Folder 20, C192-1, Indentures, Register of Wills, Baltimore City, MSA. *Michael Dorsey v. James Johnson* (a negro boy) (August 14, 1854), Box 183, T621-18, 1851–58, Petitions, Register of Wills, Baltimore City, MSA. *Michael Dorsey v. James Johnson* (a negro apprentice) (February 7 1855), T600-2, 1855, Orphan's Court Docket, Register of Wills, Baltimore City, MSA. *Michael Dorsey v. James Johnson* (negro apprentice) (1856), T600-3, 1856, Orphan's Court Docket, Register of Wills, Baltimore City, MSA. *Michael Dorsey v. James Johnson* (negro apprentice) (January 22,

1856), T621-18, Petition, Orphan's Court, Register of Wills, Baltimore City, MSA. *Michael Dorsey v. James Johnson* (negro apprentice), (February 16, 1856), C160-2, 1853–66, Appeals and Issues, Register of Wills, Baltimore City, MSA. *Dorsey v. Johnson* (negro apprentice) (June 4, 1858), T621-18, Petitions, Orphan's Court, Register of Wills, Baltimore City, MSA.

71 *Michael Moan v. William Jones* (a negro boy), T604-3, 1854–56, Proceedings, Orphan's Court, Register of Wills, Baltimore City, MSA. *Michael Moan vs. William Jones* (a negro boy) (April 25, 1855), T600-2, 1855, Orphan's Court Docket, Register of Wills, Baltimore City, MSA. "Ran Away from the Subscriber," *Sun*, September 2, 1856.

72 *Henrietta Right, by her next friend Maria Johnson v. Michael Moan* (January 24, 1855), Petitions, Orphan's Court, Register of Wills, Baltimore City, MSA.

73 "This is to Give Notice," *Sun*, February 2, 1849.

74 "Died," *Sun*, September 26, 1851.

75 *Henrietta Right, by her next friend Maria Johnson v. Michael Moan.* "Legislative Acts/Legal Proceedings," *Sun*, February 17, 1855.

76 *Henrietta Right, by her next friend Maria Johnson v. Michael Moan.*

77 Petition of Mary Johnson, *Isabella Jolly vs. Michael Moan* (January 24, 1855), Petitions, Orphan's Court, Register of Wills, Baltimore City, MSA. "Legislative Acts/Legal Proceedings," *Sun*, February 17, 1855.

78 *Isabella Jolly vs. Michael Moan* (July 6, 1855), Petitions, Orphan's Court, Register of Wills, Baltimore City, MSA. "Legislative Acts/Legal Proceedings," *Sun*, June 28, 1855.

79 "Proceedings of the Courts: City Circuit Court," *Sun*, July 14, 1855.

80 Suzanne Daly, "Belligerent Instruments: The Documentary Violence of *Bleak House*," *Studies in the Novel* 47, no. 1 (Spring 2015): 20–42.

81 On the architecture of antebellum courthouses, see Martha J. McNamara, *From Tavern to Courthouse: Architecture and Ritual in American Law, 1685–1860* (Baltimore: Johns Hopkins University Press, 2004).

8 CONFRONTING *DRED SCOTT*

1 "The First Colored Convention," *Anglo-African Magazine*, October 1859.

2 "Washington, Dec. 16," *Sun*, December 17, 1856; "United States Supreme Court," *Sun*, December 17, 1856; "The Dred Scott Freedom Trial," *Sun*, December 18, 1856; "The Freedom Trial," *Sun*, December 19, 1856; "Washington, March 6," *Sun*, March 7, 1857; "The Dred Scott Decision," *Sun*, March 10, 1857; and "The Dred Scott Case in New York," *Sun*, March 11, 1857.

3 "Free Colored Persons in Arkansas," *Sun*, January 24, 1857.

4 "Colored Persons at the South," *Sun*, February 5, 1857.

5 "Colored Persons in the South," *Sun*, February 5, 1857. "Negro Testimony," *Sun*, January 14, 1857.

6 "A Bill," *Sentinel of Freedom*, January 20, 1857.

7 "Mixing Colors," *Sun*, March 4, 1857.

8 Among the leaders of the convention was the former slave William Yates. "From California," *Sun*, January 15, 1857.

9 Gatchell served the City Court from 1845 to 1851. "Local Matters: City Court," *Sun*, February 2, 1845.

10 "The Baltimore Fugitive Slave in Philadelphia," *Sun*, January 19, 1857.

11 "Petition of William H. Gatchell in the Fugitive Slave Petition Book, January 13, 1857," Record Group 21: Records of District Courts of the United States, 1685–2009, National Archives Catalog, https://research.archives.gov/id/278903.

12 Eric H. Walther, *The Shattering of the Union: America in the 1850s* (New York: Rowman & Littlefield, 2004), 115.

13 "Baltimore Fugitive Slave in Philadelphia."

14 "Philadelphia," *Sun*, February 4, 1857. "The Philadelphia Slave Case: The Fugitive Given Up to His Owner," *Sun*, January 19, 1857, and February 2, 1857.

15 "'State Sovereignty' and Black Seamen," *Alexandria Gazette*, February 27, 1857. "Colored Seamen," *Sun*, February 27, 1857.

16 "State Sovereignty," *Charleston Mercury*, February 21, 1857.

17 "'State Sovereignty' and Black Seamen."

18 "Annual Meeting of the American Colonization Society," *African Repository*, February 1857.

19 "Thomas Wilson," *Baltimore: Past and Present, with Biographical Sketches of Its Representative Men* (Baltimore: Richardson & Bennett, 1871): 533–37.

20 In the two decades after its 1837 founding, the newspaper's attitude had been, as one scholar put it, "idiosyncratic but ambivalent." The *Sun* ran ads aimed at the recapture of runaways and promoting the sale of enslaved people. At the same time, it criticized the continuation of the international slave trade. Nicholas G. Penniman IV, "Baltimore's Daily Press and Slavery, 1857–1860," *Maryland Historical Magazine* 99, no. 4 (Winter 2004): 491–507.

21 Harold A. Williams, "Light for All: Arunah S. Abell and the Rise of the Baltimore 'Sun,'" *Maryland Historical Magazine* 82, no. 3 (Fall 1987): 197–213.

22 Penniman, "Baltimore's Daily Press and Slavery."

23 Correspondent John Reed, for example, was credited with "attending mostly to court cases" for more than twenty years. Williams, "Light for All."

24 Lawrenson's items were marked "From Our Washington Correspondent." Williams, "Light for All."

25 "Washington, March 6," *Sun*, March 7, 1857. Kingman published under the pen name "Ion." Harold A. Williams, *The Baltimore Sun, 1837–1987* (Baltimore: Johns Hopkins University Press, 1987), 269. He is said to have been the first journalist to set up as a permanent correspondent based in Washington. Rufus R. Wilson, *Washington: The Capital City, and Its Part in the History of the Nation*, vol. 1 (New York: J. B. Lippincott, 1902), 219.

26 "The Decision in the Supreme Court," *Sun*, March 9, 1857.

27 "The Dred Scott Case," *Sun*, March 11, 1857.

28 Don E. Fehrenbacher, *The Dred Scott Case: Its Significance in American Law and Politics* (New York: Oxford University Press, 1978), 155–58.

29 Institutional historians would bestow "great" status on Johnson for his "wit, moral courage, and profound mind," calling him "an undefeated hero of the forum and the bar." H. L. Mencken, *A Monograph of the New Baltimore Court House: One of the Greatest Examples of American Architecture, and the Foremost Court House of the United States; Including an Historical Sketch of the Early Courts of Maryland* (Baltimore: A. Hoen, 1899), 9–28. He would later become a border-state Unionist and support the Thirteenth Amendment. Michael Vorenberg, *Final Freedom: The Civil War, the Abolition of Slavery, and the Thirteenth Amendment* (New York: Cambridge University Press, 2001).

30 Fehrenbacher, *The Dred Scott Case*, 155–58.
31 In addition to chronicling Taney's decisions and his terms on the Baltimore Circuit
    Court bench, local papers reported on his day-to-day activities. See J. W., "Letter
    from Old Point Comfort," *Sun*, August 1, 1851 (noting Taney and his family
    vacationing in Old Point Comfort, VA); "Local Matters," *Sun*, July 16, 1851 (naming
    Taney as one of the honored guests at the St. Mary's College commencement);
    "Local Matters," *Sun*, April 28, 1851 (describing how Taney was in attendance
    at Archbishop Eccleston's funeral); "Married," *Sun*, February 10, 1852 (reporting
    the marriage of Taney's daughter Maria to Richard T. Allison); "Meeting of the
    Members of the Baltimore Bar," *Sun*, July 12, 1853, 1 (reporting that Taney was
    called from his home to preside over a memorial honoring the recently deceased
    Judge John Glenn).
32 See Carl Brent Swisher, *Roger B. Taney* (New York: Macmillan, 1935), 28–37,
    114–15.
33 Ibid., 469–72.
34 Ibid., 353–57.
35 Miner Kilbourne Kellogg's portrait of Taney, measuring just over 75 by 62 inches,
    was completed in 1849.
36 "The Dred Scott Case," *Sun*, March 11, 1857.
37 *Sun*, May 19, 1857, quoted in Penniman, "Baltimore's Daily Press and Slavery."
38 Fehrenbacher discusses these cases in *The Dred Scott Case*, 692, nn. 91 and 92.
39 See Roger Brooke Taney, "Supplement to the Dred Scott Opinion" (1858), in
    Samuel Tyler, *Memoir of Roger Brooke Taney, LL.D., Chief Justice of the Supreme
    Court of the United States* (Baltimore: J. Murphy, 1876), 578.
40 See Dred Scott v. Sandford, 60 U.S. (19 How.) 393, 529–64 (1857). See Lucas E.
    Morel, "The Dred Scott Dissents: McLean, Curtis, Lincoln, and the Public Mind,"
    Journal of Supreme Court History 32, no. 22 (2007): 133, 134–38.
41 See "Can Colored Men Sue in the Federal Courts?" *Washington* (PA) *Reporter*,
    July 22, 1857; "Important Decision in the U.S. Circuit Court: James C. Mitchell
    vs. Charles Lamar," *Chicago Daily Tribune*, July 15, 1857; *Chicago Democratic
    Press*, May 15, 1857; *New York Evening Post*, May 20, 1857; and *National Era*
    (Washington, DC), July 30, 1857.
42 "A Case under the Dred Scott Decision," *New York Herald*, July 13, 1858.
43 "Important Decision in the U.S. Circuit Court."
44 "Can Colored Men Sue in the Federal Courts?"
45 "Important Decision in the U.S. Circuit Court."
46 See, e.g., Opinions of the Justices of the Supreme Judicial Court, on Question
    Propounded by the Senate, 44 Me. 505, 508 (1857) (declining to apply Dred Scott
    when interpreting the phrase "citizen of the United States"); Anderson v. Millikin,
    9 Ohio St. 568, 577 (1859) ("The question is not, what the phrase 'citizen of the
    United States' means in the light of the decision in the case of *Dred Scott v. Sandford*,
    but what the framers of our [state] constitution intended by the use of that phrase,
    and what, in the connection in which it is found, and with the light and knowledge
    possessed when it was used, it was intended to mean."); see also Opinion of the
    Justices of the Supreme Judicial Court, 41 N.H. 553, 553 (1857) (affirming consti-
    tutionality of "[a]n act to secure freedom and the rights of citizenship to persons
    in this State," which was passed by the N.H. House of Representatives on June 26,
    1857). For an example in which a local court declined to follow the reasoning in

Dred Scott to bar an African American from suing, see generally Richard F. Nation, "Violence and the Rights of African Americans in Civil War–Era Indiana: The Case of James Hays," *Indiana Magazine of History* 100, no. 32 (2004): 215–30.

47 *Anderson v. Milliken,* 570. The court was required to interpret an 1851 amendment to the state's constitution, changing its requirement for electorship to "white male citizen of the United States" from "white male inhabitants." The latter, originally used in the state's 1802 constitution, had been widely interpreted to include not only white males but also free men of mixed-race descent whose bloodline was less than half black. *Anderson v. Milliken,* 569–70.

48 *Anderson v. Milliken,* 572, 577.

49 *Opinions of the Justices of the Supreme Judicial Court,* 44 Maine at 507. Fehrenbacher, *The Dred Scott Case,* 688n53.

50 *Opinions of the Justices of the Supreme Judicial Court,* 507–8.

51 *Opinions of the Justices of the Supreme Judicial Court,* 515–16.

52 See Heirn v. Bridault, 37 Miss. 209, 224–25 (1859); Shaw v. Brown, 35 Miss. 246, 315–16 (1858).

53 See *Shaw v. Brown,* 246, 320–21.

54 Ibid., 315.

55 For background on *Shaw,* manumissions, and the right of emancipated black nonresidents to sue for their inheritance in Mississippi courts, see Paul Finkelman, *An Imperfect Union: Slavery, Federalism, and Comity* (Chapel Hill: University of North Carolina Press, 1981), 287–90; Bernie D. Jones, *Fathers of Conscience: Mixed-Race Inheritance in the Antebellum South* (Athens: University of Georgia Press, 2009), 55–57.

56 Heirn v. Bridault, 37 Miss. 209, 224–25 (1859). The majority in *Heirn* rejected *Shaw* and its reliance on comity to hold that a free black woman from Louisiana had no right to sue for her inheritance in Mississippi, ultimately concluding "free negroes ... are to be regarded as alien enemies or strangers prohibited, and without the pale of comity, and incapable of acquiring or maintaining property in this State which will be recognized by our courts." *Heirn v. Bridault,* 233. For a detailed analysis of how Mississippi fit into the broader antebellum trend of states "denying blacks' legal citizenship and insisting on their foreignness," see Kunal M. Parker, "Citizenship and Immigration Law, 1800–1924: Resolutions of Membership and Territory," in *The Cambridge History of Law in America,* vol. 2, ed. Michael Grossberg and Christopher Tomlins (Cambridge: Cambridge University Press, 2008), 168–203.

57 See Heirn v. Bridault, 37 Miss. at 234 (Handy, J., dissenting) (arguing because plaintiff was "alleged to have been a citizen of Louisiana, and the presumption is, that her rights and capabilities as such continue. The question, then, as to her right, as a free person of color of the State of Louisiana, to take a legacy, is the same as that decided in Shaw v. Brown").

58 See Taney, "Supplement to the Dred Scott Opinion," 578–79, 598–608.

59 Roger Brooke Taney to David Perine (June 16, 1857), Box 2, Perine Family Papers, 1783–1941, MS 645, MHS.

60 Fehrenbacher, *The Dred Scott Case,* 687n42, citing Roger Brooke Taney to Caleb Cushing (November 9, 1857), Caleb Cushing Papers, Manuscripts Division, Library of Congress, Washington, DC.

61 Taney, "Supplement to the Dred Scott Opinion," 578–608.

62 Roger B. Taney to J. Mason Campbell, February 19, 1861; and Roger Brooke
    Taney to James Mason Campbell, February 18, 1861, Box 22, MS 469, John Eager
    Howard Papers, 1662–1919, 1817–68 (Roger Brooke Taney Correspondence
    [1817–72]), MHS. Taney did circulate the supplemental opinion privately, for
    example to his "friend Mr Stone, one of the Bar of [Washington, DC]." Roger
    B. Taney to J. Mason Campbell, October 23, 1863 (Washington), Box 22, MS
    469, John Eager Howard Papers, 1662–1919, 1817–68 (Roger Brooke Taney
    Correspondence [1817–72]), MHS. The supplement would finally be published,
    but only after a good amount of wrangling between his family, friends, and his first
    biographer, Samuel Tyler. Samuel Tyler to J. Mason Campbell, November 20, 1864;
    Samuel Tyler to F. M. Etting, November 18, 1864; and David M. Perine to F. M.
    Etting, March 1874, Box 22, MS 469, John Eager Howard Papers, 1662–1919,
    1817–68 (Roger Brooke Taney Correspondence [1817–72]), MHS.
63 Taney, "Supplement to the Dred Scott Opinion," 579–93.
64 Roger B. Taney, "Statement of the Historical Fact in the Opinion of the Supreme
    Court of the United States in the Dred Scott Case," Box 9, Perine Family Papers,
    1783–1941, MS 645, MHS. Taney, "Supplement to the Dred Scott Opinion," 578.
    Historian Don Fehrenbacher characterizes Taney's supplemental opinion as a
    "curious document." Fehrenbacher, *The Dred Scott Case*, 445. The opinion would
    remain unpublished until nearly a decade after Taney's death. See Tyler, *Memoir of
    Roger Brooke Taney*, 485–86.
65 Clare Cushman, *The Supreme Court Justices: Illustrated Biographies, 1789–1993*
    (Washington, DC: Congressional Quarterly, 1993).
66 Horace Gray, *A Legal Review of the Case of Dred Scott, as Decided by the Supreme
    Court of the United States* 57 (1857), 57. Fehrenbacher cites this as an article by
    John Lowell and Horace Gray in *The Law Reporter* (June 1857). Theirs was the
    "aberration" view, which concluded Taney had strayed from his usual style and
    quality of mind.
67 Gray, *A Legal Review*, 9.
68 Taney, "Supplement to the Dred Scott Opinion," 607.
69 Ibid., 608.
70 A review of the docket books of the Federal Circuit Court, Baltimore, for the
    1850s evidences no litigants identified as African American. The first black party to
    appear in that court after 1850 does so in 1863.
71 *In re* James H. Jones (April 22, 1857), Box 18, T515-21, Insolvency Papers, Court
    of Common Pleas, Baltimore City, Court of Common Pleas, MSA. On Root, see
    Wood's Baltimore Directory, for 1856–57 (Baltimore: John W. Woods, 1856),
    289. On Logue, see *Matchett's Baltimore Director, for 1855–56* (Baltimore: B.
    J. Matchett, [1855]), 209.
72 "Proceedings of the Courts," *Sun*, January 6, 1858.
73 *African Methodist Bethel Church v. Joel P. Carmack, et al.*, No. 949, Equity Papers
    A, Miscellaneous, T53-10, 1857, Baltimore City Circuit Court, Baltimore City,
    MSA (Circuit Court Order, May 13, 1857).
74 Jason v. Henderson, 7 Md. 430 (1855).
75 On restricting black testimony, see Jeffrey R. Brackett, *The Negro in Maryland: A
    Study of the Institution of Slavery* (Baltimore: N. Murray, Publication Agent, Johns
    Hopkins University, 1889), 190–94.

76 Maryland Laws of 1717, chap. 13, § 2. Thomas Bacon, *Laws of Maryland at Large* (Annapolis: Jonas Green, 1765).

77 Atwell v. Miller, 11 Md. 348 (1857).

78 See Barbara Jeanne Fields, *Slavery and Freedom on the Middle Ground: Maryland during the Nineteenth Century* (New Haven, CT: Yale University Press, 1985), 66–67.

79 See Fields, *Slavery and Freedom,* 70.

80 On Tubman, see Catherine Clinton, *Harriet Tubman: The Road to Freedom* (Boston: Little, Brown, 2004); Jean M. Humez, *Harriet Tubman: The Life and Life Stories* (Madison: University of Wisconsin Press, 2003); and Kate Clifford Larson, *Bound for the Promised Land: Harriet Tubman, Portrait of an American Hero* (New York: Ballantine, 2004).

81 Fields notes that by 1860 free blacks made up 19 percent of the Eastern Shore's total population. Fields, *Slavery and Freedom,* 70.

82 Last will and testament of William Hughes, November 25, 1850, MSA. In his will Hughes enumerates in detail the property to be left to his children, including land, cattle, sheep, and cash. No express mention is made of his holding property in persons. However, he provided that the "balance" of his estate was to be inherited by his wife, Mary, and this may well have included enslaved people.

83 Bill of Sale, Catherine S. M. Ray to William Hughes, July 8, 1842, Dorchester County Circuit Court, Chattel Records, 1852–60, vol. 776, 195–96, MSA.

84 Dorchester County Circuit Court, Chattel Records, 1852–60, vol. 776, 195–96, FJH 2, MSA CM427-2, MSA.

85 *Samuel Jackson v. Denwood Hughes, William Hughes, and Alward Johnson,* Dorchester County Circuit Court, Equity Papers, T2318-3, MSA.

86 Ibid.

87 Josiah Hughes in following year, 1852, served as a representative to the state's "colored" colonization convention, and in the 1860s he would seek ordination to the ministry in the AME Church. C. Christopher Brown, "Maryland's First Political Convention by and for Its Colored People," *Maryland Historical Society* 88, no. 5 (Fall 1993): 324–35.

88 *Samuel Jackson v. Denwood Hughes, William Hughes, and Alward Johnson,* Dorchester County Circuit Court, Equity Papers, T2318-3, MSA.

89 Bill of Sale and Deed, Alward Johnson from Josiah Hughes and others, March 15, 1851, MSA.

90 Docket entry (October 1851), *Samuel Jackson, negro v. Denwood Hughes and Josiah Hughes exors of William Hughes,* MSA.

91 The court would not remark on this turn of events. Only later, during the Civil War, would the family's manumissions be recorded. Mary and daughter Lilly received freedom papers on December 22, 1863, based on the terms of their sale to William Hughes. The three remaining children remained stayed in the possession of Alward Johnson until after Maryland abolished slavery in November 1864. Their manumission was recorded in the state's overall inventory of slaves in 1867. C-690, Certificates of Freedom, 1851–64, Circuit Court, Dorchester County, MSA.

92 Tony Allan Freyer, *Producers versus Capitalists: Constitutional Conflict in Antebellum America* (Charlottesville: University of Virginia Press, 1994).

93 See Hughes v. Jackson, 12 Md. 450 (1858), 451, 462–63. "Argument of Appellee," *Hughes v. Jackson*, S375-21, Briefs, 1857–58, Court of Appeals, MSA.

94 See *Hughes v. Jackson*, 462 (describing the question presented to the court as "whether a negro can maintain an action in this State, without first averring in his pleadings, and establishing by proof, his freedom"). "Argument of Appellee," *Hughes v. Jackson*, MSA.

95 *Hughes v. Jackson*, 450, 451, 452–55; "Argument of Appellee," *Hughes v. Jackson*, MSA.

96 See *Hughes v. Jackson*, 450, 451, 452–55; "Argument of Appellee," *Hughes v. Jackson*, MSA.

97 See *Hughes v. Jackson*, 450, 451, 452–55; "Argument of Appellee," *Hughes v. Jackson*, MSA.

98 *Hughes v. Jackson*, 455; "Argument of Appellee," *Hughes v. Jackson*, MSA.

99 *Hughes v. Jackson*, 459; "Argument of Appellee," *Hughes v. Jackson*, MSA.

100 *Hughes v. Jackson*, 459; "Argument of Appellee," *Hughes v. Jackson*, MSA.

101 *Hughes v. Jackson*, 459; "Argument of Appellee," *Hughes v. Jackson*, MSA.

102 For a history of the Maryland Court of Appeals, see generally Hall Hammond, "Commemoration of the Two Hundredth Anniversary of the Maryland Court of Appeals: A Short History," *Maryland Law Review* 38, no. 2 (1978): 229–41. Notably, the court was restructured pursuant to the state's new 1851 constitution, which provided for, among other innovations, the election of Maryland Court of Appeals justices for ten-year terms. Ibid., 235.

103 Tyler, *Memoir of Roger Brooke Taney*, 124–25; Carroll T. Bond, *The Court of Appeals of Maryland: A History* (Baltimore: J. Murphy, 1928), 153–61.

104 Tyler, *Memoir of Roger Brooke Taney*, 160; see "The Late Hen. John C. Legrand, Chief Justice of the State of Maryland," *Daily Dispatch* (Richmond), January 11, 1862, 2.

105 Tyler, *Memoir of Roger Brooke Taney*, 163; "The Late Hon. John C. Legrand."

106 See Tyler, *Memoir of Roger Brooke Taney*, 475–76; "The Late Chief Justice Legrand: Meeting of the Members of the Bar – Adjournment of the Court – Funeral of the Deceased," *Sun*, December 31, 1861.

107 Regarding Taney, see Swisher, *Roger B. Taney*, 97–99; Timothy S. Huebner, "Roger B. Taney and the Slavery Issue: Looking Beyond – and Before – Dred Scott," *Journal of American History* 97, no. 1 (June 2010): 32–37. John Carroll Legrand, *Letter to Hon. Reverdy Johnson, on the Proceedings at the Meeting, Held at Maryland Institute, January 10th, 1861* (n.p., 1861); and, Eugene S. Vansickle, "A Transnational Vision for African Colonization: John H. B. Latrobe and the Future of Maryland in Liberia," *Journal Of Transatlantic Studies* 1, no. 2 (2003): 214–32.

108 *Hughes v. Jackson*, 459.

109 *Hughes v. Jackson*, 464. For an overview of Legrand's tenure on the Maryland Court of Appeals, see Bond, *Court of Appeals of Maryland*, 153–61.

110 *Hughes v. Jackson*, 463.

111 *Hughes v. Jackson*, 463–64.

112 Ibid.

113 *Hughes v. Jackson*, 464.

114 Ibid.

115 See *Hughes v. Jackson,* 463–64. The "bundle of rights" metaphor is adapted from T. H. Marshall's view that citizenship cannot be reduced to any specific right and that many Americans throughout time have possessed only a partial version of citizenship. See T. H. Marshall, *Citizenship and Social Class and Other Essays* (Cambridge: Cambridge University Press, 1950), 10–27. While I do not share Marshall's view that citizenship rights can be characterized as progressively amassed, his metaphor displaces the view that citizenship can be reduced to a "yes or no" matter, or that it can be reduced to any one right, such as that of naturalization or the franchise.

116 Legal historian David Bogen carefully examines the legal status of black Marylanders in the early republic and demonstrates that black Marylanders experienced a decline in their standing at the start of the century. David S. Bogen, "The Maryland Context of 'Dred Scott': The Decline in the Legal Status of Maryland Free Blacks, 1776–1810," *American Journal of Legal History* 34, no. 4 (1990): 396–411, and David S. Bogen, "The Annapolis Poll Books of 1800 and 1804: African American Voting in the Early Republic," *Maryland Historical Magazine* 86, no. 1 (1991): 57–65.

117 Curtis M. Jacobs, *Speech of Col. Curtis M. Jacobs, on the Free Colored Population* (Annapolis, MD: Elihu S. Riley, 1860).

118 Ibid.

119 "The Colored Population: Important Bills before the Maryland Legislature," *Sun,* February 2, 1860. Historian Christopher Phillips recounts the struggle over the Jacobs Bill in Phillips, *Freedom's Port: The African American Community of Baltimore, 1790–1860* (Champaign: University of Illinois Press, 1997), 232–34.

120 Delphic, "Our Baltimore Letter," *Weekly Anglo-African,* February 18, 1860.

121 One white minister wrote to the *Weekly Anglo-African* to express his outrage and his objections to the bill. "The Conflict in Maryland," *Weekly Anglo-African,* March 3, 1860.

122 "The Legislature and the Colored Population," *Sun,* February 9, 1860, quoting the *Somerset Union.*

123 On Murray, see Elizabeth Dowling Taylor, *The Original Black Elite: Daniel Murray and the Story of a Forgotten Era* (New York: Amistad, 2017); Billie E. Walker, "Daniel Alexander Payne Murray (1852–1925), Forgotten Librarian, Bibliographer, and Historian," *Libraries & Culture* 40, no. 1 (Winter 2005): 25–37; and Robert L. Harris, "Daniel Murray and 'The Encyclopedia of the Colored Race,'" *Phylon* 37, no. 3 (1976): 270–82.

124 Daniel Murray Papers, 1881–1955, 1966, Micro 577, Wisconsin Historical Society, Madison.

CONCLUSION

1 "The Late Attack upon Surgeon Augusta, in Baltimore," *Lyceum Observer,* June 5, 1863. "The Late Outrage upon Surgeon Augusta, in Baltimore," *Christian Recorder,* May 20, 1863. C. Peter Ripley et al., eds., *The Black Abolitionist Papers,* vol. 5 (Chapel Hill: University of North Carolina Press, 1992), 205–11, and Claudia Floyd, *Union-Occupied Maryland: A Civil War Chronicle of Civilians and Soldiers* (Charleston, SC: History Press, 2014).

2   On *Ex parte Merryman* and President Lincoln's suspension of the writ of habeas corpus in that Maryland case, see Jonathan W. White, *Abraham Lincoln and Treason in the Civil War: The Trials of John Merryman* (Baton Rouge: Louisiana State University Press, 2011), and Brian McGinty, *The Body of John Merryman: Abraham Lincoln and the Suspension of Habeas Corpus* (Cambridge, MA: Harvard University Press, 2011). On Baltimore's 1861 Pratt Street riot, see Frank Towers, *The Urban South and the Coming of the Civil War* (Charlottesville: University of Virginia Press, 2004), and "'A Vociferous Army of Howling Wolves': Baltimore's Civil War Riot of April 19, 1861," *Maryland Historian* 23, no. 2 (December 1992): 1–27.

3   Edward Bates, *Opinion of Attorney General Bates on Citizenship* (Washington, DC: Government Printing Office, 1863). On the origins of Bates's opinion, see James P. McClure et al., "Circumventing the Dred Scott Decision: Edward Bates, Salmon P. Chase, and the Citizenship of African Americans," *Civil War History* 43, no. 4 (1997): 279–309.

4   Jeffrey R. Brackett, *Notes on the Progress of the Colored People of Maryland since the War* (Baltimore: Johns Hopkins University, 1890).

5   Ibid.

6   The precise timing of Grice's application might be explained by something as simple as his travel schedule between Haiti and the United States. Or he might have heard news that in London, black activist J. Sella Martin had been granted a passport by ambassador to Britain Charles Francis Adams. On Sella Martin, see Elizabeth Anne Pryor, *Colored Travelers: Mobility and the Fight for Citizenship before the Civil War* (Chapel Hill: University of North Carolina Press, 2016), citing "Rev. J. Sella Martin's Farewell to England," *Liberator*, February 28, 1862. Pryor explains that the secretary of state's position on passports would formally change in 1864 to make it clear that black Americans were entitled to such documents.

7   Grice's name is on the manifests of ships traveling between Port-au-Prince and New York into the 1850s and 1860s. Brig *Finance*, Port-au-Prince to Philadelphia (September 21, 1835), Selected Passenger and Crew Lists and Manifests, NARA. *General Marion*, Port Republican to New York (June 15, 1844); schooner *John A. C. Burne*, to New York (August 31, 1859); and brig *Isabel Buermann*, Port-au-Prince to New York (March 12, 1862), Passenger Lists of Vessels Arriving at New York, 1820–97, NARA. On the movement of merchants between Haiti and New York and other Atlantic ports, see Julia Gaffield, "'Outrages on the Laws of Nations': American Merchants and Diplomacy after the Haitian Declaration of Independence," in *The Haitian Declaration of Independence: Creation, Context, and Legacy*, ed. Julia Gaffield (Charlottesville: University of Virginia Press, 2016).

8   Richard P. Fuke, "Blacks, Whites, and Guns: Interracial Violence in Post-Emancipation Maryland," *Maryland Historical Magazine* 92, no. 3 (Fall 1997): 327–47. Fuke provides a rich accounting of how guns were being wielded, used, and spoken about.

9   "Work While It Is Day," *Freedmen's Record*, March 1, 1866. In 1867 the US Circuit Court, sitting in Baltimore, would conclude that the state's apprenticeship laws violated the terms of the Civil Rights Act of 1866. "Judicial," *Christian Recorder*, October 26, 1867.

10 Bettye C. Thomas, "Public Education and Black Protest in Baltimore, 1865–1900," *Maryland Historical Magazine* 73, no. 3 (Fall 1976): 381–91.

11 Bettye Gardner, "Antebellum Black Education in Baltimore," *Maryland Historical Magazine* 71, no. 3 (Fall 1976): 360–66.

12 Richard Paul Fuke, "The Baltimore Association for the Moral and Educational Improvement of the Colored People, 1864–1870," *Maryland Historical Magazine* 66, no. 4 (Winter 1971): 369–404. "An Ordinance Supplementary to an Ordinance Entitled An Ordinance Providing for the Education of Children of Colored Parents in the City of Baltimore" (April 2, 1868), Item 1649, SC5511, Deposit Collection, Baltimore City Archives Records Collection, MSA.

13 Most relevant here are Bond's letters to his wife, "Katie," most of which are undated. Hugh Lennox Bond Papers, 1850–73, MS 1159, MHS.

14 On Bond, see Norman Gross, *Noble Purposes: Nine Champions of the Rule of Law* (Athens: Ohio University Press, 2007).

15 William E. Matthews, "Maryland! My Maryland!" *Lyceum Observer*, June 5, 1863, 1.

16 "Mrs. Frances Ellen Watkins Harper," *Christian Recorder*, February 17, 1866. Melba Joyce Boyd, *Discarded Legacy: Politics and Poetics in the Life of Frances E. W. Harper, 1825–1911* (Detroit: Wayne State University Press, 1994).

17 "New York City Anti-Slavery Society," *National Anti-Slavery Standard*, May 23, 1857.

18 Bettye C. Thomas, "A Nineteenth Century Black Operated Shipyard, 1866–1884: Reflections upon Its Inception and Ownership," *Journal of Negro History* 59, no. 1 (January 1974): 1–12.

19 Thanks to historian Natanya Duncan for making the connection between George Hackett and Henrietta Vinton Davis for me. Natanya Duncan, "'If Our Men Hesitate Then the Women of the Race Must Come Forward': Henrietta Vinton Davis and the UNIA in New York," *New York History* 95, no. 4 (Fall 2014): 558–83.

EPILOGUE

1 "Maryland Court of Appeals Adopts New Foreclosure Rule," *Daily Record*, October 19, 2010.

2 Joseph Roach, *Cities of the Dead: Circum-Atlantic Performance* (New York: Columbia University Press, 1996), xii.

3 The Honorable James F. Schneider, *A Guide to the Clarence M. Mitchell, Jr. Courthouse, Baltimore, Maryland* (Baltimore: Baltimore Courthouse and Law Museum Foundation, 2009). The Baltimore City Circuit Court & Baltimore Bar Library Art Collection in Connection with the Maryland State Archives, MSA SC 5590.

4 "A Room to Chill the Blood," *Sun*, March 23, 2008.

Bibliography

Primary Works Cited

Adams, George F., et al. *History of Baptist Churches in Maryland Connected with the Maryland Baptist Union Association.* Baltimore: J. F. Weishampel Jr., 1885.

The Baltimore Directory of 1822 & 1823. Baltimore: R. J. Matchett, 1822.

Baltimore: Past and Present, with Biographical Sketches of Its Representative Men. Baltimore: Richardson & Bennett, 1871.

Bates, Edward. *Opinion of Attorney General Bates on Citizenship.* Washington, DC: Government Printing Office, 1863.

The Bench and Bar of Maryland: A History, 1634–1901. Vol. 2. New York: Lewis Publishing, 1901.

Bergman, Peter M. and Jean McCarroll, *The Negro in the Congressional Record, 1789–1801.* New York: Bergman Publishers, 1969.

Binney, Horace. *The Alienigenae of the United States under the Present Naturalization Laws.* Philadelphia: C. Sherman, 1853.

Bond, Carroll T. *The Court of Appeals of Maryland: A History.* Baltimore: J. Murphy, 1928.

Bragg, George F. *Men of Maryland.* Baltimore: Church Advocate Press, 1914.

Brent, Robert J. *Report of Attorney General Brent, to His Excellency, Gov. Lowe, in Relation to the Christiana Treason Trials, in the Circuit Court of the United States.* Annapolis, MD: Thomas E. Martin, 1852.

Brown, George William. *Baltimore and the Nineteenth of April, 1861: A Study of the War.* Edited by Kevin C. Ruffner. Baltimore: Johns Hopkins University Press, 2001. First published in 1887.

Brown, William Wells. *The Black Man: His Antecedents, His Genius, and His Achievements.* New York: Thomas Hamilton; Boston: R. F. W. Wallcut, 1863.

Carter, Nathaniel H., William L. Stone, and Marcus T. C. Gould. *Reports of the Proceedings and Debates of the Convention of 1821, Assembled for the Purpose of Amending the Constitution of the State of New York: Containing All the Official Documents, Relating to the Subject, and Other Valuable Matter.* Albany, NY: E. and E. Hosford, 1821.

Catalogue of the Library of the Massachusetts Historical Society. Vol. 2, M–Z. Boston: John Wilson and Son, 1855.

Catalogue of the New-York State Library: 1855. Albany, NY: Charles Van Benthuysen, 1856.

Cobb, Thomas R. R. *An Inquiry into the Law of Negro Slavery.* Philadelphia: T. & J. W. Johnson; Savannah: W. Thorne Williams, 1858.

Constitution and Laws of Maryland in Liberia with an Appendix of Precedents: Published by Authority of the Maryland State Colonization Society. 2nd ed. Baltimore: John D. Toy, 1847.

Cowley, Robert. "Extracts from a Memorial from the Free People of Color to the Citizens of Baltimore." In Henry Clay, *The Speeches of Henry Clay, Delivered in the Congress of the United States.* Philadelphia: Carey & Lea, 1827.

Davis, Noah. *A Narrative of the Life of Rev. Noah Davis, a Colored Man.* Baltimore: John F. Weishampel Jr., 1859.

Debates and Proceedings of the Maryland Reform Convention to Revise the State Constitution: To Which Are Prefixed the Bill of Rights and Constitution Adopted. 2 vols. Annapolis, MD: William N'Neir, 1851.

Delany, Martin Robinson. *The Condition, Elevation, Emigration, and Destiny of the Colored People of the United States.* Philadelphia: published by the author, 1852.

Dickens, Charles. *American Notes for General Circulation.* London: Chapman and Hall, 1842.

Digest of Patents, Issued by the United States, from 1790 to January 1, 1839. Washington, DC: Peter Force, 1840.

The Doctrines and Discipline of the African Methodist Episcopal Church. Philadelphia: Richard Allen and Jacob Tapisco for the African Methodist Connection, 1817.

Dorsey, Clement. *The General Public Statutory Law and Public Local Law of the State of Maryland, from the Year 1692 to 1839 Inclusive: With Annotations Thereto, and a Copious Index.* Baltimore: John D. Toy, 1840.

Foner, Philip S., and George E. Walker, eds. *Proceedings of the Black State Conventions, 1840–1865.* Vol. 1. Philadelphia: Temple University Press, 1979.

Proceedings of the Black State Conventions, 1840–1865. Vol. 2. Philadelphia: Temple University Press, 1980.

Garrison, William Lloyd. *The Letters of William Lloyd Garrison.* Vol. 1, *I Will Be Heard! 1822–1835,* edited by Walter M. Merrill. Cambridge, MA: Belknap Press of Harvard University Press, 1971.

Goodell, William. *Views of American Constitutional Law, in Its Bearing upon American Slavery.* Utica, NY: Jackson & Chaplin, 1844.

Gray, Horace. *A Legal Review of the Case of Dred Scott, as Decided by the Supreme Court of the United States.* Boston: Crosby, Nichols, and Company, 1857.

Handy, James A. *Scraps of African Methodist Episcopal History.* Philadelphia: A.M.E. Book Concern, [1902].

Hurd, John Codman. *The Law of Freedom and Bondage in the United States.* Boston: Little, Brown; New York: Van Nostrand, 1858.

Index to the Law of Maryland: From the Year 1838 to the Year 1845, Inclusive. Annapolis, MD: Riley & Davis, 1846.

Jay, William. *Miscellaneous Writings on Slavery.* Boston: J. P. Jewett & Co.; Cleveland: Jewett, Proctor, and Worthington, 1853.

Journal of the Proceedings of the Senate of the State of Maryland. Annapolis, MD: Wm. McNeir, 1831.

Kent, James. *Commentaries on American Law, in Four Volumes.* New York: O. Halsted, 1826–30.

Latrobe, John H. B. *The Justices' Practice under the Laws of Maryland.* Baltimore: F. Lucas, 1826.

Latrobe, John H. B., and Fielding Lucas. *Picture of Baltimore, Containing a Description of All Objects of Interest in the City and Embellished with Views of the Principal Public Buildings.* Baltimore: F. Lucas Jr., 1832.

Lee, Edmund Jennings. *Lee of Virginia, 1642–1892: Biographical and Genealogical Sketches.* Philadelphia: Edmund Jennings Lee, 1895.

Legrand, John Carroll. *Letter to Hon. Reverdy Johnson, on the Proceedings at the Meeting, Held at Maryland Institute, January 10th, 1861.* N.p., 1861.

Lewis, R[obert] B. *Light and Truth: Collected from the Bible and Ancient and Modern History, Containing the Universal History of the Colored and the Indian Race, from the Creation of the World to the Present Time.* Boston: Committee of Colored Gentlemen, 1836.

Lundy, Benjamin. *The War in Texas.* Philadelphia: Merrihew and Gunn, 1836.

The Maryland Code: Public General Laws and Public Local Laws, 1860. Baltimore: John Murphy & Co., 1860.

Mason, Richard. *Journal of the Proceedings of the House of Delegates of the State of Maryland at a December Session Eighteen Hundred and Thirty Eight.* Annapolis, MD: by authority [J. Green, 1839].

Matchett's Baltimore Director, or Register of Householders. Baltimore: Baltimore Director Office, 1842.

Mencken, H. L. *A Monograph of the New Baltimore Court House: One of the Greatest Examples of American Architecture, and the Foremost Court House of the United States; Including an Historical Sketch of the Early Courts of Maryland.* Baltimore: A. Hoen, 1899.

Mercier, Henry James, and William Gallop. *Life in a Man-of-War, or Scenes in "Old Ironsides" during Her Cruise in the Pacific, by a Fore-Top-Man.* Philadelphia: Lydia M. Bailey, 1841.

Minutes and Proceedings of the First Annual Convention of the People of Colour, Held by Adjournments in the City of Philadelphia, from the Sixth to the Eleventh of June, Inclusive, 1831. Philadelphia: Committee of Arrangements, 1831.

Minutes and Proceedings of the Second Annual Convention, for the Improvement of the Free People of Color in These United States. Philadelphia: The Convention, 1832.

Minutes and Proceedings of the Third Annual Convention, for the Improvement of the Free People of Color in these United States. New York: The Convention, 1833.

Minutes of the Fifth Annual Convention for the Improvement of the Free People of Colour in the United States, Held by Adjournments, in the Wesley Church, Philadelphia. Philadelphia: William F. Gibbons, 1835.

Minutes of the Proceedings of the Fourteenth American Convention for Promoting the Abolition of Slavery, and Improving the Condition of the African Race, assembled at Philadelphia. Philadelphia: W. Brown, 1816.

Nell, William Cooper. *The Colored Patriots of the American Revolution, with Sketches of Several Distinguished Colored Persons: To Which Is Added a Brief*

Survey of the Condition and Prospects of Colored Americans. Boston: Robert
F. Wallcut, 1855.

Services of Colored Men, in the Wars of 1776 and 1812. Boston: Prentiss & Sawyer,
1851.

Nott, Samuel. *Slavery, and the Remedy, or, Principles and Suggestions for a Remedial
Code.* 3rd ed. Boston: Crocker and Brewster, 1856.

*Official Opinions of the Attorneys General of the United States, Advising the President
and Heads of Departments in Relation to Their Official Duties.* Edited by Benjamin
F. Hall. Washington, DC: Robert Farnham, 1852.

Ohio Anti-Slavery Society. *Report of the Third Anniversary of the Ohio Anti-Slavery
Society, Held in Granville, Licking County, Ohio, on the 30th of May, 1838.*
Cincinnati: Samuel A. Alley, 1838.

The Ordinances of the Mayor and City Council of Baltimore. Baltimore: John D. Toy,
1838.

Pairpoint, Alfred. *Uncle Sam and His Country; or, Sketches of America, 1854-55-56.*
London: Simpkin, Marshall, 1857.

Payne, Bishop Daniel Alexander. *Recollections of Seventy Years.* Edited by C. S. Smith.
Nashville: Publishing House of the AME Sunday School Union, 1888.

Pennington, James W. C. *Text Book of the Origin and History of the Colored People.*
Hartford: L. Skinner, 1841.

*Proceedings and Debates of the Convention of the Commonwealth of Pennsylvania, to
Propose Amendments to the Constitution, Commenced and Held at Harrisburg,
on the Second Day of May, 1837.* 14 vols. Harrisburg, PA: Packer, Barrett, and
Parke, 1837-39.

*Proceedings of the National Convention held in Rochester on the 6th, 7th and 8th of
July, 1853.* Rochester, NY: Frederick Douglass' Paper, 1853.

*Regulations, Circulars, Orders & Decisions, for the Guide of Officers of the Navy of
the United States, Continued in Part and Issued since the Publication Authorized
by the Navy Department in March, 1832.* Washington, DC: C. Alexander, 1851.

*Report of Messrs. Peck and Price, Who Were Appointed at a Meeting of the Free Colored
People of Baltimore, Held on the 25th November, 1839, Delegates to Visit British
Guiana, and the Island of Trinidad.* Baltimore: Woods & Crane, 1840.

Resolutions of the People of Color, at a Meeting Held on the 25th of January, 1831.
New York: n.p., 1831.

Rules, Regulations, and Instructions for the Naval Service of the United States.
Washington City: K. DeKrafft, 1818.

Scharf, J. Thomas. *History of Baltimore City and County.* Philadelphia: Louis
H. Everts, 1881.

Semmes, John E. *John H. B. Latrobe and His Times, 1803-1891.* Baltimore: Norman,
Remington, 1917.

Smith, C. S. *A History of the African Methodist Episcopal Church.* Philadelphia: Book
Concern of the AME Church, 1922.

Speeches of John Sergeant of Pennsylvania. Philadelphia: E. L. Carey & A. Hart, 1832.

Story, Joseph. *Commentaries on the Constitution of the United States . . . in Three
Volumes.* Boston: Hilliard, Gray, 1833.

Stroud, George M. *A Sketch of the Laws Relating to Slavery in the Several States of the
United States of America.* Philadelphia: Kimber and Sharpless, 1827.

Testimony in the Case of Judge Stump, before a Joint Committee of the Legislature.
Maryland General Assembly, Joint Committee of the Legislature, 1860.
Tiffany, Joel. *A Treatise on the Unconstitutionality of American Slavery.* Cleveland: J.
Calyer, 1849.
Turnbull, David. *Travels in the West: Cuba; with Notice of Porto Rico, and the Slave
Trade.* London: Lorgman, Orme, Brown, Green, and Longmans, 1840.
Turner, Nat. *The Confessions of Nat Turner.* Edited by Thomas R. Gray.
Baltimore: Thomas R. Gray, 1831.
Tyson, John Shoemaker. *Life of Elisha Tyson, the Philanthropist.* Baltimore: B.
Lundy, 1825.
Watkins, William. *Address Delivered before the Moral Reform Society, in Philadelphia,
August 8, 1836.* Philadelphia: Merrihew and Gunn, 1836.
Wattles, A., and A. Hopkins. *Memorial to the General Assembly of the State of Ohio.*
Cincinnati: Pugh & Dodd, 1838.
Wheeler, Jacob D. *A Practical Treatise on the Law of Slavery.* New York: Allan Pollock;
New Orleans: Benjamin Levy, 1837.
Wilson, Rufus R. *Washington: The Capital City, and Its Part in the History of the
Nation.* Vol. 1. New York: J. B. Lippincott, 1902.
Wirt, William. *The Letters of a British Spy: Originally Published in the Virginia Argus,
in August and September 1803.* Richmond: Samuel Pleasants Jr., 1803.
The Rainbow; First Series: Originally Published in the Richmond Enquirer.
Richmond: Ritchie & Worsley, 1804.
The Life and Character of Patrick Henry. New York: McElrath, Bangs, 1833.
Woods' Baltimore Directory, for 1858–59. Baltimore: John W. Woods, 1858.
Wright, Richard R. *Centennial of the African Methodist Church.* Philadelphia: Book
Concern of the A.M.E. Church, 1916.
Yates, William. *Rights of Colored Men to Suffrage, Citizenship and Trial by Jury: Being
a Book of Facts, Arguments and Authorities, Historical Notices and Sketches of
Debates – With Notes.* Philadelphia: Merrihew and Gunn, 1838.

Secondary Works Cited

Abel, Laura K., and David S. Udell. "Judicial Independence: If You Gag the Lawyers, Do
You Choke the Courts? Some Implications for Judges When Funding Restrictions
Curb Advocacy by Lawyers on Behalf of the Poor." *Fordham Urban Law Journal*
29 (February 2002): 873–906.
Agarwal, Nisha, and Jocelyn Simonson. "Thinking Like a Public Interest Lawyer: Theory,
Practice, and Pedagogy." *NYU Review of Law and Social Change* 34 (2010).
Alexander, Leslie M. *African or American? Black Identity and Political Activism in
New York City, 1784–1861.* Urbana: University of Illinois Press, 2008.
Alfieri, Anthony V. "Reconstructive Poverty Law Practice: Learning Lessons of Client
Narrative." *Yale Law Journal* 100, no. 6 (April 1991): 2107–47.
Allen, Austin. *Origins of the 'Dred Scott' Case: Jacksonian Jurisprudence and the
Supreme Court, 1837–1857.* Athens: University of Georgia Press, 2006.
Allmendinger, David F., Jr. *Nat Turner and the Rising in Southampton County.*
Baltimore: Johns Hopkins University Press, 2014.

Alloy, Jason S. "158-County Banishment Georgia: Constitutional Implications under the State Constitutional and the Federal Right to Travel." *Georgia Law Review* 36 (Summer 2002): 1083–108.

Anbinder, Tyler. *Five Points: The 19th-Century New York City Neighborhood That Invented Tap Dance, Stole Elections, and Became the World's Most Notorious Slum*. New York: Free Press, 2001.

Anderson, George B. *Landmarks of Rensselaer County, New York*. Syracuse, NY: D. Mason & Co., 1897.

Bacon, Jacqueline. *Freedom's Journal: The First African American Newspaper*. Lanham, MD: Lexington Books, 2007.

Ball, Milner S. *The Word and the Law*. Chicago: University of Chicago Press, 1993.

Ballesien, Edward. *Navigating Failure: Bankruptcy and Commercial Society in Antebellum America*. Chapel Hill: University of North Carolina Press, 2001.

Banks, Willa. "Curtis Washington Jacobs: Architect of Absolute Black Enslavement, 1850–1864." *Maryland Historical Magazine* 104, no. 2 (Summer 2009): 120–43.

Banks, Willa Young. "A Contradiction in Antebellum Baltimore: A Competitive School for Girls of 'Color' within a Slave State." *Maryland Historical Magazine* 99, no. 2 (June 2004): 132–63.

Beasley, Delilah L. *The Negro Trailblazers of California*. New York: G. K. Hall, 1997. First published in 1919.

Beirne, D. Randall. "The Impact of Black Labor on European Immigration into Baltimore's Oldtown, 1790–1910." *Maryland Historical Magazine* 83, no. 4 (Winter 1988): 331–45.

Beirne, Francis F. *The Amiable Baltimoreans*. Baltimore: Johns Hopkins University Press, 1984.

Bell, Derrick. "Serving Two Masters: Integration Ideals and Client Interests in School Desegregation Litigation." *Yale Law Journal* 85, no. 3 (July 1976): 470–516.

Berlin, Ira. *Slaves without Masters: The Free Negro in the Antebellum South*. New York: Pantheon, 1975.

Bilder, Mary S. "The Struggle over Immigration: Indentured Servants, Slaves, and Articles of Commerce." *Missouri Law Review* 61, no. 4 (1996): 745–819.

Black, Joel E. "A Theory of African-American Citizenship: Richard Westbrooks, the Great Migration, and the Chicago Defender's 'Legal Helps' Column." *Journal of Southern History* 46, no. 4 (Summer 2013): 869–915.

Bogen, David S. "The Annapolis Poll Books of 1800 and 1804: African American Voting in the Early Republic." *Maryland Historical Magazine* 86, no. 1 (1991): 57–65.

——— "The Maryland Context of 'Dred Scott': The Decline in the Legal Status of Maryland Free Blacks, 1776–1810." *American Journal of Legal History* 34, no. 4 (1990): 381–411.

Bolster, W. Jeffrey. *Black Jacks: African American Seamen in the Age of Sail*. Cambridge, MA: Harvard University Press, 1998.

Boyd, Melba Joyce. *Discarded Legacy: Politics and Poetics in the Life of Frances E. W. Harper, 1825–1911*. Detroit: Wayne State University Press, 1994.

Brackett, Jeffrey R. *The Negro in Maryland: A Study of the Institution of Slavery*. Baltimore: Johns Hopkins University Press, 1889.

——— *Notes on the Progress of the Colored People of Maryland since the War*. Baltimore: Johns Hopkins University, 1890.

Breen, Patrick H. *The Land Shall Be Deluged in Blood: A New History of the Nat Turner Revolt.* Oxford: Oxford University Press, 2015.

Brickner, Paul. "The Passenger Cases (1849): Justice John McLean's 'Cherished Policy' as the First of Three Phases of American Immigration Law." *Southwestern Journal of Law and Trade in the Americas* 10, no. 1 (2003–2004): 63–80.

Brodine, Charles E., Jr., Michael J. Crawford, and Christine F. Hughes. *Interpreting Old Ironsides: An Illustrated Guide to USS Constitution.* Washington, DC: Naval Historical Center, Department of the Navy, 2007.

Brooks, Joanna. "The Early American Public Sphere and the Emergence of a Black Print Culture." *William and Mary Quarterly* 62, no. 1 (January 2005): 67–92.

Brophy, Alfred L. "'A Revolution Which Seeks to Abolish Law, Must End Necessarily in Despotism': Louisa McCord and Antebellum Southern Legal Thought." *Cardozo Women's Law Journal* 5, no. 1 (1998): 33–77.

Brown, C. Christopher. "Maryland's First Political Convention by and for Its Colored People." *Maryland Historical Magazine* 88, no. 3 (October 1993): 297–325.

Brown, Christopher Leslie, and Philip D. Morgan, eds. *Arming Slaves: From Classical Times to the Modern Age.* New Haven, CT: Yale University Press, 2006.

Brown, Elsa Barkley. "African-American Women's Quilting: A Framework for Conceptualizing and Teaching African-American Women's History." *Signs: Journal of Women in Culture and Society* 14 (1989): 921–29.

Browne, Gary Lawson. *Baltimore in the Nation, 1789–1861.* Chapel Hill: University of North Carolina Press, 1980.

Brugger, Robert J. *Maryland: A Middle Temperament, 1634–1980.* Baltimore: Johns Hopkins University Press and the Maryland Historical Society, 1988.

Budney, Stephen R. "William Jay (1789–1858)." In *Encyclopedia of Antislavery and Abolition,* vol. 2, edited by Peter Hinks and John McKivigan, 383–85. Westport, CT: Greenwood Press, 2007.

Calderhead, William. "The Role of the Professional Slave Trader in a Slave Economy: Austin Woolfolk, a Case Study." *Civil War History* 23 (September 1977): 195–211.

Campbell, James M. *Slavery on Trial: Race, Class, and Criminal Justice in Antebellum Richmond, Virginia.* Gainesville: University of Florida Press, 2007.

Campbell, James T. *Songs of Zion: The African Methodist Episcopal Church in the United States and South Africa.* New York: Oxford University Press, 1995.

Campbell, Penelope. *Maryland in Africa: The Maryland State Colonization Society, 1831–1857.* Urbana: University of Illinois Press, 1971.

Carroll, Tamar W. *Mobilizing New York: AIDS, Antipoverty, and Feminist Activism.* Chapel Hill: University of North Carolina Press, 2015.

Clemens, Paul G. E. *The Atlantic Economy and Colonial Maryland's Eastern Shore: From Tobacco to Grain.* Ithaca, NY: Cornell University Press, 1980.

Click, Patricia C. *The Spirit of the Times: Amusements in Nineteenth-Century Baltimore, Norfolk, & Richmond.* Charlottesville: University of Virginia Press, 1989.

Cohen, Joanna. "'The Right to Purchase Is as Free as the Right to Sell': Defining Consumers as Citizens in the Auction-house Conflicts of the Early Republic." *Journal of the Early Republic* 30, no. 1 (Spring 2010): 25–62.

Colaisco, James A. *Frederick Douglass and the Fourth of July.* New York: Palgrave Macmillan, 2006.

Coleman, Peter J. *Debtors and Creditors in America: Insolvency, Imprisonment for Debt, and Bankruptcy, 1607–1900*. Madison: State Historical Society of Wisconsin, 1974.

Conkin, Paul K. *Prophets of Prosperity: America's First Political Economists*. Bloomington: Indiana University Press, 1980.

Cook, James W. "Dancing across the Color Line." *Common-Place* 4, no. 1 (October 2003).

Cornell, Saul. "A New Paradigm for the Second Amendment." *Law and History Review* 22, no. 2 (Spring 2004): 161–67.

Cowan, Dave, and Emma Hitchings. "'Pretty Boring Stuff': District Judges and Housing Possession Proceedings." *Social & Legal Studies* 16, no. 3 (2007): 363–82.

Crooms-Robinson, Lisa. "The United States Constitution and the Struggle for African American Citizenship: An Overview." In *The Oxford Handbook of African American Citizenship, 1865–Present*, edited by Henry Louis Gates Jr. et al., 519–20. New York: Oxford University Press, 2012.

Cushman, Clare. *The Supreme Court Justices: Illustrated Biographies, 1789–1993*. Washington, DC: Congressional Quarterly, 1993.

Daly, Suzanne. "Belligerent Instruments: The Documentary Violence of *Bleak House*." *Studies in the Novel* 47, no. 1 (Spring 2015): 20–42.

Daniels, Douglas H. *Pioneer Urbanites: A Social and Cultural History of Black San Francisco*. Philadelphia: Temple University Press, 1980.

Davidson, George A. "The Lawyer's Perspective: Celebrating the Courthouse." *The Green Bag: An Entertaining Journal of Law* 11 (Winter 2008): 159–70.

Davis, David Brion. *The Problem of Slavery in the Age of Emancipation*. New York: Alfred A. Knopf, 2014.

DeKay, James T. *Chronicles of the Frigate Macedonian, 1809–1922*. New York: Norton, 1995.

De la Fuente, Alejandro. "From Slaves to Citizens? Tannenbaum and the Debates on Slavery, Emancipation, and Race Relations in Latin America." *International Labor & Working-Class History* 77, no. 1 (Spring 2010): 154–73.

"Slave Law and Claims-Making in Cuba: The Tannenbaum Debate Revisited." *Law and History Review* 22, no. 2 (Summer 2004): 339–69.

Della, M. Ray, Jr. "An Analysis of Baltimore's Population in the 1850s." *Maryland Historical Magazine* 68, no. 1 (March 1973): 20–35.

DeLombard, Jeannine Marie. *Slavery on Trial: Law, Abolitionism, and Print Culture*. Chapel Hill: University of North Carolina Press, 2007.

Detzer, David. *Dissonance: The Turbulent Days between Fort Sumter and Bull Run*. New York: Houghton Mifflin Harcourt, 2007.

Deyle, Steven. *Carry Me Back: The Domestic Slave Trade in American Life*. New York: Oxford University Press, 2005.

Dillon, Merton L. *Benjamin Lundy and the Struggle for Negro Freedom*. Urbana: University of Illinois Press, 1966.

Dixon, Chris. *African America and Haiti: Emigration and Black Nationalism in the Nineteenth Century*. Westport, CT: Greenwood Press, 2000.

Dunbar, Erica Armstrong. *A Fragile Freedom: African American Women and Emancipation in the Antebellum City*. New Haven, CT: Yale University Press, 2008.

Dyer, Justin Buckley. "Lincolnian Natural Right, Dred Scott, and the Jurisprudence of John McLean." *Polity* 41, nos. 1–4 (January 2008): 63–85.

Edwards, Laura F. *The People and Their Peace: Legal Culture and the Transformation of Inequality in the Post-Revolutionary South.* Chapel Hill: University of North Carolina Press, 2009.

Elfenbein, Jessica I., John R. Breihan, and Thomas L. Hollowak. *From Mobtown to Charm City: New Perspectives on Baltimore's Past.* Baltimore: Maryland Historical Society, 2002.

Ely, Melvin Patrick. *Israel on the Appomattox: A Southern Experiment in Black from the 1790s through the Civil War.* New York: Knopf, 2004.

Engler, Russell. "And Justice for All – Including the Unrepresented Poor: Revisiting the Roles of the Judges, Mediators, and Clerks." *Fordham Law Review* 67 (April 1999): 1987–2068.

Fanning, Sarah. *Caribbean Crossing: African Americans and the Haitian Emigration Movement.* New York: New York University Press, 2015.

"The Early Roots of Black Nationalism: Northern African Americans' Invocations of Haiti in the Early Nineteenth Century." *Slavery and Abolition* 28, no. 1 (April 2007): 61–85.

Fehrenbacher, Don E. *The Dred Scott Case: Its Significance in American Law and Politics.* New York: Oxford University Press, 1978.

Fields, Barbara Jeanne. *Slavery and Freedom on the Middle Ground: Maryland during the Nineteenth Century.* New Haven, CT: Yale University Press, 1987.

Fields, Karen E., and Barbara J. Fields. *Racecraft: The Soul of Inequality in American Life.* London: Verso, 2012.

Finkelman, Paul. *An Imperfect Union: Slavery, Federalism, and Comity.* Chapel Hill: University of North Carolina Press, 1981.

ed. *Slavery and the Law.* Lanham, MD: Rowman & Littlefield, 2002.

Flexner, James Thomas. *States Dyckman: American Loyalist.* New York: Fordham University Press, 1992.

Floyd, Claudia. *Union-Occupied Maryland: A Civil War Chronicle of Civilians and Soldiers.* Charleston, SC: History Press, 2014.

Foner, Eric. *The Fiery Trial: Abraham Lincoln and American Slavery.* New York: Norton, 2010.

Forbes, Ella. *But We Have No Country: The 1851 Christiana, Pennsylvania, Resistance.* Cherry Hill, NJ: Africana Homestead, 1998.

Frey, Donald E. "The Puritan Roots of Daniel Raymond's Economics." *History of Political Economy* 32, no. 3 (Fall 2000): 607–29.

Freyer, Tony A. *Producers versus Capitalists: Constitutional Conflict in Antebellum America.* Charlottesville: University of Virginia Press, 1994.

Fuke, Richard P. "The Baltimore Association for the Moral and Educational Improvement of the Colored People, 1864–1870." *Maryland Historical Magazine* 66, no. 4 (Winter 1971): 369–404.

"Blacks, Whites, and Guns: Interracial Violence in Post-Emancipation Maryland." *Maryland Historical Magazine* 92, no. 3 (Fall 1997): 327–47.

"Hugh Lennox Bond and Radical Republican Ideology." *Journal of Southern History* 45, no. 4 (November 1979): 569–86.

Gaffield, Julia. "'Outrages on the Laws of Nations': American Merchants and Diplomacy after the Haitian Declaration of Independence." In *The Haitian Declaration of Independence: Creation, Context, and Legacy*, edited by Julia Gaffield. Charlottesville: University of Virginia Press, 2016.

Gamble, Robert J. "Civic Economies: Commerce, Regulation, and Public Space in the Antebellum City." PhD diss., Johns Hopkins University, 2014.

Gardner, Bettye. "Ante-bellum Black Education in Baltimore." *Maryland Historical Magazine* 71, no. 3 (1976): 360–66.

"Opposition to Emigration: A Selected Letter of William Watkins (The Colored Baltimorean)." *Journal of Negro History* 67, no. 2 (1982): 155–58.

"William Watkins: Antebellum Black Teacher and Writer." *Negro History Bulletin* 39, no. 6 (1976): 623–24.

Gardner, Eric. *Jennie Carter: A Black Journalist of the Early West.* Jackson: University Press of Mississippi, 2007.

Gee, Harvey. "Is a 'Hearing Officer' Really a Judge? The Presumed Role of 'Judges' in the Unconstitutional New York Housing Court." *New York City Law Review* 5 (Summer 2002): 1.

Geismar, Joan H. "What Is Night Soil? Thoughts on an Urban Privy." *Historical Archaeology* 27, no. 2 (1993) 57–70.

Gellman, David N. *Emancipating New York: The Politics of Slavery and Freedom, 1777–1827.* Baton Rouge: Louisiana State University Press, 2006.

George, Carol V. R. *Segregated Sabbaths: Richard Allen and the Rise of Independent Black Churches: 1760–1840.* New York: Oxford University Press, 1973.

Ghachem, Malick W. *The Old Regime and the Haitian Revolution.* New York: Cambridge University Press, 2012.

Gilfoyle, Timothy J. "'America's Greatest Criminal Barracks': The Tombs and the Experience of Criminal Justice in New York City, 1838–1897." *Journal of Urban History* 29, no. 5 (2003): 525–54.

Gilge, Paul A. "The Baltimore Riots of 1812 and the Breakdown of the Anglo-American Mob Tradition." *Journal of Social History* 13, no. 4 (Summer 1980): 547–64.

Giltner, Scott E. *Hunting and Fishing in the New South: Black Labor and White Leisure after the Civil War.* Baltimore: Johns Hopkins University Press, 2008.

Gold, Roberta. *When Tenants Claimed the City: The Struggle for Citizenship in New York City Housing.* Urbana: University of Illinois Press, 2014.

Gordon, Sarah Barringer. "The African Supplement: Religion, Race, and Corporate Law in Early National America." *William and Mary Quarterly* 72, no. 3 (July 2015): 385–422.

Graber, Mark A. *Dred Scott and the Problem of Constitutional Evil.* New York: Cambridge University Press, 2006.

Graham, Leroy. *Baltimore: The Nineteenth Century Black Capital.* Washington, DC: University Press of America, 1982.

Gross, Ariela J. "Beyond Black and White: Cultural Approaches to Race and Slavery." *Columbia Law Review* 101, no. 3 (April 2001): 640–90.

Double Character: Slavery and Mastery in the Antebellum Southern Courtroom. Princeton, NJ: Princeton University Press, 2000.

Gross, Norman. *Noble Purposes: Nine Champions of the Rule of Law.* Athens: Ohio University Press, 2007.

Grossberg, Michael. *A Judgment for Solomon: The d'Hauteville Case and Legal Experience in Antebellum America.* New York: Cambridge University Press, 1996.

Guyatt, Nicholas. "'The Outskirts of Our Happiness': Race and the Lure of Colonization in the Early Republic." *Journal of American History* 95, no. 4 (March 2009): 986–1011.

Hahn, Steven. "Hunting, Fishing, and Foraging: Common Rights and Class Relations in the Postbellum South." *Radical History Review* 26 (1982): 37–64.

A Nation under Our Feet: Black Political Struggles in the Rural South from Slavery to the Great Migration. Cambridge, MA: Harvard University Press, 2004.

The Political Worlds of Slavery and Freedom. Cambridge, MA: Harvard University Press, 2009.

Halliday, Paul D. *Habeas Corpus: From England to Empire.* Cambridge, MA: Harvard University Press, 2010.

Hamer, Philip M. "Great Britain, the United States, and the Negro Seamen Acts, 1822–1848." *Journal of Southern History* 1, no. 1 (February 1935): 3–28.

Hammond, Hall. "Commemoration of the Two Hundredth Anniversary of the Maryland Court of Appeals: A Short History." *Maryland Law Review* 38, no. 2 (1978): 229–41.

Hancock, Harold B. "William Yates' Letter of 1837: Slavery, and Colored People in Delaware." *Delaware History* 14 (1971): 205–16.

Harper, Frances Ellen Watkins, and Frances Smith Foster. *A Brighter Coming Day: A Frances Ellen Watkins Harper Reader.* New York, New York: Feminist Press, 1990.

Harris, Janette Hoston. "Woodson and Wesley: A Partnership in Building the Association for the Study of Afro-American Life and History." *Journal of Negro History* 83, no. 2 (Spring 1998): 109–19.

Harris, Leslie M. *In the Shadow of Slavery: African Americans in New York City, 1626–1863.* Chicago: University of Chicago Press, 2003.

Harrold, Stanley. *Subversives: Antislavery Community in Washington, D.C., 1828–1865.* Baton Rouge: Louisiana State University Press, 2003.

Hartog, Hendrik. "The Constitution of Aspiration and 'The Rights That Belong to Us All.'" *Journal of American History* 74, no. 3 (December 1987): 1013–34.

"Pigs and Positivism." *Wisconsin Law Review* 4 (August 1985): 899–935.

"The Public Law of a County Court: Judicial Government in Eighteenth Century Massachusetts." *American Journal of Legal History* 20, no. 4 (October 1976): 282–329.

Hildebrand, Reginald F. *The Times Were Strange and Stirring: Methodist Preachers and the Crisis of Emancipation.* Durham, NC: Duke University Press, 1995.

Hoeflich, M. H. *Legal Publishing in Antebellum America* (New York: Cambridge University Press, 2010).

Honig, Bonnie. *Democracy and the Foreigner.* Princeton, NJ: Princeton University Press, 2001.

Huebner, Timothy S. "Roger B. Taney and the Slavery Issue: Looking Beyond – and Before – Dred Scott." *Journal of American History* 97, no. 1 (June 2010): 17–38.

James, Winston. *The Struggles of John Brown Russwurm: The Life and Writings of a Pan-Africanist Pioneer, 1799–1851.* New York: New York University Press, 2010.

Johnson, Nicholas. *Negroes and the Gun: The Black Tradition of Arms.* Amherst, NY: Prometheus Books, 2014.

Johnson, Walter. "On Agency." *Journal of Social History* 37, no. 1 (Fall 2003): 113–24.

River of Dark Dreams: Slavery and Empire in the Cotton Kingdom. Cambridge, MA: Harvard University Press, 2013.

Jones, Bernie D. *Fathers of Conscience: Mixed-Race Inheritance in the Antebellum South.* Athens: University of Georgia Press, 2009.

Jones, Martha S. *All Bound Up Together: The Woman Question in African American Public Culture*. Chapel Hill: University of North Carolina Press, 2007.

"The Case of Jean Baptiste, un Créole de Saint-Domingue: Narrating Slavery, Freedom, and the Haitian Revolution in Baltimore City." In *The American South and the Atlantic World*, edited by Brian Ward, Martin Bone, and William A. Link, 104–28. Gainesville: University Press of Florida, 2013.

"Leave of Court: African-American Legal Claims Making in the Era of Dred Scott v. Sandford." In *Contested Democracy: Politics, Ideology, and Race in American History*, edited by Manisha Sinha and Penny Von Eschen, 54–74. New York: Columbia University Press, 2007.

Kale, Madhavi. *Fragments of Empire: Capital, Slavery, and Indian Indentured Labor in the British Caribbean*. Philadelphia: University of Pennsylvania Press, 2010.

Kantrowitz, Stephen. *More Than Freedom: Citizenship in a White Republic, 1829–1889*. New York: Penguin, 2012.

Kaplan, Sidney. "Herman Melville and the American National Sin: The Meaning of Benito Cereno." In *American Studies in Black and White: Selected Essays, 1949–1989*. Amherst: University of Massachusetts Press, 1996.

Karasch, Mary C. *Slave Life in Rio de Janeiro, 1808–1850*. Princeton, NJ: Princeton University Press, 1987.

Katz, Jonathan. *Resistance at Christiana: A Documentary Account*. New York: Thomas Y. Crowell Company, 1974.

Kelly, Alfred H. "Clio and the Court: An Illicit Love Affair." *Supreme Court Review* 1965 (1965): 119–58.

Kerr-Ritchie, Jeffrey R. "Rehearsal for War: Black Militias in the Atlantic World." *Slavery and Abolition* 25, no. 1 (April 2005): 1–34.

Kersch, Ken I. "Beyond Originalism: Conservative Declarationism and Constitutional Redemption." *Maryland Law Review* 71 (2016): 229–82.

Kessler, Mark. "Legal Mobilization for Social Reform: Power and the Politics of Agenda Setting." *Law & Society Review* 24, no. 1 (1990): 121–43.

Klein, Herbert S., and Francisco Vidal Luna. *Slavery in Brazil*. New York: Cambridge University Press, 2010.

Knight, Franklin W. *Slave Society in Cuba during the Nineteenth Century*. Madison: University of Wisconsin Press, 1970.

Koger, A. Briscoe. *Negro Baptists of Maryland*. Baltimore: n.p., 1946.

Kramer, Larry D. *The People Themselves: Popular Constitutionalism and Judicial Review*. New York: Oxford University Press, 2004.

Landers, Jane. *Atlantic Creoles in the Age of Revolutions*. Cambridge, MA: Harvard University Press, 2011.

Lapp, Rudolph M. *Blacks in Gold Rush California*. New Haven, CT: Yale University Press, 1977.

Lasson, Kenneth. "Free Exercise in the Free State: Maryland's Role in the Development of First Amendment Jurisprudence." *University of Baltimore Law Review* 18 (Fall 1988): 81–109.

"Free Exercise in the Free State: Maryland's Role in Religious Liberty and the First Amendment." *Journal of Church and State* 31, no. 3 (1989): 419–49.

Leonard, William. "Black and Irish Relations in Nineteenth Century Boston: The Interesting Case of Lawyer Robert Morris." *Historical Journal of Massachusetts* 37, no. 1 (Spring 2009): 64–85.

Leslie, William R. "The Pennsylvania Fugitive Slave Act of 1826." *Journal of Southern History* 18, no. 4 (November 1952): 429–45.

Levine, Robert S. *Martin Delany, Frederick Douglass, and the Politics of Representative Identity*. Chapel Hill: University of North Carolina Press, 1997.

Levy, Leonard Williams. *The Establishment Clause: Religion and the First Amendment*. Chapel Hill: University of North Carolina Press, 1994.

Looney, Ginny. "Biting the Budget at Legal Services." *Southern Changes* 4, nos. 4–5 (1983): 257–84.

Lovit, Alex. "'The Bounds of Habitation': The Geography of the American Colonization Society, 1816–1860." Ph D diss., University of Michigan, 2011.

Mahoney, Barry. "The Administration of Justice and Court Reform." *Proceedings of the Academy of Political Science* 31, no. 3 (1974): 58–72.

Mamiya, Lawrence H. "A Social History of the Bethel African Methodist Episcopal Church in Baltimore: The House of God and the Struggle for Freedom." In *American Congregations*. Vol. 1, *Portraits of Twelve Religious Communities*, edited by James P. Wind and James W. Lewis, 221–92. Chicago: University of Chicago Press, 1994.

Mann, Bruce H. *Republic of Debtors: Bankruptcy in the Age of American Independence*. Cambridge, MA: Harvard University Press, 2002.

Maris-Wolf, Ted. *Family Bonds: Free Blacks and Re-enslavement Law in Antebellum Virginia*. Chapel Hill: University of North Carolina Press, 2015.

Marshall, T. H. *Citizenship and Social Class and Other Essays*. Cambridge: Cambridge University Press, 1950.

Martin, Tyrone G. *A Most Fortunate Ship: A Narrative History of Old Ironsides*. Annapolis, MD: Naval Institute Press, 1997.

Masur, Kate. "Patronage and Protest in Kate Brown's Washington." *Journal of American History* 99, no. 4 (March 2013): 1047–71.

May, Nicholas. "Holy Rebellion: Religious Assembly Laws in Antebellum South Carolina and Virginia." *American Journal of Legal History* 49, no. 3 (July 2007): 237–56.

Maynard, Christopher S. "Note: Nine-Headed Caesar: The Supreme Court's Thumbs-Up Approach to the Right to Travel." *Case Western Reserve Law Review* 51, no. 2 (December 2000): 297–352.

Mayne, Alan. "Tall Tales but True? New York's 'Five Points' Slum." *Journal of Urban History* 33, no. 22 (January 2007): 320–31.

McClure, James P., et al. "Circumventing the Dred Scott Decision: Edward Bates, Salmon P. Chase, and the Citizenship of African Americans." *Civil War History* 43, no. 4 (1997): 279–309.

McGarvie, Mark Douglas. *One Nation under Law: America's Early National Struggles to Separate Church and State*. DeKalb: Northern Illinois University Press, 2004.

McManus, Edgar J. *A History of Negro Slavery in New York*. Syracuse, NY: Syracuse University Press, 2001.

McNamara, Martha J. *From Tavern to Courthouse: Architecture and Ritual in American Law, 1685–1860*. Baltimore: Johns Hopkins University Press, 2004.

Meeker, Dustin. "Curtis W. Jacobs' Diary and Account Book, 1854–1866." *Maryland Historical Magazine* 106, no. 1 (Spring 2011): 135–35.

Melton, J. Gordon. "African American Methodism in the M.E. Tradition: The Case of Sharp Street (Baltimore)." *North Star: A Journal of African American Religious History* 8, no. 2 (January 2005).

Melton, Maurice. "African American Maritime Pilots in the South Atlantic Shipping Trade, 1640–1865." *Journal of the Georgia Association of Historians* 27 (2007/2008): 1–26.

Middleton, Stephen. *The Black Laws: Race and the Legal Process in Early Ohio.* Athens: Ohio University Press, 2005.

Miller, Floyd J. *The Search for a Black Nationality: Black Emigration and Colonization, 1787–1863.* Urbana: University of Illinois Press, 1975.

Morel, Lucas E. "The 'Dred Scott' Dissents: McLean, Curtis, Lincoln, and the Public Mind." *Journal of Supreme Court History* 32, no. 22 (2007): 133–51.

Moss, Hilary J. *Schooling Citizens: The Struggle for African American Education in Antebellum America.* Chicago: University of Chicago Press, 2000.

Murray, David R. *Odious Commerce: Britain, Spain and the Abolition of the Cuban Slave Trade.* Cambridge, MA: Cambridge University Press, 1980.

Myers, John L. "American Antislavery Society Agents and the Free Negro, 1833–1838." *Journal of Negro History* 52, no. 3 (July 1967): 200–19.

Nation, Richard F. "Violence and the Rights of African Americans in Civil War–Era Indiana: The Case of James Hays." *Indiana Magazine of History* 100, no. 32 (2004): 215–30.

Neuman, Gerald L. "The Lost Century of American Immigration Law (1776–1875)." *Columbia Law Review* 93, no. 8 (December 1993): 1833–1901.

Nevin, Alfred. *Encyclopædia of the Presbyterian Church in the United States of America.* Philadelphia: Presbyterian Encyclopaedia Publishing, 1884.

Newman, Kathe, and Elvin K. Wyly. "The Right to Stay Put, Revisited: Gentrification and the Resistance to Displacement in New York City." *Urban Studies* 43, nos. 1–4 (2006): 23–57.

Newman, Richard S. *Freedom's Prophet: Bishop Richard Allen, the AME Church, and the Black Founding Fathers.* New York: New York University Press, 2009.

  The Transformation of American Abolitionism: Fighting Slavery in the Early Republic. Chapel Hill: University of North Carolina Press, 2002.

Norgren, Jill. "Lawyers and the Legal Business of the Cherokee Republic in Courts of the United States, 1829–1835." *Law and History Review* 10, no. 2 (Autumn 1992): 235–314.

Novak, William J. "The Legal Transformation of Citizenship in Nineteenth-Century America." In *The Democratic Experiment: New Directions in American Political History*, edited by Meg Jacobs, William J. Novak, and Julian E. Zelizer, 85–119. Princeton, NJ: Princeton University Press, 2003.

  The People's Welfare: Law and Regulation in Nineteenth-Century America. Chapel Hill: University of North Carolina Press, 1996.

Olson, Kevin. "Constructing Citizens." *Journal of Politics* 70, no. 1 (2008): 40–53.

Olson, Sherry H. *Baltimore, the Building of an American City.* Baltimore: Johns Hopkins University Press, 1980.

Page, Max. "From 'Miserable Dens' to the 'Marble Monster': Historical Memory and the Design of Courthouses in Nineteenth-Century Philadelphia." *Pennsylvania Magazine of History and Biography* 119, no. 4 (1995): 299–343.

Palmer, Vernon V. *Through the Codes Darkly: Slave Law and Civil Law in Louisiana.* Clark, NJ: Lawbook Exchange, 2012.

Pamphile, Léon Dénius. *Haitians and African Americans: A Heritage of Tragedy and Hope.* Gainesville: University Press of Florida, 2001.

Penniman, Nicholas G., IV. "Baltimore's Daily Press and Slavery, 1857–1860." *Maryland Historical Magazine* 99, no. 4 (Winter 2004): 491–507.

Penningroth, Dylan. *The Claims of Kinfolk: Africa American Property and Community in the Nineteenth-Century South.* Chapel Hill: University of North Carolina Press, 2003.

Parker, Kunal M. "Citizenship and Immigration Law, 1800–1924: Resolutions of Membership and Territory." In *The Cambridge History of Law in America.* Vol. 2, edited by Michael Grossberg and Christopher Tomlins, 168–203. Cambridge: Cambridge University Press, 2008.

"Making Blacks Foreigners: The Legal Construction of Former Slaves in Post-Revolutionary Massachusetts." *Utah Law Review* 2001 (2001): 75–124.

Making Foreigners: Immigration and Citizenship Law in America, 1600–2000. New York: Cambridge University Press, 2015.

Perl-Rosenthal, Nathan. *Citizen Sailors: Becoming American in the Age of Revolution.* Cambridge, MA: Harvard University Press, 2015.

Petrie, George. *Church and State in Early Maryland.* Baltimore: Johns Hopkins University Press, 1892.

Phillips, Christopher. "The Dear Name of Home: Resistance to Colonization in Antebellum Baltimore." *Maryland Historical Magazine* 91, no. 2 (1996): 180–202.

Freedom's Port: The African American Community of Baltimore, 1790–1860. Urbana: University of Illinois Press, 1997.

Phillips, Glenn O. "Maryland and the Caribbean, 1634–1984: Some Highlights." *Maryland Historical Magazine* 83, no. 3 (1988): 199–214.

Polgar, Paul J. "'Whenever They Judge It Expedient': The Politics of Partisanship and Free Black Voting Rights in Early National New York." *American Nineteenth Century History* 12, no. 1 (March 2011): 1–23.

Porter, Andrew C. "Comment: Toward a Constitutional Analysis of the Right to Intrastate Travel." *Northwestern University Law Review* 86, no. 3 (April 1992): 820–1169.

Powell, H. Jefferson. "Attorney General Taney and the South Carolina Police Bill." *Green Bag* 2d series 5 (2001): 75–100.

Power-Greene, Ousmane K. *Against Wind and Tide: The African American Struggle against the Colonization Movement.* New York: New York University Press, 2014.

Pratt, Lloyd "Speech, Print, and Reform on Nantucket." In *A History of the Book in America*, Vol. 3, *The Industrial Book, 1840–1880*, edited by Scott E. Casper, Jeffrey D. Groves, Stephen W. Nissenbaum, and Michael Winship, 392–99. Chapel Hill: University of North Carolina Press, 2009.

Primus, Richard A. "The Riddle of Hiram Revels." *Harvard Law Review* 119, no. 6 (April 2006): 1680–734.

Pritchett, Jonathan B. "The Interregional Slave Trade and the Selection of Slaves for the New Orleans Market." *Journal of Interdisciplinary History* 28, no. 1 (Summer 1997): 57–85.

Proctor, Nicolas W. *Bathed in Blood: Hunting and Mastery in the Old South.* Charlottesville: University of Virginia Press, 2002.

Provine, Dorothy S. *District of Columbia Free Negro Registers, 1821–1861.* Bowie, MD: Heritage Books, 1996.

Pryor, Elizabeth Anne. *Colored Travelers: Mobility and the Fight for Citizenship before the Civil War.* Chapel Hill: University of North Carolina Press, 2016.

Quarles, Benjamin. "Charles Harris Wesley." *Proceedings of the American Antiquarian Society* 97, no. 2 (October 1987): 275–79.

Rael, Patrick. *Black Identity and Black Protest in the Antebellum North.* Chapel Hill: University of North Carolina Press, 2002.

Rafferty, Matthew, *The Republic Afloat: Law, Honor, and Citizenship in Maritime America.* Chicago: University of Chicago Press, 2013.

Reid-Vazquez, Michele. *The Year of the Lash: Free People of Color in Cuba and the Nineteenth-Century Atlantic World.* Athens: University of Georgia Press, 2011.

Reser, Heather E. "Comment: Airline Terrorism: The Effect of Tightened Security on the Right to Travel." *Journal of Air Law and Commerce* 63, no. 4 (May 1998): 819–49.

Ridgway, Whitman H. *Community Leadership in Maryland, 1790–1840: A Comparative Analysis of Power in Society.* Chapel Hill: University of North Carolina Press, 1979.

Ripley, C. Peter, et al., eds. *The Black Abolitionist Papers.* Chapel Hill: University of North Carolina Press, 1992.

Roach, Joseph. *Cities of the Dead: Circum-Atlantic Performance.* New York: Columbia University Press, 1996.

Robertson, Craig. *The Passport in America: The History of a Document.* New York: Oxford University Press, 2010.

Rockman, Seth. *Scraping By: Wage Labor, Slavery, and Survival in Early Baltimore.* Baltimore: Johns Hopkins University Press, 2008.

Rothman, Adam. *Slave Country: American Expansion and the Origins of the Deep South.* Cambridge, MA: Harvard University Press, 2007.

Ryan, Mary P. "Democracy Rising: The Monuments of Baltimore, 1809–1842." *Journal of Urban History* 36, no. 2 (2010): 127–50.

Sandage, Scott. *Born Losers: A History of Failure in America.* Cambridge, MA: Harvard University Press, 2005.

Schneider, The Honorable James F. *A Guide to the Clarence M. Mitchell, Jr. Courthouse, Baltimore, Maryland.* Baltimore: Baltimore Courthouse and Law Museum Foundation, 2009.

Schoeppner, Michael. "Legitimating Quarantine: Moral Contagions, the Commerce Clause, and the Limits of Gibbons v. Ogden." *Journal of Southern Legal History* 17, nos. 1/2 (2009): 81–120.

Schor, Paul. *Counting Americans: How the US Census Classified the Nation.* New York: Oxford University Press, 2017.

Scott, Rebecca J. "Paper Thin: Freedom and Re-enslavement in the Diaspora of the Haitian Revolution." *Law and History Review* 29, no. 4 (2011): 1061–87.

   "Reclaiming Gregoria's Mule: The Meaning of Freedom in the Arimao and Caunao Valleys, Cienfuegos, Cuba, 1880–1899." *Past & Present* [Great Britain] 170 (2001): 181–216.

Shalope, Robert E. *The Baltimore Bank Riot: Political Upheaval in Antebellum Maryland.* Urbana: University of Illinois Press, 2009.

Shepard, Kris. *Rationing Justice: Poverty Lawyers and Poor People in the Deep South.* Baton Rouge: Louisiana State University Press, 2007.

Sidbury, James. *Becoming African in America: Race and Nation in the Early Black Atlantic.* New York: Oxford University Press, 2007.

Simpson, A. W. B. "The Rise and Fall of the Legal Treatise: Legal Principles and the Forms of Legal Literature." *University of Chicago Law Review* 48 (Summer 1981): 633–34.

Skeel, David A., Jr. *Debt's Dominion: A History of Bankruptcy Law in America*. Princeton, NJ: Princeton University Press, 2001.

Slaughter, Thomas P. *Bloody Dawn: The Christiana Riot and Racial Violence in the Antebellum North*. New York: Oxford, 1991.

Smith, Rogers M. "The Inherent Deceptiveness of Constitutional Discourse: A Diagnosis and Prescription." *Nomos* 40 (1998): 215–54.

Snorgrass, J. William. "The Black Press in the San Francisco Bay Area, 1856–1900." *California History* 60, no. 4 (1981–82): 306–17.

Sobel, Mechal. *Trabelin' On: The Slave Journey to an Afro-Baptist Faith*. Princeton, NJ: Princeton University Press, 1988.

Stopak, Aaron. "The Maryland State Colonization Society: Independent State Action in the Colonization Movement." *Maryland Historical Magazine* 63, no. 3 (1968): 275–98.

Sullivan, David K. "William Lloyd Garrison in Baltimore, 1829–1830." *Maryland Historical Magazine* 68, no. 1 (1973): 64–79.

Surrency, Erwin C. *A History of American Law Publishing*. Dobbs Ferry, NY: Oceana Publications, 1990.

Swift, David E. *Black Prophets of Justice: Activist Clergy before the Civil War*. Baton Rouge: Louisiana State University Press, 1989.

Swisher, Carl Brent. *Roger B. Taney*. New York: Macmillan, 1935.

Tannenbaum, Frank. *Slave and Citizen, the Negro in the Americas*. New York: Knopf, 1946.

Thomas, Bettye C. "Public Education and Black Protest in Baltimore, 1865–1900." *Maryland Historical Magazine* 73, no. 3 (Fall 1976): 381–91.

Thomas, Lamont D. *Rise to Be a People: A Biography of Paul Cuffe*. Urbana: University of Illinois Press, 1986.

Thompson, Elizabeth Lee. *The Reconstruction of Southern Debtors: Bankruptcy after the Civil War*. Athens: University of Georgia Press, 2004.

Thorp, Galen N. "William Wirt." *Journal of Supreme Court History* 33, no. 3 (2008): 223–303.

Towers, Frank. *The Urban South and the Coming of the Civil War*. Charlottesville: University of Virginia Press, 2004.

Tuckerman, Bayard. *William Jay and the Constitutional Movement for the Abolition of Slavery*. New York: Dodd, Mead, 1894.

Tyler, Samuel. *Memoir of Roger Brooke Taney, LL.D., Chief Justice of the Supreme Court of the United States*. Baltimore: J. Murphy, 1876.

"A Typical Colonization Convention." *Journal of Negro History* 1 (June 1916): 318–38.

Vansickle, Eugene S. "A Transnational Vision for African Colonization: John H. B. Latrobe and the Future of Maryland in Liberia." *Journal of Transatlantic Studies* 1, no. 2 (2003): 214–32.

Volk, Kyle G. *Making Minorities and the Making of American Democracy*. New York: Oxford University Press, 2014.

Volkman, Lucas P. "Church Property Disputes, Religious Freedom, and the Ordeal of African American Methodists in Antebellum St. Louis: Farrar v. Finney (1855)." *Journal of Law & Religion* 27 (2011–12): 83–139.

Von Daacke, Kirt. *Freedom Has a Face: Race, Identity, and Community in Jefferson's Virginia*. Charlottesville: University of Virginia Press, 2012.

Vorenberg, Michael. *Final Freedom: The Civil War, the Abolition of Slavery, and the Thirteenth Amendment*. New York: Cambridge University Press, 2001.

Waldrep, Christopher. *Roots of Disorder: Race and Criminal Justice in the American South, 1817–80*. Urbana: University of Illinois Press, 1998.

"Substituting Law for the Lash: Emancipation and Legal Formalism in a Mississippi County Court." *Journal of American History* 82, no. 4 (March 1996): 1425–51.

Walker, Juliet E. K. *History of Black Business in America: Capitalism, Race, Entrepreneurship*. Chapel Hill: University of North Carolina Press, 2009.

Walther, Eric H. *The Shattering of the Union: America in the 1850s*. New York: Rowman & Littlefield, 2004.

Welke, Barbara Young. *Law and the Borders of Belonging in the Long Nineteenth Century United States*. New York: Cambridge University Press, 2010.

Wesley, Charles H. "Creating and Maintaining an Historical Tradition." *Journal of Negro History* 49, no. 1 (January 1964): 13–33.

White, Shane. *Somewhat More Independent: The End of Slavery in New York City, 1770–1810*. Athens: University of Georgia Press, 1991.

Whitman, T. Stephen. *The Price of Freedom: Slavery and Freedom in Baltimore and Early National Maryland*. New York: Routledge, 1999.

Whittington, Keith E. *Constitutional Construction: Divided Power and Constitutional Meaning*. Cambridge, MA: Harvard University Press, 1999.

Williams, Harold A. *The Baltimore Sun, 1837–1987*. Baltimore: Johns Hopkins University Press, 1987.

"Light for All: Arunah S. Abell and the Rise of the Baltimore 'Sun.'" *Maryland Historical Magazine* 82, no. 3 (Fall 1987): 197–213.

Williams, Patricia J. "The Pain of Word Bondage." Chap. 8 in *The Alchemy of Race and Rights*. Cambridge, MA: Harvard University Press, 1991.

Winch, Julie. *A Gentleman of Color: The Life of James Forten*. New York: Oxford University Press, 2002.

Wong, Edlie L. *Neither Fugitive nor Free: Atlantic Slavery, Freedoms Suits, and the Legal Culture of Travel*. New York: New York University Press, 2009.

Wright, James Martin. *The Free Negro in Maryland, 1632–1860*. New York: Columbia University Press, 1921.

Yamin, Rebecca, ed. *Tales of Five Points: Working-Class Life in Nineteenth-Century New York*. 7 vols. Washington, DC: General Services Administration, 2002.

Young, Ernest A. "Popular Constitutionalism and the Underenforcement Problem: The Case of the National Healthcare Law." *Law and Contemporary Problems* 75, no. 3 (2012): 157–201.

Index

Abell, Arunah, 132
abolitionists, 1, 3, 7, 45, 53, 54, 58, 91, 102–3,
  183n83; Baltimore and, 20, 39, 172n17,
  178n24, 179n31, *see also* antislavery
  movement; emancipation; slavery
Act for the Relief of Insolvent Debtors
  (Maryland), 111, 117, 207n23
Adams, John Quincy, 32, 43
African American political conventions, 37,
  43, 65, 210n8; birthright citizenship rights
  and, 36, 40–41, 63–64; black laws and, 9,
  91, 129; colonization schemes and,
  94–96, 215n87; emigration and, 40, 70;
  free African American citizenship and,
  90–91, 149; Hezekiah Grice and, 36, 40,
  48–49, 149, 182–83n79; voting rights
  and, 9, 63, 64, *see also* Baltimore; New
  York State
African American press, 3, 17, 18–19, 20,
  22–24, 34, 37, 65, 128, 149, 151, *see also*
  Freedom's Journal
African Americans, post-emancipation, xi,
  148, 155, 157, 218n; citizenship rights and,
  5–6, 9, 10, 14–15; education and, 15,
  150–51; as soldiers, 146, 149–50; voting
  rights and, 9, 100, 151
African Americans, pre-emancipation, *see* free
  African Americans; slavery
African Methodist Episcopal (AME) Church,
  6, 21, 83, 112, 179n31, 182–83n79,
  215n87; Baltimore and, 16–18, 37, 39,
  75, 78, 79; Bethel Church and, 16, 18, 78,
  79, 80, 195n42; Ebenezer AME Church
  and, 80, 84

American Anti-Slavery Society, 1, 2, 6–7, 8,
  164n4, 166n33
American Colonization Society (ACS), 37, 38,
  39, 44, 130–31
American Convention for Promoting the
  Abolition of Slavery, 45, 182n78
American Notes (Dickens), xi, 108
American Revolution, 3, 4, 16, 23, 64, 165n15
Anderson, George, 120
Anderson, John, 120
Anglo-African Magazine, 128, 149
antebellum law: birthright citizenship rights
  and, 4–5, 12, 41; Cherokee sovereignty and,
  43–44, 45, 128, 181n64; citizenship rights
  and, 12, 42, 177n12; free African American
  citizenship and, 1–6, 7–8, 9–12, 29–30,
  37–38, 40, 163n1; free African Americans
  and, 1–6, 9–12, 13–14, 19, 24–25, 26,
  41–42, 168–69n52, 169n53, 170n65,
  174n53; patents and, 43, 181nn59, 61, *see*
  also black laws; black laws in Maryland;
  Dred Scott case; free African Americans
  in court
antislavery movement, 34, 107, 108, 152;
  Baltimore and, 13, 35, 37, 39, 44, 45, 53,
  64–65, 151, 184n2, 199n28; free African
  American citizenship and, 1–3, 5, 89,
  167n41; Massachusetts and, 20–21, 57, 58;
  New York State and, 1, 8, 164n4,
  165nn22–23; William Yates and,
  1–3, 6–7, 8, 164nn4, 11, 165nn22–23,
  166n33, 167n41
apprentices, 14, 15, 100, 108, 109, 119–21,
  123–26, 150, 218n9